W9-DIL-146

FOREWORD

Surprisingly, one of the greatest challenges in writing this novel was categorizing it. Although it is a work of fiction, it was greatly influenced by what I observed during my four undergraduate college years. The story is set on the Cornell campus during the turbulent late 1960's when I was a student there. Hence, to a degree, it is a memoir. But to bring that era to life and humanize it, I have inserted fictional characters and events into the narrative. I wove together my personal observations coupled with the experiences of some of my classmates. What emerged was a hybrid, a composite-- of both history and fiction. Any resemblance to actual persons living or dead is coincidental. Therefore, I finally decided on calling this story "semi-autobiographical"-- falling between autobiography and fiction.

The background is real; the history is true. However, I took some literary license and liberties with chronology and the events themselves to keep the story flowing. My goal was to recreate those events and conversations as best as I can remember them. But to repeat: This is a work of fiction. All the characters and events portrayed in this story are either products of my imagination or used fictitiously. In order to ensure anonymity and protect the privacy of individuals, in some cases I have changed names, dates, times, locales, and even physical characteristics.Nevertheless, I tried to present history as authentically as I could within the limits of fiction-- trying never to lose sight of what this period in history was all about.

In the final chapters, I detail the infamous building takeover of the student union building and some of the darkest days in Cornell's history-- as well as American college history for that matter. This was a period some faculty, staff, students, and alumni wish could be expunged. Up to April 1969, there had been protests and demonstrations at many college campuses-- but the one that took place at my alma mater turned a page-- when shotguns and rifles were factored into the equation.

To depict those events as accurately as possible, I pieced together several different accounts. No surprise; things happened so fast and so furiously in a changing landscape. Nobody seemed to observe or report the events in precisely the same way. However, I want to single out three sources I turned to as I reconstructed what occurred-- and acknowledge their unbiased, factual, and accurate reporting as I tried to bring this chapter of my stay at Cornell to life. Their day-by-day reporting was flawless and I incorporated some of their accounts into my story: *The New York Times*... the *Cornell Daily Sun*... and an outstanding chronology, "Cornell: A History 1940-2015" by Glenn Altschuler and Isaac Kramnick.

All this being said, my overriding goal was never to lose sight of the sixties experience and capture the excitement and feverish pitch of this period. Its essence rings true. I hope you will enjoy this trip back in time as history meets fiction-- coupled with autobiography.

ACKNOWLEDGMENTS

This novel, and for that matter, everything I do in my life, is for my family. After all-- they mean the whole world to me. My wife and soulmate Sharyn... my incredible sons Todd, Eric, and Lonnie... my wonderful daughters-in-law Alyssa and Laura... and my loving granddaughters Rebecca and Kaylee-- you deserve this dedication because you have made my life complete and me the luckiest guy in the world. I want also to include "Bea" and "Lou," the best parents in the world, who always encouraged me and gave me every advantage a son could ask for.

I want to acknowledge my editor Tim Male and all the people at Amazon Create Space who guided me along the way. I also want to thank my friend and publicist Deborah Kohan, who pushed me to the finish line. And I want to mention my "legal eagle," Charlie Skop, whom I turned to for advice-- and my "computer guru," Jamey Kohn, who answered so many technical questions for me.

And finally, I want to thank you, the readers, for taking this journey through time. I hope you enjoy this saga of the sixties, that most memorable decade.

"So many things I would have done
But clouds got in my way…
I've looked at life from both sides now
From up and down and still somehow
It's life's illusions I recall
I really don't know life at all."

--adapted from Joni Mitchell's "Both Sides Now"

PROLOGUE
SEPTEMBER, 1999

#1 - Going Home

I had made this very same journey so very many times before. Like a tour guide proudly showing off his country, I could identify all the route signs, diners, billboards, pit stops, turnoffs, and even the perennial potholes along the way. No surprise; after so many runs, I had the trip down to a science. I could tell precisely where I was, not by looking up, but just by glancing down at my watch: 45 minutes to the George Washington Bridge… 45 minutes more to the New York State Thruway entrance… another half hour until the sighting of the first farm. My timetable was even more precise than that of Swiss Air.

The ride from very urban New York City to ultra-rural Ithaca, New York (they say that the cows are counted in the census) took just under five hours. From skyscrapers to silos in a matter of minutes. But that was only after the crumbling two-lane "old Route 17" was replaced by the modern (at least back then) "new 17." My parents and grandparents used to bemoan what an ordeal it had been to go "up to the mountains" in the summer on that decrepit old road. Would the '53 Hudson manage to make it up the challenging Wurtsboro Hill, the gateway to the Catskill Mountains? It was truly an endurance test at best, a crapshoot at worst.

But that was then and this is now. My 1995 Oldsmobile with power-this and power-that had no trouble whatsoever negotiating that steep incline. So, after leaving the greater metropolitan area behind, it meant slowly ascending into the Catskills Mountains and then traversing New York State, going from southeast to northwest, ending up in the Finger Lakes Region in the center of the state.

However, on this particular day and at that very moment, the trek was altogether different. As an undergraduate student at Cornell University in the 1960's, I had shuttled back and forth countless times, seemingly on automatic pilot. Today's trip was a different mission; now I was going as a *parent,* about to deliver my son to my alma mater, and my heart was racing even faster than our car on cruise control.

Identifying the *best* college in America is subject to debate-- but few will argue as to which is the *most beautiful.* Cornell University is the classic Ivy League campus characterized by its stately towers and elegant gothic architecture. That, however, is not what makes it unique. Rather than being situated in or near a large city like most of its seven sister Ivies, Cornell was somehow mysteriously deposited in the middle of a state park, complete with lush gardens, plush woodlands, thick forests, colorful flower beds, sprawling plantations, shiny lakes, dazzling waterfalls, and deep gorges, crisscrossed by picturesque one-car-at-a-time bridges. Where else can you attend college, side by side with nature's grandeur?

Perched on high atop the eastern slope overlooking Lake Cayuga in the breathtaking Finger Lakes Region of New York, the campus looks out in three directions to some of nature's most majestic vistas: north to the top of the lake, across to the sparsely populated West Hill, and south to the fingertip of the lake and the City of Ithaca. And as her alma mater proclaims about Cornell, "looks she proudly down." Little wonder people have likened the campus to the Garden of Eden. It's always been my little piece of heaven on earth. While most of the other Ivies border on large metropolises such as Boston, New York, New Haven, Philadelphia, and Providence, Cornell rests idyllically in the middle of absolutely *nowhere*-- and is damn proud of it. It's that isolation that creates its charm and makes the campus truly unique.

Nestled in the valley, downtown Ithaca, the prototype small town, sits at the southern tip of Lake Cayuga and sprawls out in two directions to the eastern and western slopes. It is an interesting mix of the old and the new. The streets bear such geographic names such as Tioga, Aurora, Geneva, and Seneca, honoring neighboring towns and counties, and further accenting the rustic charm. Although urban renewal has reclaimed the downtown area (there is now a small pedestrian mall in the center of things), many of the old-fashioned Main Street-type stores are still in business. There is the familiar family-owned drug store, the country-style post office, German delicatessen, pizza joint, ice cream shop with old-fashioned leather-top stools, and even a Chinese restaurant. This all dates back to a simpler time, well before chain stores and sprawling malls, but now they, too, are popping up on the outskirts of town.

A small brick building, recently abandoned, was home to the old New York Telephone Company that used to hire real, "live" operators, who cheerfully chirped "Long Distance" and "Information" with that friendly and familiar upstate twang. The diner *never* closes and is still a haven for insomniac college students, truckers off the highway, as well as other workers on the lobster shift. There were several movie theatres scattered about, but they are disappearing and being replaced by the new breed of multiscreen cineplexes. And, there were, and still are, countless picturesque churches covering just about every denomination.

Abandoned train tracks from the old Lehigh and Lackawanna lines as well as the small bus depot are at the west end, and must be crossed before heading up the gently sloping west bank. The eastern climb to the Cornell Campus, however, is a steep one, with San Francisco-like inclines. The Buffalo Street hill, for example, is a challenge to ascend at any time of the year, but is particularly daunting during the winter.

Ithaca is a big city by upstate standards. Neighboring towns such as Brooktondale, Slaterville Springs, Varna, Lansing, Dryden, and Trumansburg dot the map and are home to farmers and many of the hardworking service people who are employed by the University or at nearby Ithaca College which is on south hill, also towering over the lake and downtown area.

I guess that it was my destiny to attend Cornell. My parents had met there in the 1930's while taking summer courses. Whether it was for sentimental reasons or the lure of the beautiful campus, we had vacationed there as a family ever since I could remember. Both New York City schoolteachers, they would sublet student apartments for July and August, first in old Victorian rooming houses in the Collegetown section, later in professors' homes along Beebe Lake just off the main campus, and most recently in modern garden apartment complexes that seemed to be sprouting up all over. For seven weeks, they escaped the heat of the City and took advantage of the culturally rich university life set against this magnificent backdrop. As the years passed by, other teacher couples joined them, forming a growing colony of refugees from the summer in the City. Other kids went to camp; I went to the Cornell campus. Understandably, then, it became my second home and was unquestionably my first choice when it came time for the college admissions sweepstakes. In the fall of 1964, I sent in an application as soon as one became available, and received my acceptance letter some ten weeks later. For me, the nerve-shattering waiting game was over.

You can imagine my elation, then, when my son selected Cornell from among several other offers. Admittedly disappointed that he had not opted for the early decision route to Cornell, I was satisfied that at least it was one of the schools to which he ultimately applied. With several big league offers in hand, we --*he*-- had a decision to make. (I vowed not to try to influence him, at least not too much.) During the last two weeks in April, we made a marathon road trip up and down the eastern seaboard to take one last look at the colleges to which he had been accepted before committing four years and mega bucks, totaling more than $120,000. (A mere pittance by today's sticker prices!) After all, if I was moving into the poorhouse, let me go there smiling. Despite the temptation to do so with the May 1st deadline looming, I refrained from influencing his decision or pressuring him in any way, but was undeniably thrilled when he announced that he would be following in my footsteps "on the Hill," as they call it.

This trip up with my son seemed like a flashback to the day my parents escorted *me* as an incoming freshman. Hard for me to believe, but that was decades ago. Now I had to work hard to remain in the present tense and leave the past behind, at least at this very moment.

My son was uncharacteristically quiet on the ride up, reminiscent of my own reticence. After all the preparations and planning, cutting the umbilical cord was imminent. I myself had been a big talker about going away to an out-of-town college. But when the moment of separation finally came, I had some painful knots in my stomach. Now I was wondering how he truly felt. As we turned off the Interstate just past Binghamton, the last vestige of civilization for a while, following the winding country road that would carry us on the last leg of the journey, it seemed like only yesterday that I was the passenger and my father the driver. Like never before I felt the passage of time in *my* own life.

"Cornell University: 4 miles," read the sign. Destination sighted; we were on approach. The knot in my stomach further tightened. The descent from the hills began. Out of the farmlands, into the outskirts, down the hill, through Collegetown, across campus, and up to the freshman dorms. Almost on cue, the weather had changed dramatically as soon as we left New York City. The sunshine quickly faded, with a steel grey overcast taking its place.

It was raining-- teeming-- as we pulled into the West Campus parking lot. In my day, this area had been called the "Boys Dorms" as opposed to the "Girls Dorms" on the north side. Now that everything was unisex and integrated, geography rather than gender differentiated the two residence areas. The West Campus dorms, aptly titled because they were about as far west as you could go on campus, were situated at the foot of a steep hill ("Libe Slope") so named because it began the descent from the main quadrangle down to the dorms and ultimately to the lake and town below. We freshmen inched up and down that steep slope at least once or twice a day, although in winter there was a more unorthodox method for descending from the Arts Quadrangle above to the residence halls below: sliding down the hill on makeshift sleds-- cafeteria trays.

Eventually all freshmen would be housed in a new community under construction on North Campus. For now, though, there were two basic choices on West Campus. First, there were the traditional ivy-covered gothic halls omnipresent on most campuses, irregularly scattered over several acres. This was called the Baker group and was where I had resided as a freshman. In addition, there were six neatly laid-out modern brick buildings called "U-Halls" or University dorms, numbered one to six. Such cold, institutional names befitted them. Each of the cinderblock buildings was practically identical to the next; they were almost barrack-like with little distinction among them except for their number. When I was an entering freshman, the six University Hall buildings were the *last* choice in the dorm lottery. Kind of what you'd expect to find at a white collar prison colony.

Now, however, thanks to some clever fundraising that had attracted some big industrial and alumni bucks, the "U-Halls" had been completely renovated and sported names such as "Class of this," "Class of that," and the "Transfer Center." These dorms, my son had been quick to point out, was where "it was happening" and the place to be. He didn't want to hear from me that the Baker Dorms had more "character"; my recommendations fell on deaf ears.

Speaking of deaf ears, I think having a pair might have been an advantage. In those days, dorm preference was based on the date the student's deposit was postmarked. And since we had taken that eleventh hour East Coast odyssey to revisit all the colleges one more time, our rooming deposit reached Housing and Dining just under the wire. As a result, he was relegated to a remaining space in "J.A.M."-- *Just About Music.* Here, hard rock music was the norm. As a matter of fact, a freshman could play 24/7, almost without letup. *I* would have transferred out within 24 hours, but the constant racket didn't seem to bother him one bit.

The only other distinction among the six old U-Halls was the special facilities that each housed. One had a small gym, another had laundry facilities, and a third had a full cafeteria, affectionately referred to as the "Barf Bar." Who was to argue! A far cry from the Spartan existence my generation endured when furnishings were more like prison issues, consisting of a bed, desk, and lamp with absolutely *no* amenities in close proximity to the dorm.

As I noted, my own arrival day had been a soaker and so was this one. It was hot and oppressively humid to boot, with not even the slightest breeze to offer some relief. Was this Ithaca or the Tropical Rain Forest? One would have expected the monsoons to cool things off, but they didn't. Several other cars were queued up ahead of us. I hoped that by the time we reached the front of the line, the torrential downpour would have stopped. I dreaded the thought of unloading the car and, and worse, schlepping the crates, trunks, yaffa blocks, portable television, refrigerator, stereo, VCR (still around in those days), microwave, and assorted accessories in the pouring rain and then up a steep flight of stairs. Where was he going to find room for all this stuff, anyway? There was a single elevator that moved with the speed of a snail, and given the amount of traffic that day, you practically needed a reservation to get to use it. As we moved up in line, the rain began to come down even harder.

Finally, we crawled to the front. But even before we could climb out of the car, a swat team of students descended upon us.

"Welcome! We're the orientation team!" they beamed. And almost before I could close the trunk, the car was totally unloaded and a caravan of upperclassmen was methodically removing its contents and transferring them to my son's room. (They moved so fast that they inadvertently removed my luggage as well, which I didn't discover until that night.) Protected from the elements by a rain slicker, a young man with a handlebar mustache, too old to be a student, even a super senior, directed the flow.

"Oh, that's one of the assistant deans," the team leader pointed out. "They like to help out on moving-in day, too." A far cry from how this job got done when I endured this ritual what seemed like eons ago. From severely overstuffed sedan to neatly organized dorm space, the entire process took less than an hour. Truly grateful at being spared getting drenched, not to mention all those trips up and down those steps, I tried to show my appreciation. However, the captain seemed highly insulted: "Sorry, we don't accept tips, sir." This was not New York City.

Cornell may have renovated the dorms since I had been a freshman, but the individual rooms weren't a centimeter bigger. As a matter of fact, they seemed even smaller than I remembered them to be. As you entered, each of the doubles was symmetrical, with one prison-style bed on the left and one on the right. Two plain wooden dressers stood side by side up against the slider window, practically eclipsing it, at the opposite end of the room near the head of the bed; two desks were at the foot of the bunks near the entrance. Freestanding wardrobes were behind the desks to the right and left when you first walked in. There wasn't much room for anything else! A narrow aisle between the two beds "stretched," (and I use the term charitably) from the entrance door to the window. My son immediately informed me that he and his roommate (whom he hadn't met yet) had at least spoken on the phone and already agreed to follow the sage counsel of upperclassmen: They would "bunk" the beds to create more floor space for the refrigerator, TV, stereo, and computers. Where all of this was going to fit was beyond me. Worse, where the electrical power was going to come from (without setting a fire) was also a mystery. "We need to buy some power strips," I was instructed. Again, a far cry from the bare bones accommodations I had endured.

With three of us working and not much space to navigate anyway, it didn't take us long to unpack and set up shop, especially since there wasn't much maneuvering room to begin with. We were practically tripping over one other.

"Where's the bathroom?" I asked two cups of coffee later.

"Just down the hall," my son motioned.

"Men's room?" I inquired further.

"Oh, no, it's unisex," he clarified nonchalantly.

I gulped, but down the hall I went. At that urgent moment as nature called, I didn't have the luxury of searching out more private facilities. And as I entered, a cheery co-ed came bouncing out, wrapped only in a towel that barely covered the minimum essentials, but not the least bit unnerved.

"Hi!" she grinned.

"Hello," I mustered up a response. Well, at least there were stalls in there.

Times sure had changed since I was a freshman.

At least there was a semblance of a breeze in the corridor.

"Man, could it be any hotter in here?" I said wiping my brow returning to my son's room. "It's stifling."

"That's the one item we forgot to pack-- a fan," my wife reminded me.

"Your roommate is not arriving until tomorrow. There's no point in is sitting around here sweating to death." I refrained from adding, "in these claustrophobic conditions."

There were just so many times that I could test the outlets and my wife could straighten the curtains. She had painstakingly coordinated sheets, pillowcases and even the accessories to match.

"Is this the right shade of garbage pail?" She had asked me that question in earnest as we spent a small fortune in the bed 'n bath shop back in Brooklyn. Little did she know what would remain of her painstaking interior decorating efforts when we came back to visit on Parents Weekend. The dorm room would be transformed from House Beautiful to the city dump. We were lucky if we could have found a patch of floor tile amid the layers of discarded newspapers, used tissues, soda bottles, and yogurt cups piled on high.

We had done all that we could possibly do with the space allotted. The hectic pace of the day had caught up with us. We had a leisurely dinner in one of the local Italian restaurants, one of the few establishments that *was* just where I had left it. I still hadn't managed to climb out of the 1960's and my own freshman experience, and now was on the lookout for Patsy, one of our regular servers back then, forgetting that she was undoubtedly long since gone. Time hadn't stood still. I think that if I had said, "When I was a student here..." one more time, my wife and son would have disowned me. It was more than time to get back to our motel.

THE NEXT DAY

#2 - Freshman Convocation

A bright sun shone through the shades of our motel room. I shot up in bed. "What time is it?" I shouted in a panic, grabbing the clock on the night table. It was after 9:00 A.M.

My wife and son looked up. "Did we oversleep?" they said in unison.

"Why didn't you ask for a wake-up call?" My wife asked.

I had blown it. Accustomed to rising at the same time each morning, even on weekends, I had an internal alarm clock and didn't think to ask the motel clerk to ring the room. However, the emotional overload of the previous day, coupled with the unfamiliar clean country air, caused that alarm to malfunction, affording us the unwanted luxury of oversleeping.

On day number two, the major event on the orientation schedule was Freshman Convocation at 10:00 A.M. As a result, we had to nix plans for a leisurely breakfast, and instead grabbed stale muffins and weak, see-through, lukewarm coffee on the run from a very paltry continental breakfast provided by the motel. We then raced to Barton Hall, the huge cavernous armory in the center of campus.

I can't remember whether it was pouring rain or the sun was shining brightly yesterday. But I recall that the weather was absolutely glorious that morning so long ago. The previous day's downpour had swept away the heat and humidity. Cool, clear, crisp and not a cloud in a cobalt sky. Westerly winds from off the lake were exhilarating. Although the calendar still read "summer" on that early September day, there was a sharp breeze in the air-- a decided hint of the magnificent fall season waiting in the wings to make its grand entrance.

"Sorry, full." All of the parking lots near Barton were chained shut by now. We found the closest spot we could up on East Campus near the Veterinary College-- which wasn't very close-- and took hurried giant steps past sprawling fields and colorful gardens of the College of Agricultural and Life Sciences on the way to the armory. I was still in awe of the surroundings; my wife and son, not wanting to miss anything, told me to stop talking and keep walking. It was two minutes to ten; we were going to be late. As we trotted down the flagstone path leading the way, I chuckled to myself: Cornell did not operate on City time; if an event was scheduled to start at 10:00 A.M., it started at 10:00 on the dot. Convocation was certainly no exception.

The place was jam-packed. No surprise, given 3,000 freshmen, their parents, siblings, and assorted other family members. Built as an armory, Barton doubled as a gym, with high-rising bleachers on three sides. It also hosted concerts for big-name performers, who occasionally veered off the beaten path to come to Cornell, usually on the three big social weekends, "Fall," "Interfraternity Council," and "Spring." They must have been paid some mighty big bucks to come all the way up here to the Outback.

From the entrance, it looked as though every single one of the seats was taken. SRO was the price we had to pay for oversleeping. Where were we going to sit? "Up there!" I isolated a patch of bleachers in the heavens on the opposite side of the hall, space that appeared to be unoccupied. As we traversed the huge armory floor and hiked up the creaky steps to the nosebleed section, the Marching Band and the Glee Club were first joining together for a spirited rendition of the Cornell alma mater, "Far Above Cayuga's

Waters." And that's when I lost it altogether and unabashedly succumbed to my emotions. Was it recapturing my own Cornell experience, or, handing it off to my son a generation later? I guess that it was a combination of the two.

By the time the second chorus had been played and everyone was seated again (it's tradition to stand for the alma mater), we had ascended the steps and were clumsily climbing over other families--most of whom seemed quite irritated. You know that look: "We managed to get here on time; why couldn't you?" I used any shoulder or other body part I could latch onto in order to keep my balance on the steep steps, adding to the annoyance of those already seated.

"Sorry, sorry," I kept apologizing as we blazed a path up the bleachers. Out of breath, out of shape, and not used to an uphill climb like this one, I could have negotiated this incline in a gallop when I was a student, but not now. At last, we were sitting in our seats. It was a good thing; I was winded. I took a deep breath… looked around… and recalled my own induction into Cornell; now I was witnessing the very same for my son.

Just as I was settling in and getting comfortable, there was a firm tap on my shoulder. *Now what?* For a split second I feared that we had usurped someone else's seats and was prepared for a fight to claim squatter's rights. I turned around, ready to tender yet another apology. This time, though, the face was immediately familiar. It was one of my freshman classmates and first friends, someone who I had grown accustomed to seeing on a daily basis--and then abruptly lost touch with for what was truly a lifetime. A few gray strands in still a full head of hair, a fair share of wrinkles, but I still pegged him right away. I had never expected to see him ever again.

"What are *you* doing here?" I asked him with a grin.

"Precisely what you're doing here: bringing my kid to Cornell," he returned with just as wide a smile.

History was repeating itself for both of us.

"They'll also be classmates," I said nodding and shaking my head at the same time, a mixture of pleasure, surprise, and disbelief.

We did the man embrace, forgetting about the two wives who were awkwardly left to introduce themselves to each other.

"Shh!" someone chided. "The President is speaking." We humbly sat back down on the bleacher benches. Reunion: to be continued.

The President, a tall, stately Brit who spoke a veritable King's English, stepped to the microphone to a tumultuous ovation. He and his wife (the President always spoke in the first person plural "we") would be retiring shortly. As a matter of fact, this was going to be one of the final addresses of an immensely popular leader with a long tenure and just as long a list of accomplishments. His reign at the University had been punctuated by his style and charisma. The President had the gift of turning simple prose into beautiful poetry. As the thunderous applause subsided, he began to speak in his rich, sonorous British baritone.

"From that first falling leaf in autumn, the harbinger of the magnificent season to come…. to that first snowflake drifting onto the sleeping plantations of winter…." My mind started to drift… to wander away… flash back ... to all those same places, but at a much, much earlier time.

PART I

Freshman Year

SEPTEMBER, 1965

#3 - Back in Time

I guess that I was living vicariously, reliving my own induction into Cornell; I could imagine what my son was going through because I so distinctly remember my orientation experience. These days, some colleges open their doors (and their dorms) as early as mid-August with classes underway well before September 1st; classes are over by May. On other campuses, it all begins (and ends) even earlier. *What's the rush?* Back then, the Cornell campus was dead between the close of summer session in mid-August until just after Labor Day with the start of the fall semester. Frankly, I like the rhythm of the seasons; that's the way it should be. Stop tampering with the calendar. Shut down for intermission in late August, take a deep breath, and then start up all over again come autumn with renewed enthusiasm and excitement. Return to the way things were; don't rush the seasons. Back-to-school sales on July 4th weekend make me crazy. Who wants to go back to school before Labor Day, anyway?

It was the fall of 1965. There was a steady rain-- the whole time, the whole trip-- and the foul weather was in perfect harmony with my gloomy mood. My stomach was percolating. As I said, more than ten months earlier, I had jumped for joy with an acceptance letter from Cornell University in hand. It was December 8th, 1964 to be precise. It's one of those benchmark dates you never forget. Every day I raced home after school to check the mail, which was dropped through a narrow chute into the entrance foyer of my house. I bent over to gather up the pile of letters littered on the green carpet when the return address from Cornell caught my eye. Nowadays candidates don't even have to open the mail to know the verdict: A thick packet, full of forms to fill out, means an acceptance; a thin letter is a tissue paper rejection. But not back then. I tore open the envelope. "We are pleased to inform you…." That's all I had to read. *I* was going to be a Cornellian. I let out a shout that probably could have been heard all the way up in Ithaca.

But now, some nine months later, here I was on my way to campus… and was having some very grave doubts as to whether I had acted too hastily. I hadn't thought about any other college except Cornell and had filed an early decision application at the first possible moment. Had tunnel vision done me in? Maybe I wasn't ready to leave home. Perhaps Columbia or N.Y.U. in the heart of New York City would have been better choices, for me, anyway. After all, I could have gone home on weekends or even commuted each day on the subway. But it was too late now to second-guess myself. A homebody, I was strapped in. Well, I rationalized, I could always transfer after a semester. I was convinced at that very moment that I would just have to be miserable for about five months.

As we crossed over the George Washington Bridge into New Jersey leaving any vestiges of "home" behind, my stomach churned even faster. Despite my parents well-meaning pep talk that I had a leg up on classmates because Cornell was my second home and that I knew the campus like the back of my hand, for the first time in my 18 years I was about to be totally on my own. Nobody was going to tell me to get up… go to school… do my work. Nobody was going to cook for me or clean up after me. I had never been away from home before, not even to sleep-away camp. It didn't seem to bother other kids-- and that realization also troubled me. An overnight sleepover at a friend's house was about as far as I had been unleashed. Not that my parents hadn't encouraged me and pushed me out of the nest; but I always found excuses, preferring the comforts of my own B&B (bed and bathroom). I was making my first solo flight and I was ashamed to admit that back then, at that moment in time, the thought was scary. Very.

It was still raining when we entered the campus and turned into the dorms. On the one hand, I wanted my parents to stay-- forever. On the other, I wanted them to leave as quickly as possible, make the break, and get it over with already. Cut the ties so that I could test this thing out. I wondered how they felt; after all, I was their only child. In those days there was little if any orientation program for parents. Unpack and get back on the road; just cut the kid loose. These days, it's a three-ring circus, with as many activities for the parents as for the freshmen. Maybe it was easier the old way. Why prolong the inevitable? They would head back *home* to New York City the very next morning.

Over-the-shoulder, wide angle shot. I remember their waving to me as the car slowly pulled away from the dorm parking lot, leaving me standing there by myself. It was a *very* empty feeling. Looking for a stay of execution, I had remained in the motel with them the night before. Not a good idea-- only postponing the inevitable break. I admit it: I was homesick already. They had always made it easy and comfortable for me. Too bad my growing up years hadn't been more stressful like boot camp.

There was one last barrage of instructions, mostly health and safety "dos" and "don'ts" which I could recite chapter and verse. As the car passed out of view, I turned and headed toward my dorm to begin my college career. My flight instructors were gone and it was time to fly solo.

LATER THAT MORNING

#4 –The Roommate from Hell

These days, choosing a roommate is about as complicated as selecting a marriage partner. You have to complete a personal data questionnaire that inquires about all your habits, intimate and otherwise: sleeping, studying, smoking, housekeeping, and the like. It's "the like" which separates the boys from the boys! "Prefer neat non-smoker who studies in the room, but wants the lights out by Midnight." Can you imagine what they'll be asking in the future? The University then tries to match you up with a complementary partner. It's kind of like a computer dating service. There's a goldmine waiting to be discovered here for some enterprising individuals: *Roommate Finders.* But there was no such attempt at pairing back in 1965. It was luck of the draw. And, did my "situation" ever turn out to be proof positive of that!

Up to my arrival on campus, I had had no communication whatsoever with my roommate. On the advice of my guidance counselor, I had tried to make some contact with him over the summer, but none of my calls was returned. I could see from square one *why;* he and I had little, if anything, in common. "Buzz" (a.k.a. Frederick Vanadium Weiboldt) was from a fancy Philadelphia suburb and far more schooled in life than I was. You might say that he was a doctoral student, while I was just entering junior high school. Two more opposites there could not be. What sadist in the Housing and Dining Department had paired us up?

Buzz also shaved his head, not par for the course, at least not in 1965, from which he derived his nickname. I knew from the get-go that this relationship was going to be a.... challenge. He was sitting on the bed wrapped in one towel with a second over his shoulder, having just come out of the shower. A toothpick in his mouth-- which was to become his trademark-- was firmly clenched between his front two teeth. He had already arranged the room to his liking, taking the prime real estate for bed and desk near the small prison window that overlooked a courtyard between our dorm and the twin building next to it.

"Want to meet some cool chicks, dude?" were the first words he spoke to me. That was his way of introduction; he was not the type of guy to be bothered with any other amenities. Not even a "Hello" or "Hey, how are you doing?" Just cut to the chase. I didn't answer him.

"Been here three days.... already got laid twice," he volunteered proudly.

Much, much more information than I needed to know, at least at this point in our budding relationship.

Buzz was preoccupied, leafing through some kind of catalogue with pictures in it. What was he searching for, mail-order co-eds?

"What do you have there?" were my first words to him. This futile attempt at bonding was already beyond pleasantries.

"The pigbook, stupid," he snickered as he added that appellation, seeming surprised that I didn't know what he was holding. We certainly were off to a great start, and it would get even better. Buzz perused each page and circled some likely prospects. The "pigbook," known more officially as the "Freshman Register," contained the admissions picture and mini-profile of each and every member of the new freshman class.

"Let me see that," I shot back, practically grabbing it out of his hands. I quickly turned to the K's and found my mughshot. "Ouch!

They must have caught me off guard," I muttered to myself. What girl would go out with this guy with short hair, horn-rimmed glasses, and a crew neck sweater with one of the shirt collars sloppily sticking out over it?" My social life was D.O.A.

Buzz to the rescue. "Don't worry, bud," he reassured me. "This old man can get you all the action you want. I even know some of the townies already. I'll introduce you to Sure-Shot Sally." Desperate, yes-- but something told me that I didn't need to meet "Sure-Shot" or anyone else, for that matter, endorsed by Buzz. I also sensed that I might have a slightly different taste in girls. I leaned towards the more feminine types; Buzz apparently dabbled in the roller derby queens.

In the meantime, I was still preoccupied with that awful picture of me in the pigbook, which I imagined with horror was being circulated in every co-ed dorm on campus. "What a geek!" they must all be shrieking with laughter and ridicule at my expense. I would sooner have been snapped with my fly open. Oh, well, I consoled myself; Cornell co-eds were few and far between, anyway. In those days, the guy-gal ratio was about three-to-one. Besides, it was believed that Cornell women were not selected for their good looks, I rationalized. I could always "import" from nearby colleges in Elmira, Ithaca, or Cortland-- all rumored to be far more fertile hunting grounds, where the pickings weren't so slim, where a Cornell man (or *any* man, for that matter) was in demand, and most important of all, where my awful picture hadn't been circulated.

I spent the rest of the afternoon and evening silently setting up shop. As I said, Buzz had already appropriated which side of the room he was taking. He hadn't even consulted me. He had a view of the courtyard below; my window looked out at a brick wall with some obscene graffiti written on it and a rusty dumpster that obviously hadn't been emptied recently. Actually, there wasn't much else to decide: bed, desk, chair, lamp, and bureau. The "old" Baker dorm rooms were decent in size, larger than the more modern University Hall dorms, and ours at the end of the corridor was even a bit bigger than most. All that was left to decide was how to utilize the five drawers in that wobbly old bureau provided for me.

Now I was glad that my parents had talked me into the 20-meal plan (with Sunday dinner off for good digestion) because there was no choice as to where to eat. Buzz had disappeared early in the afternoon without explanation, so I ate both lunch and dinner alone. My only decision was whether to dine in the dorms at the infamous Barf Bar, or go up to campus and eat in the student union cafeteria. Desperately needing a change of scene, I opted for the latter, more than a little lonely and depressed. Two meal tickets down, eighteen to go for this week, forty weeks to go. Everyone else seemed to be in groups of three, or four, or more. I felt like a pariah. It was a long night.

THE NEXT DAY

#5 – "Look to Your Right, Look to Your Left…"

The first stop for us new recruits was Freshman Assembly at the football stadium. Still trying to develop something resembling a roommate relationship and bond with Buzz, I asked him to join me for the walk up the hill.

"Heading over to the field?" I tried. "The Assembly starts in half an hour."

He didn't even answer me, only giving me a look as if to say, "What are you on?" Buzz couldn't be bothered with such details as Freshman Assembly. So I set out on my own. Everyone else seemed to be traveling in herds. Not yet knowing anyone else in the dorm, I had no choice but to take the long walk up the hill and across the campus by myself. It was a lonely hike and a grey, dismal day in more ways than one.

Nor did the Assembly start off on a very auspicious note. After a terse, cold welcome by some officious administration suits, the freshmen were directed to line up in rows on the football field, end to end. All three thousand of us. It looked like a firing squad. What kind of stunt was this, anyway? I was starting to wonder whether they really wanted us here.

Once we were all installed in place, a cacophonous voice was heard to crackle over the rickety public address system. At $4,000 per year per student, which is what it cost back then, couldn't they afford better sound equipment?

"Look to your right," boomed the dean over the staticky stadium microphone, "look to your left: One of the three of you won't make it to the finish line." What a comforting thought! That was very encouraging and inspiring to hear on our first day of college. But, sadly, it was true. The Cornell dropout rate then hovered around the 33% mark-- and this scare tactic was meant to alert us that if we didn't pass our courses, follow University rules, and walk the straight and narrow, we, too, could become statistics and "bust out," as the phrase went.

It was starting to drizzle again, in further keeping with the glum mood of the day and my sinking spirits in particular. Where I could get hold of a Columbia University or Brooklyn College catalogue? Could I transfer for the spring semester? Even sooner? After this less-than-welcoming welcome by the University's administrivia team, I trudged back down the hill to the dorms-- still alone-- and with my tail tucked between my legs. This was not exactly how I had envisioned my college career kicking off. Forget being lonely and homesick; I was so disgusted and disillusioned that I was ready to pick up a transfer application to any college with a New York City zip code.

Enough already. I had to try a different approach if I was going to survive here. Back at the dorms, it was time to meet some of the other guys. It hadn't taken me long to figure out that Buzz was going to make himself scarce and not be the idealized lifelong "buddy" I had envisioned as a roommate. My high school counselor had chided us not to room with someone from our home high school.

"You don't go to an out-of-town college to meet someone from Brooklyn. Find someone who is different," he preached. Well, at least he had been half-right. I couldn't argue; Buzz *was* definitely *different.* Was I ever sorry that I had taken that advice. I'd have to look elsewhere, though, for that companionship; fortunately, it was just around the corner, literally. Things were finally going to take a turn for the better.

The Baker Dorm complex was not as cookie-cutter in design as the University Halls. They carried such regal names as "Boldt Tower" and "Lyons Hall," far more majestic than the institutional and impersonal "University One," "Two," etc. I was on the fourth and top floor of Humboldt Hall. Since the dorm itself was built into a fairly steep slope, if you entered from one side of the building you were on the first floor; if you entered from the other, you were on the second. From *whichever* side you entered, it was a steep climb up highly-pitched steps to the penthouse. Elevators probably hadn't been invented when this place went up. Unlike the long corridors in the other dorms with standardized rooms hanging off each, there was no rhyme or reason to the layout up here. The hallway zigged and zagged, meandering, mixing and matching singles and doubles at every turn. The only common denominator was the sloped ceiling at the top of the house that took some getting used to and could have made a claustrophobic go crazy.

The corridors were originally red brick, but had recently been painted an amber color, a strange hue. Shiny thick brown moldings provided some contrast. The restroom was immaculate (if not sterile, at least for now), tiled on both walls and floor with the same tiny octagonal pieces. The facilities themselves were "Early Ezra Cornell," with a pull chain hanging high over the commode. I was convinced that the founding father himself must have ascended this very throne some 100 years earlier. There was one telephone on each floor that, except for University dialing, only received incoming calls. I heard there was a pay phone, but not very close by. In effect, we had been cut off from civilization.

Desperate for someone, *anyone* to talk to, I paced the floor. Basically shy, I was not accustomed to making the first move, but my roommate situation called for drastic measures on my part. The door was open in the room around the bend at the opposite end of the corridor, and I heard voices and laughter inside, so I invited myself in, something I'm not wont to do. But again, I was desperate. Here at last was what looked like a more "normal" group of guys-- which it turned out to be. They were going to become my friends who would rescue me from an increasingly bizarre roommate pairing that would ultimately culminate in utter disaster.

"C'mon in." That simple yet warm greeting, after the dreary start at the Freshman Assembly and the less-than-receptive welcome by "baldy," felt awfully good.

The group had already met and bonded, but they had no problem taking in one more. They had been sitting around bullshitting, or, as they call it today, just hanging out, getting to know one another. Over the next two hours, I got to meet and learn about the guys who would become my first college friends.

We were in Ian Pierce's room. Ian hailed from Florida. The son of a local TV news anchorman there, he had inherited all of his charm and charisma, but none of the ego. Dirty blond curly hair, bronze skin, athletic build-- with his model good looks and personality, he could have been full of himself-- but he wasn't. Self-effacing and easy-going were more his style. His mom? Ian didn't seem to want to talk about her, so the others took the hint and quickly changed the subject. He had spent much of his youth in boarding schools, another subject that he seemed to sidestep.

Chester "Kip" Fulton came from Cimarron County, Oklahoma, a tiny town in the panhandle, about an hour away from civilization. His parents were both engineers-- and both were currently out of work, an occupational hazard in the economically volatile 60's. But that hadn't stopped them from sending (proudly) their only child to college. A bit on the nerd side, pocket protector, horn-rimmed glasses and all, Kip was the antithesis of Ian. But their common denominator was their genuineness. Kip was the "hick" of the group, but his lack of sophistication and sincerity were appealing. To him, Ithaca was a huge metropolis and he seemed in awe and almost overwhelmed by the size of everything. After all, the 12,000 undergrads at Cornell were far more many people than he had in his hometown. He listened a lot and talked very little.

Brant Tyler was "Joe Jock." Home to him was the Delmarva Peninsula on Maryland's eastern shore, where his folks owned a trucking and hardware business. From what I could tell, it had started out as a mom & pop operation, but his parents had parleyed it into a very lucrative enterprise-- although Brant did not seem one to boast. He looked like he fell out of a commercial for the Olympics. He was tall and trim with shiny black hair, and with the good looks and stylish clothes to match. You know, the type of guy who can make a T-shirt look good and make all the fat schlubs envious. But without a doubt, his best quality was his warm and winning smile.

Brant could have dormed with the lacrosse players, but had elected instead for a "civilian" dwelling which, he explained, was a risky business since his survival at Cornell was dependent on his athletic prowess coupled with his academic performance. Risky, because the coaches and team members were known to watch out for one another. Here, he would lack that safety net and would be in free fall if the academics proved to be too challenging. He was the first to admit that it wasn't his grades, but rather his "big stick," that had earned him a spot in the Class of 1969.

Brant knew full well that he had his work cut out for him, not only on the playing fields, but also in the lecture halls, if he was going to make it. It didn't take me long to know what I now had to do. From square number one, it was going to be my game plan to latch on to Ian and Brant; if they couldn't get the girls, nobody could.

Dwayne Jennings was from Chicago. I gathered that for him, money *was* an object. He described his parents as hardworking people who had scrapped and saved to be able to send him to college. Although he was on scholarship, his award didn't come close to covering all the bills for tuition, room, board, books, travel, and the like. His dad was a motorman for Chicago Transit and his mom was a long distance operator for AT&T when there was one phone company and before that job title was declared practically obsolete. Both his parents had paid their dues on the evening and overnight shifts, plus all the overtime pay they could stash away to make college affordable, and thereby making Dwayne the most self-sufficient of the group. He was one of the few blacks in our freshman class, and the only one in our dorm.

This was 1965 and the Civil Rights movement was still in its formative stages. Up until the mid-sixties, there was only a handful of African-Americans on campus. A concerted effort was made to rectify that situation through an intensive recruitment drive led by Cornell's president and his administration. As one faculty committee had put it, the University should "recommend and initiate programs through which Cornell could make a larger contribution to the education of qualified students who have been disadvantaged by their cultural, economic, and educational environments."

I truly believe that all this had been done with the best of intentions; however, some felt that the University had stopped short of fulfilling that initiative by failing to provide the necessary transition tools and support to ease the assimilation into a heretofore nearly all-white campus.

I am also convinced that James Perkins, then president, truly wanted to bring racial equality to campus. Records show that Cornell was ahead of the Ivy League pack in spending on minority education during that era. COSEP, the Committee on Special Education Projects, was formed; an outgrowth was the creation in 1966 of a new organization by and for black students: the Afro-American Society (AAS). All of these steps were certainly well-intentioned; but there was almost a "love 'em and leave 'em" attitude, resulting in some tough times for this new minority on campus in the short run. In the long run, it was going to prove to be extremely costly, divisive, and troublesome.

Although Dwayne stood out in a largely lily-white class, his warm grin and winning smile earned him immediate acceptance on the floor. Dwayne had finished near the top of his school class; however, he had few of the educational or cultural benefits that the rest of this middle and upperclass contingent had enjoyed, so he was at a slight disadvantage from the start. For him, there was a degree of culture shock. It became our self-appointed mission to bridge that gap.

And then there was me, until that point dubbed by the others as "Buzz's roommate." In the span of about 24 hours, Buzz had made a spectacle of himself and was already branded an outcast. Furthermore, he had declared his isolation and affirmed that he intended to have absolutely nothing to do with the rest of the guys on the floor. At best, he was a curiosity item. I had no idea that he had already made such a name for himself. I think the others felt sorry for my unfortunate pairing and willingly took me in. Ian's room was going to become safe haven and sanctuary when Buzz's antics would become more than any of us could handle. We all quickly bonded: the fearsome fivesome-- for a while, anyway.

A FEW DAYS LATER...

#6 – "You're In College Now"

Orientation was taking much too long. The class registration process proved to be even worse than we had imagined. It was the old-fashioned in-the-gym system with lots of long lines and closed sections. Seniors first…. freshmen last. By the time we made it through, most of the prime time classes were full.

"The course titles look great in the catalogue," Ian said sarcastically.

"Yeah. Too bad there wasn't any room in them by the time that we lowly freshmen got to register," Dwayne quipped.

"That's a freshman's fate," joked Brant. "Relegated to third and fourth choices, off-hours, late afternoons, and even some Saturday sections."

"C'mon guys, we gotta pay our dues," Kip rationalized. We'll get our turn someday." How sadly ironic: Kip never would.

But at last the process was completed and I had a class schedule. According to *College for Dummies* and *Cornell for Idiots,* the recipe for freshman success includes the following ingredients: a heavy reading course, a writing course, a lab course, a language course, and at least one "gut" course-- so as not to become too overwhelmed. And get the Phys. Ed. requirement over with as quickly and painlessly as possible.

I tried to follow my high school counselor's advice and opted for as wide a range of courses as I could: the obligatory Freshman Writing Seminar, Anthropology, Modern Drama, Russian, and Psychology. That last course was (and still is) a must, with as many as one thousand students packed into the largest lecture hall on campus each semester. Physical Education was mandatory three times a week. My motive for taking Russian wasn't so noble; I had signed up for that elective back in high school to appease my guidance counselor and get him off my back. He kept insisting that I needed to take another year of Science, which was my Achilles heel back then-- and which would prove to haunt me at Cornell as well. "Take Physics or you'll end up in a third-rate school," he constantly badgered me. I guess I proved him wrong.

I also vowed to follow three commandments, which I had heard again and again from upperclassmen and alumni. Their words of wisdom came to mind before signing up for classes. First, select courses by the instructor, not the title. A top prof can bring any subject to life; the converse was equally true with a dullard who can drive even the most exciting subject into the dirt. As my college career progressed, I learned that these watchwords had merit.

Second, select courses by time. Some of the guys elected their courses by the *when* rather than the *what.* They would take almost anything-- as long as it gave them the class hours and days they preferred. I was semi-successful on this front. I scheduled myself for three hour-long lectures on Monday, Wednesday, and Friday… two ninety-minute classes on Tuesdays and Thursdays, as well as a three-hour class on Tuesday afternoon.

I had managed to avoid the dreaded evening, late afternoon, and Saturday classes by sacrificing my first choices for some leftovers. I knew something had to be wrong with them when these sections were still left on the shelf at the end of the process. For a freshman, it was "choose your poison: what vs. when." Still, not a bad package for someone so low on the totem pole.

Third commandment: Don't graduate without experiencing (and quite an experience it was purported to be) the Psychology elective, "Social Deviance," a.k.a. "Nuts 'n Sluts." But fulfilling that commandment and experiencing that course would have to wait until I was an upperclassman and had cleared the required hurdles first. I eventually got around to it-- and, as we'll see, with riotous and humiliating consequences.

Once registered with class schedule in hand, I became increasingly impatient and wanted classes to begin already. I wasn't a college student just *yet.* There was still one more rite of passage to complete. That afternoon, the five of us, now traveling in a pack, hiked to the bookstore and purchased our texts and loaded up on school supplies. What I thought would be a routine shopping spree turned out to be more daunting than getting ready for the first day of junior high school. I grabbed a rainbow of folders, markers, binders, and baskets-- anything that I could color code-- with the hope that for once and for all I would acquire at least a modicum of organization, a skill that heretofore had eluded me. All I needed was Kip's pocket protector to fit the stereotype.

"Man, I didn't think that the book bill would run so high. It's mac and cheese for the next six weeks," complained the usually upbeat Kip.

"Surprise!" laughed Dwayne. "No wonder textbook authors come out with new editions all the time."

"Can't you buy some used books?" I suggested.

"Used texts don't work for most large lecture courses because the authors change *just enough* of the material and review questions at the end of the chapters to require buying the latest edition," explained Ian.

Brant grabbed a fat *History of Western Civilization* book off the shelf, ready to toss it into his cart. A "used" sticker was pasted on the front, but the shiny cover made it look like the book was in mint condition. Then just as quickly he put it back on the shelf."

"What the hell's wrong with that one?" Dwayne asked quizzically.

"Take a look for yourself," Brant said, opening the book and fanning the pages.

It seemed that the previous owner had gotten carried away with a highlighter, underscoring almost every printed word, altogether defeating the purpose of highlighting.

My parents, who were footing the bill for all this, had instructed me to buy new books; so with just the slightest tinge of guilt, I wasn't going to argue with them. Compared to the tuition, room and board, this was a drop in the bucket. After spending a small fortune and somehow managing to avoid a hernia lugging these weighty volumes cross campus and up three flights of stairs to my room, I was open for business.

The texts and workbooks were in size places on the shelf on the hutch over my desk; five color-coded spiral notebooks (and corresponding folders) were in a vertical file on the shelf below; and two plastic trays that would serve as an "inbox" and "outbox" for assignments in progress were on the desk itself. It all looked like a scene staged for a photo-shoot in a decorator's magazine. Organization, personified! Just how long was this OCD anal retentive behavior going to last? *Not very long at all.*

THAT NIGHT

#7 - "Three feet on the floor..."

At last: Classes would begin the next morning, the day after Labor Day. For me, it would be Russian at 8:00 A.M. But first, there was still one more freshman ritual that had to be completed: the address by the "assistant proctor," a.k.a. the "dean of students" about "deportment." I rarely had heard that word before. Actually, an old piano teacher had always told me I totally lacked "it." It was an SAT vocabulary word for "behavior" and we were going to be given a stern lecture about how we freshman males were to carry and comport ourselves.

At 7:30 P.M. we had a preliminary meeting to be introduced to Roy, our Resident Advisor or "R.A.," another dime word, this one for dorm counselor. He was a rather rotund, bulbous fellow with a hula-hoop potbelly. His other distinguishing features were his Eisenhower crew cut, horn-rimmed glasses, baggy corduroy pants cut about two inches too short, penny loafers, and white socks. He came to be called "Farmer Roy," both because of his appearance and his affiliation with the College of Agriculture (Ag School, as it was called back then) at Cornell. It was the job of the R.A. to dispense wise counsel to his young novitiates, both educational and personal. Instead we got a twenty-minute lecture on the virtue of cleanliness… keeping our rooms straightened up… and our stereos piped down… as well as stamping out "livestock," as he called them.

"I don't want to see no pizza cartons left in the hall," he admonished us. "They are breeding grounds for crawlin' critters," evidently speaking from personal experience. I doubted that I would ever turn to this guy for any big brotherly advice.

After that stirring lecture, everyone in our group was ordered to file down to the first floor and assemble in the large group meeting area at 8:30 P.M. *prompt.*

"The assistant proctor will be moving across campus like Paul Revere, speaking to every male resident in every single dorm. I expect you boys to be there on time. He can spend no more than twenty minutes with us," warned Farmer Roy. Was that a threat or a promise?

Since this was a mandatory meeting with attendance taken by the R.A.'s, the lounge was packed. Farmer Roy completed a sweep of the dorm, checking each and every room to make sure that nobody was hiding or staying back. Even Buzz had to show up for this one. Freshmen were still impressionable back then, and so we obeyed the command. The room, though fairly large, had not been designed for a crowd of this size.

The early birds were perched on the few battered couches and armrests. Most of us lined window ledges or sat on the threadbare carpet. Many had no choice but to stand. Little floor space was left exposed. Right on schedule, the assistant proctor arrived. He was a stout, bald, bespectacled man, mid-fiftyish in age. He was devoid of personality; he was grey in every way. Grey hair, grey suit, grey complexion, grey personality. The only color he exhibited was some redness in his puffy cheeks from being out of breath. He began his canned speech like a wind-up doll, with neither a greeting nor a welcome, probably the way he had mechanically started it so many times before this night and on every other night for so many years. I don't think he even knew what he was saying anymore. It was delivered on automatic pilot.

"The boys dorms are exactly that-- *boys* dorms-- sleeping quarters for boys only. Absolutely no other activity is permitted." There was a muffled chuckle; well, *we* could think of a few other "activities."

"And the girls dorms are just that-- girls dorms. The two do NOT mix; there is a clear line of demarcation between the two. A female is not to set foot on these premises. Just twice a year are girls permitted in the boys dorms: Fall Weekend and Spring Weekend. And then and ONLY then under the *strictest* of guidelines." The proctor spoke in a staccato style, underscoring every other word: "STRICT-est." He paused for breath after putting a triple accent on that word "strictest."

"Under *no* circumstances are members of the opposite sex to be seen in here before 9:00 P.M. and they are to be off the grounds by Midnight-- and *not a split second later.*" Once again he used a two-ton accent mark, this time on the words "no" and "not a split second later."

"Do I make myself clear, or do I have to repeat myself?" His grating voice rose to a crescendo.

You could hear a pin drop; this guy meant business. I started to wonder whether *he* ever had had a date. Ian, Brant, Kip, and Dwayne couldn't find even floor space and were standing, leaning against a wall, trying to process the diatribe this guy was spewing. Buzz, on the other hand, was sitting on the crowded floor with his back to the proctor, still laboriously chewing on that same toothpick. He was expressionless, engrossed in some other thought. I wondered how much, if anything, he was processing of the proctor's proclamation.

The proctor was far from finished: "Furthermore, while the young ladies are our guests, the following three rules will be *strictly* enforced: There must be three feet on the floor at all times... a light must be kept on in the room... and the door must remain ajar at least the width of a book. Am I making myself perfectly clear?" he asked a second time. There wasn't a sound in the room. Now, he was finished. Done. Kaput. Not a peep could be heard. "Good," he concluded with a nod. He had said what he had come to say. There was no room for discussion because there was nothing to discuss. This was 1965 and this was the law of the land and this was the way it was going to be. *And college students didn't question the law, not back then, anyway.*

I stole another glance at Buzz; he was still munching on that same toothpick with that same vacant expression on his face. I wondered whether he had absorbed any of these dictates. I wondered what was going through his mind altogether. I would find out in very dramatic fashion soon enough.

There was stone silence. Were my classmates in shock or disbelief? But those were the rules. If we didn't like them-- or worse, didn't follow them-- we could pack our bags and take the next plane or bus home. "Any questions?" The proctor asked yet again, and, not expecting any, nodded his head, moved on and we silently moved out. That's the way it was in September, 1965. There was little if any discussion on the way back to our rooms, still sensing the proctor's presence even though he had departed to perform the exact same scene in the next dorm and then the next.

These rules would be easy to enforce. The girls dorms were on North Campus, a hefty hike from the West Campus (or boys dorms) at the foot of the hill. Any male spotted in that complex would stand out like a sore thumb. The same was true for a female eyed in our sector. In those days, they were two armed camps and it was considered an act of treason to cross enemy lines. A buffer zone successfully separated them. It would have been easier to crack the Maginot Line.

Of course, there would be attempts to skirt (no pun intended) the rules. Buzz was going to be one of the prime offenders and it would turn out to be his undoing. But if you think the boys had it bad, the girls had it far, far worse. At least we guys were allowed to come and go as we chose 24 hours a day. A freshman male could be missing for days at a time, and it was possible that nobody would notice. The girls, on the other hand, were still living according to a double standard and were subject to nightly curfews. Hard to believe that back then nobody questioned the vastly different rules; it was just accepted. The co-eds had to watch the clock just the way Cinderella did. It was like medieval times.

Heaven help the freshman guy who would return his gal one second after Midnight. Fra Brunhilda, the stocky housemother dressed in a loud print frock, apron, knee socks and sneakers, lay in wait, ready to pounce on him with a "proctor's slip." I imagined her perched up in a tree, rubbing her hands together in glee, waiting for the first couple to run afoul of the law. To this day, I never really found out what happened to the female offenders. They already had a curfew; what else could they do to them, lock them up all evening and make them wear chastity belts? In the meantime, the guys had the run of the place, even back then. Betty Freidan would not have been a happy camper.

Buzz was a frequent violator of the curfew rule, or so he boasted-- but nothing fazed him in the least; nor did anything significant ever seem to happen to him. The consequences were minor for males; it was the co-eds who bore the brunt of Fra Brunhilda's wrath. However, Buzz was to meet his downfall, *big time,* on Fall Weekend.

ONE WEEK LATER

#8 - Laundry Room Woes

Finally, classes began. Maybe the prolonged orientation was deliberate to make us champing at the bit to get going. In any event, I eagerly awaited my first college class. I tried to get to bed early the night before and bypassed the usual hall gathering and rabble-rousing in Ian's room, which ran well past Midnight. But I couldn't sleep; my mind was just too active and I was just all keyed up, as if I had had too many cups of coffee.

By the time I finally dozed off at about 3:00 A.M., Buzz exploded into the room with a "Hey, dude-- what's up?" I didn't answer him and just put my head under the pillow. I gave up trying to go back to sleep. Compulsive and anal as I was, I drew a weekly chart as to how I would use my off hours and free time to study, and tacked it up over my still spotless bulletin board. It wasn't going to remain that way very much longer. Nor was that meticulously planned, neatly ruled study schedule. Nor my fastidiously organized desk. For now, though, it was "all systems go."

At 7:00 A.M., I showered, dressed, grabbed a barely edible egg sandwich at the Barf Bar, and then took the steep hike up to the Arts Quadrangle to Morrill Hall. By 8:00 A.M. I was sitting around a rectangular conference table with about twelve others students, all of whom appeared to be as groggy as I was, poised to study Intermediate Russian. Not a word was spoken among us; we just stared into space, waiting for class to begin. At least the professor was alert; if anything, she was on overdrive. My college career was under way! There were just two more hurdles to overcome, and they would turn out to be formidable ones: the laundry room marathon and the freshman swim test.

Among the five of us, we could balance any equation, perform any science experiment, speed read any book, fit carbon paper into a typewriter, or accomplish almost any athletic feat. (Well, at least the other four could). But not one of us had the vaguest idea how to wash and dry a load of laundry.

I had now been on campus for more than a week and my supply of underwear was running dangerously low, with the gauge in my bureau drawer about to read "empty." The good news was that the laundry center was located in the sub-basement of our dorm, so we didn't have to travel very far to get the job done; the bad news was that none of us knew the first thing about getting our clothes clean. We may have mastered Advanced Placement tests and captured every scholastic and athletic honor imaginable-- but were pathetically helpless when it came to domestics.

"Hey, maybe Dwayne can help us," Ian suggested.

"Yeah, he lived in an apartment building all his life," Brant added. "He can save us!" he said with mock gallantry.

"Don't look at me!" Dwayne put up his hands. My mom did the dirty duds!"

So we turned to Kip.

"Sorry guys, I'm no help either. My parents don't even own an electric washer and dryer."

Therefore, without June Cleaver in sight or Martha Stewart to come to our rescue, it meant learning by trial and error. And the disastrous results proved it.

Brant was the first casualty. Nobody had told him to separate the colors from the whites. Nobody had told him *not* to wash his bright red Cornell sweatshirt with his snow white jockeys.

"I can't wear these pinky briefs in the locker room!" he moaned. "The guys will laugh me off the team."

His attempts to rewash them after throwing in a couple of cups of bleach were equally disastrous, producing yellow stains and worse, burn holes, in all the strategic places.

"How was I supposed to know how much bleach to put in?" Things had gone from bad to worse. He held up a pair: Now his badly stained tighty whities were light pink with yellow blotches and huge Swiss cheese crater holes in them. He dabbled with the idea of going commando for a while, but then made an express trip to the local variety store, sans underpants, to buy some replacements.

Ian may have scored a perfect "5" on the Advanced Placement test in English, but obviously he didn't know how to read. The bottle of concentrated liquid detergent said "1/4 cup per load." He mistakenly thought it read "4 cups" per load. A *slight* difference--which produced suds so thick that they not only flooded the entire laundry room, but started to inch up the steps from the cellar. It was kind of like the "tomato that ate Pittsburgh."

To make matters worse (as if that were possible), he reclaimed his water-logged laundry, stuffed it into two flimsy plastic garbage bags that immediately started to burst open and leak all over the place, and dragged them up four flights of steps leaving a trail of soapy suds along his path. He then tried to rinse the sopping wet mess out in the shower, creating yet another flood on the top floor. Too exhausted to go back down to the dryers four floors below, he hung the wet clothes anywhere they would hang, so that by the following morning our entire floor reeked of mildew.

But Kip, the would-be engineer, supposedly mechanically adept, ironically caused the most havoc. Although he was not familiar with electric washers and dryers, he observed his buddies, vowed to learn from their mistakes, and do better. Dutifully he sorted his laundry into three piles: whites, colors, and no-iron pe press. He then carefully measured the right amount of de gent and bleach, and inserted the quarter (yes, that's all it cost in those days) into the machine. Nothing happened. He pounded it a few times. Still no agitation. To prime the load, he took a bucket or two of water from the slop sink and poured it into the machine with the hope that it would get things going.

The only thing he accomplished was producing the stench of burning rubber and the sight of black smoke billowing from behind the machine. Panicking, Kip did the only thing he could think of: pull the fire alarm in the basement-- causing the entire dorm to empty out.

At that point Dwayne appeared on the scene. "What are you doing, man?" A frustrated Kip explained that he had followed the directions to the letter. "Fine! Dwayne responded mockingly. "Fine. Only problem-- that's not the washing machine-- that's the dryer."

THE SAME WEEK

#9 - No Visible Means of Support

Writing and computer literacy classes were required by the time we reached twelfth grade. The laundry room catastrophe led me to conclude that every high school in America should also offer (and then mandate) a course entitled "Single Survival" or "Bachelor Living." High school graduates turned loose and sent out on their own for the first time are downright dangerous. They may possess all the book knowledge in the world, but they don't know the first thing about such domestic coping skills as doing the laundry, cooking a meal, or balancing a checkbook. Up to this point, they have had everything done for them; when left to fend for themselves, it's a frightening proposition with even scarier results.

But if our initiation into washing and drying was a rugged test, it didn't come close to the rigorous rite of passage that Cornell administered in those days to every freshman male.

We had heard about it-- but pretended that it would go away.

"Maybe this is one of those upperclass pranks," suggested Ian hopefully. "You know-- like the mythical swimming pool on the top floor back in high school."

Wishful thinking. The freshman swim test was for real, a ritual for all incoming freshman men during the first two weeks of classes. Somewhere, sometime, somehow, some sadist (or voyeur) had decreed that all freshmen were to demonstrate their "aquatic proficiency." Legend had it that some wealthy benefactor had made a huge bequest to Cornell, but contingent on the University's making passing the swim test part of its graduation requirements.

Whatever its origin (and we couldn't care less where it had come from), the directive was crystal clear: Every freshman man was directed to report to the Teagle Hall pool at his appointed time, grab a towel from the locker room, take a seat on the icy-cold metal bleachers, wait to hear his name blurted out, then march down to the far end of the pool, climb up the ladder, dive in, and then swim the full length of this Olympic-size bathtub from the front to the back. All of this-- butt naked.

There was considerable speculation as to the genesis of this last condition.

"Maybe it's a legitimate concern… you know, perhaps the toxic dyes in all those bathing suits could adulterate the pristine pool water," proposed Kip, who had been a varsity swimmer in high school.

"Or, just maybe that first Cornell lifeguard got off on this parade of male man parts," rebutted Ian, which produced a round of nervous laughter from the rest of us. Whatever the reason, it didn't really matter; the fearsome fivesome just dreaded everything about it.

As "S" day approached, the swim test became a growing topic of concern among the five of us. Dwayne was the most preoccupied and for good reason: He didn't know how to swim.

"What are they gonna do, kick me out *now*?" he fretted. "Look to your left, look to your right: One of you may be out on your ass. Hey, that dude of students wasn't kidding!" he half-joked, mimicking the dean's opening day threat on the football field. "I may be the first to go-- that's if I don't drown first." Dwayne had virtually no swimming experience. There were no oceans near land-locked

Chicago. Lake Michigan was too cold, and the only "pool" he knew anything about was in a billiards hall. Dwayne was in a panic. What *was* he going to do?

Kip, on the other hand, had been a championship swimmer in high school, so this was going to be a piece of cake for him. Although he himself didn't anticipate any problem with the swim test, he was "amazed" that the non-athletes in the group would be required to swim the full length of the Teagle pool, to and fro. "I can't believe that they make you swim such a distance," which further unnerved us. "After all, you're not trying out for the varsity swim team," he seemed surprised. "Why are they making you swim so far?" To make matters worse, he kept repeating this over and over to himself, which continued to rattle the rest of us leading to the conclusion that we were all going to drown.

Living near the Atlantic Ocean and having gone to day camp, I knew how to swim, although my style and stroke were sorely lacking; they were a cross between the Australian crawl and the dog paddle. Come to think of it, I had never swum for distance.

But Ian and I had different concerns altogether; we really weren't all that worried about passing the test or even going the distance. We just weren't all that thrilled about performing, literally, this test in the buff with a full audience. Ian cracked that he felt like he would be auditioning for *Candid Camera.* "I'll bet I'll have more viewers," he quipped. "Maybe they'll use this tape in Psych 101.

I was equally uncomfortable, and couldn't find anything to joke about. At my high school, stripping down to our shorts was about as far as it got. The shower room had been mothballed for years, turned into a storage area for generations of absence notes. For what purpose, I hadn't a clue. Now all those eyes upon me. I knew precisely how George Costanza would have felt. Even though it was just a bunch of guys, but still, I have to admit that I was really uptight.

Brant, on the other hand, was accustomed to parading around the team locker room stark naked. He was more concerned about the impact.

"What's going to happen when Mr. Johnson would... hit the tide?" he so delicately put it. "Ouch! Not even a jockstrap," he winced in pain. "Who was the sadist who dreamed this one up?" he muttered, shaking his head. His take on things was even more disconcerting.

The pain, the embarrassment, the risk of failure-- all three. I don't know which one was worse. If we didn't drown first, we could die of humiliation.

With the swim test just a day away, we didn't discuss it again, perhaps hoping it would go away, perhaps because we didn't want to reveal our own fears, insecurities, and shortcomings to one another-- and to the rest of the world. But we were all dreading this rite of passage like the plague for a variety of reasons. I was hoping to get an appointment time with one of the guys who would be there for moral support, if no other support. But since the five of us had signed up around our individual class schedules, we had to clear this hurdle "solo" with no support, *literally.*

With Anthropology 101 at 10 A.M., English Writing Seminar at Noon, and a dead hour in between, 11:00 A.M. seemed like the perfect time to get this thing over with and scheduled an appointment then. Hopefully this off-peak hour would be a bit less crowded. As the test time drew closer, I became more and more fixated on it and what could conceivably go wrong. "What if I couldn't dive? What if I couldn't swim the full length? What happened if it hurt? What if the pool was cold? What if--? And not to mention certain "anatomical concerns" with all those eyes on me...."

Anthro 101 was a huge lecture course. Huge, even by Big Red standards. Cornell was known for its large introductory courses for underclassmen and this was the prototype, surpassed in size only by the introductory Psych course. Class size at college is often a barometer of the professor's popularity (or lack thereof) and this was no exception. It was scheduled for the large theatre in Goldwin Smith Hall, the main classroom building on the Arts and Sciences quadrangle.

GSH, Cornell's flagship building, was a magnificent structure that had been renovated several times through the years. Its marble staircases, terrazzo floors, and dark wooden moldings are the stuff that Ivy League colleges are made of. The lecture hall itself had recently been refurbished yet again and had that first-day-of-school smell of varnish. The room was gently steeped to the rear like stadium seating in a theatre; the chairs were comfortable with drop-down desks to write on. Still, with a class registration way up in the hundreds, there was closed-circuit television for those seated in the rear, pretty revolutionary back in the 1960's. The professor himself couldn't be bothered with housekeeping matters; graduate assistants roamed the aisles with huge records books in their outstretch arms, seeming to monitor our every move, but at the very least-- our presence. They handled all the bookkeeping and grading duties. I think that there was even more surveillance going on than in a gambling casino.

I had expected to be assigned to a numbered seat, but such was not the case. As tends to happen, though, through force of habit, the students gravitate to the same spots at each class session. There must be a doctoral study somewhere investigating this pattern of behavior: who sits up front… who heads to the rear… and who doesn't come at all.

I had found my way next to a very pert and attractive co-ed named Diana Sheppard. Although this was only our third class together, we had already struck up a mutually convenient working relationship in which we agreed to photocopy each other's notes as insurance against missing even a single syllable of the professor's words of wisdom.

And words of wisdom they were. Actually, you really couldn't afford to miss a beat and I could see why this course was so well-subscribed and why the students hung onto every word he spoke.

In those days, many high schools did not adequately prepare their students for what they would face in college. Instead of the conventional high school staple of 40-minute self-contained lessons routinely followed by rote drill to reinforce what had been learned, college meant relatively little classroom time. You had to quickly become accustomed to crowded lectures, heavy note-taking, little or no interaction with your teachers, massive reading assignments, and self-directed term papers. The professor strode up to the podium at the top of the hour, and fifty minutes later he disappeared. In those days, he (or she) might as well have been on videotape. Class was over; there was ten minutes to get to the next class, if you had one.

At the first session, we received outlines for all our courses. Few if any reading or writing assignments were due right away. That proved to be a potential pitfall for some who saw no rush to hit the books just yet: "After all, we have until October," they convinced themselves. But before we knew it, it *was* October and these procrastinators found themselves sinking fast. As the school year picked up steam, more than a few students were having trouble negotiating this 180-degree turn in which they were responsible for themselves. They just hadn't been prepared for being on their own and so self-disciplined. The basis of that one-third dropout rate predicted at the Freshman Assembly was becoming increasingly clear.

In any event, I could see that I was going to enjoy this class for more reasons that one. The icing on the cake was sitting next to Diana. I liked her a lot and I was waiting for just the right moment to advance our partnership beyond a mere business relationship. I looked forward to going to this class, not only to listen to the professor, but also to sit with her.

Professor Maxwell Sinclair was a very distinguished man in his late thirties, maybe forty. He sported a full head of wavy reddish hair with a neatly trimmed beard. For his age (even 40 seemed old to me back then), he was tall, trim, athletically built, and meticulously dressed in a mature and preppy style. Plaid vest with matching bow tie was his trademark. In short, he looked very professorial from tip to toe up at the podium. Dr. Sinclair enjoyed an excellent reputation as both a scholar and lecturer. Furthermore, he seemed to relish his work with undergraduates, an exception to the rule. There were some lofty profs who felt undergraduate teaching (and freshmen in particular) to be well beneath them.

Despite his impressive academic credentials, which could have made him untouchable to us lowly newbies, he was charismatic, down-to-earth, and easily approachable. He had a stellar reputation among the students. I had been told by quite a few Cornell grads to make sure to take his course. Little wonder it was such a big draw. Every word he spoke in the course of the 50-minute lecture was worth hearing. Furthermore, his course outline was very explicit; he seemed to be truly invested in his students' success. The joint note-taking system that Diana and I had devised would work well in this class.

However, I was of virtually no use to Diana on the morning of the swim test. Like the condemned man waiting for execution, I was dreading my fast-approaching pool date and kept recycling in my mind the litany of "what if--" questions over and over again.

"Why aren't you taking notes?" Diana startled me. "You're missing important stuff." She prodded me, seeming puzzled that I was so tuned out. "What's with you today?" she pestered me. To silence and pacify her, I mechanically put pen back in hand and pretended, going through the motions of writing. But little was processed; my mind was elsewhere. Diana sensed that I was not myself, but did not question me further. I was relieved; after all, this was a guy thing and not exactly the first subject I wanted to confide in her about my own insecurities and myself, especially if I had more than platonic designs for her in mind. I kept looking at my watch; she kept looking at me, more than a little perplexed, almost to the point of irritation.

Usually, Dr. Sinclair's fifty minutes flew by fast; however, his lecture that day seemed to drag on interminably. While I *heard* the whole thing, I hadn't *listened* to a single word he said. Finally, the class was over. Mechanically, Diana and I said goodbye. I was glad to have escaped without having to give her any further explanation as to what was bothering me. At that point our only contact was this class, three mornings a week. I wondered if she wanted more. But I sensed that Diana was very relieved to be rid of me, at least at that moment. Frankly, I didn't care, at least at *that* moment.

It was now time. How I was dreading this. Very slowly I exited Goldwin Smith, crossed East Avenue, the main drag that traversed campus, and headed two blocks east in the direction of Teagle Hall. There was absolutely nothing I liked about what was going to happen except that "it" would all be over in about an hour. I could only hope that I would come out of it with my degree requirements, body parts, and pride all intact.

Teagle Hall was the main Physical Education building located in the center of campus near the stadium complex and the satellite sports programs. It was about a five-minute hike from Goldwin Smith Hall, although on that day, it seemed a lot longer. The building housed the facilities for just about every sport as well as the offices for most of the coaches and athletic programs. The large central locker room area made up the core of the building, adjacent to the numerous specialty areas, among them the magnificent Olympic-size pool. A steam room, sauna room, and large shower room were also contiguous to the locker area. As spotless as it was, it still sported the sweaty smell of a gym. There was no mistaking what we were all here for.

I entered the locker area. To my dismay, it was full. So I wasn't the only one with the clever idea of taking the swim test in the middle of the day. Well, I rationalized, there are hundreds and hundreds guys to test. Even locating an empty locker space was a challenge. As slowly as possible, I undressed. Subconsciously I kept hoping that someone would announce, "Freshman swim tests canceled." Dream on; no such luck. Once undressed-- there was nothing to put back on-- I realized that it was time to go. This was it. Carefully I took my Teagle towel and draped it over my arm, placing it strategically in front of me. Then, like dead man walking, I headed for the pool.

As I approached the heavy metal door (resembling the one leading to the old San Quentin gas chamber), which led inside to the deck and pool itself, there was a familiar figure holding it open for me. Who was this? For a split section I couldn't place the face. Just as quickly I realized that it was Professor Sinclair… my Anthro prof, heading to the pool for the open swim, himself not wearing anything but his broad smile. I was embarrassed… that I hadn't recognized him at first.

"Sorry, sir. I didn't recognize you… without your clothes on." Foot in mouth, big league. But he laughed in recognition; I hadn't meant to be funny. That was it! Good enough for him, good enough for me. If *he* could do this, so could I.

EARLY OCTOBER, 1965

#10 – Less Painful Traditions

Yes, four of us passed the swim test in a breeze.

"Yeah, but I'm stuck taking 'Dog Paddlin' 101' 'til I can prove that I can float," moaned Dwayne.

"And it didn't hurt all *that* much," joked Brant. "Well, a little."

"I am going to request the film and use it as a screen test for my next audition," said Ian, the wannabe actor proudly.

Somehow I had managed to overcome this obstacle while keeping my pride and package in one piece. It was easy to joke about the experience now. I don't know how long this "tradition" continued after our entering class endured it. But to this day, I'd like to deck the guy who concocted it.

There were other Cornell traditions-- far less stressful and much more civilized-- to which we were being introduced. One was Ivy League football. I purchased a season ticket book as soon as they went on sale. Fearful of a sellout, I didn't want to miss out. When I had thought about applying to college as a senior in high school, one thing was sure: I wanted a rah-rah school, big on sports. If it hadn't been Cornell, it would have been another large campus or Division I school just like it. Some things didn't matter to me, but that was tall on my short list of what to look for in a college. As the first month of classes drew to a close and October was upon us, it was time for the opening home game against Dartmouth.

The Big Red had already played its first two games away; now it was back to Ithaca for the home opener. Ever so gradually, the weather was starting to change and it was becoming autumn at its best. I needed that floor fan one day, but a portable heater the next. Clear, cool, crisp. How I wished I could have bottled that feeling! I was familiar with Ithaca during the summertime, but I had never been there in the fall and hadn't experienced anything even close to this. The leaves were turning; the foliage would reach peak in the middle of the month when the fall line passed through the Finger Lakes. Although I had been a frequent visitor to Ithaca, I never had seen it up close in the autumn. Snapshots and calendar pictures just didn't do it justice; you had to be there to catch the full flavor of that fall feeling.

Many of my classmates took the change of seasons for granted; I didn't. A Brooklyn boy through and through, I had grown up in a canyon of pavement, cement, gutters, and stoops. Trees, yet-- but few and far between-- so the changing of the seasons was muted. There were some advantages to living in the city, but spectacular fall foliage wasn't one of them.

I got a good deal of ribbing from the other guys about my "fascination with a bunch of leaves," but I really didn't care. The novelty of being in the country, the appeal to all five of the senses, particularly at this time of year, never wore off. Every now and then, I took a detour…. the long way, circumnavigating the campus: leaving the dorm…. climbing up steep Libe Slope…. passing the bustling student union building, then the library and bell tower-- the campus hub…. crossing the Arts Quadrangle and looking up at Goldwin Smith Hall and at the seven other stately stone buildings…. walking over a narrow suspension bridge and peering down and listening to the rushing rapids far, far below…. crossing a deep gorge…. coming over on the opposite side and curving around a rural street lined with neatly manicured clapboard Victorian homes and small cottages, all of them with wrap-around porches.... turning up to fraternity row with one Greek house after another.... heading over to North Campus and the girls dorms.... back down and around beautiful Beebe Lake and more waterfalls.... traversing another footbridge, this one of stone....circling back around acres and acres of unspoiled plantations.... cutting through the Colleges of Agriculture and Home Economics (that's what they were called back then) and their quadrangles, greenhouses, and gardens.... reaching one of the highest points on campus, the Crescent of the football stadium.... then stopping, for a moment to peer across the lake and at West Hill from this vantage point.... taking it all in... and then finally heading back down again across campus and to the dorms. For me, there was.... there is.... there will never, ever be a more beautiful place on earth. Yes! I had found my Garden of Eden.

Creature of habit that I am, I still follow that precise same walking tour whenever I visit campus. Whatever the season, to this day, I still love to stand atop the Crescent in an empty football stadium, all alone, and look out over campus, across the valley, and towards West Hill. But to be at that very spot in early October....

That Saturday was picture-perfect and I will never forget how it was the ideal day for football-- and to be a freshman at Cornell. The chimes were clanging continually from atop the bell tower on the Arts Quadrangle. I recognized most of the music, football fight songs or other spirited Cornell favorites. The only other sound was the crunch of leaves, which had already fallen to the ground, and an occasional gust of wind working its way through the branches. It was about fifty degrees, or sweater weather, as we called it. About an hour before game time, students began streaming across the campus from all directions: up Libe Slope, down from the girls dorms, around from fraternity row, across from Collegetown. What a great birds-eye-view aerial shot that would have made! With our boys dorms at the base of the hill, only garden apartments and rooming houses sat below us on the way to downtown Ithaca.

Schoelkopf Field was perched up on high, regally overlooking the valley and Lake Cayuga. The bright blue skies, puffy white clouds, and choppy aqua waters set against a backdrop of brilliant autumn reds, golds, and purples combined to paint a picture that was magic to the eye, along with smells and sounds that were just as pleasing to the other senses.

In those days, most of us still dressed the part. I had purchased a rainbow of Shetland wool sweaters for occasions just like this one. Companion color-coordinated corduroy pants were still in style. The other guys were similarly attired. Far from what the freshmen of today would be wearing. When kids see these old pictures these days, they laugh at how "geeky" we looked. Well, I think we looked pretty damn good.

We sat in the Crescent, on the east side of the stadium, facing due west and the Cayuga valley. The place was packed with students, their co-ed dates, or imports from neighboring colleges, as well as faculty, staff members, and townies. In those days, *nobody but nobody* missed a Cornell football game! Too bad that the stadium is half-empty these days. Going to a football game is no longer "the thing" to do. But in 1965, this was what life in a small college town was supposed to be all about. And I had not been disappointed. Nor was there anything wrong with it. Today's generation is missing out on a great thing.

I don't remember who won that game. I don't even remember the game itself; I don't really care. I do remember that the experience was everything I had hoped for-- and more. Cornell was everything I wanted it to be-- and beyond. All my interest, attention, time, and efforts were focused on my classes, growing circle of friends, and budding relationship with Diana. I didn't have another care in the world. Now New York seemed to be a million miles away. For the first time, Cornell felt like home. Unfortunately, that bubble would burst and that carefree euphoria was not going to last very much longer.

MID-OCTOBER, 1965

#11 – Roll Call

For all intents and purposes, I had a single room. Buzz was almost never there; for nights at a time he would vanish and not return. Frankly, I didn't care where he was or what he was doing. I wasn't even curious; I was just relieved when he was gone. Our relationship was strained at best. As I noted, there was still a double standard with a strictly enforced curfew for the gals, while it was come-and-go-as-you-choose for the guys. A male underclassman could disappear, be M.I.A., and his absence gone undetected for days. On the other hand, if a female student was late by even a nanosecond, the wrath of housemother Fra Brunhilda was incurred with the National Guard called in and an "all-points bulletin" sent out.

They say that opposites attract. Such was certainly not the case between Buzz and me. We couldn't have been more different in every way imaginable. And it was a very bad pairing. Horrendous. My only salvation was his frequent vanishing acts. Whenever I came back to the room, a knot in my stomach tied as I inserted the key into the lock if I even suspected he was inside. Forget the fact that he was a total slob; I wasn't exactly neat myself. But old newspapers, damp and dirty laundry, discarded food, and half-empty soda cans were starting to pile up and the place looked and, worse, smelled like the pits. His marksmanship was way, way off when he took aim at the trashcan and he couldn't be bothered with correcting his errant shots.

Among his other faults were wide mood swings ranging from his totally ignoring me to treating me like his best buddy-- with no apparent explanation for the radical shift. At least if he had been consistent. But I never knew what to expect when I crossed the threshold; nor did I know in what mental state I would find him. My gastro system was taking the brunt of his increasingly bizarre behavior. So I took my refuge and sought bonding and companionship down the hall.

Brant's roommate, a pleasant soft-spoken fellow from India, was a declared pre-med, so he spent practically every waking moment in the library or in the lab. He departed the dorms at the crack of dawn and didn't return until well after Midnight, going to bed immediately on his arrival. For all intents and purposes, Brant had a single, too. Ian and his roommate, a farmer from upstate New York, passed like two ships in the night. That guy was aloof, to put it mildly, and had absolutely no interest in making friends with anyone in the dorm. Besides, he looked soused most of the time. At first we thought it was too much study, too little sleep; we soon found out otherwise: too much time at the local bars. The two of them rarely spoke.

Kip had a "de jure" single room, although I was thoroughly convinced that it was actually a converted closet. The sloped walls on both sides seemed to come towards you. Still, the solitude and quiet suited Kip, who was known to pull many an all-nighter studying; when he had had enough of the dorm hi-jinx, he could always retreat to this hideaway. Dwayne also had a small, dark, cave-like single, but as he put it, "At least the space is all mine." Actually, I would have liked a normal roommate. But Buzz certainly wasn't what I had in mind. Fortunately, for me anyway, his total demise was fast approaching.

NOVEMBER, 1965

#12 - Troubled Waters

By November, our ship sailed into some rough waters. All of a sudden, things weren't going all that smoothly for the not-so-fearsome fivesome. Cornell had a unique grading system based on "prelims" or "preliminary exams" given after the first and second third of each course. These long, comprehensive tests were difficult to study for, given the huge wad of lecture notes that we had amassed, coupled with the voluminous reading assignments we supposedly had completed. That first round of prelims was just around the corner and those exams would converge on us all at once.

For the procrastinators who had put off the reading and writing, it was time to pay the piper. There was no way they could possibly catch up this far into the game. When we had received our course outlines at the first class back in early September, the prelims seemed many miles down the road; now they were upon us.

Brant had the most to be afraid of: busting out. He was in ever-growing danger of becoming a statistic. True, I was no scholar, with first-round grades hovering between the B- and C+ level. But at least I was passing. My flirtation with failure wouldn't come until later, when I would run afoul of Geology. In the meantime, I rationalized and found comfort in the dean's opening day remarks:

"No longer are you the big fish in the little pond. Now you have all been reduced to little minnows. Consider yourself lucky if you can maintain a C average with peers like these."

Minnows? His analogy made my classmates sound like piranhas. That dean's comments certainly did a lot for our self-confidence and self-esteem, not to mention trust. So I convinced myself (if not my parents) that I was doing just fine with at least passing marks. Of course, this mediocre grade-point average would never get me into a decent graduate school, but I was too nearsighted back then to think about the future.

Brant was equally consistent-- but with few if any passing grades. It's not that he didn't put in the study time; just nothing seemed to register. He was overwhelmed by five courses and didn't know where to begin. No sooner would he make some headway in one course when he would fall further behind in the other four. I was curious as to how he had gotten by in high school. He admitted privately to me that his coaches had sometimes covered for him. And having a bevy of beautiful girlfriends eager to help him study or write papers didn't hurt, either.

Here at Cornell, his coaches and teammates tried to help, but it was to no avail. Being isolated in a "civilian" dorm, in hindsight, had not been a wise idea. And the girls he hung out with, not exactly Rhodes Scholars themselves, weren't much more academically inclined than he was. Unfortunately, Brant was becoming the personification of the stereotypical dumb jock.

Dwayne was also having a tough time, but for entirely different reasons. Academically, he was hacking it. As a matter of fact, things seem to come easy to him. If only he put in half as much time studying as he did hanging out, he probably would have been near the top of our class. But Dwayne was facing other kinds of challenges; he was having difficulty assimilating into a white world. He was spending more and more time away from us, courted by a fledgling black student association taking shape on campus.

This was 1965 and while Civil Rights had moved to the forefront in the cities, it hadn't quite made its way yet to the wilderness, upstate New York to be specific. Although Dwayne's absence was increasingly conspicuous, the other guys were sympathetic to the inner conflict he was experiencing. I was less charitable and couldn't fathom why our friendship wasn't enough for him. Maybe I was insensitive, but back then, I just didn't get it. Something I came to regret later on.

Grade-wise, Kip was doing the best of all. Perhaps he knew what a hardship it had been for his parents to send him so far away to an Ivy League school and he would go to any lengths to make sure that he wasn't going to let them down. Besides, no sooner had he landed at Cornell as a freshman, when he already had his sights on master's and doctoral programs, at either M.I.T. or Cal Tech. Without a doubt, he put in the most study time and the results evidenced it. You'd catch Kip studying even while waiting to be served on the Barf Bar line. Gimme a break! He was almost embarrassed to admit that he was in striking distance of the Dean's List. Brant jokingly asked him to shave a few notches off his g.p.a. and throw them his way. "Anything would help," he said with a desperate sigh.

Our classes met at very different times. (Kip had some Engineering sections in the late afternoon, one in the evening, and even one on Saturday.) And even our study habits (or lack thereof) varied. But by 11:30 P.M. Sunday through Thursday, just about everyone was back in the dorm and too keyed-up to go straight to sleep, even with the specter of the dreaded 8:00 A.M. classes hanging over most of us. We were up, usually raising Cain in Ian's room because it was the largest, carrying on well past Midnight. Then the routine began all over again. We worked hard-- and we played hard. That was Cornell. Still is, today.

Although the five of us still basically hung together, Ian and I bonded most closely. Our interests and outlooks were most similar. His good looks and charm made him a magnet for every co-ed on campus, and how I wished some of that babe bait attraction would have rubbed off on me. Alas, it was not contagious.

Fall Weekend was fast approaching. We would finally reach one of those two landmark occasions when we could invite and entertain a Cornell woman (or, "import" from another college) in our room. In the meantime, my business partnership with Diana in Anthro 101 had advanced to the second stage, well beyond shared note-taking. I *really* liked this girl. But my George Costanza insecurities got the best of me and I started to wonder whether I was up to her high standards. Nevertheless, I mustered up the courage to ask her to the Weekend-- and to my delight (and surprise), she quickly accepted. I would have been out of luck if she had turned me down, having put all my eggs in her one dating basket up to that point. All was still right with the world. But our plans were upstaged by another more dramatic event on the eve of that weekend.

FRIDAY OF FALL WEEKEND, 1965

#13 - The Joke's on Us

It was tradition for the campus newspaper, the *Cornell Daily Sun*, to publish a "gag" edition on the Friday before Fall Weekend. It ran some outlandish banner headline that was totally fabricated for shock value. The freshmen, however, weren't privileged to be in on the joke and took the story at face value. Actually, they were targeted to be the butt of it. In short, the joke was meant to be on us.

The *Sun* was a tabloid-size newspaper, which came out with the regularity of a small city daily. It was very professional in appearance: well-written and well-edited with a good mix of international, national, local, and Cornell coverage. As a matter of fact, I was hoping to "com-pet," as it was called, for a job as a reporter. After graduation, staff members were often recruited by big city papers. The *Sun* was viewed as a fertile training ground for aspiring journalists and this was one of several career paths I was considering. Fall Weekend 1965 was no exception to the freshman "prank" edition tradition. However, the joke backfired in more ways than one.

Kip, who rose with the roosters, was generally the first one up each day. This morning was no different, although I could sense something out of the ordinary was going on. By the time I was up and out of bed, there was a commotion in the corridor outside of his room. Everyone, still in bathrobes or boxers, was standing, crowded around a single edition of the paper that Kip was reading. I joined the circle and peered over some shoulders to find out what the fuss was all about. That screaming banner headline said it all:

> ***COLLEGE DEFERMENTS TO END;***
> ***STUDENTS TO BE DRAFTED***

We had lots of questions, but practically no answers. None of us had given the armed services very much thought. All of us had found safe haven at Cornell, thanks to the good graces of Uncle Sam and his "2-S deferments" that enabled college students to postpone and possibly avoid military service altogether. It was almost automatic. There was some talk of "4-F," or medical exemptions, with lots of jokes about flat feet and other deformities that would cause the military to deem us damaged goods. Up to this moment, being drafted was the furthest thing from my mind. Now what had been taken for granted was being called into question. Was I no longer safe? Would *I* be drafted?

There was a war going on; but until that moment it seemed far away.... remote.... over there: Vietnam. Being sequestered in upstate New York added to the feeling of isolation and insulation. Johnson inherited that war, along with the presidency, when Kennedy was assassinated. It was baggage he did not want. Up until 1963, J.F.K. had managed to keep it more or less on the back burner, although the flames flickered and shot up every so often.

The earlier 1960's provided other distractions and hence America's attention was focused elsewhere. To this day I wonder how long Kennedy could have managed to keep Vietnam largely out of sight; at what point would it have completely captured the headlines; how he would have fared had he lived; and how American history might have taken an altogether different course.

The 1950's had been grey by comparison. General Eisenhower as President, wife Mamie as First Lady. Cold War... the "Red threat"...

Senator Joseph McCarthy... "The Russians Are Coming, the Russians Are Coming!" Kids today have fire drills; we also had shelter drills. When the bells sounded, duck and cover under your seats, turn away from the windows, and cover your face (to avoid the breaking glass). Very comforting for an eight-year-old. It was a 180-degree turn when Kennedy took over. Camelot, as it was called, proved to be an excellent distraction. People were captivated by the glamor of the White House: a young president with movie-star good looks, his chic young wife, and their two adorable children, not to mention the reality show antics of the extended Kennedy clan.

My high school years had been carefree; our biggest concern was which song to play on the jukebox. My college career started out the same way. But now this. It seemed that just as soon as the less colorful Johnson took over as president and the diversions of the Kennedy family were gone, Vietnam swiftly moved forward, front and center. In retrospect, I believe Johnson was inherently a good man who inherited the job at a most difficult time. America was being sucked in and increasing attention was being focused on that remote Southeast Asian powder keg of a country.

But would that have happened if Kennedy were still president? Historians have speculated. Who knows for sure? But I couldn't care less back then. There we were, nestled on a beautiful rural campus in upstate New York, declared exempt from involvement, at least up until that moment. Suddenly all that changed. I guess we had blocked Vietnam out of our minds. It couldn't have been further away, both geographically and spiritually. Now this bombshell shattered that complacency and brought the War into striking distance and uncomfortably close in a matter of minutes. Practically overnight, we had come of age.

The dorm was abuzz with activity for this early hour. There was an urgent need to know what this all meant in terms of our future--if we still had one. Classmates were bandying about every possible scenario:

"I'll go to Canada. They won't find me."

"I'll get married and have a kid right away. They won't take me."

"I'll tell 'em I'm gay. They won't want me."

This was *not* a matter to joke about. Or was it?

There was no such thing as a cell phone back then and so there were long lines at the two pay telephones nearby. The long distance wires to every hometown in America were burning up. But as quickly as the panic spread, calm was restored. This was a Fall Weekend prank-- and the freshmen had fallen for it hook, line, and sinker. We let out a collective sigh of relief. Back to business.

Sad thing was, it was frighteningly prophetic of what was *really* going to happen to us in the not far too distant future.

SATURDAY OF FALL WEEKEND, 1965

#14 – "It's my party and I'll cry if I want to,
Cry if I want to, cry if I want to.
It's my party and I'll cry if I want to
Because these things happened to me."

–Leslie Gore

By Saturday morning, everyone was laughing about the previous day's antics. They had gotten one over on us. Very funny; we were the butt of the joke. Just as quickly, attention was focused back where it should have rightfully been: namely, on this afternoon's football game and this evening's partying. Once again we put our blinders back on, managed to block out the rest of the world, and tuned out that War which back then seemed so far away-- although it was beginning to creep closer and closer. All we cared about was getting around the dean's directive about dormitory deportment. In short, all we wanted was some action with the females. We had waited more than two months for this moment, and were hot to trot.

It was another glorious fall day, albeit a bit grayer, colder, and crisper than what we had been experiencing earlier in the season. Sort of what you would expect for mid-November-- and all the more reason to get out the sweaters, coats, and mufflers. The autumn season was now past its peak. Over the past few weeks, never before had I seen such a brilliant array of reds, oranges, purples and golds in the trees on campus as well as in the broad vista in the hills around us. The dazzling display put on by fall, set against the backdrop of green slopes and blue and white skies, made for quite a kaleidoscope of color. This would be the mental snapshot that I would carry of Cornell, Ithaca, and the Finger Lakes for the rest of my life. Unfortunately, that picture perfect image would be somewhat tarnished by events that happened in the years to follow. Nevertheless, it was a snapshot I've held onto and treasured.

We went to the football game as three couples. Brant and Dwayne were AWOL. Ian was ticked that Brant had abandoned us for the weekend.

"He's got divided loyalties," I tried to explain. "Cut him some slack."

"Bullshit," snapped Ian, "He and his date are sitting with the lacrosse team. You know he's just trying to impress her."

"Well you gotta admit, junior and senior jocks are certainly more impressive than a bunch of lame freshmen," I conceded

I know that Brant felt guilty about splitting off from us and although Kip and I didn't show it as much, we both felt a bit irked at this crack in our solidarity, especially on the eagerly anticipated Fall Weekend. Dwayne was another story. He didn't make any excuses, but instead chose to sit with his new-found friends from the Afro-American Society. That, we could understand and deal with.

I was with Diana, Kip was with his female clone, another Engineering student with pocket protectors, and Ian escorted his latest bimbette. We were a diverse group, but a happy one, with still not a care in the world.

Diana never looked more striking than on that day. I was accustomed to seeing her in class: Her light brown hair always done up differently....her perfect skin, not a blemish and without a touch of makeup....her slinky silhouette, usually wearing a colorful peasant-style dress. This day, however, was different. Her beautiful hair was pulled tightly to the back and gathered in a French braid. She wore some light makeup that punctuated her already beautiful features. It was all capped off with a small beret. A colorful poncho, fashionable back then, kept her warm. Although I would have gladly obliged to do the honors.

By game's end, the sun was already setting in the western skies. The days were growing shorter and colder; winter was well on its way. Without the sun, it was more than a bit chilly. We headed for Bailey Hall, the stately old concert theatre in the center of campus and "Fall Tonic," which featured a series of college singing groups delivering a cappella renditions of old barbershop quartet-type favorites. The Cornell Glee Club came on last and wrapped things up with the "Evening Song" and "Alma Mater." Each performance was followed by a long and loud ovation. There was a very warm feeling inside in more ways than one and a great time was had by all. Once again, this was what the college experience in 1965 was all about, certainly for me, and probably for most others.

The six of us then proceeded to march down the steep hill to the city of Ithaca, where we had dinner at our favorite inexpensive Italian red checkerboard tablecloth restaurant. We had little choice; pasta was cheap and it was a stone's throw from campus. Again, we had little choice; we had no wheels. Dinner was finished just in time to get back to the campus and to Barton Hall for the concert featuring the *Mamas & Papas*, then one of the hot sixties groups. The armory was packed to the rafters.

This was the place to be on Fall Weekend. As much as I enjoyed the music, most of the time my mind was focused on the "encore" that would follow directly after. Now it was finally time to head back to the dorms for the long-awaited open house and my dalliance with Diana. I had been patient; but it had been a very long wait and there was a limit as to how long I could contain myself and my energy zipped up.

Humboldt Hall was unusually spotless that night. Under Farmer Roy's command, the freshmen had done an impressive job of scrubbing and prepping for the Big Event. Actually, he couldn't have cared less about our dates; he wanted to pass inspection and score points under the assistant proctor's close scrutiny. That was probably the only "scoring" he would do. Even the bathroom was presentable, with the ubiquitous random sheets of toilet paper stuck to the floor, not to mention the hanging underwear, having been removed for this special night.

However, an odd odor permeated the building that challenged the olfactory sense-- a strange combination of cheap after shave, aerosol deodorant, and powerful disinfectant-- all of which had been quite liberally applied earlier in the evening. A vain attempt to rid the place of the malodorous stench by opening up all the windows only resulted in nearly freezing us out. The weird smell lingered right up to show time; we couldn't get rid of it. Still, Farmer Roy appeared pleased with the efforts of his charges. As I said, he wanted to score some points on the proctor's watch; we just wanted to score.

Since freshmen were not permitted to have cars on campus, we had become fast walkers. After more than ten weeks, I was accustomed to the hike up and down Libe Slope. We Cornell men probably have the strongest calves in the country. However, I don't think Diana was quite prepared for the trek down the hill to Humboldt Hall and then all the way up to the top floor. Her dorm had elevators; mine was built before they were invented.

"What is that odor?" Diana looked puzzled as she followed behind me as we climbed up to the penthouse.

"What odor?" I replied, pretending not to notice what was starting to smell like ether.

"Why is it so cold in here? It's freezing-- like a meat locker," she complained.

"I guess they haven't turned the heat on yet," I tried.

Finally we reached my room-- only to find the door bolted shut.

First come, first served. Squatter's rights. Buzz was *already* in the room by the time we had reached our destination. And he was already "entertaining" his date behind locked doors, already in defiance of the proctor's edict. I was a little put out and more than a little bit annoyed. All these weeks he had successfully found other venues for his romantic exploits. Why did he have to encroach on my turf the one and only night afforded me? Now all I could do was wait my turn. However, the aftermath of his amorous tryst turned out to be well worth my momentary ire.

The Proctor's rules were omnipresent, tacked up on every door and corridor bulletin board in bold print:

SATURDAY NIGHT OF HOMECOMING
"Three feet must be on the floor at all times...."
"A light must remain on in the room all evening...."
"The door must remain open at least the width of a book."

None of these rules was very conducive to romantic pursuits. But once again, this was 1965. And what the assistant proctor says, goes. Or, *you* go. That had already been made abundantly clear to us by the proctor, reinforced ad nauseum by Farmer Roy. Who were *we* lowly students to question anything, anyway? Most of us did what we were told to do. Most-- not all.

Ian and Kip quickly disappeared behind their partially closed doors, dutifully following these edicts. I, on the other hand, had been evicted and was left with no place to go, standing there lamely with my tail between my legs. Every few minutes I gave a knock. The first few times, I got a response, expletive deleted; thereafter, Buzz just ignored my banging. I cooled my heels with Diana, trying to buy some time while waiting my turn. Actually, it wasn't my heels that needed cooling. I looked longingly at the other doors down the hall and just imagined what was going on inside. Then I looked again at my door. The one difference was that my cubicle remained sealed shut in direct defiance of the proctor's edict.

More than a bit ticked off, I was still trying to stall for time, making some small talk with Diana. I was running out of things to say, standing in the corridor, just short of jumping into a cold shower-- when it happened. The proctor was making a sweep across the freshman dorms and he was patrolling our floor like a guard inspecting prison cells.

"Is anyone in there?" he growled as he stopped in front of our room. I said not a word, but motioned with a sweep of my outstretched arm.

He gave a loud rap on the door. Obviously Buzz thought it was still me who was doing the knocking.

"Get away, drip. Wait your turn!" he shouted, among other things, at an increasingly enraged proctor. Another two thuds on the door. "I said, 'Get the hell away!' Keep it in your pants." Buzz ordered.

That was all the proctor needed to hear. Buzz had touched a nerve; I think it had been in the proctor's pants for much too long a time. The opening salvo had been fired. He started to boil over like a volcano, taking direct aim at the doorknob. It was locked; another violation, but that didn't stop him. With considerable effort, he managed to slide a passkey out of his overstuffed pocket, nearly splitting his overstuffed pants in the process, and quickly gained access to the room. He interrupted Buzz and his paramour at a most inopportune moment. Diana and I had a great over-the-shoulder vantage point of the drama about to unfold.

"You've violated the rules! Every one of them! You've abused the privilege!" he roared at Buzz who frantically tried to cover up as did his partner du jour who took protective refuge behind the sheets.

"No, I didn't," bounced back Buzz, who made a quick recovery. What a sight-- the two of them shielded behind the bed covering with cigarettes dangling out of the corners of their mouths. Violating the "No Smoking" rule was the very least of their troubles.

"Three feet on the floor!" shouted the proctor.

Buzz motioned to a bridge table that had been set up standing on three legs.

"Four legs if I'm counting right," Buzz bounced back with the innocence of an altar boy.

"A light on at all times!"

Buzz smirked and with a sweep of the arm that would have made Vanna White proud, he motioned to the lit candles placed all around the room; the proctor scowled. "Gotcha on that one, Prock."

Anticipating the next challenge, Buzz signaled with his pointer to a *match*book that had been placed in the door-jamb to comply with the third edict.

But the proctor was not amused. He turned a beet red. Plump as he was, he now resembled a ripe tomato.

"Get dressed. I said, *get dressed!*" wailed the proctor at the top of his lungs. I bet they heard his lion's roar on the other side of campus.

Buzz and his bimbo continued to snicker. But the proctor, a man devoid of any humor whatsoever, did not think it at all funny, to say the least. He stepped out into the hall and shut the door behind him. Diana and I watched this entire scene unfold without uttering a word. We were in shock.

The proctor in no way acknowledged our presence, acting as though we were not there. This noisy row could have wakened the dead. By this time, a few curious heads were taking an intermission and poking out from behind partly closed doors. The decibel level had drawn them away from their own exploits to the dramedy unfolding before my eyes. I wondered which show was better: the performance inside their rooms or this side show outside in the hallway.

A few minutes later, Buzz and his lady friend emerged fully clothed but totally disheveled. The pair was led out like a couple of convicts caught in the act. In fact, they had been.

THE MORNING AFTER

#15 – Free at Last

I never saw Buzz again. To this day, I don't know what became of him. Frankly, I don't care. He had been the roommate from hell. By the following evening, his belongings had been swiftly and efficiently packed up and cleared out by a SWAT team of university security officers, or the "Proctor Police," as we called them. Not even the slightest trace of his brief Cornell stay remained. It was as though he had never existed, disappearing altogether, vanishing into the Witness Protection Program: "See yah."

But in time, Buzz came to be viewed as a martyr. It became a legend in the dorms of what can happen to you if you don't adhere to the rules set down by the big, bad proctor. "Pack up your bags and go home." That's the way it was back in 1965. Rules were rules and they were to be enforced. There was no appeal, no recourse, no compromise. "Zero tolerance" had its genesis then and there. Buzz was history. As for me, I'd just have to wait-- for *spring* weekend. The only silver lining to the Fall Weekend debacle was that he was gone, this time for good.

Now I had single room to rattle around in. I immediately rearranged the furniture to *my* liking. At first I enjoyed the freedom of coming and going as I chose without having to seek permission from Buzz. Nor did I miss having that pit in my stomach much of the time, a malady that I attributed to his extreme mood swings. My gastrointestinal condition took a turn for the better. However, that short-lived novelty of living alone soon wore off.

At the same time, Ian was becoming increasingly turned off to his roommate.

"This guy is drunk more than he is sober," he complained.

"Maybe we should do something to get this clown some help, rather than watching him go down the tubes," I proposed.

"What are you, Mother Teresa?" Ian hit back. "Besides he's rejected my offers on several occasions after his drunken rampages."

"What about Farmer Roy? It's the R.A.'s job to do something," I suggested.

"Now *there's* a novel idea," Ian smirked. We both knew that enlisting his counsel was pointless.

"Well, we could try," I said half-heartedly.

"His only concern is cleaning up the mess and restoring sterility after this jerk is finally through throwing up."

So we rationalized that either he didn't need or want our help. And as the weeks passed, he became the object of some very cruel jokes. Who said it's just the girls? Guys can gossip maliciously and be plenty mean, too.

The final straw came when "Plastered," as he had come to be called, exploded into his room at 2:00 A.M., totally blitzed out of his mind, shook Ian out of a deep sleep, picked him up, hauled him out of bed, doused him with a can of beer, barfed on his pillow, and then roused the whole corridor with a wild stampede, banging madly on every single door, waking every guy up-- all this on the night before a major prelim. Ian decided then and there that it was time to move out of his room and move into mine.

From that point on, we rarely saw this guy, and if we did, just plain ignored him. No surprise that "Plastered" would drop out at the end of the first semester. Like Buzz, another casualty at Cornell. That 33% dropout rate was starting to register. But the circumstances this time were very different. Looking back, I guess someone should have tried even harder to help "Plastered." I still wonder who that "someone" was.

For the rest of the year, Ian and I moved in step, seemingly attached at the hip. He was far more schooled in the ways of the world and I had a lot to learn from him, and fortunately for me, unlike Buzz, he was willing to take on the job as tutor. I liked the way he dressed, I liked the way he acted, and most of all I like the way he attracted the girls. He could have been full of himself given his stellar looks and magnetic personality-- but he wasn't, probably because of some not-so-obvious, deep-rooted insecurities. I, on the other hand, knew precisely what my strengths and shortcomings were, and was up front about them. Perhaps for that very reason, we bonded so closely. Unlike my relationship with Buzz, this *was* a case of opposites attracting.

I came from a small but tightly-knit family with whom I was in constant contact by mail and telephone. Of course in those days there was no such thing as e-mail and long distance calling was a luxury reserved for weekends, with sky high rates, making every minute precious. Ian, on the other hand, was lucky if he got a two-line postcard per month from home, wherever that was. Although I had never met them, his parents struck me as cold and distant, just by the way he rolled his eyes at their mere mention.

At first I thought my close ties with my family and my regular contact with my parents irritated Ian. To the contrary, he was envious and seemed to relish what I had and he lacked. His parents were divorced and not exactly Mr. and Mrs. Ward Cleaver. Almost as far back as he could remember, he had been raised in boarding, military, and prep schools. Now his bicoastal folks were a continent apart, his father still rooted in Florida, and his mom having transplanted herself to California. Neither place seemed like home, he frequently lamented. Ian seemed to long for the family attachments that I took for granted. We were a good pair, alike in some ways, different in far many more. We became extremely tight friends and remained that way for quite some time. Until our own personal tsunami.

THANKSGIVING, 1965

#16 - Homecoming

Ian didn't have to be asked twice about going back to New York with me for the four-day Thanksgiving break. He jumped at the invitation. The dorms were rather bleak and lonely at holiday times with the campus practically emptying out, except for those who lived too far away to make a long trip home for a short stay either worthwhile or affordable. Even Okie Kip had a place to go; his aunt and uncle lived in Connecticut and he was excited about spending Thanksgiving in picturesque New England. Otherwise, I would have taken him home, too. My parents' attitude was that there was always room for one more at the table, albeit a very crowded one.

Up to this point, Ian had used distance as an excuse for not going back "home" for the holidays. Actually, there was nothing to go *home* to. Although they listed Florida and California as their respective residences, his Dad was usually "on assignment" and his Mom was-- somewhere. I could see how much he longed for the family stability that I had grown up with and simply took for granted.

That's something missing in my generation-- and in our culture in general. Everyone's on the run; what happened to roots? Maybe I am a bit old-fashioned. Actually, in previous generations, after college most people returned home and settled near where they had been raised. Not anymore! We're a nation on the constant move. Most of my cousins with whom I grew up and used to be very close have long since scattered all around the country. I missed that extended family.

Despite my parents' vehement protestations, Ian and I went to the "ride board" in Willard Straight Hall, the student union building, in search of a car traveling to Brooklyn. The drivers, in turn, viewed this as a moneymaking proposition, in the hunt for car-less people to help defray (or pay for altogether) the cost of gas and tolls for their trip. We reasoned that ride-sharing was cheaper, quicker, and more comfortable than the Interstate express bus, which localed through every whistle stop in the southern tier of New York and Pennsylvania. It turns out that we had reasoned wrong. In the meantime, my parents, perennial worriers, asked me if I knew anything about the driver.

"Does he drive safely? Does he speed?" they seemed anxious to know.

"I'll write to the Department of Motor Vehicles and demand a copy of his driving record," I joked, trying to pacify them. My parents pleaded with me to take the bus; I just brushed them off.

"Make sure he doesn't drive too fast…. make sure you wear your seatbelts…. make sure he's wide awake…. stop every two hours for coffee." A comprehensive list of guidelines, all for a five-hour car trip. Funny, now I say the same things to my own kids-- and they blow me off the very same way.

Ian and I ripped through the index cards in the Brooklyn box.

"This one looks like a good prospect," I said as I took the card and copied down all the pertinent information. We hooked up with a guy named Leon who lived a stone's throw from where I had grown up. I later learned that he had attended my high school, but we had not known each other given the age difference and the size of the graduating class. Just to strike up a conversation, I mentioned this bit of trivia to Leon, but it didn't seem to impress him one bit. To be blunt, he couldn't have cared less. As far as

Leon-the-mercenary was concerned, Ian and I were but a business investment; he wasn't in the market to make friends or even conversation, for that matter, but just to make some money. We were nothing more than dollar signs to him. Besides, we were at our driver's mercy and Leon didn't want to leave until 3:00 P.M., after his last lecture class-- which turned out to be our undoing.

Thanksgiving is the one "national" holiday, and Thanksgiving eve is the time when the whole country hits the road at just about the same time. Little did my parents know that they had nothing to fear about Leon's driving too fast. Nor was this going to be a routine five-hour trip. Sluggish traffic south of Binghamton slowed down even further to a bumper-to-bumper crawl, stop 'n go for fifty miles or so down Route 17 below the Catskill Mountains to the George Washington Bridge. This was the biggest backup I had ever seen, with no let-up in sight. At dusk, all I could see were two solid lanes of red brake lights for miles and miles ahead, going nowhere fast.

To make matters worse, Leon refused to make even a single pit stop as if it would have made a significant difference in our arrival time. Nor would he expend any fuel on heat in the car on that raw November afternoon. We inched along; I was cold, hungry, nauseous, tired, and desperately in need of a restroom.

The two of us were crammed into the back seat with our luggage; Leon had reserved the trunk for his own baggage and the front passenger seat for his stereo, which got far better treatment than we did. The guy must have had a rubber bladder; we weren't going to make it to Brooklyn without a bathroom break.

"Watch out!" Ian warned me as he took matters into his own hands. Without the slightest hesitation, he bolted out of the car, into the bushes off the shoulder of the highway, took care of business, and bounded back into car, all this before we had traveled fifty feet. Leon never batted an eyelash. If traffic had suddenly and miraculously started moving, he would have stranded Ian there without the slightest bit of remorse. When we finally got dropped off shortly after 10:00 P.M., home never looked better and a home-cooked meal never tasted so good. Then and there, Ian and I succumbed and conceded to make the return trip by bus.

Our small, square, tan stucco house was on a residential street in the Brooklyn College section of the borough. All the houses on the block looked the same, although each was painted a different pastel color. The front door opened into a tiny vestibule with a coat closet and then turned left into a fairly large living room, leading into a dining room behind it, followed by a small corridor connecting to the kitchen, bathroom, and two bedrooms. That was it. Like everything back then, simple. For a family of three, it was just fine. A far cry from the palatial estate which I later learned Ian was accustomed to in West Palm Beach. To him, this could have been the servants' quarters. But it was a warm and wonderful home in which to have grown up. And I'm willing to bet Ian would have traded places with me in a flash, giving up those fancy digs for what I had and he lacked.

Luck was on my side: This was the year that it was my parents' turn to host Thanksgiving. (Our tradition was for the aunts and uncles to rotate holidays.) Following the previous day's trek, I couldn't be happier to stay at home, stay off the road, and have the company come to us. The last thing I wanted to do was get back into the car, any car, for any trip. Furthermore, my mother was a terrific cook. In Yiddish, they called her a *ballaboosta.* Her only "fault" was that she overdid it, cooking enough to feed an army. She was forever fearful that there wouldn't be enough. It was explained to me that this was a byproduct of the Depression mentality. I recall eating over at a friend's house in high school. That mother opened up one can of corn, whether there were five or fifteen people at the table.

"Better there should be leftovers," was my mother's defense as she prepared enough rations to feed the whole neighborhood. Turkey, brisket, meatballs, stuffing, puddings, and vegetables galore. Nobody ever went hungry in my house or on my mother's watch. What a cook! The desserts were just as good, although most of these were store-bought. It was custom for everyone else to bring a cake; I held out for the hard-icing chocolate layer with fudge filling or, better yet, the chocolate blackout. I associate those good times with the wonderful aromas that filled our house on a holiday morning as we got ready for the relatives to arrive.

My parents let Ian and me sleep late after the long trip the night before. I woke to the delectable smells of turkey and stuffing in the oven. By the time I got up, having recovered from the previous day's travel odyssey, my mother had already been awake for hours, donning her apron, doing the cooking. Our small kitchen was crammed with dishes she had already prepared, lined up, and labeled on the small table. My father had gone to the local deli to get egg and cheese sandwiches, o.j., and coffee for the two of us, not wanting to break Mom's rhythm in the kitchen and not be under foot. But even before taking a bite, the first thing I did upon rising was to make a quick call to Diana in Chicago.

"What's going on in the Windy City?" I asked.

"A lot of hot air!" she joked.

"I miss you already," I gambled.

"I miss you, too," she replied.

That's all I had to hear; she had made my day.

Even though I had temporarily moved out and was away at college, I still retained my age-old assignment of helping my father piece together the seating arrangement for the 20+ aunts, uncles, and cousins who would be converging on our house. Every card and bridge table was appropriated and appended to the small dining room table; even the piano bench was pressed into service for another two people. The adjacent living room was annexed for a folding table that would serve for kids' seating.

By 2:00 P.M., there was a full house. It was cold, grey, dark, and threatening outside-- a typical New York November day-- but warm, welcoming, and inviting inside. My parents somehow always managed to make it that way. I don't know how we were able to pack all those people into that small space in the dining room, but we did. Yet once seated for dinner, it was virtually impossible to get up or get out. You were locked into place.

After dinner, stuffed to the gills, we piled into the adjoining living room when someone invariably called for "pictures." Out came the old slide projector and we hooted and howled at shots of the same family gatherings taken five, ten, or more years ago. Corny, yeah… I took those good times for granted. How I long for them now. I think that the new generation is missing a great deal; they are searching for that secure, extended family feeling that has been practically eradicated and replaced by a new, fast-moving and mobile world with everyone either on the run or running away altogether. Just too many moving parts.

Ian seemed more than at home with the two dozen relatives whom my parents had assembled for my homecoming from college. They, in turn, welcomed this stranger into their midst with open arms and treated him like a member of the family, rather than a guest. He seemed to relish the presence of all those aunts, uncles, in-laws, and cousins. I sensed a tinge of envy. I thought he would be bored to tears, but he even seemed to enjoy the slide show. I think he was more entertained by the reaction to the pictures than to the pictures themselves, although, granted, some of them were pretty funny.

"I remember when you were this big," reminisced Aunt Ida, cradling a pillow in her lap. I looked at the now bulbous Aunt Ida and thought to myself, "I remember when *you* were *this* big," but diplomatically kept my comments to myself.

"I remember when you used to sit my lap," she cooed. "I remember when you had a lap to sit on," I thought, but contained myself again. They were all so adoring. How much I miss them now.

By Sunday afternoon, it was time to pack up and return to Cornell. I almost said, "to return *home*." That's what Cornell was fast becoming to me. How things had changed. Less than three months ago, I was talking about transferring out. "Be patient; give it a chance," my father coaxed. "Don't make a decision you'll regret." He was right, as usual.

My mother repeated over and over how relieved she was that we had come to our senses and decided to take the bus. We, on the other hand, weren't exactly relishing the thought of being cooped up for seven hours with forty or so strangers on a whistle stop sightseeing trip through the likes of Pennsylvania or the southern tier of New York. Worse, to extend our stay in Brooklyn, we were taking the "red eye" which wouldn't get us back to Ithaca until the following morning. There was no express bus at that hour of the night. I'd just have to go straight to class on arrival, and that's assuming we got there on time. Still, it was a lot better than being stuck with Leon and freezing to death in the backseat of his crammed car. At least there would be heat, a bathroom, and some breathing room.

Ian had taken to my parents and they had taken to him. So after prolonged hugs, kisses, and the standard good-byes, we left with my father for the drive to the Port Authority Terminal in Manhattan for the bus trip back.

But on arrival-- not so fast. As we waited to board the coach, there was a loud commotion at the front of the line.

"What do you mean-- you're not going to drive this bus?" a frantic dispatcher demanded to know.

"You heard me. I'm not even boarding the bus," the driver barked back.

Rubberneckers that we were, Ian and I rushed up front to find out what the fracas was all about. It turns out there was a snake charmer and his groupies heading for Buffalo. Exotic snakes on a bus? And, this driver was deathly afraid of snakes:

"If they're getting on the bus, I'm not," he shouted.

After delicate Kissinger-like negotiations that went on for some time, under the aegis of a supervisor who was trying to satisfy the snake charmer while assuaging the driver, a compromise was at last reached: The snakes could come along for the ride, but they had to remain in the locked undercarriage of the bus. No stops, no visiting. He would get off the bus in Buffalo-- and so would they. Almost an hour late after this brouhaha, we were ready to roll. Could we make up the time or was I going to miss my 8:00 A.M. class?

As soon as the bus roared out of the terminal and pulled away from the City, my attention shifted back to campus life. Next on the agenda were final exams and fraternity rushing.

DECEMBER, 1965

#17 - Changing of the Seasons

With Thanksgiving behind us, the last leaf had fallen off the last tree. The glorious fall season was just about over. The bleakness of winter was waiting in the wings to make its unwelcome entrance. And once it came, it would stay much too long, like an unwanted house guest.

On the first Sunday in December, we put books aside, and watched an afternoon football game on the television in the dorm lounge.

"Hey, how about some dinner at the Olde Inn on the Lake?" Ian suggested excitedly.

"You're kidding, right?" exclaimed Dwayne.

"That place ain't cheap!" added Kip.

"C'mon. Let's splurge. The five of us together. It's a special occasion," said Brant.

And how are we supposed to get there? No matter how good the grub is, I'm not hiking 12 miles," Kip chimed in.

As I've mentioned, automobiles were verboten for freshmen in those days. I love to eat, but no restaurant is worth that trek.

"Brant to the rescue! I can borrow a car from an upperclass teammate. He owes me, anyway."

So for one night, anyway, we had wheels and decided to put them to good use. Upstate New York folds up for the winter season and this restaurant would be shutting down after this weekend. Cabin fever loomed.

The four other guys were paired in conversation. A city boy, I had never seen anything like this before. The days were growing shorter and shorter; lit pumpkins on the roadside, a last vestige of the fall season, guided our way. There was the smell of burning leaves in the air. And it was starting to turn *cold.* Having grown up amid the cement canyons of New York City, this was a whole new wonderful rural world for me. I had always liked the rotation of the four seasons; here that change was even more pronounced.

The five of us traveled as a unit on that particular night. Brant had managed to pull away from his teammates. Even Dwayne had decided to join us. It was the first time in a very long time that our original quintet had been in the same place at the same time, so we were in a rather celebratory mood. It would also be the very last. Leaving campus meant leaving some troubles behind as well.

The Olde Farm Inn was perched atop a promontory on the west shore, overlooking Lake Cayuga. The restaurant had been a huge mansion converted into one of the finest eateries in the Finger Lakes Region. The oversized picture windows offered a stunning view of the lake and Cornell across on the eastern bank. Up until this point, my frame of reference was from the other direction, from the East, looking west, so this panoramic view itself was worth the price of admission. Everyone asked for a window table; students rarely got one. As a matter of fact, students rarely frequented a place such as this. Only for special occasions. And *this* was a special occasion.

There were no menus; the waitresses were these hospitable, folksy types donning big white bows in their hair and frilly country aprons. Among their trademarks was the ability to recite the complete menu of offerings, which rarely changed. From soup to nuts, everything was home grown, freshly cooked, and elegantly served family-style. It was a far cry from the institutional cafeteria cooking to which we had grown inured. Here, no lunch lady counted the number of lukewarm undercooked peas dispensed in a cold white dish. So a great time was had by all. Too bad, it would be the last, at least with all five of us together.

As if Mother Nature knew how to read the calendar, the weather changed drastically with the new month. The winter season made its appearance-- and as I just said, it was going to be a long, unpleasant visit, overstaying its welcome. Central New York is known for its cold, grey, bleak winters. "Ithacating" became a meteorological term for a mixture of overcast skies, raw winds, and misty precipitation. There is an old line that every Cornellian knows: "Ithaca has just two seasons: winter-- and the Fourth of July." Or, "Stick around: If you don't like the weather, it will change in a few minutes." Legend has it that Mark Twain once lived nearby and recorded over 100 different types of weather in a 24-hour period. In any event, after the glorious fall season, I now felt as though I had been marooned on the tundra.

Cold and grey on the outside for at least five months. Friends who went to colleges in warmer climes forever asked me, "How did you ever manage to survive those winters?" We Cornellians adapt quickly and easily, redirecting our energies. Snow and ice just don't get in our way. And for the cold weather buffs, nearby skiing and intercollegiate hockey couldn't be better. The academic year was in full swing, the party season had heated up, the bars were full, hockey tickets were on sale, and fraternity rush was just one month away. No doubt about it: Cornellians are a special breed; they have to hit the books hard-- but they also know how to have a damn good time.

Besides seeing Diana in class every other day, I now spoke to her every evening and saw her both nights of the weekend. I guess taking for granted that we would be together without making a date meant that we were, as they used to say, "going steady." Admittedly, at first I felt I didn't deserve such a good-looking girl. Alas, my old insecurities were surfacing again. But Ian took over the controls:

"Listen, dude. Trade in those glasses for some contact lenses. Ditch those duds. You look like Urkel or Eddie Haskell. Get some new threads. If you want to keep a girl like Diana, dress the part." So then and there, Ian performed what is now called a "makeover." Before long Diana and I looked like a matched pair. Well, not quite. But at least I was out of the geek zone.

Our favorite haunt was the "Commons," a coffee house located in the basement (or, "lower level," as they preferred to call it) of Annabel Taylor Hall, the religious center, and a block down from Willard Straight Hall, a.k.a. "the Straight," or student union building at the core of the campus. This supplanted the Ivy Room cafeteria in the Straight as my number one hangout.

It was here that I acquired my lifelong addiction to strong coffee and sixties tunes. Early on in the freshman year, the music consisted solely of mindless love songs spun on a quarter-gets-you-four-plays jukebox. Most of us still didn't have a care in the world and our music reflected it. Those are the songs still played over and over again on the oldies stations: "I Will Follow Him," "Runaround Sue," and "Donna, the Prima Donna"--just to name a few. Who listened to the meaningless lyrics, anyway? They all had a great beat, and that is all that mattered.

The Fall Weekend hoax had been just that, a hoax. Campus life returned to normalcy, just as quickly as that tranquility, security, and complacency had been shattered by the *Cornell Sun* headline. Tucked away cozily in upstate middle-of- nowhere, we felt protected. Most of us still managed to ignore *The New York Times,* which devoted increasing coverage with screaming headlines to the War in the rice paddies and civil rights protests in the cities. There was an advantage from being in such a remote place: We could just block it all out. College campuses in the big cities weren't so insulated.

But we couldn't escape it altogether. That social consciousness was starting to creep into our music. Local folk singers began appearing at the Commons. The music was no longer so mindless. Naïve as I was back then, I enjoyed the guitar music, but still paid little attention to the words. That irked Diana no end. I sat there mimicking the beat of the drums at our table with the silverware, bobbing my head, humming along.

"Don't you hear what they're saying? Aren't you listening?" she chided me on more than one occasion with great exasperation in her voice. "Why do you tune these things out?" she rebuked me.

Maybe she was right; maybe I did. It was the Pollyanna in me. But at that point in time, these heavy-duty issues still hadn't hit home or touched me personally. That would come later. For the time being, I sidestepped them and took things at face value. To this day, I am still accused of seeing the world through rose-colored glasses.

Not Diana. If anything, she was the direct opposite and took it upon herself to be the world's savior and made every political and social issue her business. She was the only child of two prominent Chicago attorneys. I was starting to feel that being only children was about the only thing we had in common. Her family lived in a well-to-do suburb, just north of the city proper. They were liberals even before it had become fashionable to sport that label. Ironic that she and Dwayne hailed from the same city, but from two opposite ends of town as well as two opposite ends of the economic spectrum. When I complained about his forsaking the fearsome fivesome, she became even more irritated and impatient with me.

"Can't you imagine what he's going through, being the only African-American in the group? Don't you have any sensitivity?" Diana shook her head, somewhere between disbelief and disgust.

"No, I don't," I half-mocked. "I guess I'm just an un-feeling type of guy," I snapped back, uncharacteristically, surprising even myself. But I had about had it with her put-downs. And I kept on beating the table to the rhythm of the music, which seemed to annoy her even more.

"It was *his* choice to pull away; he didn't have to," I argued. I pretended that it didn't bother me, but in truth, it really did. Selfishly I felt a betrayal at his withdrawing from the group without understanding where he was coming from. Besides, who was Diana to complain, anyway? She didn't exactly live in the slums. But I didn't want to become too contentious for fear of wrecking our relationship, so I bit my lip and kept my mouth shut. I had fallen for this girl, head over heels, like none ever before.

Fortunately, these verbal fisticuffs between us remained on the surface and didn't last very long. Other common denominators, such as the music, attracted us and we continued to draw closer and closer together, despite the differences in our politics and viewpoints.

JANUARY, 1966

#18 – Intermission

Winter break was uneventful. The five of us, even Ian, scattered cross-country to our hometowns. The days passed by quickly, doing what, I can't say for sure. I was restless, eager to get back to school for fraternity rush and final exams-- in that order, which showed my pathetic lack of priorities. Back on campus, much of the first few weeks of January were spent cranking out papers and cramming for the fast-approaching make-it-or-break-it exams. Pulling all-nighters became a way of life as my caffeine addiction heightened. I had fallen prey to the common Cornell malady: namely, procrastination. I'd use any excuse to get out of studying. "Want to hang out?" Sure. "Want to go down to the diner?" Why not? I'd follow anyone who'd lead me by the nose. In short, I didn't know the word "no." Avoidance became my mantra. I had put off much too much until it was almost too late.

Miraculously, though, I managed to get everything turned in at or near the deadline, although the assignments were rush jobs. Papers were returned with disappointing results; alas, the content was good, but they were rife with typographical errors that I could have easily corrected if I hadn't waited until the last minute and reserved just a little time to proofread. For one project, I carelessly omitted a page altogether when I had collated and stapled it. As a result, the final grades weren't what they could've and should've been. Then and there I promised myself to have learned from my mistakes and would never let this happen again-- a vow that I never quite managed to keep.

We experienced our second casualty at the end of that first semester. First it had been Buzz; now it was Brant.

When I got back to the dorms, as usual, everyone was gathered in our room. But the mood was heavy; you could cut it with a knife.

"Who died?" I asked, trying to break the spell, but nobody appreciated my pathetic attempt at humor.

After a pause, Brant stepped forward. "I've been asked to leave Cornell." At that point he shoved a notice in my face which had been hand-delivered from the dean. All the tutoring in the world couldn't save him. He ended up with an anemic grade point average a smidgen below 1.0

"You are being asked to continue your studies elsewhere." The letter ended with some ray of hope: conditions under which he would be allowed to return.

All of this was hardly a surprise to Brant; he had sensed for some time that this directive was coming and so he was philosophical about it. He blamed his poor performance on his athletic pursuits. He had learned his lesson, or so he said.

"I should have come as a student first, athlete second," he moaned with a sigh. He pledged that from this point on he would hang up his cleats and crack the books. Brant had it all worked out.

"I'll attend a local community college at home in Maryland for the spring semester, and then re-apply for admission to Cornell for the following fall. So I'll be just a year behind the rest of you guys." But Brant was never to be a student at Cornell ever again.

Relationships change; people move in and out of your life. I still recall one Sociology professor who compared marriage partners to constantly moving circles: "Sometimes the circles stand still, other times they keep moving; sometimes they move together, but often they move apart; sometimes they touch, and other times they even overlap. They may stay together for a while, or even forever; but other times they may be on the move again, and, sadly, in very different directions." I think the same is true of friends. You gain some, you lose some as the years go by.

As time passed, I realized I had lost a friend-- a very loyal one. I was just too foolish to realize it then. Forever surrounded by people at home, at work, and at play, "friends" seemed deceptively cheap, plentiful, and expendable. There was, there is, there will always be-- a significant difference between an "acquaintance" and a "friend." Superficiality separates the two. That was, it still is-- one of my biggest regrets-- never being able to distinguish between them. And still a third category: "frenemies"-- those people who *pretend* to be your friends.

Poor Brant: athletic prowess, yes; academic depth, nil. As I said earlier, he was the personification of the dumb jock. But with that simplicity came a naiveté which I privately scoffed at… then appreciated more and more as the years passed by… and now value so much today. For a variety of reasons, I have lost some close friends. That's a flaw in me to which I plead "guilty."

With Brant, what you saw is what you got. He had no airs or phoniness or duplicity about him. There wasn't a mean bone in his body. His lack of sophistication was not a weakness; on the contrary, genuineness was a major strength. It was one of his finest qualities, something I didn't appreciate then and wish I could emulate now. As life has gone by, I have been duped in many dealings and relationships; but Brant was simply incapable of deceiving anyone. Ultrasensitive, he would do anything to please, willing to give you the proverbial shirt off his back. He was one of those people who needed to be liked. At the same time, he liked everyone.

Strikingly handsome like Ian, but in a different way, Brant had no trouble getting dates. The co-eds seemed to line up to go out with him. But during his abbreviated stay at Cornell, I realized that he had very few *second* dates-- because the girls were looking for someone deeper. What's the opposite of "slick," anyway? Sad, they didn't give it time to realize what a really great guy he was. Regrettable, that back then, I didn't realize it either-- what a rare commodity he was and what a solid, potential life-long friend I was losing.

Dwayne was a different story altogether. He became increasingly scarce, spending most of his time with his fellow black students. I had repeatedly extended my open hand, but only got a clenched fist in return; that offer was soundly rebuffed. As a matter of fact, I sensed hostility directed at me alone. What had I ever done to him? Looking back-- now I fully understand; I was far from faultless in the demise of our fast friendship. I failed to realize how difficult it was for him to be such a small minority those days. Never mind, I tried to convince myself. First Brant, now Dwayne. A double dose of disappearing. I brushed it off cavalierly. Deep down, I had to admit that it really stung.

Kip was still around, but he was spending more and more time at the Engineering Library and less and less time in the dorms. What spare moments he had left were reserved for his girlfriend Margaret, that female clone. They looked alike, they acted alike, and they were in complete tandem. Lucky Kip; he had found his soulmate. The two of them moved in step. I questioned whether Diana and I would ever have that kind of relationship. It certainly wasn't coming naturally; rather, it was something we had to work at. They took it for granted. It bothered me that I had to wonder about that, envious of what Kip and Margaret had. In the meantime, I liked their honest, down-to-earth, unsophisticated country bumpkin ways and worked to keep my friendship with Kip alive as best I could, although from a distance.

And then there were two. As the fearsome fivesome began to disintegrate, Ian and I became even tighter. I looked to him as a big brother while he viewed me as the source of stability missing in his life. Too bad that this best friendship would eventually be tested and also short-lived.

LATE JANUARY, 1966

#19 - "On your mark, get set...."

During the fall semester, "fraternities," "sororities" and "rushing" were strictly verboten words in the freshman vocabulary. "Hands off!" was the University's clear and distinct message to the fifty or so national houses, part of the elaborate Greek system that was very much alive and well on campus. "Leave 'em alone!" was Cornell's cry and it meant business. Other colleges permitted students to enter the fraternity/sorority system on arrival.

Not Cornell! Freshmen were untouchables, to be left alone for the first half of the year, so they could make the adjustment to college and concentrate on their academics before they practically cast aside their studies in favor of pledging nonsense. Otherwise, the dropout rate might have been 50%. Violators-- who were immediately reported by tattletale rival houses competing for the same desired pledges-- were swiftly and severely dealt with. It was a veritable spy system.

The University was prepared to put muscle behind its mouth, with tough penalties meted out for those houses that ignored the ban-on-contact decree. Like the proctor's three-feet-on-the-floor rule, there was zero tolerance for violators. Our only link to the Greek world was via classroom association with upperclassmen, which the University (alas) conceded, was something it just could not control. After all, there was a smattering of sophomores and even juniors and seniors in some of our elective courses, and like wolves in search of prey, they were on the constant lookout, obviously reporting back to their rushing chairmen, getting their contact lists ready to roll once the moratorium was lifted. Recruiting "hot" prospects was as competitive as trying to sign superstar athletes. I started to feel that signing bonuses were being paid. Perpetuating the breed was what it was all about.

Of course, this hard and fast rule didn't prevent us freshmen from talking about fraternities and rushing; as a matter of fact, all during January, it was the *major* topic of conversation in the dorms, pre-empting the upcoming final exams, which should have been our primary concern. As soon as the fall semester was officially over and those exams were behind us, the Interfraternity Council fired the opening shot-- and it was all men (and women) for themselves. Rushing was on, no holds barred.

Cornell was a big fraternity-sorority school, which is not surprising given its size. It's easy for 12,000 underclassmen (a total that doesn't include the graduate students) to fall between the cracks and get lost in a very impersonal shuffle. The system provided an opportunity for the large cell to divide into smaller, more manageable ones. Put another way, those looking for a home could find one. Back then, about 40% of the freshmen ended up going Greek. How many actually stuck it out without depledging or de-activating (once initiated) is another story.

Of course, there were other alternatives for those who wanted to find that "home." One of Cornell's greatest strengths is its size: huge student body… but also a collection of smaller communities. You don't have to conform to fit in. For example, if you're a harmonica-playing Icelander maturing in botany… odds are you'll find more harmonica-playing Icelanders with the same major. Not that other colleges don't have a wide array of activities from which to choose; but they also have adjacent cities which serve as an extension of their campuses.

Cornell's unique isolation and remote location turn out to be a major advantage, at least as far as campus life is concerned. The University is not what college students refer to as a "suitcase school"; there is really no place to go on weekends and traveling home is costly, in terms of time, distance, and money. In some ways, it has become a "walled city."

As a result, on-campus activities became the outlet for that energy. Glee Club, Asia Society, Students Against Cruelty to Reptiles, intramural sports, Gay Activists Alliance, Coalition for a Clean Environment, Young Marxists, Society for the Prevention of Circumcision of Buffalos-- just to name a very, very few which attracted hundreds and hundreds of students. Though hard to believe, if there wasn't a club or organization to your liking, then you could start one, which is what some students did.

There were those who rejected fraternities from the start, as did Kip. In essence, his "home" was the Engineering Quad where he spent so many hours with his classmates. For all intents and purposes, he was in a de facto "fraternity" already. Others elected to get immersed in extracurricular activities. For example, the drama troupe, which put on five or six full-scale productions each year, could also become a base for those looking for a place to hang their hats or just plain hang out. Ditto for the staff of the *Cornell Sun* and WVBR, the radio station.

And then there were other more independent souls who didn't want or need a group or home; they preferred to be by themselves, looked down their noses at the fraternity-sorority scene, and by mid-freshman year were already hunting for roommates or single apartments, generally in old rooming houses in the Collegetown section, or on the outskirts of campus, for the next school year.

I'm surprised that the "Idiot's Complete Guide to Fraternities" or "Rushing for Dummies" has never been written. Mastering the Greek system is indeed an art, if not a science. Each of the 40 fraternities and dozen sororities was "typed"-- and prospective pledges were pigeonholed into those categories. (Of course, each house strived to find its "token" minority members to disprove this theory.) There were houses for: animal jocks, pretty-boy jocks, rich city guys, poor suburban nerds, animals, farmers, pigs, artsies, engineering tools-- and the list went on and on.

The fraternity directory could have taken on the look of a real estate catalogue, with a photograph of each house along with a capsule description of its membership profile. For example: "Soccer and lacrosse jocks preferred; New York City types need not apply; token minorities considered, but only one or two." Then we could have avoided this madness and done the whole thing by computer matching. But nobody has ever written such a guidebook. And I suppose that getting there was half the fun. So the race was on. Let the games begin!

No surprise, but just about every house on the Hill took aim at Ian. Why not? Between his "strong profile" and being the son of a quasi-celebrity, he was a hot ticket. Although active rushing was not permitted in the fall, I later learned once I was on the inside, that pledge committees had been assembling their "preferred" or "A" lists all along, which would be activated the split second the recruitment ban was lifted. Every house would have liked Ian as a pledge.

An elaborate inspection procedure had been devised through the years to sift, sort, code, categorize, and label prospective new pledges. During the fall, rushing committees assembled lists of potential recruits whom they would go after as soon as the starting gun was fired in January. These were based on campus contacts in classes, on teams, and in activities, which were beyond the control of the University's "hands off" policy. Recommendations also came from siblings, upperclassmen, and even alumni. Pigbook pictures were posted on poster boards with pithy comments about each.

The rushing chairman was one of the most important, if not the most important, officers in the fraternity house. He took on the air of a powerbroker; the future of the chapter rested on his shoulders. After all, even one weak rush could doom the house by failing to perpetuate the breed. Even the high and the mighty could not rest on their laurels.

Freshmen received invitations to smokers at which they were systematically passed around like hors d'oeuvres, handed off like partners in a square dance, and herded past the brotherhood like cattle for branding. The rushing chairman and his henchmen stood on high and choreographed these smokers. It was as simple as A-B-C. Literally, A-B-C! Potential brothers were being rated "A" rushes (hottest prospects), "B" rushes (so-so candidates), or "CC's"-- closet cases (not even worth talking to). A "CC" was moved around the rushing floor like a hot potato, with each brother trying to unload him as quickly as possible to the next. It didn't take long for us freshmen to figure out how these smokers worked.

As soon as the smoker was over, the pledges were quickly driven back to the dorms and the brother escorts raced back to the house. There, the membership immediately assembled for "hash sessions" at which time the pigbook picture of each prospective pledge was flashed on the screen. While the images were fresh in their minds to dissect their prey, the brothers labeled them with such witty descriptors as "hot prospect," "geek," "grunge bucket," "closet case" and so forth. As each new picture went up, sound effects from the audience enhanced the individual ratings. Yet another generation about to be born to perpetuate the old stereotypes.

Dwayne had long since committed to the black co-op. If it were up to him, he would have moved in there by now; but he, too, had to wait until his sophomore year to become a full-fledged member. Instead, he spent all his waking moments over there, returning to the dorm late at night just to sleep. It was understandable. We didn't see him for days on end.

As I said, Kip had declared from the outset that he was going to remain an "indy." Although he halfheartedly went along to some of the smokers with us after considerable coaxing, he decided the Greek life just wasn't for him. He planned to take an apartment in Collegetown for his sophomore year with some fellow tools. Ian and I pledged to pledge together. Unfortunately, though, for me anyway, that didn't work out the way we had planned.

"Contacts" came to the dorms to deliver bids to prospective hopefuls during a three-hour stretch on the appointed evening. For some, it was a long and painful evening; they were eagerly expecting guests, but none ever arrived. It was like getting stood up on a blind date. In some ways, it was worse than waiting for college acceptance letters; the news could determine your social life for the next three and a half years-- or more. Imagine making an offer to one roommate and having to come empty-handed to the other. I saw it happen again and again in Humboldt Hall.

Without a doubt, this ritual was one of the most hurtful things I have ever observed. Watching some guys rack up offer after offer while others ended up with zip must have been an ego-blowing, humiliating experience. "Whatdidyaget, whatdidyaget?" Not only does a left-on-the-shelf freshman have to answer to his classmates, but he also has to answer to himself. "What's wrong with me?" he questions. "How come nobody wants me?" Simply put, the system sucked.

On bid night, Ian had a full house, with offers from more than a dozen fraternities. But I did "okay" as well, receiving several good offers myself. My first choice was Chi Alpha Theta, the "CAT house," as it was called. It was stocked with some great New York City guys with whom I fit in, and they gave me a bid. I was ignoring yet another piece of wisdom dispensed by my guidance counselor about dorming and rooming and hanging out with guys from the same background.

"That's not what you go to an out-of-town college for," so went the sermon. I had taken his sage advice about a freshman roommate. And what had I ended up with? Buzz. So much for his words of wisdom. Frankly, I wanted to be comfortable. And I was very comfortable and at ease with the brothers of CAT. I just took it for granted that Ian would go along with me as we had planned, in what they called a "package deal."

I could see, though, that something was eating away at him. The morning after bids were handed out, I cornered him.

"What's the story? You've been avoiding me last night and today."

We had vowed to stick together; and I had assumed, then, that we were both bound for the same house. I knew that he, too, liked and felt comfortable at CAT. It was the only bid we had in common. But Ian was reluctant to tell me something; he was holding it back. For a moment I assumed that maybe he, too, had decided to buck the fraternity system and not pledge.

"OK, pal, let's hear it. What's going on?

After a long pause, Ian finally came clean. He hit me right between the eyes.

"You asked for it." After another interminable pause, he blurted it out: "I also have an offer from Gamma Rho."

His pronouncement fell on me like a ton of bricks. Gamma was, without a doubt, *the* most prestigious house on campus. How could CAT compete? I knew how torn he was and how guilty he felt. I made it abundantly clear that I had no intention of standing in his way. We had established a close bond and had developed a degree of friendship and trust I never had been lucky enough to have had before. Heretofore many of my relationships were either superficial to the point of being worthless or based on destructive competition. And so this one, too, I feared, was destined to be cut short. I would be losing a close buddy, but I knew how desperately he wanted that bid from Gamma.

"I'm not going to send you on a guilt trip. If this is what you want, so be it. I'm not standing in your way. Go for it."

Ian, who had been looking down during this whole conversation, suddenly looked up and directly at me. He stretched out his hand; I did the same. Unrealistic as I tend to be and dreamer that I am, I just expected this friendship to remain intact despite the fact that we were going our separate fraternity ways.

"We're still on the same campus. It's not like we're leaving Cornell," we consoled each other. But it was like Abbott without Costello. And so Ian and I parted ways, pledging different houses.

However, this wrinkle in our relationship was mild by comparison to future bumps in the road, and only the first chapter in what would be an up-and-down and stormy friendship in the years to come.

As strange as fraternity rushing was, the sorority brand was even more bizarre. There were only a dozen or so houses, each with a clear and distinct pedigree. It was fair game to tag a girl and predict where she would end up. From the "Miss Americas" to the "Miss Piggys," we guys were right on the mark with our sorting system, cruel as it now seems.

I had Diana earmarked for Beta Theta Omega. It was a lock. I just took it for granted that's where she'd pledge. "Betas" were known to be the best-looking girls on campus; they were also pegged as the snobbiest. Assume nothing. When I casually mentioned my prediction to her, I was not prepared for her volatile outburst as she uncharacteristically flew off the handle.

"How could you even *think* that I would lower myself to that level?" She had no intention of joining a sorority; furthermore, she seemed annoyed and almost indignant that I was of such "low moral fiber" that I would consider being part of a fraternity. Frankly, I didn't know back then what "moral fiber" meant; the only fiber I was familiar with came in oatmeal. As it turned out, that single exchange soured our relationship irreparably and was going to mark the beginning of the end. Our worlds and our value systems were just too far apart. The pot had been simmering for months; now it was going to come to a boil.

FEBRUARY, 1966

#20 - Breaking Up Is Hard To Do

Second semester picked up where the fall semester had left off. The only difference was that with one term under my belt, I knew the ropes and was better able to navigate the system. I also had a newfound home in my fraternity. And although I wouldn't live in the building until the following fall, much of my existence became centered around the "CAT house," that big rickety old wooden building on one of Cornell's several fraternity rows.

I still returned to the dorm at night and often hung out with Ian and Kip. But from early morning through dinner and then again until after libe time, we were all away from the dorms. Now our first loyalties were elsewhere as we were all being pulled in different directions. It became a yeoman test of our friendship. We had to work at getting together; just finding time for hanging out was no longer taken for granted.

My relationship with Diana co-terminated with the end of the fall semester. The differences over fraternities and sororities was the immediate cause. But I rationalized that if it hadn't been that issue, it would have been something else. I had fallen for her hook, line, and sinker at first sight; maybe it was just too much too soon.

As we had gotten to know each other better and better, we realized that our ways of looking at things were too diametrically different. At first I thought that I could be the one to change to conform to her expectations. But try as I did, we seemed to agree on less and less and bickered more and more. Appeasement didn't work. The more I bent over backwards to her way of thinking, the more fault she found in me. There was no explosion at the end; the relationship just petered out; it ended in a whimper. The flame extinguished itself. The game had been called on account of indifference before I could get to second base.

Mercifully, we didn't have any classes together in the spring semester. Out of sight was, hopefully, out of mind. The Cornell campus is so huge that I could go for weeks at a time without running into her-- which is not what I wanted, but which is what happened. The Commons was still my favorite hangout and I think that subconsciously I went there hoping to run into her. But she never showed up anymore.

While we had been going out, it had been convenient not to have to work at making dates and just to take it for granted that she would be there for me, especially on weekends. Now I had to throw myself back into the mating pool and play the dating game all over again. Admittedly, I was rusty. I was a single guy again, and not liking it very much at all. Although Ian and I were still roommates in the dorm, we were living in two different worlds, and he was no longer much help.

I used my newfound celibacy to concentrate on my studies. After an anemic albeit passing 2.6 grade point average for the fall semester, I vowed to take advantage of the fresh start (and current single status) to put in more time in the library. That was my defense mechanism: trying to convince myself that I had to get over Diana and my mind off of her. But a challenging obstacle loomed: wrestling.

MARCH 1966

#21 - Wrestlemania

Fortunately, my newfound friends in the fraternity were chock-full of advice when it came to selecting Physical Education classes. During the course of the freshman year, everyone-- well, almost everyone-- (except those, like Dwayne, who had flunked the swim test) was required to pass through a 30-week rotation, with three weeks spent at each of ten activities before rotating to the next. The purpose of this exercise was to expose us to as many different lifetime sports as possible. This seemed harmless enough, even for a non-jock like me: badminton, bowling, gymnastics, soccer, swimming, and so on. It was the "so on" that would prove to be my downfall. I was cautioned to expend the maximum three cuts allowed per semester very judiciously.

Not exactly the athletic type, I sometimes felt it was my fate to be relegated to a retirement village at an early age, getting my exercise from horseshoes, shuffleboard, bowling, and bocce. In high school gym class I never made it up to the top of the ropes; as a matter of fact, I never managed to lift myself off the floor. I rarely if ever got the ball over the net when I played volleyball. And I retreated to the back row when it came time for dodge ball for fear of getting hit. Even punchball, a Brooklyn phenomenon, was a major challenge for me. Forget about golf; and tennis was even worse: I could barely make contact with the ball, rationalizing that there must have been a hole in my racket.

After surviving the freshman swim test back at the beginning of the year with both body parts and dignity unscathed, I had become almost a regular in the Teagle Pool, still weighing in at a svelte 149 pounds, quite trim for a tall guy. Not exactly a championship swimmer, I nevertheless found this form of exercise to be relaxing and one that kept me in pretty good physical shape. I had swimming under control and was totally at home in the pool.

At the bowling alley, we were on the honor system, just having to sign in at the desk. For all they knew, I could have spent an hour in the TV lounge. At badminton, I just prayed the shuttlecock was never hit in my direction. I muddled my way through those two. But it was going to be wrestling that would prove to be my downfall. After several sessions, I decided then and there that this was where I would elect to "spend" my three cuts.

The drill was the same each time. On entering Teagle, you went right to the "cage" where a grumpy curmudgeon, who must have been Ezra Cornell's classmate, dispensed the rations: skimpy grey flannel shorts, a washed-out tee shirt, a towel that reeked from bleach, and a threadbare jockstrap.

"Size?" My answer produced undoubtedly one of my most embarrassing moments. I didn't know whether he was referring to the waist or the cup, so this skinny merink was in a great deal of discomfort until I got the measurements down pat. In the meantime, it was obvious that my tuition money certainly wasn't going towards new gym uniforms. You had to change and get to the assigned activity by the prescribed starting time or else be marked late and, perish the thought, run the risk of having to suffer this indignity all over again.

Carl Crumm, the wrestling instructor, was this short, stocky, neck-less drill sergeant-type who looked as though he had been transplanted from boot camp, crew cut and all. He seemed to take delight in the pretzel-like contortions he demonstrated on the mats, using members of the class as his unwilling props. I cringed every time he raised his pointer finger; I only hoped he wouldn't call on me for one of his demonstrations. Fortunately, I lucked out. But I still shuddered when I heard the joints and other body parts of my classmates creak. I kept glancing at my watch; this class couldn't end soon enough. Towards the end of the hour, it was our turn to show what we had learned. I was randomly paired with this rather rotund fellow who looked as though he hadn't shaved and smelled as though he hadn't showered since he had arrived on campus.

The first two subjects were called forward to demonstrate what they had learned. Once again, I sighed in relief that I had been spared this indignity. Instead, it was Ralph who had been pulled out-- actually *volunteered*-- this arrogant s.o.b. wiseacre whom I recognized from the dorms. Nobody liked him. Look up "creep" in the dictionary and you'll find his picture there. He was the type of guy who, when you ran into him coming down the corridor, just assumed *you* would step out of the way because *he* was coming.

Nor did he have any compunction about cutting the cafeteria line at the Barf Bar, as if the food were worth fighting for. Still, everyone seemed afraid to challenge him. The world existed for Ralph, or so he thought. I despised guys like this. He owned the air space-- just very impressed with himself. And for little reason: stocky, scruffy, and swarthy. We couldn't imagine what any girl would see in him. Yet I had been amazed on Fall Weekend at the pretty decent-looking co-ed he had managed to corral.

Still, I felt his physical pain (and mental anguish) when I saw his partner, this gorilla-type-of-guy lift him up five feet off the ground, hold him like a statue with one hand on the chin and the other on the crotch-- and then proceed to fling him down on the mat, completely knocking the starch out of him, all of this to the delight of his classmates, most of whom found him just as thoroughly repulsive as I did.

As if that indignity wasn't enough, the ape lifted him up again, even before he could get his wind back, this time propping him up by holding him under the arms. However, it became very obvious that poor Ralph had broken one of the cardinal rules of P.E. class; as his gym shorts rode up, the poor guy wasn't wearing his "official" Cornell-regulation-threadbare-athletic-supporter dispensed by that old guy at the Teagle cage. Unbeknownst to King Kong behind him, the victim was *very* aware himself that he was increasingly "hangin' out" and flapping in the wind, flailed his legs wildly to cut himself loose to the roar of the other guys. But it was to no avail; the more he tried to break loose, the greater the public display of his package popping out of his shorts. And it couldn't have happened to a more deserving fellow. Payback time! Even usually straight-laced Carl managed to snicker at the spectacle. Roger landed on the mats a second time; overcome with embarrassment and to the delight of the class, beet-faced, he bolted back to the locker room.

This was it! I didn't want any other guy picking me up; nor did I want to handle anyone else, especially some smelly, sweaty Neanderthal. Now if this had only been a co-ed sport... But it wasn't-- and this was the perfect time to exercise my escape mechanism. Like a "Get Out of Jail Free" card, I had scrupulously saved my gyms cuts all semester and would now put them to very good use.

LATER THAT WEEK

#22 - In Flew Enza

As luck would have it, though, I ended up not having to go to *any more* wrestling classes. For a day or so after that ugly encounter, I had a dull headache and little appetite--which itself was very strange for me. After all, I could run the table at dinner. Was this my penance for ridiculing Ralph during his humiliation? Two days later I succumbed and headed for the health clinic with a severe headache (the kind that even extra strength aspirin doesn't mask), cold sweat, and violent stomach cramps. I was burning up; yet I felt the chills-- hot and cold at the same time. Conveniently, I went during wresting class. I didn't know whether this constituted a cut. Frankly, the way I felt-- I didn't care.

The wait to see a doctor seemed endless. An old black and white TV in the reception area was broadcasting little more than snow and static; a few badly tattered magazines on the battered end tables were more than a year old. It really didn't matter. I was too sick to watch television, read, or do anything else. All I wanted to do was see a doctor, get some medicine, and start to feel better.

After what seemed like an interminable time, I was summoned to walk behind the large swinging doors into the examining area. Where was the doctor? The receptionist mechanically pointed to a bench.

"Sit down," she ordered me.

"But where is the doctor?" I panicked.

"Sit down, I said," she repeated herself, not amused. After all that time, I was expecting to get to see the doctor. Instead, this nurse, a rather huge, humorless, frightening creature, appeared on the scene. She was a portrait in white, with the old-fashioned cap holding down blond curls and dressed in crisp hospital whites, white stockings, and white shoes. Even her face appeared powdered. Her only color was ridiculously bright red shiny lipstick, something only a clown would wear. Surely her cold hands weren't going to handle my burning body. Or were they?

"Open your mouth so I can spray your throat," she directed me without even a "hello" and with the tenderness of a tarantula.

"But I don't have a sore throat," I mildly protested, too sick to put up a better fight.

"I said-- open your mouth," she barked the order once again.

"Shut up," advised the fellow who suddenly appeared out of nowhere sitting next to me. He somehow managed to talk to me despite having a thermometer flung in his mouth. "She sprays *everyone's* throat. You could have a hemorrhoid and she'd spray your throat," he mumbled. This guy seemed to know the drill. So I gave in and opened my mouth.

The doctor, whose bedside manner was not much more compassionate than that of this Florence Nightingale, finally appeared and after a cursory examination, determined that I did in fact have a wicked case of the flu. Like a prisoner in shackles, I was transported by station wagon to the infirmary down the hill and informed that my "sentence" would probably be about a week. The only thing missing were the handcuffs.

But I was too sick to run away, anyway. Also like a prisoner, I was permitted one phone call, which I made to my parents, who would have called out the National Guard if they didn't find me in the dorms. It took some convincing to keep them from racing up to Ithaca. I reassured them that I was in good hands and I'd be fine in a few days. What I didn't tell them, though, is that I longed to be back in Brooklyn, in my own bed, under my own cozy comforter. It's no fun feeling so sick and being so far away from home, especially in that cold (in more ways than one) infirmary.

Maybe this was psychosomatic; perhaps I had brought this malady on myself, I confessed, guilt-ridden-- just to get out of the rest of wrestling. Or, maybe it was my punishment for relishing Ralph's mortification. I don't which was more torturous, burning up in this prison or being tossed around on the mats by a stinking gorilla. My head was killing me so I couldn't think straight.

The admitting nurse assigned me to a spot. The infirmary bed was high and hard. The sheets were coarse with an army blanket tightly wrapped around the mattress. Slipping under was itself a project. What I would have given for my own pillow and blanket from home. All I wanted to do was to go to sleep.

And sleep I did, for most of that week. I remember little else until my temperature finally broke. I was in a ward with five others, but there was little if any communication among us. We were all too sick. My roommates were also feeling the wrath of the epidemic sweeping campus and none of us was in the talking mood. The only thing that interrupted my snoozing was having my temperature taken at seemingly all hours of the day and night, and the appearance of trays of food, most of which I turned away untouched. I don't know whether it was the fact that I had zero appetite, felt so sick, or the rations were so unappetizing. Maybe it was a combination of all three.

The only other thing I recall was the constant blaring of a black and white television that rested precariously on two brackets high up on the wall. It broadcast non-stop, twenty-four hours a day, a mélange of raucous game shows and monotonous soap operas. Nobody ever took the trouble to turn it off or even change the station, even on the overnight.

There was also a great deal of news on the television, more than I was accustomed to hearing. At home, I had grown up with the TV constantly on, one of those kids who did his homework all the time in front of the set. Try as they did, my parents h cess in curing me of this addiction. This was one of the few points of conflict between us back then. Some people can't study with the least bit of noise; I, on the other hand, growing up, couldn't study in silence. The library made me crazy.

I recall friends who were limited to the number of hours they could watch television each day and just assumed that their parents would be carted off by the child welfare authorities for inflicting such cruel punishment. On the rare occasions that my parents suspended this privilege (they knew my weakness), I went through withdrawal symptoms. It was about the worst deprivation they could inflict on me. It would have been less painful to have been sent to bed without supper. So on coming to Cornell, this TV junkie had been forced to go cold turkey, having been removed from television and the news in particular. The few sets were in the lounges and the reception, pre-cable, was lousy at best.

How times have changed since 1965. These days, college students bring with them every creature comfort from home, including their own Smart phones, beepers, answering machines, televisions, cable boxes, DVD players, stereos, speakers (that can eat up half the dorm space), refrigerators, hot plates, grills, and even microwave ovens. Rooms take on the look of appliance stores. I'm surprised nobody's added a smaller washer & dryer, but I wouldn't be surprised if that's next. Back in 1965, we were permitted *none* of those amenities. You couldn't even have a hot plate in your room for fear of incurring the wrath of an R.A. like Farmer Roy, who, in turn, would relish the opportunity to rat you out to the assistant proctor.

For me, television was the most painful deprivation. Most college students experienced some degree of this separation, but it was especially keen in Ithaca, so sequestered in the hills and valleys of upstate New York, so removed from any city. Even if we had our own TVs (there was that broken-down set in the dorm lounge), there was little to watch. With cable still in its infancy, we were lucky to be able to pick up any signal out in the sticks, and the reception was snowy at best. For a city boy like me, this was really roughing it.

I was caught in a time warp. The world was changing faster than ever… but my connection to it had been severed. The *Cornell Sun* contained world and national news headlines and I did steal an occasional look at *The New York Times.* But having been so preoccupied with campus life, I had really lost touch with the outside world and what was going on. Now I was about to get a dose of reality. The focus had changed: Johnson had been catapulted to the forefront….the War in Vietnam was percolating….our participation in that War was being debated….and a peacetime draft was at issue. On the domestic front, civil rights protests had taken to the streets with large-scale demonstrations and even riots in some cities.

Suddenly I was jolted back in touch with the real world. The tranquility of campus life was also about to be shattered. For several months I had successfully tuned out and turned off what was going on beyond the borders of the insulated Cornell campus. Thanks to my unanticipated infirmary confinement, I had become a captive audience, and now I knew everything that was happening in the outside world. It wasn't a pretty picture.

On the fourth morning of my confinement, I woke up in a drenching sweat. The fever had finally broken. Apparently there had been some cause for concern about the high temperature I had been running. A kindly old nurse, a far cry from the battle-ax who had admitted me, assured me that this was the turning point and the first step to a full recovery. Soaking wet, I asked to take a shower. Permission granted. However, while the spirit was more than willing, the flesh was hardly able. My legs, about as sturdy as rubber bands, barely supported me for the short walk down the hall-- which seemed more like a mile. Almost a week in bed had taken its toll. I felt as though I had run the marathon.

Still, piping hot water, change of clothes, and freshly made bed all contributed to making me feel a great deal better. My appetite came back, which was a sure sign to me that I was on the mend. I could expect to be released, return to the dorms, and resume a normal routine very shortly. Never mind that I had missed almost a week of classes and had fallen hopelessly and helplessly behind in my schoolwork. So much for doing better during the second semester. I'd be lucky if I could get up to speed. The only silver lining was that I had gotten out of going to wrestling. Well, maybe it *was* worth all *this* pain and suffering to escape *that* one.

By the following Monday, I was back in the swing of things, albeit five pounds thinner and very behind in my work. At least wrestling was history. Handball? That I could handle. And it was great to be back on my feet and back home in the dorm. Just in time for the rock that would soon be dropped on us and shatter our closed little society.

APRIL, 1966

#23 - CAT House

Any plans to "com-pet," as it was called, for the *Cornell Sun* or get involved with any other campus activity had to be put on temporary hold while I tried to dig myself out of the deep hole that I had dug for myself. To begin with, I had to play catch-up ball with the class lectures I had missed, volumes of reading I had put off, and papers I had managed not to write. One thing I had mastered at Cornell was "avoidance," and it was not a good "major." My father had half-kiddingly accused me of having the "manana syndrome": Don't do today what you can put off until tomorrow, had become my guiding principle.

At least I had made the right decision in the choice of a fraternity. However, the CAT *house* itself was not one of its biggest draws, to say the least. It was a tired, old, dilapidated two-story Victorian building that desperately cried for a coat or two or three of paint, both on the outside and the inside. The antiquated kitchen, dining room, large living room, and a few tiny bedrooms were on the first floor. The furniture in the commons area looked as though it had been rejected by the Salvation Army. During rushing, the brotherhood had made every effort to clean things up as best they could. Since the smokers were jam-packed, standing room only, wall to wall with brothers and prospective pledges, the décor was mercifully obscured.

Now, the house was fully exposed and reverted to its usual messy state of disrepair. A staircase at the front entrance climbed halfway up to the second floor and then split left and right, leading to two identical corridors of bedrooms, mostly doubles. Except for those few rooms on the first floor, almost all of the sleeping quarters were located here. What impressed me immediately was that there were no locks on any of the bedroom doors. Well, that was 1966.

The bedrooms, of various sizes and shapes, shared one thing in common: All sported paint-over-paneling-- with an added coat applied by the incoming brothers every fall. A common trademark was that the new inhabitants were too lazy to remove the tape from the posters hung by the previous tenants-- so they just painted over the tape, a detail that further detracted from their redecorating efforts. I would be a rich man if I had dollar for every coat of paint that had been put on those walls.

The narrow dorm corridor area had been carpeted-- probably about twenty or thirty years ago. The "broadloom" was very stained, beaten down, and even threadbare in spots. The upperclassmen joked that each of those stains had a story behind it. There was one bathroom on each floor; I doubt it would have received a four-diamond rating from the AAA. As a matter of fact, I am quite certain that it would not have received *any* approval rating at all. The stiff shower curtain probably could have marched out on its own. So that none of the five senses should be neglected, the blended smells of deodorant and cheap cologne seemed to have been absorbed into the carpet and paneling and the combined stench permeated the entire second floor.

But I couldn't care less what the place looked (or smelled) like; none of this physical stuff mattered to me: This was my new home and I loved it. However, I think that my parents were ready to pass out after their initial visit to the house.

"This is a fire trap," they concluded. And they were probably right. But at age 19, you don't think about those things. Gamma Rho, where Ian would live, was a showcase of expensive stained glass windows, shiny marble banisters, beautiful terrazzo floors, and polished wood moldings. How could you compare the two houses? From a physical standpoint, they were in different leagues, with CAT mired in the minors. Yet I wouldn't have traded places with Ian for anything. His house was cold and sterile, in more ways than one. There was an indomitable spirit here at CAT that overcame the ultra-shabby surroundings.

The fraternity house was home to about 40 guys, mostly sophomores and four upperclassmen who served as officers. By privilege, they occupied the king (relatively speaking) double rooms on the second floor corridor at the back of the building with a panoramic view overlooking the unpaved gravel parking lot, the overflowing garbage dumpster, and some rusty lawn furniture. With rank comes privilege, and the prospect of an officership gave me something to aspire to when I would be a junior or senior. All in all, I was delighted that this would be where I'd be spending my sophomore year, no matter where they put me.

The house had two full-time employees: First, there was Otis, the ancient houseman, who had taken the job many years ago after his retirement from the local gun factory where he had worked as a "lifer" on an assembly line since coming over from Yugoslavia more than 50 years ago. Widowed with no children, he had made the brotherhood his family. Otis boasted that not only could he name every frater who had passed through the house over the past 20 years, but he could also pinpoint the room in which he had lived. There were other fascinating facts that he claimed he knew, including where all the skeletons were buried. Fact or fiction? Otis spoke with the voice of authority; I sometimes wondered whether he made this stuff up as he went along. As a matter of fact, sometimes I wondered whether his imagination had gotten the best of him altogether. If even a fraction of those "legends" were, in fact, true...

Furthermore, it was not always easy to understand Otis, given his thick accent and tendency to revert to some Slavic dialect when he became upset, forgetting that most of the brothers understood not a word of his native tongue. He also had the habit of gesticulating wildly with his hands when he got agitated. Otis took care of the (very) light housekeeping and (very) minor repairs. Nobody knew exactly what he did all day. But I quickly learned that the guys overlooked his flaws and sincerely loved him. After all, he was the glue that kept the generations together. Furthermore, his loyalty to the house was unwavering.

There was also a cook who provided three meals a day, six days a week, as well as brunch on Sunday. In those days, there was no such thing as a day off. He (or she), unlike Otis, was far from a permanent fixture in the house. On the contrary. Maybe those working conditions, or lack thereof, contributed to the fact that there was little or no stability in this tenure area; as a matter of fact, a series of chefs had come and gone in recent years with none of the transients staying on for more than ten months at a time, many far fewer. Otis proudly boasted that he knew the "true" stories surrounding the comings and goings, hirings and firings, of these men (and women). He seemed to develop a love-hate relationship with all of them as they filed through CAT's revolving kitchen door.

Henny was the current cook-of-the-month when I started pledging and was on the verge of setting a new record for longevity-- one full year. She was a woman of enormous proportions whose toothy grin was her most conspicuous characteristic. I never saw her out of her white uniform, which included a big chef's hat at least one size too big, even for her huge head. Although all of her meals were appetizing, breakfast was her specialty. She would rise before dawn and go over to the Cornell plantations to pick up fresh eggs, cheese, and milk. These were unheard of commodities for a city boy like me, who was accustomed to plucking his less-than-fresh provisions out of the supermarket dairy case, where you always had to check the expiration date on each item.

Breakfast was served short-order style: eggs, omelets, hash browns, pancakes, French toast, you name it-- on demand. Henny effortlessly rustled it up off the grill, cooking multiple orders at one time. I marveled at how she did it. Although we freshman pledges were still on meal plans, it was well worth the trouble of getting up half an hour early, wasting our meal plan tickets, and trekking from the freshman dorms to CAT on foot-- just to start the day with Henny's big breakfast. None of us guys could care less about saturated fat, trans fats, triglycerides, calories or "good" and "bad" cholesterol back then. How could you compare this fresh, impeccably prepared food with the watery eggs or doughy pancakes dished out at the Barf Bar cafeteria in the dorm complex?

So with the cooks doing their disappearing acts, the only other "constant" besides our beloved Otis was the omnipresence of dogs. Sometime in the past, according to folklore, it was proclaimed that they were to be given free rein to roam as they pleased. A professor could be at the very climax of a serious lecture, driving home a point-- when a huge St. Bernard would wander aimlessly on stage. But we became accustomed to these intrusions, and almost welcomed them. "Mavis" was my personal favorite and I actually kept an eye out for her whenever I crossed the quadrangle.

Back to CAT House: The living room or "commons" area, as it came to be called, had a U-shaped arrangement of couches and chairs, all of which had seen better days. Obviously they had been purchased (or donated) during different eras as evidenced by the fact that few, if any, matched in style or color. "Eclectic," one might rationalize. But at least they were comfortable. All this furniture wearily rested on washed-out wall-to-wall carpet full of stains and lacking any color whatsoever. I couldn't begin to guess what hue it originally had been. I shuddered to think what dust and food particles had been ground in. As I said, during the rushing smoker, the standing-room-only crowd of prospective pledges had successfully concealed it. Now it was in full view. Otis proudly boasted that he himself had shampooed it six years ago.

And facing the "U" was a "big" screen TV, my nemesis. ("Big" screen in those days meant 19 inches.) Somebody always had the tube turned on. Round-the-clock it blared; rarely, if ever, was the set given a reprieve. It's a wonder the thing didn't overheat or burn out altogether. One of those upholstered chairs became my nesting place for the remaining weeks of the spring semester.

While the viewing fare consisted of a menu of loony tunes, cartoon frolics, soap operas, sitcom reruns, and game shows, there was an increasing number of news reports. Civil rights protests became the focus. Naive as I was back then, I still couldn't fully fathom what was happening. But it proved to be the proverbial rude awakening. First Dwayne, now these very shocking images-- which jolted me into reality.

Perhaps it was my personal frame of reference. I had grown up on a quiet, maple tree-lined street back in Brooklyn. Our block consisted of the Bellos, Butlers, Castillos, Cavanaghs, Clearys, Goldbergs, and Gustaffsons. In the 1950's, it was drummed into our little heads that America was a "melting pot"-- with all the ethnic differences "melting" away into a single assimilated culture. I just took it for granted that my elementary school teachers knew what they were talking about. My street couldn't have been a better example of that fifties phenomenon. Just look at the names; it was a veritable United Nations. Everyone got along beautifully. Hence, I had been sheltered. This was *not* the real world.

Today, the melting pot is gone; nowadays our country is likened to a "salad bowl," in which all of the ingredients are mixed together, each retaining its own flavor and identity.

My confusion was further exacerbated by Dwayne's behavior back at the dorm. This at-first friendly and fun-loving guy who seemed to fit in so well was becoming increasingly withdrawn and militant. He cut short my advances of friendship and had little use for his former friends in the dorm. He became confrontational, pulling away from us more and more. But I would later learn that this turnabout was in no way his fault. After all, I had not walked in his shoes; nor did I experience the tough road he was traveling. I should have been more sympathetic. His behavior, coupled with what I was observing all around me, was starting to add up. Nevertheless, given my background, it all came as quite a shock. I was having a tough time reconciling what I had grown up with as opposed to what I was observing.

At about the same time, the War in Vietnam had moved front and center. President Johnson frequently appeared on television to justify our involvement. His hangdog, dour, and sullen countenance was in such sharp contrast to the presence of the charismatic Kennedy. But Johnson's attempts to provide a rationalization for our involvement seemed to backfire, and ended up in his digging a deeper and deeper hole for himself. The harder he tried to be convincing, the more doubts he raised.

As LBJ tried in vain to explain the reasons for our being sucked into such an unpopular war, he was being upstaged by more compelling news stories, which contained graphic footage of the bloody carnage straight out of the battlefields. "If it bleeds, it leads"-- became the news editors' mantra. The evening newscast was a far cry from what I was used to seeing. It wasn't very appetizing, not what Americans wanted to watch over the dinner table.

MAY, 1966

#24 – Growing Dissent

Up until this point, that picture postcard perfect perception of the Cornell campus was impenetrable to the ugly war images bombarding the outside world. But that veneer was wearing thin and about to fall apart altogether. For the first time, the War in Vietnam and Civil Rights movement were becoming regular topics of conversation on campus, even filtering down to the fraternities, which heretofore had remained immune. Some students, though few in number at first, became increasingly outspoken, and were quickly branded outright activists; their extracurricular activity became their involvement in fledgling protest groups and took the cause with a passion. From the classroom to the dorm room, they doggedly fought America's involvement in the War. I sensed that the idealism of these students jaded their judgment. After all, I wondered, who was backing these anti-war groups?

At the other extreme, there were the more conservative students, who still staunchly stood supporting America, right or wrong, no matter what. Their country and its leaders deserved our unbending support, and so they practiced what appeared to be a blind patriotism. A widening chasm was forming in the country and soon after even within the student body, which was a microcosm of the population at large.

And then there was a third group, the vast majority back in 1966, whose members still turned a deaf ear to politics, oblivious to the world around them, and continued to be preoccupied with fraternity pranks, Animal House hi-jinx, and pledging nonsense.

Where was I on this wide political spectrum? Admittedly confused, I was waiting to be won over; not committed to one side or the other. I had grave misgivings as to what was motivating the two opposing sides. But at least I was beginning to do a lot more listening and asking a lot more questions, although, I'm ashamed to admit it now: I was a frater first, diving into the pledging routine hook, line, and sinker. It was my brand of copping out.

By the spring of 1966, it was still possible to escape the growing restlessness. After all, I was safely ensconced on this beautiful campus and both the Civil Rights protests in other parts of the country, as well as the War in Vietnam on the other side of the world, seemed figuratively and literally a million miles away. At first they had been rather easy to ignore; but now they were encroaching into our lives and could not be easily sidestepped. Instead of reruns of Mission Impossible, the nightly network news broadcast became a regular viewing staple at the house. And those newscasts spawned some pretty heated debates, indicative of the deep divisions on campus and to some degree, even within the brotherhood.

"Sure, sure, they're gonna show you what they wanna show you just to tug at your heartstrings," vehemently argued another one of the brothers, the son of a career military man. "We all know who controls the news, anyway. All they show you is those poor gooks being blown to bits and carted off in body bags. How about what they did to us Americans first, huh? Why don't they show *that* on television?" I winced at his obnoxious choice of words to describe Asian-Americans. But since he challenged anyone who dared to differ from his point of view in a most belligerent manner, I kept my mouth shut. In hindsight, that was wrong, very wrong on my part.

Rather than face the ugly fact and get into an argument that I'd probably lose anyway, I bit my tongue and took the line of least resistance. In retrospect, I chickened out. It was easier to change the subject simply by flicking the channel and watching innocuous, apolitical Roadrunner cartoons instead, something I'm ashamed to admit that I did on more than one occasion.

Why I backed down so easily, I don't know. There was no doubt about it: My conscience was being touched by what I was viewing on the evening news. Americans were sitting down to dinner with an unfamiliar guest and it was a very grotesque one. But looking back, I'm sorry to say-- at least in 1966-- that I was not willing to drop everything, stand up for what I believed was right, fight for my convictions, or demonstrate that commitment by enlisting in one of the various protest groups springing up all over. Could I trust what I read in the newspapers and saw on television? The fact of the matter is, at that moment in time, I just didn't know what was really right. In short, I plead guilty of having left it to the others.

MID-MAY, 1966

#25 - Super Pledge

Instead of taking sides, as a diversion, I threw myself into pledging whole hog. I enjoyed the sense of belonging, the social life, and the bonding (or whatever they called it back then). During that spring semester, our sole raison d'être seemed to be plotting never-ending revenge against the pledge master and his henchmen for the various and sundry tortures, indignities, embarrassments, and humiliations they inflicted on us. It was all (almost) harmless fun, operating on the maturity level of junior high school boys. You might say that it was reminiscent of "how many pledges can you stuff into a Volkswagen?" Actually, it was a form of escapism, blocking out the scary images steadily thrust in our faces by newspapers and television. Looking back, it's hard to believe that we were so preoccupied with such nonsense while there were life and death issues creeping ever closer.

The brothers laughed with us and they laughed at us. Psychological torture and humiliation, it was theorized, were supposed to bond us closer together as a group, and ultimately to the fraternity house, a tribe-like mentality. That hazing of pledges ran the gamut. Of course, every one of us had to know the name, rank, and serial number of each upperclass brother. We could rattle off the pedigree of all the brethren in our sleep: name, hometown, class, major, minor: "James Knight, Akron Ohio, Class of 1967, Political Science major, Economics minor."

There were more creative assignments as well. For example, there was no such thing as a multiplex theatre in those days. Each pledge had to be able to recite the movie schedule of the four theatres in downtown Ithaca, never referred to by their rightful names (such as the "State" or the "Ithaca"), but rather identified by their proximity to the fraternity house-- the "near-near," "near-far," "far-near" and "far-far." It was twenty push-ups for the pledge who couldn't reel off the starting time of every feature film playing in town.

Then there was the time we were blindfolded, driven three miles from campus, unceremoniously dumped in the middle of a cow pasture, manure and all, and had to devise a way to get back to campus-- wearing nothing but our boxers or briefs. That was about the closest to streaking I ever got. I was always told to be wearing clean underwear-- just in case. Sorry I hadn't listened, at least on that particular day.

But without a doubt, the most embarrassing stunt was having to obtain 30 signatures from Cornell co-eds. Sounds simple-- except for one small hitch: the purple-inked pen used to obtain the Jane Hancocks was tied to a string which, in turn, was wrapped around the male member. Most of the gals were wise to this fraternity ritual and took added pleasure in giving the writing instrument an extra yank when it was handed over. My goal was to find some unsuspecting co-eds, or at least a few who would have some mercy in gently handling the family jewels. I escaped relatively unscathed, but this ritual landed one poor pledge in the infirmary with something resembling rope burn and a lot of explaining to do. Wonder if that same Neanderthal nurse at the health clinic sprayed his throat first before she applied the requisite first aid.

Not to be outdone, we pledges concocted our own acts of revenge. Taking advantage of the open door policy, we once sneaked into the president's bedroom upstairs in the back of the house and, while he was in the shower, emptied a bottle of Ben Gay into his underwear drawer. Then we watched him squirm at the dinner table until he suddenly couldn't take the heat anymore, and bolted out of the dining room, grabbing himself in a most undignified manner, all to the raucous laughter and applause of the pledge class and the puzzled looks of the unsuspecting brothers.

Ben Gay was old hat. But we could be more creative. For example, there was the time we wrestled poor Ridge, the super stud pledge master, to the floor and then dangled him by his wrists outside over the front porch, wearing only his jockeys. All this to the roar of the other pledges and the delight of passing sorority co-eds from across the street. Everyone got a big laugh out of that one. Well, almost everyone. Ridge was now part of the public domain and, understandably, didn't surface for the next several days. Maybe we pushed the envelope on that one. But that incident wasn't going to pass without some further counter retaliation and triggered yet another round of juvenile stunts concocted by the upperclassmen, with the pledges returning the favor and upping the ante yet again.

All seemingly harmless fun. *But what a dichotomy, what a juxtaposition of two such different worlds!* Those two separate and distinct spheres managed to co-exist a while longer. Juvenile fraternity pranks and shenanigans on the one hand..... blood and guts, life and death, for real, on the other. The poor pledge master had lost his pride and dignity; but there were some classmates who were about to lose their lives.

There were some pledges who just couldn't handle the hazing-- psychological, physical, or both. A few crossed over to the fledgling anti-war movement. "Sour grapes," we concluded. For whatever reason, coming into the home stretch in May, the pledge class had dwindled down to 25 from the original 30. This attrition was far greater than in past years, the upperclassmen nervously conceded. It takes years to rebound from a weak pledge class, even for a strong house, so a concerted effort was made not to lose anyone else.

JUNE, 1966

#26 - Initiation

The spring semester was entering the home stretch and the end of classes was in sight. Yet the summer season in Ithaca was still a long way off; as late as the first week in May, we still had to endure a nasty ice storm. Beautiful to look at-- but it made navigating the huge campus treacherous. Final examinations were just days away. With a little bit of effort, I might muster enough points to match my anemic fall grade-point average of B-, but it was highly improbable that I would improve upon it. If I had devoted as much time to mastering Macroeconomics as crafting my pledge paddle, my g.p.a. might have been a tad higher. But pledging had taken its toll and my grades paid the price. The damage had already been done. And, now there was still one more obstacle to hurdle: fraternity initiation.

It was amazing that I was doing as well as I was doing, academically speaking. Pledging had sapped me of a great deal of time and effort that could have been more productively spent: pledge skit, pledge project, pledge raids, pledge pranks, pledge paddle. If only I could have gotten course credit for the time I put into the fraternity... Schoolwork became secondary; library time took a hard hit. But I was into it. I was a star pledge-- at the expense of being a star student. Few of my pledgemates were as committed; as a matter of fact, the original class had further dwindled down to 23. If I had spent a fraction of the time I did on pledging by studying… I can just imagine what Diana would have thought of the depths to which I had sunk, at least in her opinion. Hell Week was the last lap before the dreaded Hell Night and initiation ceremony.

The University had put the screws on the Greeks to curtail their physical and psychological abuse after some very damaging publicity about one fraternity stunt that had gone awry, leaving a freshman critically injured. It was made perfectly clear that this was non-negotiable and that these were not idle warnings. Houses violating the directive would be summarily thrown off the Hill. Having heard horror stories about the hazing, hurt, and humiliation during these rituals, I had been dreading the ceremony, almost as much as the freshman swim test. Myth or fact?

Fortunately for me, the fraternities were on their best behavior during this time period, fearing the powerful hand of the University and the firm muscle of the image-conscious Interfraternity Council. Still, expecting the worst, several pledge buddies and I decided in advance where we'd draw the line in terms of physical and psychological abuse. Our imaginations were starting to get the better of us.

But the actual initiation was far milder than I had feared; the script was borrowed from the movie Animal House with a bunch of near-naked nineteen and twenty-year olds, running around in their briefs, performing all sorts of stupid stunts a la Beat the Clock. About the worst of it was a weird relay race requiring us to transport an olive between our butt cheeks from one end of the dining room to the other. By the end of the evening, we had been stripped down to a white sheet and a jock. The psychology was to strip us, literally, of our defenses, and to bind us to the brotherhood. Supposedly these rituals are to create a bonding of sorts.

At about 2:00 A.M., after a brief candlelight initiation ceremony in which we recited the creed and took our pins-- we were anointed full-fledged brothers. Each of us was given his fraternity name, such as "Eczema," "Grunge Bucket," or "Vermin." From that point forth in time, I was to be called "Fungus." The total membership then piled into a caravan of cars and headed downtown to the diner to celebrate our new status over greasy eggs, burnt hash brown potatoes, and strong coffee.

I returned to my dorm room at about 3:30 A.M., a mixture of emotions-- exhausted, exhilarated, and above all, relieved. Certainly far too keyed-up and caffeined-up to sleep. Now, I had to get back to my studies in earnest, alas, a bit late to salvage the spring semester. Final exams were around the corner and I wasn't anywhere near ready for them. Another semester down the tubes.

Ian wasn't back yet, but that was par for the course. Hard to believe, but pledging had taken even more of his time, than mine. There were all sorts of "requirements": a service requirement, a stay-awake requirement, and a slave-to-a-brother requirement. Gamma Rho owned its pledges, or so it seemed. That house didn't appear to be intimidated by the University's warnings about hazing. Drained to the point of total exhaustion, I was too wide awake to fall asleep and replayed the whole pledge experience again and again in my mind. Just as I was finally drifting off, I heard some fumbling for keys at the door.

Before I could turn over, Ian was inside. The minute I looked at him, I knew something was very, very wrong. Nothing ever bothered Mr. Cool. On the other hand, I did enough worrying for the both of us. Every concern rolled off his back, like water on a duck. Super sensitive, I took everything to heart. But tonight was altogether different. Ian had the reputation of being easy-going. "No sweat," his trademark line. "Worry is a wasted emotion," he frequently chided me. "Chill, brother," he would say. Never before had I seen him as on-edge as this.

His eyes were glassy. My first thought was that he had been drinking. No, but a couple of beers would have provided a good analgesic. Ian was perfectly sober. I think he might have been crying. This is the first time I had ever seen a crack in his smooth veneer. When I split up with Diana, he was my sounding board. When I was in the infirmary, he dropped by almost every day. When I was desperate for a fix-up, he was the first to snag me a blind date. When I misplaced a term paper, he helped me reconstruct it. Ian had always been there for me when I needed him. True, we had gone our own separate fraternity ways. Still, now it was my turn to be there for him. He just sat there in his desk chair at the foot of his bed. After a few moments, I felt it was time to break the silence:

"Just got in myself. Tonight was the night. Initiation," I tried.

He shot upright as if a bolt of lightning had struck him at the mention of the word "initiation." But still he said nothing.

"When do the brothers put it to you?" I tried again.

After a long, long pause, he said in a half-whisper. "Tonight... It was tonight." Well, at least he was talking.

"Mine was nowhere as rough as I imagined it was going to be. All they did to us was--" Ian cut me off. With a shake of his head and wave of his hand, he wanted me to stop talking. Obviously I had struck a raw nerve.

"Hey, why don't we talk--"

"Lay off," he signaled me again, this time more assertively. He, too, had been initiated this night, but he made it clear that he didn't want to discuss what had happened. Obviously things hadn't sailed so smoothly for him. One more time I tried to reach him.

"Ian, let's--"

"I said, 'shut up!'" before I could get any more words out.

But I persisted. "What the hell happened tonight?"

"Don't go there," he motioned. I took the hint. His rite of passage evidently didn't go as routinely as did mine. Whether there had been physical or psychological torture, he would not say. As I said, I had made up my mind in advance to respond "No!" if matters had gotten out of hand. There were some things I just wouldn't do, even it meant sabotaging my future with the fraternity. I wasn't going to submit to extreme physical pain; I wasn't going to risk life and limb; and there were limits to public humiliation I would endure. Some guys have no inhibitions; I'm not one of those guys.

What Ian had been subjected to-- I never found out. And although we were the closest of buddies for some time thereafter, this subject was always strictly off limits. Admittedly, it didn't stop me from wondering. To this day, I don't know what happened to him that evening. I do know, however, that whatever it was-- it changed him forever. He just sat there, staring in silence for the rest of the night in almost a catatonic trance.

Ian never returned to Gamma Rho. But his disenchantment with the house was long in coming and evident way before initiation. Whatever happened at this rite of passage was just the immediate cause. He just didn't fit in. The brothers showed him off like their "trophy" pledge. Gamma Rho couldn't have been more different from CAT. The house was a five-star hotel. From the polished-to-perfection glossy interior to the wrap-around porch overlooking the Cayuga Valley, this was some chunk of real estate. Forget Otis, the octogenarian houseman! Maid service was par for the course here.

With a well-endowed national fraternity backing it, not to mention super supportive alumni, mega bucks had been pumped into this place. Money was no object here. But what "Rho" offered in physical comfort and all the trimmings, it lacked in humanity. The brothers were plastic-- and from day number one, I never understood how Ian didn't see through them. At least up until now, he hadn't.

At first blinded by the lavish building, opulent setting, and highly pedigreed and manicured membership, this down-to-earth straight shooter just didn't belong in a place so ostentatious. The only things he had in common with the brethren were neatly-creased chinos (that's what they called khakis back then) and highly polished penny loafers. I guess-- or so I was told-- that in the game of life, you scored a few points when you said you were a "Gamma Rho." Who could turn down a bid from "Rho"? Well, it was evident that Ian should have. Whatever happened on initiation night was evidently the straw that broke this brother's back.

Ian had been initiated less than a week when he went "inactive." This was probably record time for a newly-initiated brother. For a few days, he went through the motions, but showed little affect; it was almost as if he were in a trance. The big guns at the house wined him and dined him in a last-ditch effort to get him to change his mind. As a matter of fact, even the huge cannons from the powerful and mighty national office were summoned to sway him, but to no avail. Gamma Rho had always wanted Ian on its team; now they didn't want to see a high-profile guy like him call it quits so quickly. This was an image thing; *nobody* quits Gamma Rho. The way Ian tells it, they didn't "give a shit" about him; all they cared about was "how it looked" and how his leaving damaged the reputation of the house.

However, Ian didn't remain an independent for long. He declared his intention to join me at CAT, bemoaning the fact that he should have joined here in the first place, but was blinded by the glitz of Gamma Rho. My fraternity brothers welcomed him with open arms. Now, however, he would have to wait to join the next pledge class. Fate works in strange ways: I would be assigned to be his big brother.

JULY, 1966

#27 - Nine to Five

I did a bit better on my finals than I had expected and ended up with a grade point average just a hair shy of a 3.0. Not bad, I rationalized, given the demands of pledging and the time it stole away from what I should have been doing. I didn't want to think about what I could have achieved *if* I had put academics first. I hadn't had my priorities on straight. I vowed to do better in my sophomore year.

Summer in the City: With one quarter of my Cornell career behind me, it was time to earn some money. "Where?" was the question. With Ivy League resume in hand, I headed for all of the temporary employment agencies in Manhattan, expecting the red carpet to be rolled out as soon as I announced that I was from Cornell. I would have been better off with a certificate from Katherine Gibbs Secretarial School. Temptimes, Office Temps, Tempos, etc. etc. Similar names… same responses. "Don't tell us about your college credentials; just let us know how fast you can type. Show us your clerical skills." It was a rude awakening.

Unfortunately, thousands of my college classmates were hitting the pavement at exactly the same time with precisely the same idea in mind. Come to think of it, I had absolutely no marketable skills to offer. Why should anybody hire me? I wouldn't even hire myself! What could I do? Even before I could utter my name, the receptionist was saying, "Sorry," and pointing to the door.

Then I caught a break at one agency that specialized in account temps. I didn't know the first thing about accounting; as a matter of fact, I could barely balance my own checkbook. I had fallen into this lousy habit one of my brothers taught me of rounding up the dollar amounts of the checks I wrote: $58.60 became $60, $127.80 became $130. So when my bank statement arrived, if I had done the math calculations correctly, I ended up with a surplus-- which I immediately used to buy something I wanted. Pretty clever, heh?

While my bookkeeping left a lot to be desired, my typing skills were halfway decent, a talent acquired from one-fingering all those term papers. It was certainly cheaper than paying some starving student to type them for me at the rate of $1 per page, or $1.25 with footnotes. That's what it cost back then to outsource the work.

Forget technique; I had mastered the keyboard and could get the job done, which was all that mattered. In junior high school, when I had taken, under duress, the ten-week typing course required of all seventh graders, the teacher kept shoving an orange under my fingers to correct my lousy typing technique and shoving my chest back against the chair to fix my slumping posture. These days they'd hang her high for child abuse.

"Stop slouching! Curl your fingers!" she berated me. "A-s-d-f, a-s-d-f," she monotonously droned on like a drill sergeant, as she marched up and down the aisles, tapping each desk with a yardstick to the rhythm as she passed by. I wondered if she recited this in her sleep. Worse, or so she said as she tried to correct me, is that I kept straying from the home keys. I was only afraid that she was going to slam my fingers with that wooden ruler if I didn't perform up to her expectations. But she quickly learned that I was a hopeless case and gave up on me as I reverted to habit, bad ones at that, as soon as she passed by my desk. To her dismay, she had to pass me because the work I turned in was correct.

The agency handed me a week-long assignment, which, I was informed, could very easily extend for the rest of the summer if I performed well. On Monday morning, I was officially a commuter, riding the subway with newspaper in one hand and container of coffee in the other, heading for Maiden Lane in the heart of the financial district in lower Manhattan. For that first day, anyway, the trip was a novelty. It wasn't going to last.

The subway stop nearest to my house was a ten-minute walk through my quiet residential neighborhood with its modest yet immaculately manicured homes and tree-lined streets. I bought my subway tokens in this rustic little cottage on street level that served as the train station. It was a steep climb up to the platform and tracks, two heading into Manhattan, two coming from it. Ours was a local stop. As I reached the crowded platform, not surprising, since this was the heart of the rush hour, a city-bound express was bearing down, flying past on one of the center tracks. But I didn't have long to wait for the local, which chugged into the station at a considerably slower speed.

Today, the trains are signified by their letter or number designations: the B, D, N, and Q or Number 1, 4, and 7 lines. In those days, the subway system identified its many routes with more colorful names: the Brighton Line, Sea Beach Express, West End Local, Nassau Loop, Times Square Shuttle, or Lexington Avenue Limited. I prefer those more descriptive designations much better. Just like the all-digit telephone numbers we have these days. What was wrong with exchanges like Trafalgar 5, Esplanade 7, Chelsea 4, or Butterfield 8? I, for one, liked it the old way.

So much for leisurely reading the paper or sipping my coffee; the train was jam-packed. And forget about a seat. Since I'm tall, I was lucky that I was able to grab a piece of the floor-to-ceiling pole that many other straphangers were holding onto for dear life, just to keep their balance as the train jerked out of the station. I didn't dare open the coffee container for fear of getting drenched. Reading was also out of the question; I couldn't fold the paper, let alone focus on it as the train started and stopped, lurching from side to side. I had all that I could do just to hold on.

Every so often the train stopped short and my fellow passengers practically fell on top of me. And people did this five days a week? To make matters worse, there was no such thing as air conditioning on the subways-- and it was a sweltering day, so the heat in the train was oppressive. The car had a malodorous stench of deodorant and dime store perfume. We were packed in like sardines. And, yes, there was that smell, too.

Fortunately, there was an express stop just ahead, and the speeding bullet that had passed us by, was patiently waiting to take on transfer passengers. A number of my fellow commuters made the mad dash across the platform, leaving the local train far less crowded, although I was still left standing for the next half-hour's ride into New York City. At least I could unfold my newspaper. But by now the still unopened container of coffee was squashed and leaking all over the place and I got some disapproving stares and glares as to the mess I was making, not only on the floor, but on myself as well.

I was starting to wonder whether I would be late for my first day on the job. But the train picked up speed, relatively speaking, after it left Brooklyn and I arrived at my assignment with ten minutes to spare. This was some place! I was impressed with the opulence of the surroundings. The boys of Gamma Rho would have fit in fine around here. Dark wood predominated: the doors, the desks, the moldings. The mood was dark as well. On arrival, I filled out some forms in the personnel office (which is what "human resources" was called in those days), and then was escorted to the spot at which I would be working.

By the time I had been "processed" by the office manager, there were at least two dozen other people already laboring away in a large open area with huge desks scattered haphazardly. Nobody took notice of me, only an occasional curious glance as they mechanically moved through the motions of their own tasks. Lots of paper was rustling, but there was very little conversation. Word processors hadn't been invented yet. The pounding of typewriter keys and the clanging of the typewriter bells were the only audible sounds.

My job, processing investment inquiries in response to a magazine advertisement, was explained to me. I could handle this, I said to myself. A roly-poly middle-aged woman who looked like Humpty Dumpty in a short-sleeve flower-print dress that did nothing to conceal her granny arms and liver spots sat at another large desk directly across from me. I was told to ask her if I had any questions. She forced a constipated smile; I reciprocated with a smile back. There was no further exchange between us.

The task was simple enough. I comfortably kept pace with the pile of applications that was periodically replenished into my in-box. Once or twice, the supervisor came over and peered over my shoulder, nodded once, and without further comment or feedback, moved on. She was a thin, officious type, whose most notable characteristics were her tightly tied, copper-colored ponytail and pointed chin just below her horn-rimmed glasses attached to a thick chain that dangled her over small chest. I didn't have to look up to know she was coming; the bath she must have taken in toilet water telegraphed a clear signal that she was on approach. So the most I got was a nod and nothing else. I assumed I was doing OK.

At 10:15 A.M., a bell sounded, much like that on an ice cream truck. At first I thought it was a fire drill judging by the rapid response of my pencil pushers who seemed to jump out of their seats. No, it was the coffee wagon coming off the elevator. I observed a Pavlovian response. On cue they proceeded to drop whatever it was they were doing and nearly knocked one another over to queue up for their midmorning caffeine and cruller fix that they seemed conditioned to get at this very moment. I shuddered to imagine what might have occurred should the cart have been a minute or two late, or worse, hadn't come at all.

Rations were dispensed by this squat woman neatly dressed in blue blazer, grey pleated skirt, white blouse, and red tie. She looked as though she was ready for a grade school assembly. I watched her do her job mechanically without any show of emotion whatsoever. There was little conversation, even among those on the line.

"Cruller... coffee... seventy five cents." That was the extent of it. She certainly fit in with this deadbeat crowd. Not sure whether or not I was entitled to a break, I decided to remain seated and let the cart roll by, although I would have killed for a cup of coffee and piece of Danish about then. It was already mid-morning; I still hadn't had that first cup following the drenching debacle on the subway and I was beginning to experience caffeine withdrawal symptoms. But I just kept working.

At 11:45 A.M., a menu was dropped on my desk by that same supervisor who breezed by like that morning express train. There was no explanation or comment. Now, finally, I did have a question for my neighbor with whom I hadn't exchanged a single word for the past three hours. Even before I uttered a syllable, she explained in an impatient tone and with that same constipated smile:

"If you eat at your desk, they pay for your lunch."

"Thank you," I curtly responded returning the same sort of forced smile.

Well, how was I supposed to know that, I said to myself, but kept my mouth shut. I had never heard of anything like this before. But it made good business sense, I reasoned: They stuffed your face, a good quid pro quo, expecting increased productivity in return. Didn't I learn that in my Economics class? I went back to work without any further exchange between the two of us.

I was hungry. But I didn't want to make a pig of myself, at least not on the first day. Maybe they weren't used to a college man's appetite. So I ordered very conservatively: a tuna fish sandwich on rye with lettuce, tomato, & onion-- with extra mayo on the side-- and a cherry Coke. That request certainly wouldn't send the company into bankruptcy.

After a walk around the office just to stretch my legs and make a quick pit stop in the men's room, it was back to my desk. I wasn't used to sitting this long at a time. At about 4:30 P.M., I saw my colleagues starting to pack up. I just kept working. None of them had spoken a single word to me all day. As a matter of fact, they had spoken very little to one another. This certainly was a very business-like place with no room for small talk. At 4:45 P.M., my supervisor returned yet another time. She curtly thanked me for the job I had done. I was a bit surprised; wasn't this supposed to have been at least a week's assignment, maybe longer?

"No," she responded in an icy tone with practically no emotion. "We won't be needing you after today."

That was it. Fired from my first job. Had I done something wrong? Frankly, I knew I had done a very *good* job. The stack of papers in the out-box was testimony. Wild and crazy thoughts raced through my mind. Maybe I shouldn't have asked for lettuce, tomato, & onion or extra mayonnaise on that tuna sandwich. And a *cherry* Coke? Hey, this was really getting to me. Sure, this was only a temporary summer job. But now I was 0-for-1 in the working world. The lady across the desk sensed my consternation so she mercifully stepped in and provided some much-needed closure.

"You don't understand," she said, finally showing at least an ounce of humanity. "They don't hire your kind around here."

"My kind." What "kind" was I, anyway? This had been my first exposure to anti-Semitism. How did that supervisor know that I was Jewish, anyway? What did she have, X-ray vision into my shorts? Actually, this wasn't the first occurrence. When I had gone up to the course change desk at Cornell registration, I gingerly asked about switching out of a Saturday section into a weekday one. The advisor snapped at me, "If you religion forbids you from taking classes on Saturday, you shouldn't have applied to Cornell in the first place." *In the first place*-- I wasn't the one who had brought up religion-- he had.

I sheepishly left the building without protest but feeling a mix of both abject failure and raging anger at the same time. When

I recounted to friends and family the discrimination I had encountered on the job, they weren't surprised, especially when I mentioned the name of the company. Apparently, it had that reputation. Still, this was a brand new "welcome to the real world" for such a naïve guy like me.

"Then how come nobody does anything about it?" I kept asking. There was just a shrug of the shoulders. People just don't bother to pursue these things. They just move on and leave it to the next guy. Well, then, I reasoned, maybe *I* should be the "next guy" and put a stop to it. Strange. I had dodged any thought of social or political activism on campus, and now I was suddenly eager to run with the ball because I was the one who had been targeted. All of a sudden I knew where Dwayne was coming from; I even started to question why nobody had come to "Plastered's" aid when he was in freefall back in the dorms. Now, I was moved to action only because it hit home. Another dose of self-imposed guilt; someone else might accuse me of hypocrisy.

I called Ian for solace. He was spending some time in California with his mother.

"Sue the bastards!" he coaxed me, half-jokingly. But I wasn't any more persistent; it just didn't seem worth the time or trouble back then. I probably couldn't have proven anything, anyway. Pure rationalization, just trying to convince myself that it really wasn't worth the effort. Besides, I hadn't been blackballed; the temp agency quickly found another spot for me, although this time the intellectual demands were, hard to believe, even less challenging. I would be working for a Fortune 500 company. That was the good news. The company advertised in newspapers and magazines around the country. That was the bad news.

"Your sole job is to file our advertisements in huge storage cabinets according to the name of the publication in which they appeared: Time, Newsweek, Sports Illustrated, etc. etc. "Do you want this job?" I think he was expecting me to walk out of there, given the moronic work this Ivy Leaguer was being asked to do-- but I surprised him and said "yes." After all, there was nothing better on the horizon.

Huge file cabinets? I mean *huge;* I needed a step stool to reach the top drawer in each cabinet. I am a six-footer, but I was dwarfed by the furniture.

That's what I did-- seven and a half-hours per day, five days a week, for six more weeks. No coffee wagon, no free lunch, no roly-poly co-worker, no super-perfumed supervisor hovering over me. It was a solo operation. The single amenity was the elevator music piped into the overly-air conditioned, windowless file room to which I had been banished. That place was little better than solitary confinement. For all that time, I was the only one in there. No human contact.

But who was I to complain? It was supply and demand and in the summer of 1966 there were plenty of college students who couldn't find any work at all and would have gladly jumped at this "opportunity" for want of a better word. It was a job, not a career. And besides, the pay was halfway decent-- $3.50 an hour, which in those days seemed like a lot. Furthermore, I viewed myself as a mercenary. However, I used every minute of my thirty-minute lunch break to sit outside on a bench and savor the fresh(?) New York City air. As polluted as it was, a welcome relief from all that frigid a.c. inside.

The one fringe benefit came when I was let out of jail, sent like a schoolboy on an errand to the mailroom, but accidentally stumbled into the telephone room. All I could hear was a cacophony of the word "Operator" over and over and over again. Stretched across the back wall were about twelve women, all ages, shapes, and sizes-- some of them quite good looking-- perched high up on wooden stools, working on the old-fashioned cord and plug switchboards. What a waste of womanhood to have them so sequestered behind closed doors. It was evident that this room was off limits to everyone else.

From that day on, I found every excuse to find my way into the central telephone room. As the number and frequency of my visits increased, I ran afoul of Edna Quigley, the chief operator, whose job, among other things, seemed to be to protect "her girls" from the ferocious "wolves" (like me). Edna was a sour old bag, with grey curls that looked as though they had been sheared from a Persian lamb coat. She always looked as though she was ready for a fight. Whenever I entered, I could read the expression on her face: "What the hell are you doing here now?" She marched up and down behind those women and seemed to monitor their every move.

The pace seemed rapid, with that big board always lit up like a Christmas tree and the operators always trying to keep up with the calls. Yet I never heard any of "her girls" complain when I would stop by, and was usually greeted with some giggles and some winks. This reception did wonders for my male ego, although I think the sight of anything wearing pants would have gotten them going in this females-only domain. I was in my prison and they were in theirs.

I seemed to catch the attention of one very attractive brunette, Donna, who cautiously nodded my way whenever Edna's back was turned-- not wanting to get in trouble with her supervisor. Donna was two years older than I. She had a willowy figure, sensuous moves, a touch of the devil in her eyes, and one great smile. Having just graduated from Queens Community College, she would be transferring to a four-year school in Colorado, near where her recently divorced mother lived. This job was certainly not a career, only a summer moneymaker for her, too.

If it hadn't been for the distance factor, I might have pursued this office romance, but we both realized after a few dates that this was just a summer fling with very little future. Donna was lot of fun to be with, in more ways than one. She was Diana-- but without the political baggage. She didn't know (or care) the first thing about what was going on in Vietnam. She was a true-blue, red-blooded, healthy American girl. I got my soldier stripes that summer to prove it. All she wanted was a good time and it was my job to provide it. Which I did willingly.

To ease the boredom after a while, I started to make it a challenge to see how many times I could escape the file room and sneak into the telephone room and linger near the switchboard each day. It became a game of cat and mouse and the other operators played along, sometimes running interference for me when Edna's back was turned. The good times I had with Donna that summer made all that mindless and backbreaking filing worth it.

My college buddies weren't faring all that better finding summer jobs. Kip, for example, was back home in Oklahoma working for a lot less and doing what I deemed to be pure water torture-- proofreading the upcoming edition of the local telephone directory-- letter by letter, number by number-- comparing the information on index cards to page proofs of the new edition. Tedious, laborious. By comparison, my filing job was "stimulating."

Ian, on the other hand, was having a field day. Actually, he didn't need to work, but to keep himself busy (after all, you couldn't surf every day), his dad got him a job with one of those mail order sweepstakes companies. His task-- opening and sorting the responses into the "yes" and "no" piles ("purchase" or "pass" on the offers) sounded routine, but was anything but. He shared with me stories of what messages people added to those sweepstakes entry forms. For example, one man included a detailed roadmap to his home so that the Prize Team wouldn't get lost. Another politely requested that they show up with the million dollars after lunch because "I sleep in." Yet another demanded advance notice when she won and before "they" came to her house; this was a woman who said she wanted to get her hair blown out so that she would look good on national television. I guess Ian's job was more exciting than filing or proofreading for 40 hours per week.

AUGUST, 1966

#28 – Off Hours

At nights and on the weekends, I hung out with some of my high school friends. But except for a few very close ones, most of those encounters were strained. Each of us had moved on; our lives centered around college now. New friends... new interests. Most of those relationships had not withstood the test of time. The commonality was gone. In some cases it had been replaced by competition. Sometimes I felt these guys were just trying to outdo each other. What was your g.p.a.? What fraternity did you join? How many girlfriends? How many times did you score? In short, it became a game of "Can You Top This?"

To this day, I am envious when I hear stories about high school buddies who remained friends for a lifetime. They were in one another's bridal parties, served as godparents to their offspring, played poker or racquetball once a week, and then approached advancing middle age supporting one other. Didn't happen for me. One of life's regret. Yes, there *were* a few close high school friends, but they scattered to the four corners of the country and it became increasingly hard to maintain those long distance relationships.

And so by early August and the dog days of a particularly hot and humid summer in the City, I was bored by day, restless by night, and couldn't wait to return back "home" to campus and take up residence in the CAT house.

I picked up the phone and called Ian, as I was accustomed to doing whenever I was down. His employment had been short-lived, a two-week assignment. He had no need or desire to do anything else except veg out. His summer was truly carefree; his biggest concern was which beach to surf. Although Kip was going to be "in exile" from the rest of us residing in fraternity row, we pledged to stay in touch, so we spoke several times during the summer. Brant was working for his family's business. He had enrolled in a community college for the spring semester, but found it too hard to join in midstream. So now his latest plan was to re-enroll there this fall and then return to Cornell the following September.

Although we were pulling ahead of him as well as pulling for him, we had our serious doubts whether he could pull this off. He was now a full-year behind the rest of us-- and according to his "Plan B," it would soon be a full two. Dwayne was a lost cause altogether. After the insurance company fiasco and my first-hand encounter with discrimination, I decided to give it a try and give him a call. Maybe we finally had experienced something in common. But the call was strained at best and I found him to be impatient, bored, patronizing, and disinterested-- eager to get off the phone.

"So you got a taste of what's really happening out there. Gotta go," he said, cutting me off rather abruptly. I deserved that treatment; after all, how sympathetic had I been to him? Except for running into each other every now and then in class, that would be the last time we would speak-- until our stormy senior year. Although I blamed him then, I was far from faultless in the implosion of our fast friendship as arriving freshmen.

PART II

Sophomore Year

LABOR DAY, 1966

#29 - Back on the Hill

After a tedious summer, I couldn't wait to get back to campus and move into the fraternity house. The high point of the past two months had been my fling with Donna and even that was forgettable. Both of us knew from the outset that it had no future and provided us only momentary nighttime diversion from our dreary day jobs. Our final date was little more than, "Nice knowing you. Have a good life."

As returning sophomores, we felt like big men on campus. Actually, we now lived *off* campus, and had wheels. We passed the entering freshmen first arriving-- remembering what it had been like for us, now liberated from the dorms, and remarking how much had happened over the past year. We also scouted the incoming co-eds, "fresh meat," as Ian called them. And, we knew the drill: registered early, got the courses we wanted, and bought our books-- all before the lines got to be too long. More important to us, at least then, was purchasing paint, posters, and paneling to decorate our rooms in the fraternity house.

Sometimes I think we lost sight of why we were in college. Then again, maybe that was what the true college experience was all about. Sure, I learned a lot inside the lecture halls-- but just as much on the *outside*. Before classes started up again, we made the rounds to a seemingly non-stop series of parties, mixers, and drunken revelries with such apt fraternity titles as "Bake on the Lake" and "Spawn on the Lawn." For the time being, we had been drawn back into the protected, shielded cocoon of Cornell. Life was damn good; but the clock was ticking-- and we were running out of time.

My parents referred to my room in the fraternity house as that "fire trap" and implored me to live elsewhere. I was only afraid that they would blackmail me by refusing to pay the tuition bill unless I moved out immediately. That was a moot point; living space on campus was at a premium, and besides, I loved CAT. But they persisted.

"How would you escape from here if there was a fire? There's no place to go," my mother said in horror as she put her hand over her mouth. I didn't have an answer; she was right.

"Don't worry, ma," I tried to allay her fears. "Guys have lived in this room year after year. Nothing happened to them."

But she wasn't satisfied. "Then they were just lucky. This place is an accident waiting to happen." All I could do was change the subject every time she brought it up, which painfully seemed like every few minutes.

The six-by-eight-foot cell was a dungeon located on a short corridor off the kitchen, one of the few bedrooms on the first floor of the fraternity house. It had a bed on the right when you first walked in running the length of the short wall. A decent size wooden desk with a hutch on top, designed for books and papers, was on the opposite wall. A tall but narrow wooden dresser next to the doorless walk-in closet was on the sidewall, to the right. Just to the left of the desk and directly across from the entry door was a large window that looked as though it had never been washed; it faced out on a tiny courtyard that led nowhere and offered no means of egress, to my parents' chagrin. You could touch the window of the bedroom on the opposite side with a slight stretch, not that you'd want to. That mini-courtyard in between was strewn with occasional garbage that the second floor brothers had tossed out last spring-- and which Otis hadn't quite gotten around to picking up yet. A generous supply of condom wrappers piled high added to the ambiance. The carcass of a dead squirrel was also lying there. Otis had missed that, too.

"Don't worry. I'll hang a curtain over the window," I promised. That didn't appease them.

But I didn't care how microscopic the room was, how remote it was, or how dingy it was. I didn't even mind the squirrel or the condom wrappers. This space was all *mine.* After last year's catastrophe with Buzz, I wasn't going to take any chances and practically *demanded* a single, even though there were quite a few brothers with whom I had bonded who would have made good roommates. Evidently the powers that be who decided these things were apprised of my horrendous freshman experience and honored my request.

Next to my room was a small bathroom (which obviously hadn't seen a mop and pail in recent memory) and beyond the bathroom was a fairly large double room looking out on that back parking lot, directly under the president's room, so royalty was right above us.

The renovation took but a day: I painted the walls royal blue, put up a few posters purchased at the Campus Store, rigged up my own stereo and speakers, brought my own blanket and pillow from home, neatly filled the closet and bureau with my clothes and toiletries, and organized my books and school supplies in that bookcase atop the desk. Even my parents had to admit it: The room had been transformed nicely. And, most important of all, it belonged to me. My parents left for home, still shaking their heads, but finally accepting the fact that I wasn't budging on this one.

With a last-minute decision by some juniors to room in the house when their apartment plans fell through, Ian was "bumped" and forced onto a waiting list for a room in the fraternity, a list that didn't hold too much promise. I would have gladly put him up in my room, but the only place he could have slept would have been in one of the bureau drawers. As was, my room was claustrophobic, even for just one person. The always-magnanimous Kip had offered to temporarily house Ian in his already cramped Collegetown quarters until something else opened up.

But as was so often the case, one of the brothers didn't return to the fraternity house at the last minute (or rather, like Brant, he wasn't asked back by the University) and "pledge" Ian was sharing a second-floor double with Jordan Sheridan, one of the other sophomores in my pledge class. My classmates were starting to drop like flies, for one reason or another.

I quickly established a routine: work hard, play hard. Classes by day, library (and some fun) by night. I desperately wanted to avoid the trap of just playing hard-- both day and night-- and then busting out, becoming part of that 33% statistic that was constantly thrust in our faces.

Hanging out was the line of least resistance. There was always that temptation. At any given time, there would be some guys who were just "hanging out." Then they hit the books. But there were those who just moved from group to group and *just* hung out-- all day, all night-- always managing to find someone to join them. I was determined not to become that "someone." And then there were the procrastinators who just kept putting off reading, writing, and studying until it was too late. Sound familiar? I lived in constant fear of becoming a statistic.

On the other hand, I had absolutely *no intention* of studying every waking moment, which is what some students did. There were the pre-meds, who had no life. I realized that they were sacrificing now for the future. But the existence of a drone wasn't for me. Between classes, after classes, at night, and on weekends. Just like Kip, you'd catch them even reading a book on the cafeteria line, with not a second to spare. All they did was hit the books. I rationalized that they would eventually burn out. Besides, I didn't want to be a doctor anyway; I could barely make my way through a science course. Even the sight of ketchup made me squirm.

Instead, I sought a balance. I quickly learned to use my "dead" hours between classes in the morning to at least dent my heavy assignments, resisting the temptation to hang out at the Straight. Having targeted English as my probable major, I discovered there was never an end to the reading and writing that was expected. Cornell was not giving its diplomas away; they had to be earned. And the demands were rigorous.

Although I didn't have to declare my major until the end of my sophomore year, I had to worry about getting past those pesky distribution requirements as well as the English major prerequisites before I was accepted by the department. Some tough hurdles were coming up. Well, at least this year there wasn't a swim test to pass. Nor did I have to wrestle anyone.

I had many, many poor study habits, but if I had one strength, it was that I was highly regimented, and to a degree, self-disciplined. Dinner at the fraternity was over by 6:30 P.M. Miraculously, Henny, the cook, had returned. She must have set a record: same cook, two years in a row. Well, Otis seemed to like her-- and his endorsement went a long way. Her meals were never a disappointment. She worked wonders with the shoestring budget allotted to her by the stingy steward, one of the upperclass officers who collected room and board and meted out the money for the provisions as if he were disbursing dollars from this own bank account. That didn't stop Henny! She could do wonders with pasta bought wholesale, perform amazing feats with surplus cheese, and work miracles with government-wounded turkeys.

Student waiters served for their supper. We took great joy in busting their chops as they tried to balance those huge round metal trays that every so often came crashing down, dinner plates and all. No sooner were the evening announcements made by the house president while dessert (Jell-O in assorted colors or cardboard sheet cake) was being served, when I bolted across campus to Teagle Pool for my workout routine of ten laps… steam room calisthenics… showering, dressing… and getting ensconced in my study carrel at the library by 7:45 P.M. Like clockwork. I was, I still am, a creature of habit. If I deviate from the routine even by a minute, my system goes haywire. Change the maze and the rats run wild.

Trying to get any studying or writing done at the fraternity house was a lost cause. I preferred the business-like atmosphere of the graduate school Olin Library and always took an end carrel with a side view next to a huge picture window overlooking the Arts Quad. What a great place to study! And that was my hiding spot for the rest of my Cornell existence. Miraculously, it was always available.

To this day I wonder why Olin is sidestepped in favor of the older, more crowded Uris undergraduate library just next door. Actually, I shouldn't have been surprised. Uris was far more social and where all the action was taking place. But from 7:45 to 11:30 P.M., I didn't want any "action." This was sacred time for getting my work done. I'd play later. I can count on one hand the number of times I studied in Uris. I knew my Achilles heel-- how easily I could be led by the nose to distraction-- and needed that uninterrupted study time that I could get only at Olin. In retrospect, it was one of the wisest decisions I managed to make.

Again, like clockwork, at 9:15 P.M. I took a brief milkshake break at the Straight, and was back at the library for another hour and a half of hitting the books. I prided myself on having at least this modicum of self-discipline and resisting the temptation to join the guys at Uris, or worse, back at the house. Doubtful I'd ever make dean's list, but my work got done-- and except for my close brush with a disaster in Geology, I never felt in jeopardy of failing a course, or worse, busting out. More about that debacle, coming up.

Slow but steady wins the race. Those three-to-four hours of intensive study time paid off. I may not have put in the quantity of hours others did, but I managed to do some quality libe time. Day and night, there would still be plenty of opportunity to hang out and "play." This routine worked perfectly for me.

The major culture shock from high school to college is how little time is actually spent in the classroom. A college student has to structure all the remaining hours for himself or herself. Many find this to be a formidable challenge.

Cornell gave me my book knowledge; the older brothers in the house provided me with my carnal knowledge and my social schooling. All would prove valuable in the years ahead. The juniors and seniors introduced us to all the popular hangouts: Popcorn plus vintage cartoons and fifties flicks in a converted old railway car permanently stationed about five miles east into the farmlands; beer and pizza at the Big Red Barn in Collegetown, when I didn't give a second thought as to how many slices I wolfed down; fresh eggs and greasy home fries at the diner in downtown Ithaca, particularly tasty after pulling an all-nighter during prelim week; Sunday dinner at small, inexpensive Italian restaurants around town; and those rare and (very) special occasion dinners at that Olde Inn on the west bank of Lake Cayuga.

And, of course, there was the Commons coffee house, still my favorite hangout-- maybe because that's where I had spent so much time with Diana. But she was past tense, ancient history. I was now back in the hunt. We sophomores were tutored in the intimate secrets of each sorority house, which girls made the best dates (and for what reasons), and all the good pick-up lines to get 'em. Fall 1966: life was good, very good. All of that, however, was abruptly about to change.

NOVEMBER, 1966

#30 - No Joke

The breakfast routine was the same day in and day out. Since my first floor room was a stone's throw from the dining area, I observed the regimen up close and personal, from the vantage point of a front row seat. Nor did I have to rely on an alarm clock; I was a light sleeper and the early birds invariably woke me up. No wonder this single room was so easy to get; there had to be a catch and strings attached. The brothers would stumble in, half asleep, and line up across from the grill back in the kitchen area while Henny served up breakfast fare short order style.

"Whatcha havin', boys?" was her standard line. She could rustle up anything cooked to perfection in a matter of minutes. There was little conversation at this uncivilized hour in the morning. An 8:00 A.M. class was the lowest blow you could possibly get. Most of the bleary-eyed were still not fully functioning, particularly if they had been up late, studying, or whatever. A few syrup-stained copies of the *Cornell Sun* were casually scanned over pancakes and eggs and then left on the sticky tables for the next wave of brothers to arrive.

But there was one morning that was very different from the rest. I had overslept that day and emerged from my room, slightly disoriented, still in my robe, rubbing my eyes. The kitchen area was far more crowded than usual and I sensed something was up. Several groups of brothers were huddled together, sharing copies of the *Sun*, which usually doubled as place mats by the time the second shift was on the scene. Why this sudden interest today? They were obviously engrossed in their reading, uncharacteristically alert for this hour of the morning. I sensed a tension in the air.

The banner headline screaming across the top of the front page said it all:

COLLEGE DEFERMENTS TO END;
STUDENTS TO BE DRAFTED

"That's the big fuss?" I yawned, wanting to go back to sleep. "You have short memories. That's the same scare headline that ran last year," I said bursting their bubble. It was déjà vu. But the other guys totally ignored me as though I weren't there. I tried again to allay their fears: "Hey, guys: It's the Fall Weekend prank. You know, the freshmen. Now you're falling for it." A few heads turned toward me, seemingly quite irritated, but not a word was spoken. I didn't like the way they were looking at me. I wanted to see this for myself so I swiped one of the papers. This time, it was *no joke.*

Effective immediately, all 2-S student deferments would be suspended. The draft boards around the country had let Washington know that they had declared a severe manpower shortage; they could not meet their quotas. The War in Vietnam was revving up and the United States was becoming more and more entangled in it. Men were needed for this undeclared war-- and *we* were *those men.* Individual draft boards could start calling students to come home, drafting them for military service almost *immediately.* The long arm of Uncle Sam was reaching onto college campuses. And Cornell was no exception.

All of a sudden, we were exposed, out there, and very vulnerable, stripped of our student-status protection. Few if any deferments were left. Those draft boards were just licking their chops; they couldn't wait to get a piece of us college men. A frightening thought: Lake Cayuga one day…. Mekong Delta the next.

The optimist in me took over. "*Could* start calling students home. It doesn't say *will* start." Still not a word from the others. What had been a seemingly harmless prank a year ago….a parody, a satire….had become *reality*. How ironic that that phony headline-- precisely as it had been written-- was so prophetic, repeated one year later. The only difference was that this time it was for real. It had been an omen of what was actually going to occur.

The news spread like wildfire across campus. And this time, it was not a prank. From fraternities to the dorms….from lecture halls to the library….from the cafeterias to the gyms... it had become the sole topic of conversation. And well it should have been. We had lost control. *We college men felt that our futures and our fates were no longer in our own hands.*

Feelings of helplessness, hopelessness, and panic spread. Once safe, ensconced in rural and rustic upstate New York, impenetrable to danger, far removed from the real world and that remote war- - suddenly we were being served up to the enemy. It was a bad dream relived. Only this time, it *was* for real. Last year as quickly as the panic spread, we were told it was all a harmless prank. "Never mind." Resume your routines; the laugh is on you. This was double jeopardy, because now that headline wasn't a prank. There was no waking up from this nightmare. After last year, it now seemed to be a practical joke that had gone bad, very bad.

Our seemingly impenetrable fortress had been invaded. In one fell swoop our sense of safety and security had been shattered. No longer did we have a sanctuary from war. Instead of being preoccupied with fraternity pledging, rushing, and dating games, we now had to deal with the real world, life, and… death.

If I had to pinpoint a single day, that one would be it: the turning point. *Cornell University was changed forever. My generation was changed forever.*

The rumor mill was running overtime. Students were handling the news in a variety of ways. There were those who practiced avoidance-- business as usual. They acted as though nothing had changed. For the time being, anyway, there was nothing to worry about. They carried on as they normally would have, pretending "it" to go away, and never touch them. This type of guy knew how to live for the moment. I guess they were lucky; I certainly wasn't one of them.

At the other extreme were the fatalists who just gave up; they expected the next call, letter, or telegram to be from Uncle Sam, telling them it was time to pack up and ship off to the rice paddies. They were prepared to call it quits on the spot.

"What's the point of going to class? Studying? Doing any work?" Ian mused. It doesn't matter anymore. Who knows how long we'll be at Cornell anyway?"

And then there were those who were looking for an escape route.

"Get married… run off to Canada… develop some malady or mental condition overnight!" mocked Jordan, Ian's new roommate. We all knew what it would take to entitle us to that highly coveted 4-F deferment.

"I'll confirm that you are cra-zy!" Ian joked to break the tension, at least for a moment. However, just for a moment. This turn of events was nothing to joke about.

"Getting hitched, running away, pretending you're nuts… Isn't all of this a little bit far-fetched?" I commented.

But the others jumped down my throat when I questioned these extreme steps. "Isn't that better than ending up in a body bag?" was the group retort. Drastic times… call for drastic measures.

Kip was bandying about a term "C.O," conscientious objector, which at least at that moment in time, I didn't know all that much about. He explained that C.O.'s refused to serve based on their beliefs.

"Are these people sincere-- or are they just looking for a way out?" I questioned.

"Can you blame them?" explained Kip. "If it's a question of survival"

Survival: No, that word no longer meant making the grade at Cornell. Nor did it signify obeying the proctor's edicts. Rather, "survival" now had come to mean simply-- staying alive. So with a growing sense of desperation, everyone was in search of that elusive escape route. The rigid dorm rules which we had lived by up to that point seemed absolutely irrelevant and obsolete.

There were those who said "Yes" and agreed it was time to fight-- not in Vietnam, but in Washington, at the Pentagon, and against the big chieftains who were controlling their destinies and they vowed then and there to take up arms against them. But, most were still like me: somewhere in the middle, just plain confused, insecure, and increasingly fearful-- not knowing what was in store for us, what the next day would bring. How quickly things had changed; the campus was in a state of turmoil.

1957, BROOKLYN, NY

#31 - Turning the Clock Back

How I longed for simpler times, when there was perfect order and things were predictable.

I am a product of the fifties, a throwback to Leave It to Beaver. The Kussins could have been the Cleavers. I lived in a middle-class neighborhood in which, as I described before, everyone got along. The schools were the anchor; they were tightly run. Very. Nothing was questioned. Nothing. Although both of my parents were schoolteachers themselves, they would never second-guess *my* teacher, let alone the principal. After all, would a patient dictate to a heart surgeon how to operate --or-- would a driver instruct the auto mechanic how to repair an engine? They were deemed to be professionals, experts in their respective fields. In those days, educators were also put on a pedestal. The lines were so clearly drawn; roles were so carefully delineated.

There are many other things about the 1950's I miss. Just three television networks is one of them. It seemed that the entire country sat down and watched together. Today, not only are there more than 500 different channels, but there is a set in every room in the house, with each person retiring to his or her own quarters to watch alone. Yes, it felt like one country back then; the "United States" was not a misnomer.

Imperfect as she was, we relied on Ma Bell. There was only one telephone company, with live operators who could connect you from Portland, Maine to Portland, Oregon. No confusing menus stating "that our options have changed recently" with a seemingly endless number of buttons to press.

There was an efficient railroad system with routes which criss-crossed the country and coupled all the big cities. Trains proudly sported such names as the Silver Meteor, the California Zephyr, the Texas Crescent, the Hiawatha, and the City of New Orleans.

We knew the cop on the corner and the name of the school crossing guard. There was a "Main Street" or at least an avenue close by with a candy store and ice cream shop. We were given an allowance which slowly grew as we grew. If we needed more money for something, we had to save or earn it. For a dollar we could buy a piece of pizza, a soda, a bus ride, a rubber ball, and a copy of *Mad* magazine.

Parents knew they had to be our parents, not our friends. Every mother belonged to the PTA. We called other adults "Mr." or "Mrs." Above all, there was respect.

Authority was never questioned; it was patently clear who was in charge and in control. There was a great deal to be said for the way things worked in the 1950's. We had rules, we had boundaries, we had limits-- and we knew what they were. We also knew that there would be consistent *consequences* if we crossed the line.

So going back to my first day at Cornell the previous fall, when the assistant proctor scowled, "Don't do it," most of us, products of the 1950's, had not even the slightest thought of "doing it." That, however, was all about to change. And for very good reason: Our lives were on the line, our futures on the chopping block. We had to "do" something about "it."

In most ways, I couldn't have felt more secure growing up back then during this golden age; but in a few others, I felt very frightened. Nikita Khrushchev, Russia's leader, was the arch villain. I was too young to understand, but there was a lot of news about this senator named Joseph McCarthy and the "red menace." There was also a great deal of talk about mushroom clouds.... hot lines... bunkers.... bomb shelters... and blacklists.

By the early 1960's, following the Bay of Pigs Invasion and the Cuban missile crisis, my generation grew up overnight as things suddenly became even tenser. To this day, I recall sitting on the floor in our living room, legs folded, watching those pointed missiles on our small-screen, black and white television. My parents didn't want to alarm me, but I could sense how apprehensive they were. Back then, there were times the world wondered whether it would see another daybreak. *Would America survive?*

But if I had to pinpoint one event which marked the end of an era with a single shot, it was John Fitzgerald Kennedy's assassination. Much has been written and said about how the Age of Camelot came crashing down on November 22, 1963. Through most of the fifties, Eisenhower had been president. A great general, but not exactly a charismatic leader. World War II was in the rearview mirror; now we were in the "Cold War," with some self-imposed isolation.

Kennedy's razor-thin victory over Nixon in 1960 changed all that. Our revised images of the presidency now consisted of touch football at the family's compound, sailing off Cape Cod, horseback riding, a beautiful and charming first lady, and two adorable children who were known to upstage their father at press conferences. JFK and Jackie trotted the globe, putting America back in the limelight.

However, the era of Camelot was short-lived. Whoever is old enough will always recall precisely where he or she was at the horrific moment when the news bulletin interrupted regular programming and shattered our heretofore carefree existence. We were told that this young, handsome, dynamic leader, who literally had promised us the world and had started to deliver it, had been shot and killed. CBS news anchorman Walter Cronkite, himself a close Kennedy friend, wept as he broke into *As the World Turns* to make the grim announcement. First scenes from a soap opera, and then the words *"CBS News Bulletin"* in a bold, italic font, white lettering on a black background. Quite a jarring juxtaposition. We had become conditioned to know that good news was not forthcoming.

Assassination was just not part of the sixties experience, at least not up to that moment. It was unheard of, something we only read about in high school history texts. There had been the Lincoln assassination and then the attempt on the Archduke Ferdinand of Austria that catapulted us into World War I. Prior to 1963, "assassination" was an abstract concept; Kennedy made the word concrete. And of all people... someone so beloved and so revered by so many.

But after 1963, assassination became more commonplace. We gradually became hardened: Dr. Martin Luther King... Robert Kennedy... Indira Gandhi... John Lennon... Shimon Peres. And then there were the attempts on Ronald Reagan, Pope John Paul, and George Wallace--just to name a few. The shock value began to wear off. Not a good thing. The first slaughter or killing or butchering is gut-wrenching for the executioner. But the second? And then the third? Frighteningly routine after a while. Remember the first school shooting? After a while, such massacres were so frequent that they didn't always make the front pages.

Vietnam produced an altogether different kind of fear during the mid-sixties through to the early seventies: Individually, each of us wondered whether we would have a future. But at least the children no longer had to worry about the Russians coming.

And now all of a sudden our lives had become so complicated. Overnight, my world had become topsy-turvy; taking the proverbial 180-degree turn. No longer was my existence so orderly or so prescribed. This abrupt turnabout was very scary. It was a loss of control-- and I was understandably frightened. *Who was in charge?* It wasn't all that clear anymore. Very soon I, too, would be asking a lot of questions.

DECEMBER, 1966

#32 - The Debate Heats Up

The War became our sole topic of conversation. It was discussed and debated everywhere from the coffeehouses to the dorm corridors, from the bars to the steam room, from the classrooms to the library, often accompanied by very heated exchanges. For many it had become all-consuming; yet for others, it was something that they still tried their hardest to block out. In either case, overnight it had hit home and become very real, infecting our sense of well-being.

The New York Times became required reading; the network evening newscast replaced sitcom reruns and cartoons as our TV diet. Vietnam bolted to the front and center of our thoughts.

Over the next few weeks, things subsided a bit. We found a means of escape with talk of Cornell hockey, winter concerts, and fraternity mixers. Perhaps it was avoidance, perhaps it was denial, or perhaps it was our belief that "it" would all just go away. But we could not eradicate these thoughts altogether. They continued to hang over us like a dark cloud. Would the storm pass the way it had a year ago? No, not this time. For now, "the War" was very much with us and would continue to dominate our thoughts, our lives.

As much as I was starting to believe that this war was wrong, as angry as I was at our involvement, as vulnerable as I felt to the draft, as horrified as I was at the images of death and dying plastered across the television screen-- I loved this country passionately then as I do now. I continued to be one of those who were still deeply divided about our role in Vietnam-- and for those reasons, was not so quick to jump on the anti-war bandwagon. I couldn't help but question the motives of some of my classmates who shredded the flag, burned their draft cards, damned our leadership, and chanted "Hell, no, I won't go." Were they reacting out of anger? Moral indignation? Or, perhaps fear? Or, were they just following the crowd? Most important, to me, anyway-- who was instigating these demonstrations and protests? I needed to know the answers to those questions before I could come off the fence.

My ambivalence towards joining the anti-war bandwagon, even by the late 1960's, is not all that difficult to understand. It traced back to my own education. World War II and the War in Vietnam couldn't have been more different.

Vietnam had divided the country. It was becoming Civil War II of sorts. World War II, on the other hand, had united us. Extended families gathered around the radio in what they used to call the "parlor," listening to reports from Europe and FDR's fireside chats. Americans were eager to catch any news they could about their boys overseas as the conflict heated up on all fronts. It was a Rockwellesque portrait of America.

Television had been unveiled at the 1939 World's Fair but quickly vanished; in a war economy, factory production of tanks and guns took precedence over consumer goods. Hence, the 1940's became the Golden Age of Radio, when the news provided information and the entertainment offered some diversion. There was a growing field of network radio correspondents in the European and Pacific theatres, men who earned their stripes overseas and then returned home to anchor and report the nightly newscasts during the next two decades.

While those newsmen informed us, some of the greatest performers of all time got their start on radio and entertained us. Above all, the picture in the 1940's was a country united, almost 100% behind this war effort. There was a common enemy and almost full consensus that it had to be defeated. The mood at home was much like it was after September 11th and the terrorist attacks here. We became one nation and patriotism rocketed to an all-time high.

Then came D-Day and Victory; the boys were coming home! Throngs of people were there to welcome them, hugging, and kissing, literally dancing in the streets, holding up newspaper headlines, heralding our victory. Those who didn't return were considered true heroes. Once again, we were truly a *United* States.

Not so with the War in Vietnam. The mood and tone of the country produced a deep chasm when it came to this conflict. There was no such consensus; quite the contrary. There were so many issues that had to be resolved and agreement was hard to come by. Without a doubt, the most significant of which was whether we should have been involved in Southeast Asia in the first place. There were many who didn't identify an enemy, at least not to the United States. This was simply not *our* war; Vietnam was none of *our* business. So why get sucked into a hopeless struggle that we couldn't possibly win, anyway?

On the other hand, there were those who maintained it *was* our responsibility as the number one superpower to play policeman and monitor the globe, making sure that the Communists didn't get a foothold in Southeast Asia. *Who was right?*

Despite their sharp differences, there was one thing that both sides agreed upon: Once we went in, it would be extremely difficult to get ourselves out. The "hawks" felt that we were *already* entrenched and had to achieve a victory to preserve our nation's honor. After all, America had never lost a war before. On the other hand, the "doves" didn't want us to get involved in the first place, but as we got dragged in deeper and deeper, they wanted us to take our losses, lick our wounds, and extricate ourselves from this quagmire.

With each passing day, not only did it become increasingly clear that the country was split down the middle, but it was also evident that both sides had their heels dug in and were not going to budge. We were at war abroad… and at war at home. As I said, you might call it, "Civil War – part II."

The end of student deferments resulted in a bandwagon effect. But while many of my classmates, friends, and fraternity brothers wholeheartedly embraced the anti-war and anti-government movements, I continued to have some misgivings and reservations about their knee-jerk reaction, and worse, what might truly be behind their motives for jumping on board. I wasn't ready, just yet, to follow the crowd.

FEBRUARY, 1967

#33 – Rocks for Jocks

Despite all the talk about the War, I couldn't lose sight of my academics and why I was at Cornell. Protesting became a raison d'être for some, but not for me. From freshman frolics to fraternity rushing last year, I had always found an excuse for mediocrity. Now I was trying to stay on the straight and narrow and not get so distracted during my sophomore year. Excuses, excuses; I always had them. But I was determined to do things differently. And in fact, academically speaking, "things" were rolling along better than expected-- until I hit, *literally,* a huge boulder in the road.

Cornell's graduation requirements were fashioned after a Chinese restaurant menu. "Take one from Column A, one from Column B" and so forth. I was able to skip the egg roll and bypass Math altogether, which was a huge relief. However, there was no way around the science distribution requirement; you had to take one course in either the biological or physical sciences.

At first, I thought I would register for "Concepts in Physics," or "Physics for Poets," as it was more aptly dubbed by those students who sought refuge in this watered-down version of the traditional course. However, no matter how it came camouflaged, Physics still intimidated me, as it had in high school. My new fraternity brothers advised me that "Geology" a.k.a. "Rocks for Jocks" was the easiest way to meet and beat the science requirement. After all, it was reasoned, if football players could hack it (no aspersion intended!)-- so could I. Wishful thinking on my part.

Science had always been my Achilles heel. In elementary school back in the 1950's, the subject had been practically sidestepped altogether; it wasn't one of the three R's. Back to basics? They had never left: reading, (w)riting, and 'rithmetic-- end report. The only things I recall learning even remotely connected to science were the names of the planets, and we memorized them ad nauseum for five years in a row: Mercury, Venus, Earth, Mars, Jupiter, Saturn, Neptune, Uranus, and Pluto. Or, as one of my elementary school teachers relentlessly drilled us, "Myrtle Very Easily Makes Jelly Sandwiches Nightly Under Pressure." Even that ridiculous sentence was a challenge for me to master; I just seemed to have a block against science.

I hoped for better in junior high school; actually, it got worse, if that was possible. In seventh grade, we had a home economics teacher who was assigned to teach a section of science out of her certification area-- so most of the class knew much more than she did, which was not very much. Even seventh graders had enough savvy to figure out that she was struggling to stay one lesson ahead of us.

"Don't ask questions, don't ask questions! We're not up to that yet," she admonished us constantly when we dared to raise a hand and be so bold as to ask one instead of constantly copying notes off the blackboard for 45 tiresome minutes, which she, in turn, had transcribed from a review book. Her efforts were futile. I think I learned everything there is to know about the use of brome thymol blue (whatever that is) that year, which was her favorite subject to talk about. Actually, it was her *only* subject to talk about.

In eighth grade, we went from bad to worse. The ditzy brunette was having a torrid affair with the lab technician who was evidently on overdrive, and (to our glee) was caught in the act in the adjacent science prep room by a snoopy assistant principal when he appeared on the scene to find the class left unattended. She quickly vanished from the scene, much the way Buzz was exterminated after his encounter with the assistant proctor.

Things were looking up in the ninth grade when we started off the year with the superstar of the department, a kindly old gent who was a legend, having taught our parents-- and possibly our parents' parents, for that matter. His snake collection was his prize, and once he brought his companion boa constrictor, Solomon, to school, wrapped around his waist. Feeble from the start, he (the teacher, not the snake) became even more sickly early on, and we proceeded to endure a parade of substitutes, all of whom looked as though they had been sent by central casting, and none of whom knew the first thing about science. Once the novelty wore off of tormenting and torturing them to the point of getting them to vow never to return, we settled down to learn the subject, but alas they had little or nothing to offer. Chalk up another goose egg.

High school science wasn't all that better. My Biology class was tapped for an "experimental workbook approach" in which we never even touched a test tube, let alone performed a dissection. We *read* about microscopes, but never handled them; they were off limits to us, left to gather dust in the central science prep room. I didn't fare very well with Chemistry, either, with the class under the aegis of a woman whose desk was littered with off-track betting slips. Everything she taught was in terms of "odds." Hard as I tried, I couldn't get those equations to balance. When she mercifully passed me, I decided to quit while I was ahead and told my guidance counselor "Don't even think" of putting Physics on my schedule. So, try as I did to get out of it, when I found that there was no way 'round the science requirement at Cornell, I took what I thought was the easy way out with Geology 101.

Was I ever wrong! If the two lectures per week were totally unintelligible (at least to me), the labs were even more challenging, but for different reasons. I had enough trouble keeping track of what happened yesterday and couldn't care less about what happened five zillion years ago. The course took advantage of the fact that Cornell is located in the heart of the Finger Lakes Region of New York State. The gorges, lakes, and valleys provided a natural outdoor laboratory. During the Ice Age, glaciers had moved from the North to the South through these parts and scooped out those beautiful waterfalls and gorges. That much I could comprehend. Even I was impressed with that little bit of knowledge. But it was downhill, literally, from that point on.

Every Tuesday afternoon, rain or shine, we donned hiking shoes and traveled to one of these geological sites. The lab instructor, a young South African working on his own doctorate, was extremely enthusiastic about the subject matter. He really seemed to get off on this rock stuff. The proverbial absent-minded professor, rather disheveled, with creased shirt and baggy pants, his most salient characteristic (besides his thick accent) was that his fly was usually wide open. The fact that he lectured with his hands in his pockets only made the display even more gaping. When he would get excited about some geological phenomenon, little did he know that the class wasn't laughing with him, but at him. But he was a nice sort of chap and I felt a little guilty that he was the butt of our jokes. One of my classmates actually did a take-off (no pun intended) of his lecturing during Improv Night at the Commons. At least he made the lab work somewhat palatable. The lecture part of the course made little or no sense to me at all. The two-hour lab made it seem a bit more real.

My most unforgettable experience was traipsing to the very bottom of one of the deepest gorges to study fossil formations. I had passed over this area, crossing the suspension bridge way above it, almost on a daily basis. Was it ever a strange but beautiful sight looking straight up from all the way down there! From far above we barely heard the roar of the rapids, sound effects that enhanced nature's spectacular picture show down below. Dutifully, we removed our shoes and left them on the banks before gingerly walking on the rocks amid the bubbling stream of water.

My lab partner, to whom I had been alphabetically assigned, was this country girl, blond with twin pigtails, who always wore gingham dresses and horn-rimmed glasses. Unlike my fortuitous pairing with Diana in Anthro 101, there was no romantic attraction, none whatsoever, this time. These days, I'd probably refer to her as the "anti-Viagra." The only thing we ever talked about was our joint lab reports, which seemed to come easily to her. So at least there was something for me to gain from this arranged marriage. She had absolutely no sense of humor whatsoever and didn't know how to smile. Well, once-- but I think it was gas. Of another place and time, she looked as though she had fallen out of the 1950's. But on this occasion, she did speak to me.

"I wouldn't be stepping on that rock down there if I was you," she warned me in a dispassionate, monotone drawl. I looked down. "That there is a snake." That's all I needed to hear. This city boy became a bit more circumspect on future sojourns into the wilderness. For that reason, to this day, I refuse to sit through a screening of the *Revenant.*

For the first time in my academic life, I was in distinct danger of failing a course. Now I understood the sense of utter helplessness that Brant had experienced. Always a high achiever in high school, I felt as though I was flunking if I ever got a grade in the 80's. Even in elementary school, I longed to be awarded a "self-control" button, which was the consolation prize for just mising honor roll; it was given to those whose behavior was exemplary, but achievement was lacking. Alas, its attainment was elusive. No, I was never able to walk around with that little round button proclaiming "I have SELF-CONTROL."

Up to this point, high school Chemistry had been my toughest challenge; however, it paled by comparison to what I was facing in Geology 101. At this moment in time, however, I would have gladly gotten a 65 on the prelim and settled for a mere passing grade in the course. The lectures made absolutely no sense to me. Who cares what happened in the Ice Age? This was 1967. Besides, I concluded, it was all guesswork, anyway. I was a concrete sequential kind of guy, not an abstract thinker. Well, that's how I rationalized my frustration. I found myself passing some tests and failing others. I felt as though I was sinking-- like a rock! And it was rock identification that proved to be my downfall. To me, a rock was a rock was a rock. It didn't matter what fancy name it was given.

The upcoming lab practical would make me or break me in terms of passing this course. According to the rules of the game, each member of the class would start off at a rock station. We had 45 seconds to identify the type of rock and write down its name in the space provided on the answer sheet. After 45 seconds, an egg timer would sound and we would rotate to the next station where the process would be repeated. All in all, we had to identify 25 specimens in about twenty minutes.

As I surveyed the room, all the rocks looked the same to me: They looked like-- rocks! The politically correct term was to say that I was "geologically challenged." I had gone to the kindly South African during his office hours for extra help, which he gave freely, but to little avail. He tried to be helpful, but there was a language barrier between us. To begin with, I didn't understand a word he was saying through his thick accent and rapid delivery. I just kept nodding my head like a bobblehead doll, "uh huh, uh huh" so as not to offend him. He, in turn, perceived this as a sign of my comprehension and kept babbling, progressively faster and faster, using geological expressions making him even more incomprehensible. It was almost as if he were speaking a foreign language. I guess that in a way, he was. Furthermore, when I did manage to make out what he was saying, it didn't make a bit of sense to me anyway. To make matters worse, he used highly technical terms, which further compounded the language barrier.

He continued to coach me; the only thing I could recall was that if you put sulfuric acid on the rock sample and it bubbled, it was-- quartz?? And if you tasted a rock and it was salty, it was-- marble?? Or was it the other way around? So I would have to alternate between dropping acid on the rock and then licking it, hopefully on virgin territory, in mortal fear of burning my tongue irreparably.

The race was on. Those 45 seconds at each rock station seemed to pass by awfully fast. The sound of the egg timer seemed to come sooner and sooner. After a while, I was just writing down-- "marble… quartz… marble… quartz… marble…" I somehow managed to eke out a 56 on that exam, which translated (mercifully) into a D- that (miraculously) was a passing grade. Actually, I think that the South African took pity on me and passed me-- which only made me feel even guiltier about jumping on the bandwagon that had ridiculed him through the semester.

I did, however, learn one thing from that experience: I wasn't going to be a science teacher or a rock climber. For several days, I held a vigil by the glass case outside the Geology office where the final course grades were posted. Since they were listed by student identification number, to this day nobody ever knew about that D-, which jumped off the page, sandwiched in among all those A's and B's. I vowed then and there never to darken the doorstep of the science building, ever again.

MARCH, 1967

#34 – As Luck Would Have It

It was about this time, in the early spring of my sophomore year, that I met Norma. She was from a prominent family in Memphis, Tennessee. Norma, too, had it "good" and sympathized with my ambivalence, not yet wanting to be suckered into the anti-war frenzy overtaking the campus.

We had met at a fraternity-sorority mixer. She was from Omega, heretofore an "untouchable," from the sisterhood "across the tracks." Apparently a joint party between her house and Gamma Rho fell through when "GR" was put on social probation for a hazing incident in which two pledges had been severely injured. No surprise; I already sensed that the brothers of Gamma Rho were capable of practically anything, judging by whatever had happened to Ian on initiation night.

In the meantime, a band had been hired and the bar had been stocked. The only thing missing were the guys. We became the stand-ins, the second bananas. Otherwise, Norma and her sisters would never even have condescended to give us a second look.

The mixer, moved to our house, went passably well, although some of the girls looked extremely bored and started their vanishing act half-way through the evening. We CATs were just not up to their highfalutin standards; nor was our décor or lack thereof. They were accustomed to something a lot spiffier. No surprise, Ian was the star attraction, drawing the sisters around him like bees to honey. Most of us got the feeling that Omega was going through the motions and wanted this evening over and done with as quickly as possible. For them, it was one big yawn. It certainly wasn't for me.

Norma Cooper was short, pert, and attractive. I had managed to reel in a lively little one. She had the softness that Diana lacked. Diana was a "career girl" at 18, mature beyond her years; Norma was homier. She was a college student, knew it, and was content with herself. We hit if off right away. Most of my brothers were not faring nearly as well, passing around co-eds like cocktail franks. But Norma seemed to enjoy being with me-- and the feeling was certainly mutual. I was just fearful that she was only being polite and would tail out of there, giving me the heave-ho as soon as the opportunity arose. As far as I was concerned, that evening could have gone on forever. Most everyone else viewed it as a chore, glad for it to be over with, but not me. On the contrary, I didn't want the proverbial Midnight to come.

"I don't know whether she really liked me or just didn't want to hurt my feelings," I kept asking myself as well as Ian, my sounding board, over the next few days.

"Well, then call her and find out," he said in an exasperated tone, as if this were a no-brainer. Easy for him to say, I said to myself; Ian wasn't used to rejection. So I made the call.

"You really don't want to go out with a guy like me, do you?" I sheepishly asked her. Well, not exactly in those words. But I was hardly exuding confidence in that initial phone conversation. Yet before I could pop the question, she accepted: "I'd love to!" I was sailing.

Over the next few weeks, we spoke on the phone, met on campus, and saw each other every chance we could. We made the rounds at all the events. Weekends were automatically spoken for once again. It was nice having a serious relationship, not having to resort to blind dates, or getting fixed up by the house matchmaker. I wasn't into the bar scene, either; I didn't like to drink all that much. Nor did I care for the "meat market" which was the M.O. there.

Furthermore, besides Ian, Norma was the only other person who understood me and my reluctance to jump onto the anti-war bandwagon. What I didn't know at the time was the nature of her father's business and his close connections to the big wigs in Washington. That would come shortly thereafter in a most dramatic fashion. But for the time being, ignorance was bliss, and we were, as they used to say, an item. I didn't have to constantly be on my toes. Norma was Diana, without the political baggage.

APRIL, 1967

#35 – Uncle Sam Comes Knockin'

Happily, very much so, I continued to date Norma that spring. In the meantime, the anti-war sentiment was simmering on campus. Before too long the pot would boil over.

Up until that moment, the War was still amorphous. It lacked a face. Nobody I knew had been touched. I hoped that maybe it all would just disappear. Wrong. Everything was about to change. My sense of security would start to unravel. My world was about to be turned upside down.

This was a time when long distance phone calling was still a small luxury and there was no such thing as e-mail. I spoke with my parents every Sunday morning; it became a ritual. These days, long distance rates are cheaper than first class postage; but not then. Ma Bell had us by the short hairs and each minute was precious. A letter from home was a coveted prize. Fortunately for me, my parents were prolific writers, so rarely a day passed by without some missive from them, be it just a post card. The news wasn't very exciting: items about the neighbors, the weather, and so forth. But it was mail. When I was a freshman, whenever I was feeling even a pang of homesickness, I would go to the central mailroom at the lunch hour and watch the sorting into those little postal boxes. To this day, I still remember my three-number combination.

The mail ritual was altogether different in the fraternity house. The local letter carrier dumped, with considerable contempt I might add, all the mail for these spoiled rich kids. It was our job to search through the pile and ferret out what belonged to us.

I was buying review books in Collegetown on the day that changed Kip's life-- and in some ways, mine, too-- forever. In the walk-up apartment where he lived, the mail was sorted into metal boxes in an alcove on the first floor. He stopped to collect his pile of letters before we went upstairs. He opened the slot and out poured the contents onto the floor. I had no reason to take much notice of what he was doing as he picked them up. He leafed through several envelopes, bills, junk mail, or whatever. Then I noticed that he seemed preoccupied with one piece in particular. At first glance it looked like one of those "official" notices you get for a prize sweepstakes. But this was *not* Kip's lucky day. The return address caught my eye: **United States Defense Department - Selective Service System**. Immediately— we both knew what this meant. A chill shot up my spine. I could just imagine how Kip felt. This was definitely not good news; this was a contest he definitely *didn't* want to win. His number was-- up.

Kip didn't wait to get up to his apartment to see what was inside. He ripped open the envelope and snapped out its contents in the small vestibule, letting the envelope fall to the floor, out-of-character for someone so compulsive-obsessive neat. I didn't have to read the letter to know what it said; I just read his expression.

It was his draft notice. Kip would be going to Vietnam. He was told to report home to his local draft board in Oklahoma immediately. Washington had said, "Get ready, get set, go! So, they couldn't wait to get their hands on him, not even letting him finish out this semester, which was entering the home stretch. Go to jail, don't pass GO, don't collect $200. No longer was the war impersonal; now, for me, it had hit home. It had that face.

Kip said absolutely nothing. There was nothing to say. I accompanied him up to his apartment. The silence was very uncomfortable. I tried to break it, but I just fumfered. Whatever babble came out of my mouth only seemed to make things worse, so I just shut up.

Of the five of us, Kip was by far the best student, sailing through Cornell, near the top of our class. Now, all his best-laid plans would have to be put on hold. Worse, he was about to be shipped off to Southeast Asia, fate unknown. I knew in my heart that he could very easily become a statistic. But not the type the proctor had talked about. And I'm sure Kip was thinking precisely the same thing.

How life's course can take a bad turn in a split second. Should I leave him alone? Stay? What to do? I remained in his apartment for a while longer. Still, I said nothing; I was at a loss for words. I guess I was fearful of saying the wrong thing at this delicate moment so I continued to keep my mouth shut. But how I wanted to console my buddy!

Yet there was nothing I could possibly do to make him feel any better. "Don't worry-- everything will be all right," just didn't work. Who was to say that everything *would* turn out all right? Just the fact that Kip was being forced to leave Cornell was not "all right." He didn't deserve this! I cried out to myself. I wanted to be there with him and for him at this moment; and yet a different part of me wanted to tear away as fast as I possibly could and run away as far I could from this trainwreck. I tried to put myself in his place and imagine what he was going through.

There was a tinge of guilt. Maybe I wasn't as scared for Kip as I was for myself. After all, I was equally vulnerable; the very same thing could happen to me at a moment's notice. Whatever the reason, I was extremely on edge and uncomfortable. After about an hour-- which seemed a lot longer-- I found some bogus excuse to extricate myself from this bad scene.

I needed to talk to someone, and as I had become so accustomed to doing, I turned to Ian. But he was of little use. The news hit him, too, like a ton of bricks.

"What a bummer," he kept saying, shaking his head in disbelief. Sure, we felt terrible for Kip. But there was the selfish side to this as well. Ian validated my self-doubts. If it could happen to Kip, it could happen to any one of us. For the first time, I knew someone who had been touched by the War. Also for the first time, I felt as though I was losing control of my future.

Talking to Ian had only made me feel worse. But I still needed to unload on someone, so I decided to call Norma for comfort. Although she still hadn't met Kip, she was mildly sympathetic. Yes, she cared that I was upset; but she just couldn't seem to grasp *why*.

"Look," she consoled me, "get used to it. This is the price you're going to have to pay to keep our freedoms," she sighed. I must admit that I was a bit unnerved by her casual attitude. But I brushed it off, rationalizing that since she didn't know Kip, it hadn't hit as close to home for her. Nevertheless, her nonchalance irked me, especially when she saw how upset I was by what was about to happen.

SEVERAL DAYS LATER

#36 – "Bring him home."

"He is young; he's afraid.
"Let him rest, heaven blessed.
"Bring him peace, bring him joy.
"He is young; he is only a boy.
"Bring him home."

–*Les Miserables*

Ian and I planned to accompany Kip to Tompkins County Airport for what undoubtedly would be a long and lonely flight back to Oklahoma, for more reasons than one. We weren't going to let him be alone for this sendoff. At least for this part of the trip, he'd travel as a civilian. After boot camp and before too long, he'd be flying in a different direction, in a different mode, and in different class, all courtesy of Uncle Sam.

It was near daybreak. The sun was trying to rise, but fierce-looking storm clouds were winning over. Kip's roommate, a pleasant Korean fellow whom I knew only in passing, also an Engineering student, wanted to go with us. Kip's girlfriend was too devastated, beyond consolation, and said her final good-byes back in

Collegetown. I think she was afraid of breaking down at the airport, which would have made it all the more painful for Kip.

Ian and I picked the two of them up at their apartment. We left a half hour for the fifteen-minute trip, not wanting to risk being late and missing the plane. However, with virtually no traffic at this hour of the morning, we made it in even less time. What's the rush, I said to myself, teeth gritted? To serve Kip up to the warmongers?

Little was said on the short ride to the airport. I sat in the back seat, shivering, whether it was from the cold or a very bad case of nerves. I was trying to suppress my anger. I tried to break the uneasy silence with some small talk and encouraging words, but it didn't work; as a matter of fact, I think it was so forced that it made things worse. I could read Ian's mind: "Shut-up. Just shut-up." There was no way around it: Kip was leaving Cornell and soon after going to Vietnam. That was it. There were no words which could cushion the blow or make that plain and simple truth any easier to swallow.

Not only did we get to the airport ahead of schedule, but on arrival we discovered that his plane would be delayed for at least an hour, due to inclement weather coming from the North. All of this further prolonged the good-byes and compounded the pain.

"Let's get this over with already," Ian muttered to me when we were alone for two seconds. "This is torture."

"For all of us. For all of us," I answered back in a hushed tone.

The cold, grey April skies, not unusual for Ithaca at this time of year, only added to the dreary mood. At last Kip's flight was called.

"You'll be back soon," I pretended, forcing a smile as I embraced him tightly.

Ian slapped him on the shoulder. "Hang in there, big guy, until you come back to us," was all he could muster up, fighting back tears. I had rarely seen Ian get so emotional before. The roommate just stood there, expressionless, almost as if in shock.

Kip half-smiled, but said nothing, trying to remain stoic. But deep down he must have sensed that none of this was ever going to happen.

We accompanied Kip as far as we could until we were abruptly ordered to stop at the gate. Just as well. Frankly, I was glad to have to make the break; the scene was all so excruciatingly heart-wrenching.

So this was it. I was still shivering, and it wasn't just from the raw wind that cut through me. Kip gave us one more forced smile, one more silent set of hugs, a wave-- almost a salute-- and it was over. We watched him climb the gangplank and board the prop plane, not even looking back. Then we watched his flight take off, holding on to Kip as long as we could, not leaving until his plane rose and disappeared into the swirling storm clouds. He faced a long and lonely trip ahead of him, first to New York, next to Chicago, then to Oklahoma City, and finally to his hometown in Oklahoma. Layovers and all, it amounted to more than eleven hours of traveling, grueling even under the best of circumstances.

Heads hung low, we walked back to the car in the parking lot in total silence. I was really shaking by now, from both the cold and emotional overload. I also had a splitting headache. Little was said on the ride back, either. Kip's departure had hit us hard. He had been snatched out of the womb. We were scared for him. But we were just as scared for ourselves.

I wrote to his parents. They immediately responded, thanked me for contacting them, and sent me his mailing address, first in boot camp, and then, ultimately-- in Vietnam. Kip quickly answered back with a detailed letter describing everything from what boot camp was like… to the flight over… to the conditions on the other side. His mood actually seemed upbeat as he even joked about the food and some of his fellow soldiers in his platoon. Apparently sending and receiving mail was a major diversion. Over the next few months, playing pen pal was the very least I could do for Kip; it may me feel good, too.

So I wrote back just as fast… and he answered just as quickly, with a play-by-play account of what combat was like, up close and personal. I responded-- and then waited and waited for his next letter in return.

Yes, I waited and waited. That response never came. Certainly not standing on ceremony, I wrote again. But my next letter went unanswered as well. And so was the next.

I never heard from Kip again. For a long time, I was tempted to write to his parents, but I just couldn't muster the courage, fearing the worst. Kip never came back to Cornell. I don't know what happened in Vietnam… whether he finished college… or what. On several occasions, I have been tempted to inquire at the Alumni Office, but for some reason, I stopped short and never followed through. Maybe I'm afraid of finding out the truth. At least by not knowing, I can keep some hope alive. Even now, whenever I pick up an alumni magazine or college directory, I keep an eye open for his name to appear. Nothing. To this day, I don't know whether Kip is dead or alive. And it pains me greatly.

Kip was only the first. The long arm of the Pentagon was reaching onto the college campuses all around the country and plucking students into its grasp. Cornell was no exception. There started to be more and more missing persons in the lecture halls. One shuddered to ask: "What happened to--?" when he was absent for a few classes. Sick, hung over, overslept, cutting? Those would be the best answers you could hope for. Instead, there was an uncomfortable silence. But everyone knew the real reason. We lived in constant fear, wondering who would be the next to get that call, who would be the next to leave an empty seat.

MAY, 1967

#37 –Worlds Apart

I continued to date Norma for the next few weeks and during these uncertain times. I still hadn't recovered from the blow of Kip's being abruptly snatched from our grasp and eagerly welcomed the diversion of dating again. Unlike Diana, she had no interest in politics whatsoever. I think that it was a big bore to her. I found that I didn't have to be on guard that what I said might incite her. I did know, however, that she had her strong beliefs about the War and she knew that I had mine. We respected those differences and steered clear of that topic, which became strictly off limits. The biggest potential stumbling block in our relationship was not politics, but rather the difference in religion: This was the first time that I had seriously dated a girl who wasn't Jewish.

After growing up in New York, coming to Ithaca was a rude awakening for me. I had never been a minority before. Being in that distinct minority, it wasn't easy to find a "nice Jewish girl"-- which was what I was looking for. I hadn't told my parents about Norma; I wasn't sure how they would react to the news. After all, I wasn't marrying her. Yet. Not even close. But who knows what could happen? These things have to start somewhere. Well, I rationalized, I'd cross that rickety bridge if I ever got to it. For now, I would enjoy the ride.

Actually, I was going to get to meet her parents first. Her mother and father, along with her two brothers, were coming to pay a visit the following weekend. I was invited to join them for dinner on Saturday night. Admittedly, I was more than a little apprehensive. I must have had a foreboding; little did I know then what a colossal disaster this evening would turn out to be.

I hadn't been to the Olde Inn on the Lake for a while, so the meal itself was going to be a treat. My diet consisted of tiresome fraternity food fare with the same menus recycled again and again. How many different ways could even Henny camouflage mystery meat? Nobody faulted her; she did the best she could with the paltry provisions she was provided. The only break from the tedious routine came in the form of a meal on campus, a hero from the sandwich truck, an occasional visit to the diner, or an even more infrequent restaurant trip, usually reserved for the weekends. Still swimming regularly, I had no problem keeping my weight at that svelte 149 pounds, pretty trim for a six footer. So I looked forward to Saturday evening when I would get to meet Norma's parents and get a square meal out of the deal. Little did I know what else would be on the menu.

"Walter Harmon, here," he introduced himself when the family came to pick me up in their roomy Buick, which once inside looked more like a living room than a car. Her father was a fiftyish fellow, maybe even pushing 60, on the short, stocky side, with a ruddy complexion and silver hair styled in a bad comb-over. His hanging jowls did a good job of covering up his neck. He certainly was well-dressed, in a navy blue pinstripe suit with everything else complementing it perfectly, from the crimson necktie to the handkerchief neatly folded in the breast pocket of his jacket. Now I could see where Norma's height, or lack thereof, came from. I didn't know much else about him. Norma had told me that he owned some sort of factory back in Tennessee.

"This here's the missus, Norma's mom," as he introduced me to her. No Women's Lib here; dad was clearly in charge and did most of the talking. Norma was a carbon copy of her mom, only the mother was an inch or two taller and quite a bit stouter. As a matter of fact, she looked as though she had been inflated with a bicycle pump. But like the father, she, too, was exquisitely dressed and arrayed in shiny, splashy jewelry. Come to the think of it, the mother and father were a matched pair and looked like each other. Brother and sister?

In the back seat of the car were Norma's two older brothers, Walter, Jr. and George. They were somewhere in their early twenties, close in age, and I couldn't make out which one was older. When they got out of the car I would see that both boys, though not exactly giants, were considerably taller than their father. Although they politely greeted me, it was hardly with enthusiasm; neither was particularly outgoing or friendly, not to me, anyway. I would characterize their mood as "reserved." Junior and George did more listening than talking. Much of the conversation on the twenty-minute ride to the restaurant was dominated by Norma's dad, with an occasional question fired at me. They all seemed to be fishing for something.

Mr. Harmon (I didn't dare call him Walter; nor did he invite me to) had made sure that a table was waiting for us when we arrived. This time, I *did* get to sit at a window overlooking the lake. Money talks. The waitress quickly came over to recite the menu. Mr. Harmon took over from there.

"I'll have the Beef Wellington; the missus will have the Chicken Marsala." He picked his side dishes-- and her sides as well. But Mrs. Harmon didn't seem to mind at all; she was too busy chitchatting with Norma, catching up with girl talk and paid little attention to the men. The older brothers stoically sat at attention, like Twiddle Dee and Twiddle Dumb. They gave their dinner choices to the waitress, but said little else. There was no question as to who wore the pants, big pants, in this family and who was in command at this table.

"So tell me a little about yourself, young man," Mr. Harmon petitioned.

"Nothing too exciting, sir," and I proceeded to give him a short resume, going back to high school and bringing him up to the present.

"And what do your parents do?" What was this, *This Is Your Life*? Well, I reasoned, it was his only daughter and I was her current boyfriend, so I gave him the full pedigree.

"Both are teachers in the New York City school system." He exhibited no reaction.

"And are you planning to become a teacher, too?" Now I didn't know what answer he was looking for, so I decided to just tell the truth.

"Still not exactly sure. I have a hankering to do something in journalism. Or, maybe television. But I also might consider teaching. I can go several ways with an English major." I thought that would satisfy him-- but it didn't.

"Teaching?" he queried. "To get out of the war?" Both his eyebrows and intonation became raised while his lips frowned down, as he continued to interrogate me, suddenly scratching his bald spot. Apparently he had heard about the students' run on Education courses to avoid the draft as it crept closer and closer to the college campuses.

"No, sir," I snapped right back at him. If I go into teaching, it will be because I *want* to." I put that overemphasis on the word "want." He seemed to like that answer a bit better. But I was still on guard. This exchange was going downhill, fast.

"So tell me, young man, what *do* you think of this War?" He blurted out, no holds barred. This was casual table talk for our first meeting? I knew what he wanted to hear-- but I wasn't prepared to give it to him. Trauma now or trauma later: I had to let him know where I stood.

"I'm still on the fence, sir. I want to support our country, but I don't know if we belong in Vietnam. And I certainly don't like the way my classmates are being dragged into this with no say whatsoever. As a matter of fact, one of my closest buddies was just snatched up and carted off in mid-semester." I stopped short to assess his reaction; he was OK with the first part, but winced at the second.

For the first time, the mother and daughter stopped gabbing, sensing some tension at the table. At this point, Twiddle Dumb spoke for the first time.

"Nobody is being dragged into nothin'. If called, I go," Junior proudly proclaimed with a rather disapproving glance at me.

"So you'd just get up and go without any protest?" I tossed the ball back to him.

"Walter Junior doesn't *have* to worry about that. He's in R-O-T-C," Mrs. Harmon chimed in for the first time, obviously quite proud. Both sons gave one quick nod in sync. So that's how he'd get out of it; somehow I didn't see this pair of three-piece suits on the front lines.

Sensing this was not going in the right direction, Norma piped in. "Let's talk about something else. I'm kind of sick and tired of all this war stuff, anyway."

But Mr. Harmon was on my case. "So what *would* you do if you were drafted?" he demanded to know.

I had no easy answer for him; nor did I feel I owed him one. "I don't know, sir. I just don't know, I'm very torn on this issue.'

"Torn about *what?*" the other brother jumped all over me. So I reprised my earlier answer.

"I just saw one of my classmates taken off campus and carted to Vietnam in the middle of the semester," trying my hardest to keep my cool, avoiding the temptation to answer him in the same tone he took with me. "He was yanked away without the slightest warning whatsoever. He had no absolutely no say in what happened to him and whether we should be involved in that War in the first place. Frankly, I don't know whether he'll end up dead or alive. You want to talk about *un*-American? That's not American." I couldn't contain myself nor hold back any longer. I let it all pour out, telling them just what and how I felt.

"Not American?!" I had touched a nerve. Mr. Harmon shot up in his seat, as if he had been struck by lightning. "Then who's supposed to fight for this country? Just because you're in college, you're exempt?" he snapped, shaking his head all the while.

"Now don't raise your voice, Walter," Mrs. Harmon tried to calm him down, spearing his elbow with her pudgy hand. "You don't want to get your pressure up." But the horse was out of the barn. It was too late. He just ignored her.

"Do you want to know what's going to happen to this America of ours if we don't fight and if we don't win this war? I'll tell you precisely what will happen," he practically roared, drawing the curious stares of other diners at neighboring tables. "The Reds will take over another country and we'll look like a second-rate power. That's what'll happen. The rest of the world will be laughing at us. We have to go in and we have to win-- and win *big* over there." He supersized that word "big" as he looked me squarely in the eyes with fire raging in his own. I was expecting smoke to come out of his ears. The four members of his captive audience were nodding in approval like puppets on a string.

What was I going to do-- argue with him? I'd never win anyway. He practiced a blind jingoism. There *was* no other side. America, right or wrong. Besides, I was outnumbered. I still hadn't formulated an opinion. But it wouldn't have mattered anyway; in Mr. Harmon's mind, I wasn't entitled to any opinion other than his.

"And what do you do?" I feigned politeness towards Mr. Harmon, baiting him just a bit, having been clued in by Norma as to what answer I should expect.

Mrs. Harmon answered for him. "Walter owns several factories in Tennessee and Ohio," she said proudly.

"He's helping support the war effort," Junior jumped in.

"And what do they manufacture?" I matter-of-factly asked, full-well surmising the answer by now. The two of them looked at each other, seeming not to want to answer this question, so Norma, naïve to the trap I had set, filled in the blank.

"Daddy has a number of munitions contracts with the government. He's helping to fight this war," she said proudly.

So *that* was it! I bit my tongue; I would have liked to have said that "the War is helping to support Daddy"-- but I didn't want to ruin this evening altogether, or worse, jeopardize my relationship with Norma. I was searching frantically to get off the subject and out of this snare when the dinner was mercifully served. For the next half hour, everyone was too busy gobbling up their grub to converse.

Intermission over, it was time for Act II-- which would end up making Act I look like child's play. As the plates were cleared away, I made a point of restarting the conversation and picked the topic, just to avoid any further discussion of the War. "Do either of you guys play sports?" I directed it at the brothers, figuring this was innocuous enough. Judging by their reaction, I thought they liked that question and I was on neutral territory. Wrong.

"I play soccer and lacrosse; Walter Junior plays baseball," George answered.

"Both boys got scholarships for their ath-e-letic prowess," Mother Harmon proudly proclaimed. Junior received an honorable mention for the All-American Team," she boasted. I caught a glance at Mr. Harmon who was beaming with pride. Actually, though, this was *not* a very safe question. I had gone down the wrong path once again, and knew what was coming. My fault; I had set myself up this time. Here it comes:

"And you? What sports did *you* play in high school?" they turned the tables, seeming to know what my answer would be. At first I thought I'd get myself out of this mess with some humor, by saying "Chess and checkers" --or-- recounting the freshman swim test story or wrestling debacle. But I was tired of playing verbal fisticuffs and ceded this round.

"I was on the JV volleyball team in high school," I sheepishly tried.

That was a cue for the two of them to roar in unison.

"That's no sport," snapped one.

"Hell, no. If you don't have to wear an ath-e-letic supporter, it just doesn't qualify," shot back the other, also amused at yet another put-down.

The two women just giggled, almost embarrassed; Mr. Harmon just stared at me in mock disbelief. I just sat there, motionless and expressionless. There was no retort worth offering up. For a split second, I wanted to say "figure skating" or "gymnastics" but wisely I kept quiet. I guess the Harmon definition of a true sport demanded inflicting pain and shedding blood while brandishing a jockstrap. I decided to surrender this round before they could get any more digs in.

"Well, then, I have to say *none*, sir. I'm no super jock," I conceded on this one. Chalk up another win for their side. I was "0" for two so far. The third and final strike was about to be pitched.

This response didn't sit too well with Mr. Harmon, to say the least. "Ath-e-letics" was in their DNA. The brothers seem to gloat at my response. Mercifully, the check was delivered to the table just at this moment. But there was more to come; they were saving the best for last.

Mr. Harmon put on his reading glasses and scrutinized the bill carefully as though he was auditing a business statement. "Hey, they didn't charge for the a la carte desserts not on the dinner special," he pointed out to his wife. Now how would the All-American couple handle this moral dilemma?

"Maybe we can Jew them out of a couple of dollars," Mrs. Harmon giggled. The boys laughed as well. I shot up in my chair, trying to conceal my shock. I had never been referred to as a "verb" before. "To Jew" them-- this expression was alien to me in more ways than one. Norma sensed my distress. She was more tolerant (relatively speaking) than her parents. As far as I was concerned, this time Mr. Harmon had crossed the line. Nevertheless, I just kept quiet; I was just too outnumbered.

The check was paid with dispatch, we left the restaurant, piled into the car, and returned to campus. Little of consequence was said on the return trip. I could tell by Norma's expression that she could sense that I was ticked off, big league. She knew that I was Jewish. Hadn't she told her parents? Couldn't they figure it out? It wasn't obvious from my last name, but I had been told that I "looked" Jewish-- and that was something I was proud of. Had that remark been made inadvertently? Or, even worse, consciously? It didn't matter. For whatever reason, I had a strong distaste for this man and his family and had no intention of making any bones about it.

I said good night to Norma, but did not kiss her. I matter-of-factly thanked her parents for taking me to dinner with a robot-like acknowledgment. I doubted that I would ever see them again. I totally ignored the brother act. They didn't deserve any homage or respect.

By the time I walked the few steps to my room, I felt totally stressed out and flopped face down on the bed. Too bad the gym wasn't open at that hour; I would have liked to have punched something, or some *one.* I had restrained myself, held in my anger, and contained my rage all evening. Now it was pouring out. These people were *awful.*

Norma's parents absolutely personified the enemy of the anti-war movement: the fat-cat war monger who was getting fatter and fatter at the expense of the college students and other poor helpless souls. Worse, they were outright bigots. It was easy to dismiss them. The only problem was, I still *loved* their daughter Norma. Yes, *loved.* If we were going to have a relationship, where would they fit in? Could I get past this? Not a very auspicious beginning.

However, that matter was quickly resolved for me. I went to bed, but, no surprise, couldn't sleep, being so torn and twisted. At about 1:00 A.M., the phone rang. It was Norma.

"I just want to apologize for Daddy," she said softly.

That was a big step for her to take, so I quickly softened my stance. Maybe there could be some peaceful coexistence. I didn't want to make it even more painful, so I didn't suggest that both he and she and the mother and the brothers-- they should *all* be apologizing. She was trying, or so I thought, to negotiate some détente. I stepped lightly, not wanting to risk ruining our relationship. Then she hit me right between the eyes:

"I can't see you anymore," she blurted out. That blow certainly blindsided me; her punch was a knock-out one. I said nothing, waiting for her to speak further.

This time after a brief pause, and what I thought was a muffled sob, she filled in the blanks. "Daddy says that we're just too... different." I could tell that she was trying to hold back tears.

"Daddy says"-- I said to myself. I didn't know whether to hope that she would buck "Daddy" or to take the lead and answer her back myself. I should have kept quiet and ridden things out. But impulsive as I am, I let loose, full force.

"Norma, 'too different' means two things: that I don't agree with his stand on the War. And that I am Jewish. Well, if you ask me, he's a fat old bigot with no sense of morality."

What had I said? He was still her father. My temper had gotten the best of me. No wonder I had never earned that "SELF-CONTROL" button in elementary school.

Once again, there was silence at the end of the line. Had she hung up? No, Norma was still there; I could tell by the sniffles. And I knew her well enough to know that the tears were streaming.

"As I said, I don't think we can see each other again," she sobbed. I heard the phone hang up on the other end. That was the end of it.

For days after, I was heartbroken. This little girl from Tennessee had taken my heart and had me hooked. But to a degree, I blamed myself: I should never have started with her in the first place. We *were* just too different, worlds apart. For a relationship to start... for it to last-- there has to be at least some commonality. Religion.... culture.... political beliefs-- *something!* We had none of that stuff. Norma and I just were not meant to be. Too much, too soon.

I can just imagine the lecture and tongue-lashing she received from her parents, her father in particular. The mother probably just sat there nodding her head in agreement, bobbing up and down. I was clearly not the man they had in mind for their little girl for so, so many reasons.

Norma and I did run into each other from time to time over the next few months, either on campus or on the party circuit. Her greeting was cordial enough-- as if I were a distant cousin. She recovered from this break-up much more quickly than I did. The very next time I saw her, she was arm and arm with another guy, this one much more in her own style. She certainly rebounded fast. Some say that a girl marries her father; in this case, the guy was a clone of her two brothers.

I somehow managed to get over Norma before too long, but I was left severely scarred by the whole Harmon family experience.

SUMMER, 1967

#38 - "...like you lost your best friend."

The summer following my sophomore year was a ho-hum one. I still hadn't gotten over what had happened to Kip, which had jolted all of us into reality. All of a sudden, it was a whole new world in which we were living. The operative words were "exposed" and "vulnerable." By now I had lost total contact with him while seeing other classmates forced to follow the same script. The Cornell Class of 1969 was taking a hard hit.

To make things worse, the debacle with Norma, though hardly a life and death matter, was highly disconcerting and certainly deflating. Frankly, I wasn't looking to do anything too exciting for July and August; I just needed some time off to heal from a double blow. That, however, was not in the cards. Little did I know that the third leg of a tripleheader was in store for me.

Once again I took a series of highly forgettable assignments courtesy of the temporary agency. Actually, my typing skills had advanced from hunt 'n peck to intermediate so I was able to land some positions that commanded more than the then minimum wage. It was July, 1967 and I was earning four bucks an hour, which was a very decent rate of pay for college students in those days. However, none of those short-term stints is even worth reporting.

Simply put, I was in it for the money. In retrospect, I should have been using that time to fine-tune some career decisions, perhaps with an internship or some volunteer work. After all, when I would go back in the fall, I was one step closer to the on-deck circle in the game of life. Also, it was coming ever closer to a time when I had to formally declare a major. Both were extremely scary propositions for which I was in no way prepared.

But this was summertime. Enough, already. For two months, I didn't want to think about college, courses, or careers. And, furthermore, I rationalized that I had worked hard enough all year to deserve a break, not to mention all the other trials and tribulations of this past spring. My grade point average had climbed to the 3.2 or stratospheric B+ range and I was feeling pretty good about that.

It turned out to be an especially hot and humid July that summer with a long, unbroken string of 90+ degree days. Walking outside felt like entering a blast furnace. The only good thing about my summer jobs was the frigid air conditioning in those Manhattan skyscrapers. It was almost too cold. By the time the dog days of August rolled around, I just plain had enough. I didn't have to think very hard when Brant invited Ian and me to come to spend a week on the Maryland shore to close the summer before returning to campus for junior year.

I drove down from New York. Ian came in from California. He flew the skies much the same way I hopped the turnpikes. Actually, it had been quite some time since the two of us had seen Brant. He had picked up a few credits at a local community college, but had little else to show for the past two years, other than working in his parents' business. Entering our junior year, we were a constant reminder to him of what might have been. Despite all our academic and romantic misadventures, we were making steady progress towards a degree and still on track to graduate on time. However, if that fact bothered Brant, he didn't seem to show it. He seemed genuinely glad to see us and quizzed us endlessly about our future plans-- which neither of us was very certain about.

Brant's family lived in a converted old farmhouse not too far from the Maryland shore. The apple didn't fall far from the tree. I could see where his kind, gentle, and genuine manner came from. His parents couldn't have been nicer or more hospitable and seemed eager to meet his old college friends. They were the veritable opposites of Norma's folks. I thought that we would have been a thorn in their side, a reminder of Brant's failure at Cornell thrown in their faces, but that was definitely not the case. I also could see where his extreme good looks came from. Although he was a replica of his father in his build and stature, he carried many of his mom's fine-looking features.

Their house was furnished in a country motif through and through. It was evident that money had been no object when it came to decorating it. That "ma and pa" business they had started and built up evidently had paid off many times over. The first floor consisted of a sprawling maze of rooms with few walls separating them, only an occasional step up or step down. One room seemed to roll into the next. Considerable attention had been paid to every detail.

The rustic flair was followed through, from the large and friendly country kitchen with hanging pots and copper kettles, to the living room with its oversized and overstuffed couch and fireplace, to a formal dining room still in the country style, and finally a huge family room with tremendous picture windows that overlooked the sprawling fields behind it. A screened-in porch adjacent to the kitchen was also beautifully furnished. It was filled with wicker furniture, huge pillows, lush plants, and a big screen television-- well, big for those days.

All kinds of sports memorabilia adorned the walls and curio cabinets. Many of the trophies that Brant had won in high school were also on display. That's the kind of room I wanted to have in my house someday, I thought. (Well, probably without the sports trophies.) The bedrooms on the second floor were equally well-appointed, all with matching wallpaper and bedspreads. The house was rich without being ostentatious. In short, each room could have appeared in a Macy's furniture catalogue.

After a terrific home-cooked dinner that culminated in chocolate seven-layer cake (Brant's mom had been clued in to my favorite), we called it an early evening after a tiring travel day. Besides, we had the rest of the week to go out at night. Brant's mom was up early the next morning, preparing a sumptuous Maryland breakfast reminiscent of what our old cook Henny used to dish up.

By 10:00 A.M., we headed for the shore and one of the best beaches around. And to my amazement, it was practically empty, to boot. After being cooped up in an overly air-conditioned high-rise office building for the past six weeks and in my car for six hours the day before, I had acquired a severe case of cabin fever, and was thrilled to be outdoors, especially on a quintessential beach day like this one. This was precisely what the doctor had ordered.

Of course, there would be no competing with these two guys. Ian, forever in search of that first acting break, was in better shape than ever. No matter how many hours I would spend in the Teagle Gym, I'd never have his build. Not even close; I was also muscularly challenged. Tall and thin, built like a rail back then, a flick of the fingers could have knocked me over.

On the other hand, bronzed from the California sun with his dirty blond hair bleached by those weeks spent surfing, Ian sported red swim trunks that perfectly complemented his tan. It was a no-brainer that the girls would be chasing after him. Brant was just a darker, even more muscular version. He was wearing a black racing suit that left little to the imagination. I, on the other hand, was wearing far more conservative swim trunks, baggy and down to the knees. Sandwiched between these two Adonises, I felt like the odd man out. All I needed was a pair of white sox and brown lace-up shoes to complete the sorry picture. At least it was a beautiful day, even if I wasn't going to be competing in the hunt.

The waves were wild that day, and after about a half hour splashing in the surf, the three of us came back to the beach. Brant went to buy us some beers and Ian was off just as quickly, scouting the girls. I sat down on a large towel, knees bent, with my arms wrapped around them, facing the ocean, taking it all in. It was the perfect summer day: balmy, not too hot, no humidity at all, with bright blue skies and the sea gulls humming. Just what I needed to decompress. Then all of a sudden I realized that I was not sitting alone.

"Hello there," chimed in the friendly female voice. I turned to my left. Who was this sitting next to me? I didn't have to wait long to find out. "I'm Holly," she cheerfully introduced herself. The name seemed to fit perfectly. She was pretty and perky. Oh well, I quickly concluded, she must have been eyeing Brant or Ian. I was the seat-saver until the two of them returned. But I'd milk this as long as I could. I introduced myself; to my continued surprise, she still seemed interested.

"What are you doing here?" she inquired.

"Two of us are visiting an old friend before heading back to Cornell for our junior year."

"Cornell?" she seemed impressed. In the meantime, I felt like Cinderella. As soon as Ian or Brant would return, I knew I would be shunted aside, unable to compete. The jig would be up. Too bad; she was one of the most beautiful girls I had ever seen. Her scant navy blue bikini did justice to her near-perfect, perfectly tanned body.

"I'm from New York. My buddy Ian-- he'll be back in a second-- is from California. We're visiting... an old classmate who lives around here." I felt I didn't owe her the details of Brant's situation, even if meant advancing my own position by knocking him down a peg.

At that very moment, the two guys converged on the scene, coming from two different directions.

"And whom do we have here?" Ian already was making his move.

"I'm Holly," I let her introduce herself.

"And I'm Ian. And this ugly guy is Brant," they all laughed.

The only question that remained was whether the redhead would opt for the blond or the brunette. In any case, I was the weakest link and it was just a matter of time before I would be scratched from the competition. But that's not what happened.

"We two guys were, uh, kinda talking," she motioned, rubbing her left toe against mine in the sand. I shot up a bit. In other words, she was saying, "Get lost" to Brant and Ian. And they took the hint.

"Hey, Ian, let's play some frisbee," suggested Brant, sizing up the situation and coming to my rescue.

"OK," answered Ian half-heartedly. I could see he would have liked to have hung around and made his moves on this gal. For as long as I had known him, Ian was forever in "drive." But he knew he would be encroaching on my territory so he reluctantly followed Brant's lead. The two of them headed right, down the beach, and practically out of sight, with Brant dragging him a comfortable and safe distance away leaving us alone.

"Good friends?" Holly questioned.

"*Very*," I underscored. Especially now, I thought to myself, with the potential rivals nowhere to be seen. I didn't deserve a girl like this, especially with the likes of those two guys lurking in the wings. How easily they could have moved in and shunted me aside. But they didn't. And Brant saw to that by being Ian's caretaker. I had found Holly first.

"So now that you know a little about me, tell me about yourself."

She smiled. And, what a smile. "I'm in college, too. I'll be a junior this fall at the University of Maryland. But I'm from Arizona. I'm staying with my aunt and uncle who live around here."

"Pick a major yet?" I asked.

"Oh, yeah, Education. I always wanted to be a teacher," she said with confidence.

Something else we had in common. "Me, too," I rushed in. Well, I was sort of telling the truth; I had "kinda" decided on Education at this point. Or, Journalism. Or, something else. But who cared? This situation was looking better and better. This girl was for me! "Both my parents are teachers," I added. At least that was totally true.

"I want to teach Special Education," she added.

"How come? Isn't that awfully tough?" I fired away, then realizing that maybe I was asking too much too soon. But she was eager to respond.

"My brother is severely handicapped. Is that the 'politically correct' term these days? Or, should I say, 'physically challenged,'" she said in a self-deprecating, almost mocking tone. "I've seen how far the school has taken him. I want to do the same for other children." Beau-ti-ful, and what a kind soul, to boot! And, she was interested in me. This was too good to be true.

We talked for about another half hour. Brant could keep Ian at bay just so long without hosing him down, so the two of them returned. Anyway, the hour was growing late and we had to get back to Brant's place for an early dinner and a night in town.

"When am I going to see you again?" I boldly asked her in front of the other two.

"My aunt and uncle are taking me to Cape May tonight. But I'll be back tomorrow night, if that's OK," she proposed, scribbling her phone number on a discarded napkin.

"If that's OK?" I repeated to myself. The question was whether I could contain myself until the following night.

Brant, Ian, and I left the beach, crossed the parking lot, and climbed into his pickup-- all three of us still covered with sand. (That's the one thing I hate about the beach.)

"Details, details," Ian demanded to know from me. Brant just grinned.

I shared with them our discussion leading up to the date. Both guys seemed genuinely happy for me. Then they became engaged in some meaningless babble about the game plan for the upcoming night, which I tuned out. All I could think about was Holly. And I'd be seeing her again the following evening. I couldn't wait!

Brant's mom prepared another great meal for us that we gobbled up quickly so we could head for the bar scene in town. The other two guys would be on the prowl; I didn't have to be. All I had to do was cool my heels, among other things, and be patient until the following night. We made the rounds, met some of Brant's local friends, and were introduced to a few more girls. An okay evening, but not a very memorable one. My thoughts wandered elsewhere.

The next morning, Brant had planned to give the two of us a grand tour of the family business. Ian begged off; privately he told me that he just didn't feel like wasting any part of his mini-vacation cooped up indoors and came up with some lame excuse for staying back. But my good-old guilt got hold of me; how could I say "no" to this invitation after he and his family had treated me so royally. So the two of us headed into town for a more-than-I-needed-to-know look at their trucking and hardware business.

I tried to be as enthusiastic as I could be while Brant and his dad lectured me about vinyl siding and caulking. Frankly, nothing could have interested me less than hardware. Furthermore, I had my mind on meeting Holly that evening. Still, I played the role of the polite guest and tried to respond with interest to each and everything they showed me, from sprockets to socket wrenches. Admittedly I was a bit curious as to how they had taken a small family-run business and turned it into a huge store competing with the largest chains.

But I'm not that a good an actor and after a few too many yawns that I just couldn't suppress, Brant sensed that I was getting a bit bored, so mercifully he cut the tour short after a brown bag lunch, telling his dad that we had big plans for the night coming up. Well, that *was* the truth. The drive back to the old farmhouse took about twenty minutes.

"So you really made it, big guy," Brant said, as we pulled away. Frankly, I didn't know what he was talking about: finishing two years of college or landing a girl like Holly.

"You'll be graduating before you know it," he quickly clarified. "You're half-way there." I detected a sense of envy and sadness in his voice, although he tried his best to conceal it. What did he have to show for the past two years? Not much at all.

"It's scary. I still don't know what I'm going to do with the rest of my life. And the War...." I tried to downplay it all, making it sound as though things were not all that rosy. And it was the truth: I was confused about the future for a variety of reasons. Vietnam... the danger of being drafted... then picking a major... choosing a career. The lack of certainty.

Still, everything's relative. I knew that Brant would have traded places with me in a minute. I didn't want to gloat; he had been just too good a friend to me. I knew he was hurting. Having Ian and me around threw it all in his face. I was still surprised that he had invited the two of us to visit. So I attempted to change the subject.

"Are you going to take over the family business?" I tried.

Brant didn't even answer. Either he was deep in thought, didn't know, or it was just a sore subject altogether. I probed no further; he kept quiet as well. We finished the last few minutes of the trip in silence.

The cook's tour had taken much less time than expected. We got back to the farmhouse a little before 2:00 P.M. The evening's itinerary called for us to head into town, meet Brant's current girlfriend (another in a long line), have dinner, and do some bar hopping. I welcomed this layover, wanting to catch some *zzz's* before another late night out. Quite a pace-- and the ocean air had made me even sleepier.

Brant opened the fridge and offered me a beer; I took a Coke instead. Actually, anything cold and wet would have quenched my thirst on that blistering summer afternoon.

"Catch you later," I signaled to Brant as I headed upstairs to the guest room.

He was still downing the beer and gave me a thumbs up signal in acknowledgment. Climbing the steep flight of steps, I hung a sharp left turn at the landing, and headed toward the guest room I shared with Ian. No lock and key here. I wish there had been one. I opened the door. To my utter shock and dismay, there was Ian --with Holly-- under the sheets.

I don't know who was more taken aback, the two of them, or me. For a split second, the scene reminded me of the assistant proctor barging in on Buzz on Fall Weekend some two years ago. But this wasn't nearly as funny. It wasn't funny at all. Just yesterday Holly had made it perfectly clear she was interested in me. And now this turn of events... with my supposed best friend. What could possibly be worse; I had never, ever felt as low as at that very moment.

Ian bolted up, into his boxers, and out of bed.

"I can explain, brother, I can explain," he hurriedly spoke. I was still in too much disbelief to speak. Holly wrapped herself in the sheet, knees bent back pressing against the headboard, with a cross between panic and embarrassment on her face. I don't know whether I was angrier with him or with her. *How could she do this to me?* I knew him a lot longer and a lot better: How could *he* do this to me?

"Let me explain," Ian said imploringly.

"There's no *possible* explanation," I said with obvious furor, regaining my speech. I glowered at him and then turned to Holly and did the same to her.

She started to speak. "I came over this afternoon to see you," she tried to explain. "I didn't know you were going into town with Brant. We were left here alone..."

"Oh," I said mockingly. "You were alone... so that gave you the right to hop into the sack with my *friend* here," I fired that salvo at Ian, accentuating the word "friend." The initial shock was wearing off. It was turning to rage. Very soon it was to become disgust.

"We got talking," Ian sighed. "It was so hot outside. We came in... we were alone... things just got out of hand. One thing led to another."

"I can *see where* they led to," I snapped back. No matter the explanation, I didn't want anything further to do with Holly. It had been just too good to be true. But now I had to wonder whether I wanted any more of Ian. Some best friend. The bionic pecker had struck again.

We were standing there in silence for a few seconds when Brant broke in with a rap at the half-opened door. He just walked in and then stood there gaping.

"Oops. Bad timing. Guess I'd better leave," he said highly embarrassed by this obvious turn of events. And he quickly made a literal about-face and retreated from this ugly scene. I had nothing more to say, either, and exited the room. I joined Brant in the kitchen. He did most of the talking, nervously, just to fill the vacuum; I was still too overcome with conflicting emotions to speak.

Minutes later, just enough time to get herself dressed and together, Holly flew out of the house with not even a goodbye, let alone an apology or further explanation. I thought I detected a muffled cry. Or maybe that was just wishful thinking on my part. Shortly thereafter Ian came bolting down the steps, dressed in jean shorts and a T-shirt. Fortunately, Brant had the good sense to walk out and leave the two of us alone.

"I don't know what to say you, buddy," he said with earnest. But I wasn't going to let him off so easily.

"There's nothing to say," I hit back at him. "This was my girl. You've had more than your fair share," I fired at him with a mixture of anger and pain in my voice. "Finally I had a chance. Where did you come off moving in on her?"

"I told you... it just happened. One thing led to another. She took me from neutral into drive. There was no turning back. We didn't plan on this. You've got to believe me," practically begging.

"Yeah, it just happened; I know the male plumbing," I replied. I wanted to believe him. Supposedly he was my friend. But no matter what the situation, how had he betrayed me like this?

"You gotta forgive me," he pleaded, his voice cracking. I think he realized that he had crossed the line and put our friendship in serious jeopardy. Ian seemed so sincere-- or was this "Ian, the actor"? Obviously, that friendship meant something to him as evidenced by the plaintive tone in his voice. And yet, he had cost me Holly. I felt torn apart. Neither of us said anything further; I retreated back to my room, but the sight of the rumpled bed was an uncomfortable reminder of what had just taken place. So I took a long walk through the farmlands instead, just to clear my head.

Forgive, yes... forget, no. I ultimately did forgive Ian. But I never, ever forgot what happened. And although it recovered, our friendship was never quite the same after this, as hard as he tried to make it up to me in the two years which followed.

For Brant's sake, the plans went on as scheduled that night, although the strain between Ian and me was readily apparent. Brant tried to lighten the mood, but to little avail. It was a good thing that we would be joining other people, Brant's girl, and some of their friends, so I could get lost in the crowd and not have to face Ian all night. I simply went through the motions, mixing in and trying to forget my woes. I was never a big drinker, but that night I surpassed my usual limit of four beers to blunt the pain.

We were scheduled to leave for home the next afternoon, but I moved things up a bit, itching to get away from what was tantamount to a crime scene, at least in my view. I woke up the next morning with a splitting headache. I don't whether it was from the tension of the day before, a hangover, or a combination of the two. My temples were pounding in precisely the same way they had the morning we took Kip to the airport for his rendezvous with Vietnam. Once again, it was the kind of head-splitter that even aspirin doesn't dull.

In any event, I just wanted to get away from there as quickly as I could. I thanked Brant and especially his gracious parents (who seemed oblivious to this turn of events) for their supreme hospitality; I wondered when, if ever, I'd see Brant again. I gave Ian a perfunctory "so long" as if nothing was wrong and then hit the road. There would be two more weeks until the start of the semester before I'd have to face him again, so there would be a stay of execution and a chance to sort things out.

What should have been a four-hour drive back to New York became a lot longer. The trip seemed interminable. For one thing, the shore traffic during the summer months is always heavy, so it was stop-and-go, bumper-to-bumper much of the way; I think it would have been faster to get out of the car and walk home. For a second, my air conditioner was straining to produce anything cooler than tepid air.

I played the radio, but the reception was staticky: first some music, and then the Yankee game, but I couldn't focus; instead, I just kept replaying the miserable events of the past few days. I really liked this girl, and, still better, she seemed to like me. Ian had managed to screw it up royally for the both of us-- and for the two of us guys, as well. It was double hit. After almost eight hours on the road (and it seemed even longer than that), I staggered into my parents' house.

I did not share this nightmare of a vacation with them. They were in the process of packing for a Labor Day trip to Cape Cod and Martha's Vineyard. This benchmark holiday marks the unofficial end of the summer, especially significant in a schoolteacher family, with the cycle ready to start all over again. This was the last hurrah of the season, a weekend followed by a family barbeque. It was tradition, and growing up, it was something I always looked forward to. I still had a few days before I had to return to campus, and so to their surprise and almost shock, I took them up on their offer to join them on the annual trip to New England.

I am glad that I did. The Cape was just as beautiful as the Maryland shore, just an extension of the Atlantic coast. The balmy weather hit the spot. A powerful breeze combined with a strong late summer sun to produce a spectacular effect. A keen smell of the ocean was also in the air. The only sounds, besides the crashing of the waves, was the squawking of the seagulls. I could have sat there forever. Whether it marks the end of summer, the heralding of a new year, or the passage of time, there is something special, wistful, pensive, and in some ways sad, about the last days of August. I recall just sitting on the beach, just staring and reflecting.

I think my folks sensed that something was troubling me, but I was grateful that they didn't give me the third degree. Time, I hoped, would heal these wounds. I still was so angry-- I felt like *wounding* that *heel*: Ian. But I would try to forget and forgive and remember the good moments we shared. It might take more than a little time, I concluded. As far as I was concerned, I had to recover from yet another blow.

PART III

Junior Year

SEPTEMBER, 1967

#39 - Round III

I was still licking my wounds when I returned to campus for my junior year. Kip's abrupt vanishing act, not of his own volition... the too much-too soon, doomed relationship with Norma (not to mention the reasons for it imploding)... and then the double whammy of losing Holly to my supposed best friend. All these events had combined to hit me like a ton of bricks. How much could a guy handle in a single year? I was hoping that my junior year would be less eventful, more "tranquil," for want of a better word. I've heard it said: "Boredom ain't always a bad thing." Perhaps I could've used a dose back then.

And so I returned to campus in September, midway through my college career, with two years at Cornell under my belt. The upcoming junior year was supposed to be the "peak", or so everyone told me: my advisor, my professors, my parents, and even my fraternity brothers.

Besides, I knew this was make-it or break-it time for two reasons. To begin with, my three-year grade point average that would be submitted to graduate schools, should I choose to apply, would be locked come June. This would be the last chance to raise it. Second, I was coming closer and closer to having to make some life-changing career decisions. I was going the route of English major, really by the process of elimination. Actually, the choice was made with only mild enthusiasm. I reasoned that this was the best bet because it would buy me some more time before committing to a career choice. Teaching, television, and journalism had emerged as the frontrunners vying for my attention. A degree in English would serve me well for all three.

I was psyched! I started off in September with every intention of making the most out of the months ahead.

The previous spring's rush was anemic at best and yielded the smallest pledge class in years. There was plenty of space in the fraternity to fill. In an attempt to lure juniors and seniors to room in the house rather than taking apartments elsewhere, the larger double and single rooms were put up on the trading block. Ian and I had taken the bait at the last minute, deciding to spend one more year living in CAT, not by choice but by default. The simple fact is, with all that was happening last spring, we just never got around to apartment-hunting in earnest, and before we knew it, finals rolled around and the school year was over. The few places we checked out were the leftovers-- overpriced, dilapidated, claustrophobic, or all three. So, the two of us took the line of least resistance and found ourselves back at CAT-- together.

Of course, that deal was struck well before the Holly debacle in Maryland over the summer. Up to that point, Ian had been talking of rooming with me again, a rerun of freshman year; but he felt that it would have been awkward dumping his sophomore roommate Jordan, so they stuck together and moved into one of the largest doubles. That worked for me, especially after the events of the past few weeks. A little distance is what the doctor ordered…

Was I ever glad now that I had decided to stick with a single, at least twice the size of the room I had lived in during sophomore year. A room with a real view, without a dead squirrel for scenery and condom wrappers for decorations.

On the surface, Ian and I were friends again, but I hadn't fully gotten over what had come between us during the visit to Brant, and I needed some time and space for the tension to abate. After all, I had been betrayed. We hadn't spoken since leaving Maryland; there had been no attempt at communication from either direction. I used this break in the action to convince myself of all the good things he had done: "I always have your back," he used to say. Well, he had used "my back"-- and stuck a knife into it. Quite frankly, I was on edge about seeing him again after these two weeks. He had screwed me royally. I tried to wipe it away, hearing him plead that it was not intentional. Still, good friends don't do things like that to each other. It had hurt and the pain had not fully subsided.

Nevertheless, when we were reunited on campus, you'd never sense that there had been a problem between us. If there were any bad blood or strain in our relationship, it didn't show. Actually, I got over Holly much more easily than I would have expected, convincing myself by rationalizing over time that obviously she wasn't the "nice" girl I thought she was.

Ian greeted me as if nothing had happened and I decided to do the same, although the aftereffects of what had taken place would continue to fester inside of me for some time to come. But, it was time to move on, and that we did.

I had other concerns those first few weeks of the semester. Admittedly, I wasn't all that thrilled with the required courses in the English department. I had been leafing through the thick course catalogue as if by magic something new would appear. If the 200-level courses were abstract, the 300-level courses were the occult, while the 400-level courses were outright esoteric. "What was I doing in this department, anyway?"-- I kept asking myself.

Most of the offerings dealt with the analysis and interpretation of literature. I had already sampled several of those courses during my sophomore year, in preparation for becoming a department major. They were all the same. The professor would spend the full fifty minutes lecturing to us what the writer or poet was *trying* to say, on occasion focusing on a single word or phrase for the full fifty-minute lecture. Shaking my head with a combination of disgust and disbelief, I watched as some of my classmates hung on every syllable that was spoken; they were really into this stuff.

I couldn't care less; frankly, if the author's message was so important, why didn't he just *tell* us? I wasn't into all that flowery speech and fancy imagery. Maybe it was a "guy thing," not to get so worked up over the interpretation of a few words or phrases. I concluded that it was not my lot in life to ferret out the hidden meanings. I had become restless and bored in those classes and started to second-guess my choice of major.

In the meantime I had become more interested, relatively speaking, in the drama courses. I came up with an idea about devising a combined major in "dramatic literature," with courses from two departments. I arranged three meetings, first with my advisor, and then with the deputy chairs in both the English and Theatre departments, to propose an interdisciplinary major, drawing on courses from both disciplines. I even put together a written plan, enumerating the specific courses I would take to meet the requirements. I really thought I was on to something revolutionary. This was so uncharacteristic of the "conservative me."

All three of them, with the two department heads being extremely territorial and protective of their turf, soundly rebuked my idea. They succeeding in making me feel guilty about coming up with such a preposterous notion in the first place.

So, I was resigned to the fact that if I was going to remain an English major, I would have to join in on the authors' guessing games. In the meantime, the concept of "make-your-own-major," a.k.a. interdisciplinary studies, is now a big draw at Cornell, as well as at most other colleges.

OCTOBER, 1967

#40 - Let's Get Physical

I used to look forward to getting the mail; now I dreaded it. Imagine how any draft-age man of my generation felt when he received a letter with a return address from the "Selective Service System." You can understand, then, my panic when I got such a greeting from Uncle Sam. I didn't have to read any further than the upper left-corner of the envelope. My stomach instantaneously knotted up. Death sentence?

"First Kip, now me," I shuddered, recalling that awful day when he was abruptly whisked away. Was history repeating itself? Was it my turn? I ripped open the letter, expecting to find my draft notice, coach ticket to Saigon, and marching orders for the War. However, it was only half as bad. I was being told to report for an army physical. At least nothing imminent; "just in case... a stand-by," the letter implied. Was I physically fit for military service?

So, I breathed a sigh of relief; it was a veritable stay of execution. Now I, too, had my membership card for the club to which every other young male of my generation belonged. Suddenly there was the dreaded sword of Damocles, with the threat of being drafted, dangling over my head. I was one step closer to a call-up.

Magnanimously, the powers that be gave me a choice: Have the physical back home at Fort Hamilton in Brooklyn, or at an upstate army base outside of Syracuse. Just wanting to get the thing over with, I opted for the latter, and also scheduled the earliest possible date.

As with the dreaded freshman swim test, I didn't want to go by myself and would have preferred traveling with someone I knew, anyone at all. I was so desperate I would even have gone with that creep Ralph, whom I had shunned in the freshman dorms and ridiculed in wrestling. But nobody I knew was so summoned, at least not on my appointment date. Face it, I said to myself: I was in this one alone.

I'm sure that the same scene was playing out in cities and small towns across the country. I was told to report at 7:00 A.M.-- *prompt.* The Army gets you up early in the morning. For fear of arriving even a minute late and having to incur whatever consequences that gross violation might impose, I set the alarm for 4:45 A.M., leaving plenty of time to get up, get showered, get dressed, and make the one-hour drive north. However, there was virtually no traffic on the country roads or even the Interstate at that pre-dawn hour. As a result, I got to the base way ahead of time.

It was dark and chilly outside, so I sat in my heated car, killing time, until the last possible second. I had no intention of going in early, not even a second sooner than I had to. By 6:45 A.M., I had the neatest glove compartment in the county. How many times could I rearrange road maps, gas credit card receipts, a can opener, and a tissue box? No, no condom wrappers; wishful thinking. The parking lot was filling up with guys streaming in from all over. I hadn't expected such a crowd. Although they were from different regions of the state and different backgrounds, they shared one thing in common: Nobody looked happy to be here, especially not at this hour of the morning.

I had expected to get a cursory once-over by some doctor, much like the one at the clinic when I had the flu, and then sent packing. What followed, however, was far different. The army physical was as cold and clinical as it could possibly be. They checked p ... body I didn't even know I had.

A brief induction was given by a drill sergeant who was a cross between Carl, the wrestling instructor, and the assistant proctor: "Are my dee-rections clear?" he roared; it was more of a command than a question. We were assigned lockers to secure our street clothes and then ordered to strip down to our shorts. "Nothing else, not even your socks," barked GI Joe. A parade of nearly naked men was then led from station to station for all sorts of medical testing. We were, literally, all shapes and sizes. Some of the guys were in perfect condition while others looked as though they would collapse if they had to run more than two steps. Our country was in sorry shape if these were the recruits who had to defend us.

The lineup looked like an underwear convention, with everything from boxers to briefs to bikinis. One guy put up quite a kick when he refused to take his pants off because he said he wasn't wearing underwear. He was led off kicking and carrying on by two soldiers and probably placed in a stockade.

Hurry up and wait; the lines were long and we were led around as though on a leash from station to station. It had the appearance of elephants herded around on ropes at the circus. There was this fat fellow in front of me for the whole journey, who looked as though he was in his ninth month. Then he stopped short while I wasn't paying attention; it was no fun rear-ending him in the caboose, although it generated quite a bit of laughter from those behind me and even a faint smile from that stern sergeant who led us around.

While waiting my turn at some of the stops, I looked around and managed to recognize a couple of guys from campus, although not by name. I even saw several college instructors and grad assistants, also in their skivvies, and realized that they weren't that much older than their students, and also subject to the draft call. Nobody was exempt from this 60's rite of passage. They were no doubt especially uncomfortable to be part of this spectacle, having to endure this public indignity in front of their students.

For the next two hours, I produced just about every bodily function from "cough" to "breathe"…. and just about every command from "bend down" to "spread 'em" to "drop 'em"…. while I was methodically poked, prodded, and dissected to ascertain whether I was fit for military service. The grand prize at the end of the competition was to be awarded a "4-F" classification-- physically unfit-- which meant almost zero chance of being called for military service. For once my parents had let me down. Why couldn't I have been born with flat feet or a pilonidal dimple-- both reported to be deal-breakers?

While the "hernia check" won top honors for being the most humiliating examination, without a doubt the "psych station" was the most entertaining. Several of the potential recruits pulled out all of the stops as they displayed the symptoms of every possible mental disorder from schizophrenia to paranoia and every possible diagnosis from fear of the dark to homosexuality. One pair even seemed to have a rehearsed comedy bit `a la Laurel and Hardy in which the first appeared to be deranged and the second appeared to be his keeper. They performed to the delight of the crowd. As funny as they were, I was afraid to crack a smile for fear of incurring the wrath of that sergeant standing over me who saw absolutely no humor in any of this. Obviously, the examining doctor was not amused with their theatrics either, and routinely stamped "passed" on both fellows' section sheet, no matter how bizarre their outburst.

After about three hours, I cleared the final hurdle, was instructed to get dressed, and summarily dismissed. I couldn't get away from there fast enough, for a variety of reasons. All I wanted to do was return to campus, take a long, steaming hot shower, and go to class, any class. Never before had a dull philosophy lecture looked so appealing. Until that moment, I had taken for granted the joys of just being a carefree student. What a difference two years had made. What a difference this morning had made. I had been "accepted" into a club which I definitely didn't want to join. It was becoming increasingly difficult to block out the War from my mind and daily existence.

I was informed that I had passed my physical exam with flying colors. This, however, was one test that I wish I had failed.

NOVEMBER, 1967

#41 – Movie Star

Despite my thinly-veiled contempt for most of my English literature courses, I was actually acing most of them. The early returns were in, and so far I had inched up to a grade-point-average approaching B+. Little wonder; my recent state of celibacy in the early fall had given me the study time I should have been devoting to my schoolwork all along. Admittedly, I even came to enjoying some of the English classes and acknowledged to myself that I had, in fact, made the right choice of majors.

The Shakespeare elective, for example, was a cross between a trip through history and a theatrical performance. With lectures delivered by a wannabe Elizabethan actor, I hung on every word he spoke-- and spoke so eloquently. Academically speaking, I was riding high. Still, all of this did little for my social life, which was practically nil at that point. The needle on my ego scale was about as low as it could go.

I had successfully managed to finally get Diana out of my system for once and for all, but for some reason, I was still feeling really crappy over my breakup with Norma. After all this time, I was still licking my wounds. Yet, as much as I had liked her, I knew this relationship never would have gone anywhere; we were just two too different people who looked at the world in two completely different ways. I could never conform to her lifestyle nor she to mine. To compound the differences, were her parents. There was no common meeting ground. At least that is what I tried to tell myself, although not very convincingly. We had parted friends.

However, as I said, I had taken the abrupt breakup hard and was hurting for quite some time. Running into her on campus arm and arm with someone else didn't help matters, either, especially when she acknowledged me as though I was nothing more than a casual acquaintance. And my encounter with Holly over the summer, although so fleeting, just added insult to the injury. Where was Donna, the switchboard operator, from the summer of '66, when I could have used her?

Once again my fraternity brothers threw me into the dating pool but, alas, they managed to scrounge up another series of very forgettable co-eds. No lifelong soulmates in this mix. My confidence hit an all-time new low, if that was possible. So as I had done after my breakup with Diana, I used this dry spell to plunge into my studies, forget my social life or lack thereof, and get my grades up even higher. Some reason!

It was about this time that a group of guys from the house dragged me to a showing of student-produced films at the Statler Auditorium on campus. One of the seniors was screening a flick he had made during the fall semester, so the brotherhood was coming out for him to see the debut and cheer him on.

I really intended to pass on this outing, but it was Ian who gave me no choice. He practically ordered me to join them. As of late we had traveled as a pack, kind of like the good old days back in the freshman dorms. At least the camaraderie was there, while my social life was still running on empty. With nothing better to do than face studying 150 pages of a textbook that was as about exciting as memorizing the telephone book, I unenthusiastically agreed to go along.

The Statler was the center of the School of Hotel Management, another one of the separate colleges that are part of the University.

The auditorium adjoining the hotel itself was a first-class facility, seating several hundred. The cushiony armchairs were so comfortable that I was ready to go to sleep when the lights went out. Glad I didn't.

We suffered through some pretty amateurish efforts, mostly feeble attempts at humor, including a Charlie Chaplin parody and a takeoff on the Munsters. Even our brother's film was disappointing and I had to force myself not to doze off. For this I gave up watching Mission Impossible reruns back at the house? None of the entries, mercifully, lasted more than fifteen minutes, maybe twenty at the most, although they seemed a lot longer. All of them were the end result of student film-making projects in a fledgling cinema course being offered for the first time. Ian and the others were also squirming in their seats, looking at their watches, waiting for this ordeal to be over; now they, too, were sorry that they had come and schlepped me along. Then, however, came the final entry which made the wait worthwhile.

This was a silent film, with no dialogue, no music. The simple story was told with action. There was a beautiful young girl with long red hair, almost copper in color, waist-length, reading a magazine. Seated near her in a waiting room was a young guy, nondescript in appearance, about the same age, say 20 or 21. It looked as though they were in the anteroom to a doctor's office with cheap furniture around the periphery.

A wide shot revealed that they were the only ones left in this waiting area and the guy was trying to get closer to her. But the harder he tried, the more she pulled away, ignoring his advances. He sat down next to her... she slid two seats to the left. Tenaciously, he followed her. It was a kind of clever cat-and-mouse chase scene.

Actually, this bit managed to hold my interest; I wanted to see what he would do next to catch her. I didn't have to wait long. Without warning, the guy stood up, turned his back to the camera, and dropped his pants. To my amazement, the girl responded immediately in kind with no inhibition. The camera zoomed in on her with a full frontal attack. In a matter of seconds they were going at it.

"I can't believe this," Ian shrieked.

"Holy shit!" exclaimed the other guys.

Reactions from the rest of the nearly full theatre ranged from gasps to shouts of "Go for it!" as if this were a sporting event.

This was the still the late 1960's. The rest of the audience, mostly students with some faculty members sprinkled in, was just as shocked as we were at this unexpected plot twist-- and what we were seeing uncensored. The deed was done, the film short came to an abrupt end, and the lights very slowly started to come up. In a matter of seconds I had shifted from neutral to drive: What kind of girl would do this on camera? I didn't have to wait long to find out; she was sitting all by herself in an aisle seat, unnoticed, about five rows down from me, all the way on the right.

The other guys from the fraternity behaved worse than junior high school boys seeing their first skin flick. Only I realized that the "star" was seated so close. She sat there, alone, expressionless, with her chin resting on her hand, in a pensive mode. The theatre was emptying out. Everyone was still buzzing about what they had just seen. But given the dim lighting, I was still the only one who recognized that the star performer was seated so nearby. The rest of the crowd was left in the dark, in more ways than one.

Ian and his band of brothers were still oblivious as to whom I had stumbled upon, and for whatever reason, I had no intention of telling them; why, I wasn't sure, but I wasn't sharing. This was my private discovery. The brothers started to exit from the center aisle.

"Will you c'mon already," Ian motioned.

"He just wants to get back to the house and get off on this," chuckled Jordan.

"Shut up," Ian laughed, slapping his buddy on the back. "You're the one who can barely stand up straight."

"At least I'm not stuck to my seat," Jordan bellowed back, practically howling.

"You haven't had this much action in years," Ian answered him back, still doubled over in laughter. "You're the one who needs the cold shower."

Then they all signaled me in unison to get up. "Let's get outta here."

"Go on without me; I'll join you in a couple of minutes," I motioned them on. They seemed a bit puzzled as to why I wasn't joining them, but didn't question it further.

"Well, hurry up," Ian commanded. "We'll meet you at the Big Red."

"Don't let it take too long," scolded Jordan in a mocking tone as they broke out laughing hysterically once again. I just ignored them and their schoolboy behavior.

I waited until Heckle and Jeckle and their gang had exited the theatre. I was in no mood for their clowning. This exquisite young girl was still sitting there like a statue. Her expression had somehow changed. She appeared even more radiant, obviously having been pleased by her performance, and more importantly, the response to it.

I just stared at her. I could read her mind and wanted to tell her that anyone could have done what she did on the screen and gotten that kind of response. It didn't exactly take talent. Just the same, I really wanted to talk to her; I just didn't know what to say. I certainly didn't want to compliment her on her "acting."

The remainder of the crowd was moving up the aisles toward the exit, still buzzing about what they had just seen, still unaware that the "star" was sitting in their midst. Like a salmon trying to swim upstream against the tide, I slowly made my way down the aisle and then slid over to where she was sitting. As soon as we were just about alone, I gave it my best shot.

"Wasn't that you in that picture?" I tried, preparing myself for being ignored or, worse, outright rejected.

To my pleasant surprise, she looked up at me and nodded, and then turned away again. By now the theatre had totally emptied out and the house lights had come on. Except for the janitor who was methodically sweeping each row, it was just the two of us left.

After a beat, she turned her head towards me and asked, "So what did you think?" she posed the question with an inquiring stare. Her deep, dark, dazzling eyes mesmerized me.

Usually I don't say the right thing, especially in these kinds of situations, but for once my mouth worked the right way while I managed to keep my foot out of it.

"What do you say I tell you over a cup of coffee at the Commons?" I propositioned, avoiding the question while at the same time trying to advance this relationship. I eagerly awaited her response, sitting there with my mouth agape, looking like a panting dog.

"I was supposed to meet my boyfriend after the screening," she answered rather matter-of-factly. My heart dropped. "But I guess that he isn't sticking around," she tacked on.

This seemed awfully strange. "Who's that?" I inquired.

"The producer. You know, the guy who made this film," she blurted out.

This beautiful girl was dating the producer? She allowed *him* to do *this* to *her*? What kind of guy was this anyway? Now I had no qualms whatsoever about asking her out. I was going to assume the role of her protector.

"Well, then I guess you *are* coming with me," I said affirmatively. She nodded with a smile and we were off.

Aubrey, as she introduced herself, certainly wasn't shy, in any which way. She took me by the arm and cuddled against me as we walked across campus on that raw and chilly evening. She said little as we headed toward the Commons. I had totally forgotten about the plans to meet Ian and company at the Big Red. They had been pre-empted. Anyone passing the two of us by would have assumed we were a couple. A few minutes ago, we didn't even know each other.

We were quickly seated, ordered hot chocolates right away, eager to get acquainted. Both of us were oblivious to the music being played in the background-- and how that had changed so drastically in just two years. Gone were those mindless love songs of the early sixties. The singers and the strumming guitarists were protesting everything from the War in Vietnam to civil rights... from the plight of the migrant farm workers to equality for women. Peter, Paul & Mary was my favorite group: "Where have all the flowers gone?" *Where had they gone?*

Aubrey seemed to have no qualms about having left her producer-boyfriend at the starting gate. I certainly didn't mind. And the guys at the Big Red? I had forgotten them altogether. This girl had dropped into my life.

My biography was boring. I wanted to know all about her. This beautiful young girl was a junior, like me, but in the College of Home Economics, as it was called then. She was from Texas, which sort of surprised me, considering how relatively conservative people are in the South, and with some trepidation I dared to ask her.

"That last scene, did you--?" I said in a hesitating way.

"Plan on doing it?" she helped me get the words out. "No, the whole film was kind of impromptu. I've been with this guy who's into making movies. We just started to shoot. No script, just an idea," she explained simply. "He told me this film would get me noticed."

Did it ever get her noticed! I was about to ask her if she realized that she had been exploited, but that would have been an instant relationship-killer. Besides, she kept talking-- and I absolutely no intention of interrupting.

"All of a sudden he got this concept," she explained somewhat excitedly. "So, we just *did* it," adding with a shrug and a simple smile, almost non-chalantly.

"Just *did it,*" those words reverberated. I was afraid to ask her the next question. "Do your parents have any idea?" I sheepishly inquired, curious to find out.

"They don't know... and even if they did, I wouldn't care," she callously remarked. Aubrey explained that she had very little to do with her folks, anyway. I detected some very bad vibes. I almost felt that she was trying to get back at them in some way. When the opportunity came, she jumped on it.

"Besides," she continued, toying with her spoon, "my boyfriend said this flick could make me a star."

I couldn't help blurting it out. "This guy didn't make you anything but a --," I left the last word off. "He exploited you." And so I said it. Again, this was the late 1960's... and this was a college campus.

Aubrey's expression changed suddenly. If was as if I had put a dagger through her heart. But I couldn't help it. Was her self-esteem so low that she would allow someone to do this to her? Worse, what kind of guy would do this to his girlfriend, whom he supposedly loved? "He exploited you," I said to her yet again, expecting her to get up and walk away. But she didn't.

"By the way, who was that guy in the picture with you?" I inquired, quickly changing the subject.

"Oh, him? Some dude who thinks he's going to be the next teen idol. I barely know his name," she said with a look of repulsion.

"Did he know what was going to happen next?" I kept going.

"Who knows? And does it really matter?" she protested. Now her emotions were getting the best of her. "How come he's a big hero when he drops trou?" she added angrily with fire in her eyes. "But when I--" she was too overwrought to finish the sentence.

Aubrey was absolutely right. There was that double standard back then-- and she was a victim of it.

Her eyes welled up with tears. Maybe I had said too much. Having put down her guy, and then, her, too, I felt that I just needed to defend her. There was nothing that could be done now. The film had been shown. Aubrey, all of her, had been on camera. She was public property. At least the male "star" had his rear-end end to the camera. I was totally at a loss at what to say now. She had viewed herself transformed into a minor celebrity on campus. I didn't see it that way at all; that's not exactly the type of attention she should be looking for. Wisely, I changed the conversation to something far more innocuous.

It was getting late and I walked her home, an old rooming house on Dryden Road in Collegetown. We said little on the return trip. Now I asked myself if my big mouth had blown it for me and I wondered whether I would ever see this girl again. When I got her home, I walked up the steps to her porch. She pivoted around, wrapped her arms around me, and gave me a passionate kiss.

"Good night," she said in a soft voice and with a gentle pat on the cheek. "See yah tomorrow." I floated back to the fraternity house after that. All I could think about was Aubrey.

LATER THAT NIGHT

#42 – Crowd Pleaser

"What the hell happened to you?" demanded Ian when I got back well after Midnight.

"What are you, my babysitter?" I snapped at him.

"What did you do, watch the movie a second time?" he laughed. That hurt; he still didn't know that there had been a sequel. I knew I had to tell him to shut him up. We kept few, if any secrets, from each other.

"You mean you went out with that slut?" he exclaimed in amazement.

"Don't call her a slut!" I shouted back at him, highly out of character for me.

"No, no, not a slut. *Every* girl you go out with screws on camera," he said mockingly.

"I said, 'shut up!'" even louder and angrier.

Ian seemed startled at how upset he had made me, and fortunately, had the sense to back off.

"OK, OK, guy. But is this the kind of girl you want--?"

I cut him off. "She's a *wonderful* girl," I said affirmatively. "She's weak; she's vulnerable, she's defenseless. She got taken advantage of."

"Just wait a minute," he cut in, suddenly a bit skeptical, "Nobody forced her to—"

"Shut the hell up!" I ordered him. He had never heard me speak that way before. Frankly, I surprised even myself.

"You really fell for her," he said, suddenly softening, pedaling more gently, now nodding his head.

"Yes. Yes, I did." I replied.

Nothing else was said between us that evening. Nothing else needed to be said. I retreated to my single room. I had fallen for Aubrey like I had fallen for no other girl. All the others were ancient history now.

In the days that followed, I had one and only one thing on my mind: Aubrey. Her old boyfriend? She had made short shrift of him anyway. He didn't care; he had used her-- and was ready to move out and on to the next and then the next. So the timing was perfect for me to move in.

Forget evenings and weekends. The two of us met on campus whenever we could during dead hours. I even ditched class once or twice just to be with her. Unfortunately, though, the film was shown for the rest of the week, and there was nothing I could do about that. Word spread and the Statler Theatre was SRO just about every night, giving her quite a bit of notoriety. The rest of campus did not view Aubrey the way I did. But they didn't know her the way I did. To them she had become public domain.

I could tell by people's faces and even by some rude finger-pointing that she was recognized wherever we went. Frankly, I didn't care. What Aubrey had done was past tense; now she was with me and nothing like this would ever happen to her again. I would see to that. But in the meantime, she had to live with it, and seemed to have major league regrets. Still, the subject was never openly discussed between us, and we spent as many waking moments together as possible. I took her to dinner, I took her to the movies, I took her to the fraternity. I sensed she had never been treated this royally nor respectfully before. Bingo! Maybe that had been her problem. And that's precisely where I entered the picture. We complemented each other perfectly. I had struck gold.

Ian, who was forever trying to make it up to me after the ill-fated Holly affair, took charge at the fraternity house. It was evident that he had done some advance work to make sure that none of the brothers made any snide comments to or about Aubrey. She was politely accepted by most, although at a curious distance, and it was obvious, to me anyway, that a few of the guys were looking her up and down.

Fall Weekend was fast approaching and there was no question this year as to whom I would be taking. We had worked out to the last detail how every minute would be spent, from the first mixer on Friday afternoon to the closing brunch on Sunday. I was sailing, socially, like I never had before. I wasn't sure whether Ian was genuinely happy for me, or just relieved that with this intervention on my behalf, his debt had been paid, and the last vestiges of the Maryland cataclysm were finally gone.

On Friday afternoon, I took her back to my room and we lay in bed, my arm around her, for a long time, not uttering a single word. I spun some soft mood music on my stereo. She started to slowly unbutton my shirt, from the top down and then ran her finger down my chest. All of a sudden, without any warning, she started to cry uncontrollably.

"What's wrong?" I tried to comfort her, holding her tighter and tighter. But she just continued to sob. "We don't have to do anything more," I said softly. And she stayed huddled and cuddled in my embrace for the rest of the evening.

She had told me that she wanted to skip the football game. But I wasn't going to miss that, so I decided to go it alone, although I was bored to tears and paid little attention to the score.

On Saturday afternoon, I arranged to have flowers delivered to Aubrey's rooming house in advance of my picking her up later on. Friday night of the big weekend was just the appetizer; tonight was the main course. I had blown my budget on the most expensive arrangement possible, but to me she was well worth it. More important, I wanted her to know that *she* was well worth it.

The evening would kickoff with a cocktail party at 7:00 P.M.; I told her I'd be by at 6:45 P.M. I rang the bell and waited a few seconds. Nobody answered. I figured that she was probably in the bathroom or still getting dressed. So I waited a few seconds more and tried again. And then again; still no response.

A little concerned now, I rapped on the wooden door. Then I squinted, trying to peer through the grimy window leading to the staircase that led up to her apartment. I managed to see that the bouquet of flowers that had been delivered earlier in the day had been dumped on one of the steps, still in its original cellophane wrapper, having never been opened. I tried yet another loud knock. This one drew the wrath of the landlady, an old vetch with a kerchief in her hair and a cigarette dangling from her yellowed teeth.

"You lookin' for Aubrey?" she quizzed me with her raspy voice.

I nodded "Yes," apprehensively.

"Sorry, fella. She done packed up and pulled outta here early this afternoon."

For a few moments more, I stood there trying to process what I had just heard; then I did a quick about-face and retreated back to the fraternity house where I spent the big weekend in solitary. I offered no explanations to anyone. I didn't need a lecture from anyone.

To this day, I don't know why Aubrey left. I sort of guessed. Had I said the wrong thing? I kept blaming myself for screwing up. If only I could have talked to her just one more time. But I couldn't; I didn't even know where to begin searching. She disappeared from Cornell without a trace and left no forwarding address. Efforts to track her down at the registrar's office came up empty. Aubrey had vanished off the radar screen. She had-- evaporated, disappearing into thin air. I never heard from her again. Another one, in and out of my life, so fast.

THE LATE FALL, 1967

#43 - Percolating

Once again I threw myself back into my studies to drown my social woes and yet again I did a half-way decent job of doing it. Schoolwork successfully took my mind off of a whole bunch of other things. I seemed to possess this weird chameleon-like ability to go in and out of academia as the occasion warranted it.

I could see Ian wanted to give me an "I-told-you-so," but had the sense to keep quiet and backed off.

During the late fall and early winter of 1968, I bumped into Diana periodically, usually at about the same time and at the same place each week. It was no coincidence; our classes must have been in close proximity. That's not unusual at such a large university consisting of hundreds and hundreds of acres; if your paths don't happen to cross by design, you can go months, or even years, without running into someone. Three other students had come to Cornell from my high school and I had gone more than two years without ever bumping into one of them. I rarely saw the other two, either, lost in the shuffle.

The pace of campus activism was accelerating fast and furiously, almost reaching a feverish pitch. More and more students were getting drafted; still others like me, though not sent off to war, had been sent for physicals, which felt like the first step. A dress rehearsal, so to speak. *Nobody* felt secure anymore. The innocence that we had enjoyed during our freshman year and even part of the sophomore year had all but disappeared and was replaced by growing uncertainty and fear.

Diana had absolutely no use for me now, treating me cavalierly on those few occasions when we did meet.

"I heard about what happened to Kip," she commented to me rather snidely.

I didn't give her the satisfaction of an answer.

"And what about you? Have they caught up with you yet?" she shot back almost in an accusatory tone. I almost thought she would have been delighted to see me drafted and in uniform. Again, I held myself back from responding. But I must admit that her condescending air irked me.

Yet with all that had happened in the world since our break-up, I still couldn't subscribe to her way of thinking. She was so engrossed in the anti-war movement that she had time for little else. No time for makeup or clothes, she appeared thinner and wan by now, almost washed out. Nevertheless, I was forced to admit to myself, she was still a knockout. But it didn't matter; the pilot light had been extinguished. I felt as though she looked at me with contempt. I hated these occasional encounters, as brief as they were.

At these moments, I thought about that summer fling with Donna. But she went to the other extreme-- not knowing what time of day it was. She was just too much of an airhead. The only connection she could make was on the switchboard. I tried to convince myself that there was no potential there for a long-term relationship and it was just as well that we had gone our separate ways. Norma? Holly? Aubrey? I had successfully managed to all but blot them out of my memory, probably because they had caused me so much pain, each in her own way.

Dwayne and I also met up again, this time in a second-level government class that became a forum for discussing the War. The prescribed course content was deep-sixed altogether. To our teacher, it was "meaningless pap."

"Current events taking place... history happening before our eyes-- that's the best textbook," the bearded young professor proclaimed as he gesticulated wildly, walking around the pit of our windowless, horseshoe-shaped seminar room, in the basement of one of the new classroom buildings. He hardly fit the conventional professorial mold. Long beard, mustache, granny glasses, and white shirt rolled up to the elbows, baggy workman's pants. Occasionally he substituted a checkered flannel shirt buttoned to the top. He was 30, maybe 35. I couldn't tell for sure. But there was absolutely no doubt whatsoever as to where his sympathies lied. He had abandoned the curriculum in favor of proselytizing us. This was not the class I had signed up for. It made me angry that college professors could get away with this sort of thing and were hardly supervised at all.

Too bad for Diana that she hadn't discovered this course; she would have been in her glory with this guy. Then again, there were probably plenty of others just like it on campus at this point in time. Suddenly Cornell was simmering, both outside *and* inside the classroom. It was understandable; the War had advanced to our doorstep.

On the few occasions when I dared to share my ambivalence about our role in Vietnam, the professor pounced on me mercilessly.

"Did our friend here check his convictions at the door when he came to this venerable Ivy League institution?" he posed the question sarcastically. Remarks like that always engendered snickers from several of the other twenty or so in the seminar and made me feel lower than the basement floor. I don't know whether my classmates were trying to ingratiate themselves to the teacher or truly felt that scorn towards me. How come they never spoke up? In either case, I became the constant target of his rhetoric and jabs and decided it was just safer to retreat into my shell and keep my mouth shut.

But the damage was done; I had become his convenient punching bag, focus of his venomous speech, and the butt of his jokes, even though I kept uncharacteristically quiet. After a time, I dreaded going to this class as much as I had detested wrestling, maybe even more so, although for very different reasons. In retrospect I could laugh about wrestling; this episode, however, wasn't the least bit funny. If there was any humor, it was at my expense. Once he pushed me so far that for a moment I considered going to the department chairperson. But only for a moment: Who knew where *his* sympathies lied in this politically charged climate?

Dwayne, in the meantime, was piggybacking the civil rights cause onto the anti-war movement and seemed to relish this class--and the abuse I was getting. He was still hostile toward me, maybe even more so, and I just couldn't fathom where all this malevolence came from. Except during this class we took together, we exchanged not a single word. He seemed to delight in seeing me under attack. If we happened to exit the room together, he would brush past me, with obvious scorn. On one occasion, it almost became physical when we went shoulder to shoulder. At the same time, he was becoming increasingly visible in the anti-war groups that were gaining momentum across campus.

Dwayne and Diana shared something in common: They both looked down at me, with great derision, and succeeded in making me feel angry and uncomfortable. I didn't want to talk to Dwayne any more than I had wanted to see Diana, and I made a conscious effort to avoid him. He was no longer the same person I had met in the dorms some two years ago. Then again, neither was I. In retrospect, I faulted myself for not trying harder to understand him and where he was coming from-- which would have salvaged this friendship and could have led to an altogether different outcome. Hard to believe, but despite all this overt hostility, I still liked Dwayne and regretted that our friendship had run aground and become a different type of casualty of the escalating conflict and turmoil.

Ian was as ambivalent and as confused as I was about the War. Our own vulnerability, coupled with what had happened to Kip, had made us frightened and angry. Our doubts were increasing; yet we remained suspicious of some of those in the vanguard of the anti-war movement. How to separate the two? Ian had had it good, very good. What was there to complain about? Why all the fuss? Don't look a gift horse in the mouth, was his attitude. But Ian also had a conscience, albeit sometimes hidden and hard to see through his tough-guy veneer. He understood that we were being sucked into a faraway war over which we had no control. College students were likened to pawns in the power struggle.

"Why are we over there?" he kept asking. "What's in it for us? What do we have to gain? We certainly have a lot to lose." These were the difficult questions with which we continued to wrestle.

Losing Kip to the draft had made the War hit home. Who would be next?

EARLY JANUARY, 1968

#44 - Diversions

It had been nice to spend some time at home for winter break, but I was very eager to get back to campus. For one thing, I wanted to get my first semester final exams over with. Actually, I had only two tests to sit for. As an English major, I had to write a paper in lieu of taking an exam for the other two courses. Never the greatest test-taker as evidenced by my SAT scores and performance at Cornell thus far, I preferred that type of assessment, feeling I had at least a modicum of control. Second, I wanted to view fraternity rushing from the perspective of a house officer. I had become a member of the "inner circle," so to speak, and got to call some of the shots. The whole process was far more fun and far less stressful being on the inside.

Both objectives were accomplished nicely. I did better than expected in my fall semester courses, ending up with a grade point average in the B+ range. Still nothing to crow about, but as long as I could manage to not totally screw up the spring semester, I would be in the hunt for a half-way decent graduate school-- if I could make it that far without being plucked off campus.

By the beginning of 1968, "If?" was a question, not a statement. Many of us were starting to wonder how long we would beat the clock and remain college students. No, the fear of busting out wasn't priority one any more. That, was yesterday's news. There was growing uncertainty and insecurity among Cornell men as to their futures. It was a day-to-day proposition. No longer were we protected, shielded by the now defunct 2-S draft deferments. No longer did I take it for granted that I would have the full four years to finish my studies.

If it could happen to Kip, it could happen to me. Now I lived with the fear that I, too, could become a statistic at a moment's notice. Perched on the cliff had become a very precarious way to live-- and would grow even scarier in the months ahead.

Fraternity rushing provided a good distraction from the growing turmoil on campus and the increasing preoccupation with the anti-war movement. To my surprise, there was still a large pool of prospective pledges who wanted to go Greek. I sensed that like me, they were searching for some escapism and distraction.

Rebounding from the previous year's mediocre rush, we ended up with a strong pledge class numbering two dozen. Overall, however, pledging was significantly down on campus, and there were several houses that were in danger of closing their doors because of low numbers. I was relieved that CAT wasn't one of them. There was even talk of some mergers, with stronger houses, like ours, subsuming the membership of those chapters going out of business.

In the grand scheme of things, pledging-- and all the nonsense that went along with it-- must have seemed highly incongruous at this perilous and unstable moment in time. I could just imagine the tongue-lashing that I would have gotten from Diana if she knew that I was still caught up in the fraternity madness. However, it was precisely the antidote, the escape, which the doctor had ordered for me to keep my sanity during these unsettling times.

LATE JANUARY, 1968

#45 - Campus Cook Killers

Unfortunately, Henny didn't remain on as house cook very much longer. Just when we thought we had finally broken the jinx, there was a big blowup between Henny and Otis, from which Otis emerged victorious. She yanked off her apron, tossed off her chef's hat, threw down her spatula, vowed never to set one big toe in our kitchen again-- and never did. With the all-important second semester of my junior year about to begin, this couldn't have come at a worse time. I felt as though food was the only constant in my life; I loved to eat; still do. I eagerly looked forward to my meals. Some eat to live; I've been accused of living to eat.

In the meantime, until we could find a replacement for Henny, the older brothers took turns playing cook. Reluctant volunteers were recruited with the incentive of getting rebates on their room and board bills. Their lack of training in the culinary arts became obvious.

Simply put, this plan was nothing short of a disaster. The meats were served either burnt to a crisp or severely undercooked. "Rare" is one thing; altogether "raw" is another. The vegetables were cold, tasteless, and on occasion, still frozen. And who can kill pasta? We did. All you have to do is know how to boil water, or so we thought. The finished product was all stuck together in one big glop. A knife was needed to saw off a piece. Hardly appetizing, especially with tepid tomato sauce or cold ketchup used to drown it.

Cooking for one is hard enough, but for a house full of college men was a whole other story. The other brothers kept uncharacteristically quiet; they probably couldn't have done any better and refrained from razzing the make-shift chefs.

Breakfast was a total debacle, with the French toast and pancakes sticking to the grill. Most of the bread and batter had to be scraped off. Henny had made it all look so easy.

"Try some more shortening," I gently suggested one morning, just wanting to be helpful to my brother who was doing his best, but failing miserably. To wit, the cook-of-the-day poured about half a cup on the grill and handed me a piece of blackened French toast drenched in more oil than you'd find in Texas.

"Here: satisfied?" He shoved it my face with a disgusted look, not taking my helpful hint too kindly.

So, we just plain starved for about two weeks. The Barf Bar food at the freshman dorms never looked so good. At least it was barely edible. The sole beneficiary of our cooking catastrophe was the diner downtown, to which we escaped now and then to avoid starvation. That greasy fare was a veritable feast by comparison.

Our steward then announced a breakthrough: A retired short order cook named Milo had responded to the ad that he had placed in the *Ithaca Examiner,* one of the local fish wraps, and we decided to get him in for an interview as fast as possible. Some interview; all we wanted to know was whether he'd take the job. Milo was a short, stocky man who looked as though he had been a prizefighter. His face, the most notable feature of which was thick lips, resembled that of a bulldog, and sported about two days of beard growth. On top, he had a short, salt 'n pepper crew cut. His clothes were slightly stained and he spoke (actually, grunted) with a small cigarette stub hanging out of the corner of his mouth. It was nice to see that he had come dressed to impress for the interview.

"This is the best they could come up with?" muttered in disgust one of the seniors sitting at my table.

"Shut up," motioned another, "We're not auditioning for Miss America. Can the guy cook?"

"Beggars can't be choosers. We're desperate," added a third. "For what we're willing to pay, we're lucky if we can rustle up Barf Bar Bill."

As it turned out, and to our pleasant surprise, Milo was a half-way decent cook. At least the kitchen was up and running and the food was edible again, if not gourmet. Apparently Milo had honed his craft as an army cook. However, that cigarette constantly flapping from his mouth, even on the rare occasions when he spoke, bothered everyone and we wondered how many ashes ended up in the eats. "Aw, c'mon. A little tobacco's not going to hurt you," kidded one of the older guys.

During his "break-in" period, each of us was assigned kitchen duty once a week. I drew Sunday morning brunch. And it was that experience that soured my taste for restaurant food for some time to come. The meal was served buffet style, starting at 10:00 A.M. I had to report for duty at 8:00 A.M.

Milo, having arrived much earlier, seemed to have everything under control so there was very little for me to do except watch. By now, he had become accustomed to the brotherhood, and his grunts were a bit more intelligible. I marveled at his ability to crack an egg with one hand. He saw me watching: "Uh, now you try it," he commanded me. My results were less successful. The shell broke in the palm of my hand with the contents dripping all over my shirt. I signaled to the cartons of eggs still waiting to enter the mix. "You better do the rest," I instructed him, still trying to clean myself up from that sticky mess.

As soon as Milo had mechanically cracked about 200 eggs, it was time to mix them. But where do you stir eggs in that quantity? Milo motioned to a large aluminum garbage pail next to the slop sink. I dragged it over to him. I gulped at the thought.

"Don't worry," he squawked in his gruff, gravelly voice. "Don't worry-- it's clean. I rinsed it out yesterday."

Rinsed it out? Yesterday?? What are the symptoms of salmonella poisoning? Obediently I poured all the eggs into the can. Milo left the stove, waddled over to the corner, and grabbed a giant wooden oar to start the scrambling process. He lifted the stick over the top. "See how easy," he grumbled, with the cigarette still bobbing up and down in the corner of his mouth. At that point, however, he lost it. The cigarette, that is. A full-length butt fell right into that can of scrambled eggs. Unnerved for a split second, he quickly recovered. He reached over the top, passed his hand through the thick yellow mix, and went on a fishing expedition to retrieve as much of it as he could find. I just reeled back in stunned disbelief. When he came up for air, he stared right back at me, knowing full well what I was thinking.

"Well, what did you expect me to do-- just throw 'em out and waste all those eggs?"

I didn't have breakfast that Sunday-- or for the next few Sunday mornings after that. When the huge mound of eggs on the table reached me, I just let it keep going: "I'll pass." But Milo's hygiene, or lack thereof, didn't seem to bother anyone else.

"Nobody's croaked from his cooking," commented Ian, who seemed to relish whatever he dished out. Still, I just didn't find it "appetizing" to say the least. I guess that I knew too much. Ignorance would have been bliss.

Fortunately (for me, anyway), Milo's tenure with us was short-lived. It was an amicable parting; he just didn't show up for work one day. The steward made some inquiries (Milo didn't have his own phone) and learned that he had gotten a better-paying job with two days off at a roadside café on the outskirts of town. We couldn't possibly compete with that deal, so nobody could blame him. It just would have been nice if he had given us some notice. We never saw or heard from him again. First Henny, now Milo.

The advertisement for a cook was placed in the local paper yet once more. I think that the editor of the classifieds had a standing order, ready to run that same want ad at a moment's notice. This time it was Dolores who responded. She was a short, stocky African-American woman whose trademark was her toothy grin. She had recently transplanted herself from Louisiana to be closer to her son who worked at the gun factory and she was in dire need of *any* kind of work immediately. When Otis heard "gun factory," his alma mater, his ears shot up. This, we wanted to believe, was a good omen. And the timing was right. We desperately needed someone in the kitchen and Dolores desperately needed a job. This was going to be a good match, at least for a while, anyway.

Henny certainly had been a very good cook, but Dolores was even better. Besides the standard fare, she came to us with dozens of other recipes, many reflecting her southern upbringing. She could have written a cookbook, "101 Ways to Make a Meatloaf." Nor was chicken ever prepared the same way twice. And besides knowing her way around the kitchen, not only was she was immaculate, but she was also very friendly. She seemed to fit right in at the house-- and the brothers responded enthusiastically by making her feel at home. What more could we, or she, ask for? At last, we had struck pay dirt. Unfortunately, the brothers ended up doing her in as well, although this time it was purely unintentional.

That semester, CAT was hosting an exchange student from Denmark. One morning, Henrik woke the whole house up well before daybreak to participate in a traditional Danish candlelight ceremony honoring one of the Saints. Nobody liked being roused out of bed, especially at 5:00 in the morning... especially on a frosty winter morning. But how could you say "no" to a great guy like Henrik? So most of the brothers got into the spirit of things and went along with his orders.

Obediently we each donned a sheet to be worn toga style. (Perhaps you can see where this is going.) I hadn't worn one of these things since my initiation into the fraternity. At least this time

I had something on underneath. Henrik also instructed us to take a white candle and stand it in a drinking glass. He would lead the procession out of the house, up the small hill on the street in front, and then back down where a repast of Danish delicacies would be waiting for us on the porch to conclude the celebration.

That was the way it was *supposed* to go. It all seemed harmless enough. Unfortunately, that's not how it played out.

At about 5:15 A.M., we emerged out of the house onto the street, walking in pairs, toward the top of the small knoll beyond the fraternity house. As luck would have it, the transit bus that delivered Dolores to work each morning let her off at the top of that hill at just about the same time. As she stepped off the bus, all she could see on this normally quiet street usually deserted at this hour of the morning, were two lines of men wearing white sheets heading toward her. And all that I can recall is hearing her shriek, "I done thought I left them behind back in the South," as she turned around, flailing her arms in the air and running the opposite way.

"Dolores! Dolores! Stop! Stop!"

But it was too late; we couldn't catch up with her then and never did again.

That was the last we saw of Dolores-- who was added to our kitchen's Hall of Shame. She, in turn, was followed by a string of chefs, all of whom performed as though they had never seen the inside of a kitchen before, and none of whom lasted more than several weeks, some as little as a day. Little wonder that CAT quickly acquired the reputation as, "The Campus Cook Killers." And little wonder that I had no trouble at keeping my weight below 150.

WINTERTIME

#46 - The Lottery

The War was really heating up now, reaching the boiling point. It was the lead story in the newspapers every morning and on the evening network newscasts almost every night. For one thing, Vietnam had become a money pit. The number of troops being shipped overseas was surging, bleeding every city and town in America. So was the number of military and technical advisors. And so was the number of tanks, trucks, and war planes. The War was becoming a drain on the economy. Worse, the number of those maimed and killed, on both sides, was steadily climbing. The casualty count was mounting. All of this was being broadcast, in graphic detail, to the American public.

Hollywood's portrayal of war with its unflappable generals in their neatly pressed uniforms `a la John Wayne had been supplanted by images of those bloodied and massacred, with body parts flying and body bags literally piling up. "Stay tuned for video at eleven," promised the anchor during station breaks throughout the evening. Not a pleasant sight to see on the tube.

More and more Americans were starting to take sides; fewer and fewer were left still sitting on the fence. Those doggedly supporting the War were highly critical of the media, claiming they were using selective editing to turn the tide of public opinion against it; but their protestations fell on deaf ears and the nightly display of carnage and blood 'n guts kept appearing on a regular basis.

On the other hand, those opposed to the War were becoming increasingly vocal and appeared to do almost anything to end our involvement. Protests of one sort or another were also a daily occurrence.

With each passing day, the United States was becoming more and more entrenched in Vietnam. The harder we struggled, the more determined President Johnson seemed to dig in his heels. It all reminded me of a gambler who kept losing, but trying to recoup his losses, kept saying "just once more, just once more."

America had never lost a war and we were not going to lose this one-- no matter what the cost in dollars and lives lost. That is what the Conservatives had to say. The lines were drawn; the country was polarized. The college campuses were becoming increasingly divided on a daily basis, although the vast majority of students were lining up behind the anti-war movement. That sentiment was clearly starting to win out.

That orderliness, predictability, and regimentation of the 1950's looked awfully good to me back then. Also gone was the innocent and carefree living of Camelot and the early 1960's. And who cared about curfews or how many feet were on the floor? The assistant proctor and his mindless rules had been declared null and void. There were far more important things to be concerned about. People were dying practically before our eyes every single day and although the bitter debate had risen to the Congressional level, little was being done to apply the brakes.

As I said, there were two wars going on. Besides "Johnson's War," a.k.a. the "undeclared war," as some had called Vietnam, there was a *civil* war taking place in the United States. It split the country into the "hawks" and the "doves," and while there may not have been combat in the streets, (those on the college campuses might disagree with that statement), we were a nation sharply torn on this one issue. It was a tug of war-- with neither side budging. So, in 1968, we were fighting on *two* fronts.

As the need for manpower steadily increased, so did the draft, so did the number of students called away from Cornell and every other college for express shipment to Vietnam. And, concurrently, so did the level of activism on campuses across the country. We had come a long way from the fall of 1965 and couldn't care less about all those silly rules that once governed our existence. To hell with the proctor; for all intents and purposes, he was declared defunct, his rules obsolete. We had more pressing concerns. Survival topped the list. An evolution; really, a revolution-- and I had a front row seat.

How students were going to be selected for the draft had to be determined. No longer was it going to be "oldest man first." Up until this point, the decision had been largely left to local draft boards that had to meet their quotas. Pity poor Kip, for example, had been the victim of one such call-up by his local board in Oklahoma that just couldn't wait to get its grips on a college boy the split second that the 2-S deferments were shelved. Except for those fortunate enough to have failed their physicals thanks to some documented malady and earned a coveted 4-F draft status, every one of us was highly vulnerable, a potential 1-A and ripe for picking. Our draft card became far more important than either our driver's license or Social Security number.

The government, now in absolute and complete control of our destinies, decreed that the draft order would be determined by lottery and that the drawing would be televised. In short, I felt like a sitting duck.

I guess you might say that the lottery was the precursor of "reality television"-- *Survivor* or *Fear Factor.* Of course, the stakes were *slightly* higher. According to the rules of this life and death game of chance, on the appointed evening, 366 dates of the year would be drawn one at a time from a drum. The first date drawn would be number one and those with that birthday would be the first to be drafted... the second date drawn would be number two and those with that birthday would be the second to go... and so on. The process would continue until each and every one of the 366 birth dates had been assigned a priority number.

As mentioned already, televisions were few and far between at Cornell in the sixties. Furthermore, the reception without cable was lousy in this remote area removed from civilization. And college students, in those days, anyway, couldn't afford it. So the viewing would necessarily take place in a communal setting.

The mood at dinner in the fraternity house on the night of the lottery was unusually somber. The dining room, arranged with eight or nine round tables, was always packed, and always boisterous. No surprise: so many college guys getting together and letting loose after a day of being cooped up in classrooms, labs, and libraries. Not this particular evening, however. Surprisingly, there was very little conversation; most of the brothers were engrossed in deep thought. Forget about their futures at Cornell, which were on the chopping block; their very lives were at risk. Their fates were to be sealed very shortly, not *by* them, but *for* them. And that loss of control was the prime sticking point.

I recalled the most anxiety-producing times in my life up until that moment: first waiting to get back my SAT scores; and then waiting to hear if I had been accepted to Cornell. But that anticipation was nothing compared to this wait. Twenty-four hours from now, those of us in the lottery would know whether we would be free and clear-- or bound for Vietnam. I'd likened it to a doomed prisoner waiting for a call from the governor to halt his execution. Yes, it was a matter of life and death.

The only sounds to be heard at dinner were the clanging of the large metal dinner trays, the shuffling of wooden chairs on the linoleum floor, and an occasional "Pass the mustard." As the brothers finished dinner-- some barely ate a morsel-- they quietly got up from the table and piled into the living room. Not me. For some reason, I wanted to be alone for the lottery. Most crowded around the old set. Going through this agonizing experience, most guys would have sought some company, support, and solace from their friends. I had feelings I felt uncomfortable sharing: my ambivalence about the War, the protesters, the fear of having to leave Cornell, and the terror of being drafted. In short, I was on emotional overdrive. My destiny was up to the luck of the draw.

I didn't need anyone gaping at me or feeling sorry for me, so I headed over to the Straight, solo, where I had at least a degree of anonymity. I had tried to talk Ian and Jordan into joining me, but both declined, albeit for different reasons.

"Where the hell are you going?" Ian quizzed me. I explained why I was going to watch the lottery on campus. He looked at me as if I had two heads.

"Well, I'm not leaving here to watch my fate decreed with a bunch of strangers. I don't need a public execution." He muttered and just walked away from me shaking his head, almost in disgust. Jordan on the other hand, was a different story altogether. He wasn't even sticking around. His defense mechanism was avoidance.

"Can't do anything about it anyway," he tried to convince himself-- and me. "Why even bother? I'll read about it in the papers tomorrow morning. I'm going over to the gym," he said resolutely. At least one thing was certain: Teagle gym wouldn't be crowded this night; he'd have all the workout machines to himself. So, I ended up going it alone; I couldn't bear waiting until the next morning to find out if I had a future.

By the time I got there, the social hall in Willard Straight Hall was packed SRO with students lining the walls. I found a small open space in the very back and propped myself up against the rear coat rack. This was going to be a long and uncomfortable evening in more ways than one and now I was forced to stand. I had second thoughts about having left CAT and for a moment thought about going back to the fraternity house. However, the strange need to be alone and deal with this by myself at this moment trumped everything else.

The room was long and rectangular. I could barely see the TV screen, perched on a shelf, from the back where I stood. No matter tonight; all that I needed to know was in the numbers. There was nothing I really had to see. At least I had a panoramic view of everything going on in front of the screen. About ten rows of cheap couches, like those you'd see in a doctor's office, faced the television. Not only was every seat taken, but some of the co-eds sat on their boyfriends' laps. Here, too, the mood was somber; there was some buzz of conversation, but nothing audible. All waited in silence for the ceremony to begin and to hear their fates decreed.

There were a few familiar faces-- from the dorms, from the gym, from my classes-- but nobody I really cared to sit with or converse with. I remained determined to get through this ordeal all by myself. The CBS network had pre-empted its regularly scheduled broadcast of *Mayberry RFD* to carry the drawing live. After all, this was *real* drama-- with life-changing outcomes.

The "program" had the aura of a game show. I guess I had expected there to be some slick, smooth emcee assisted by a lady from the auxiliary with white gloves and a crescent hat with an ostrich feather in it, and a boa scarf around her neck, who would be picking the numbers out of a hat. A forerunner of Vanna White, she would have pulled out each birthday from the rotating drum with the finesse and cheery smile of a game-show model.

But that's not how it happened. The process was far more surgical... clinical... and business-like. A number was drawn and that birth date would be affixed to a number on a board. It was kind of like "Dialing for Dollars"-- only the stakes were much higher and there were no consolation prizes. Instead of getting a year's supply of panty hose or a toaster, the "losers" got an all-expense paid trip to Vietnam, round-trip if they turned out to be really lucky.

Let the games begin. The "stage" was bare-bones, with some office furniture pushed together for the occasion. The ranking Republican on the House of Representatives Armed Service Committee was given the "honor" of drawing the first number. *Honor?* Like ringing the opening bell on the New York Stock

Exchange? No, this was hardly an "honor." I would have felt like an executioner.

Slips of paper containing 366 birth dates were placed in blue plastic capsules. They were mixed up in a shoe box-- and then dumped into a huge glass jar perched on a stool. The capsules were drawn from that container, one at a time... opened... read aloud... and then the date affixed to a giant "game board" in the rear with a list of numbers from 1 to 366. The process continued until all 366 days had been posted.

According to the advance news reports, the Selective Service System estimated that the first third (approximately numbers 1-120 in the lottery) could expect to be sent packing to the rice paddies with almost certainty. The third at the other end (numbers 241-366) were *probably* safe-- at least for the time being. It was doubtful that their numbers would be reached, although nobody ever felt truly "safe" during this era of uncertainty. Things could change at a moment's notice. Those in the middle had to keep their fingers crossed that the first batch of new draftees was sufficient to fill the manpower quotas for their respective draft boards. Though better offer than the first group, they would still be left out there hanging on tenterhooks and in jeopardy during those unsettling times.

Normally, the large TV lounge in the Straight was noisy and full of life. But not on this evening. The mood in the room was best described as reserved; the tension could be cut with a knife, just the way it was back at the fraternity house during dinner. You could hear the proverbial pin drop as the procedure was explained. Even the usual catcallers and hecklers were reduced to silence. This was no laughing matter. In a matter of minutes, the young men in the room would know their destinies: Would they be allowed to finish their Cornell education --or-- would they be whisked away and shipped off to Vietnam with dispatch, having to put their schooling *and* lives on hold?

And, there were those in the middle who would *still* be left up in the air, having to live in daily fear of the next call-up. They dreaded going to their mailboxes to find that unwelcomed letter with the "Selective Service System" appearing in the return address corner of an envelope. Yes, the answer *was* in the numbers. Each and every one of us would know our fates in a matter of minutes. It was all beyond frightening and *without a doubt* the *most anxiety-producing moment of my life.*

The preliminaries were finally completed and the first birth date was called out... and then the second... and then the third. Just by the law of odds and averages, someone in that packed room had to have the first number drawn: September 14th. A shiver ran up and down my spine as I tried to imagine what that must have felt like, having the finger of fate pointed against you so early in the game. "Why me?" he must be asking. "Why me? What are the odds?" Yeah, 1 in 366. I just couldn't imagine what it must have felt like to be the one picked right at the start. Well, someone had to be first.

Surprisingly, little or no emotion was shown on screen during the drawing; it was all very routine and matter-of-fact. One would think that numbers were being called at a bingo game. My stomach knotted up a bit tighter as each birth date was announced. This was one time I did *not* want my number to be called. I did not want to shout "Bingo!" Nor was there much response in the lounge, for that matter. As the drawing progressed, I would have expected eruptions of anguish or glee. None came. Methodically, mechanically, date after date was drawn and announced. There was an occasional outburst. But most Cornell men accepted the outcome with resignation.

Gradually the room started to empty out and I slid into an empty space on a now-vacated couch. Those with the low numbers understood precisely what was going to happen to them; they knew full well what tomorrow would bring. In deference to the "losers," there was no celebration among those who had lucked out. They just quietly slipped out of the room as the drawing winded down. Why rub it in the faces of those less lucky?

I watched the drama unfold on the screen; I wa ma going on in the lounge. Guys, who like me, ha muttered, although their cursing was barely audible. ples embraced silently; there were muffled sobs. Besides finishing their college education, they now faced a double whammy, the added burden of having to put their future lives together on hold, fate unknown. I could just imagine what was going through their minds and shared their pain. Still others, enraged, cracked under the pressure, and blurted out expletives. But I was surprised that there were no prolonged outbursts. And there were those all ready to bail out with escape plans already formulated.

"Canada, here I come," shouted out a guy seated two rows in front of me.

By the time the number 250 had been reached, I was getting a bit antsy. Maybe my birthday *had* been called at the beginning and I had missed it. After all, I hadn't given the drawing my undivided attention, watching the drama in this room unfolding before my eyes. When number 300 was reached, about half the original audience had departed the lounge. Those who were lucky enough to fall in this final third silently slid out as soon as they heard their numbers; strange as it sounds, they felt almost guilty that they had been spared. I've heard it said that there is a sense of "guilt" experienced by survivors of any catastrophe. And this *was* a catastrophe. Still no sign of celebration by anyone.

By now I wanted my birthday announced already. I didn't have much longer to wait. My priority number was 319; I hadn't missed it after all. Safe. At least for the moment. But nobody was truly "safe." It looked as though I had been spared the wrath of Uncle Sam, at least for now; in all probability, I was not going to be touched, although it was constantly shoved in our faces as we were repeatedly reminded that there were still no guarantees. *Nobody was really safe.* Talk about a mix of emotions. I should have been euphoric; instead, I was nauseous and sick to my stomach. For me, I deemed it merely a stay of execution. And what about my friends and classmates...

What a difference a few minutes had made in the lives of so many. What occurred in Willard Straight Hall at Cornell University took place on hundreds of college campuses all across the country. The pie crust, comprised of a mixture of the ingredients of fear, anger, and apprehension remained the same; only the filling, the students from campus to campus, was different. *The well-spring of rebellion and fury was being fomented and fired up then and there.*

How would I have felt if I had been one of "the chosen"? Still, I had that pang of guilt that I had not been. My mind was racing, full of competing emotions, from conscience to anger. Given scenes like this, it is easy to understand the mentality of the sixties college student. We had been victimized… violated. We had done absolutely nothing wrong; yet our futures were being torn away from us without being given any say whatsoever in the matter.

I raced back to the fraternity. As much as I wanted to know how my friends had fared, at that moment I just wanted to go to bed, and flung myself face down, burying my head in the pillow. But being so emotionally exhausted, I was too keyed up to sleep. My beaten body was battling my racing mind, which ultimately won out. Over and over again I replayed the events of the evening, their short-run and long-range implications, not just for myself, but for college men everywhere. I tossed and turned for several hours before finally lapsing into a deep, deep sleep.

That rest did absolutely nothing to refresh me. I woke up with a splitting headache and burning stomach ache, a hangover without the benefits. All told, I had slept little more than three hours. I didn't give a shit about going to class. Give me a cut, or two, or three. What else can "they" do to me? Big deal, in light of all that had taken place the night before. A lottery connotes something good: a million dollars, a better dorm room for next year, priority seating in a closed course. Not this one! There was little good about its outcome. At this moment in time, college seemed totally irrelevant. But I did need to know how Ian and Jordan had fared.

Ian also had lucked out, with a lottery number in the low 200's, ensconced in that gray zone. Jordan didn't do quite as well, ending up right on the cusp of the second tier with a 131. But it didn't seem to faze him in the least. That was Jordan; like a duck, he let the news just roll off his back. "Can't do anything about it, anyway," he repeated. "So why worry?"

Remember in high school when you asked your friends after you got a test back, "Whatdidyaget? Whatdidyaget?" Well, all of us guys were asking one another "Whatdidyaget? Whatdidyaget?"-- but it wasn't test scores we were talking about. Our futures-- perhaps our lives-- rested in the answer. It was a very, very scary time. It became an extension of a person's identity. "Hi, I'm Joe Shmoe. Pre-med from Osh Kosh. Draft lottery number 75. Vietnam, here I come."

THE NEXT DAY

#47 – The Aftermath

I ditched all my classes that morning. So did Ian and so did Jordan. Classes, cuts, tests, papers. They all seemed absolutely meaningless, a bunch of irrelevant bullshit that day. And "three feet on the floor at all times"? Who gave a crap now?

Little surprise; we had all slept through breakfast at the house, and so we headed for the Ivy Room cafeteria at the Straight. The sole topic of conversation was the lottery. The reaction around campus ranged from rage to reprieve to resignation. Those in the "safe" zone expressed a sigh of relief, stepped into the background, and kept their mouths shut. Some others threw their hands up in defeat and accepted their fate, albeit with black humor. "What is the zip code for Hanoi?" Many, however, started talking about plans they would devise to avoid the draft; I overheard bits and pieces everywhere I went, from the cafeteria line to the men's room:

"I'll leave the country. My uncle is from Brazil. Canada is too cold."

"I'll get married; we'll have a kid right away. So I'll have to learn to change a diaper. If that'll get me out of it--"

"I'll become a teacher; they're not drafting teachers. So what; who cares that I hate kids?"

"Forget about becoming a lawyer. They make too much money, anyway. I'd end up in another tax bracket."

"I'll become a C.O., a conscientious objector. Whatever that is."

"Hey, I'm gay. Gotta towel to snap? Just let me loose in the showers! Then they certainly won't want me."

"I'll come up with some illness. Who has a medical encyclopedia?"

"Turn on the TV to one of those medical shows. What's the disease of the week?"

"Can you get a 4-F for flat feet?"

Humor-- blended with fear and anger: a strange concoction.

The news media had a field day with stories about the lottery and its outcome. One statistician, for example, faulted the method altogether and claimed the drawing had not been fair; nor had it been left to chance. He demonstrated that there was a disproportionate number of low priority numbers (first to be drafted) for November and December. Perhaps the dates hadn't been mixed sufficiently before the picking began. That result was statistically improbable if the lottery had been truly random.

Hence it was agreed that in the future a dual drawing would be devised. The birth dates would still come out of the first drum. But instead of just being listed in the order that their owners would be drafted, a second drawing would be used to pair the birth dates with one of the 366 numbers. So, say that June 5th was the first date picked; it wouldn't necessarily be priority number one. A number would be picked from the second drum-- say 179. June 5th was paired with… 179. How equitable; it was so comforting, so reassuring to see that someone really cared about being "fair" and the government was watching out for us...

Thanks to the draft lottery, my career planning came into sharper focus. If I decided to become a teacher, it would not be because I *had* to, but because I *wanted* to. Up to this moment, I wondered whether the threat of being drafted was subconsciously tempering my career choice. Although I was far from being completely out of the woods, at least I had a stay of execution.

Such was not the case for many of my classmates. With the fear of being drafted hanging over this generation of college males, the ranks in the Education classes started to swell. This was to become a generation of teachers who entered the profession to avoid the draft. Some went on to get their degrees, put in their time, and then pursued their true passions and chosen professions after the storm had passed. However, happily for the sake of the school children, many (to their own surprise) actually liked what they had been "forced" to do-- and remained in teaching, making a career of the classroom. The number of male teachers had never been so high, a boon to children everywhere. Fate works in strange ways.

MARCH, 1968

#48 – "What if?" Contingency Plans

And what *would* happen if my lottery number *wasn't* high enough to keep me safe? In the days which followed, the sense of security I felt immediately after the drawing started to dissipate as paranoia set in and replaced it. After all, there was no guarantee; things could change dramatically overnight. I had seen that happen already. Future generations would need to understand: There was no such thing as feeling truly safe or secure in those days; I felt that things were spinning out of control. At least out of *our* control. First, Kip's banishment; then the army physical; now the draft lottery. All these events were wake-up calls for me. I felt extremely vulnerable and ill-at-ease, to say the least.

The weeks following the draft drawing proved to be particularly unsettling. One would think that I would have felt a degree of protection. But "one" wasn't in my shoes. Of course, guys with much lower numbers would have traded places with me in a heartbeat. "What are you balking about?" I could just hear them saying to me with envy. Everything's relative; that was little consolation. I felt much unprotected, vulnerable-- like a boxer in the ring without his helmet, gloves, mouthpiece, or cup; though not probable, things could go south overnight and I could be reached at any moment-- and that was a scary thought for all college men of this era. "That" letter in the mail could come sending for me at any time.

Banner headlines on the front page of *The New York Times* were screaming every day: more troops, more casualties. The United States was sinking deeper and deeper into the Southeast Asia pit, as if it were quicksand. If the War took another bad turn, I very easily could be out there fighting it. The modicum of security I felt after the lottery diminished; suddenly the possibility of being drafted once again seemed a real and a distinct possibility. I became increasingly agitated.

I needed someone to talk to and sought some solace down the hall in Ian's room.

"C'mon in. Pull over a bed he motioned," obviously in the same funk I was in. Ian was working at the desk, but otherwise preoccupied, and was just going through the motions of studying. He seemed to welcome the excuse to stop and swung his chair around to face me, his legs straddling the sides, his chin resting on the back.

"I keep telling myself that my lottery number is going to provide me with a safe cushion. Doesn't it?" I asked him plaintively, really just trying to convince myself, looking for some reassurance.

"Go tell that to Kip," was his bitter response, never having fully recovered from the way our buddy had been plucked away from us practically overnight.

"Think back to freshman year when Vietnam seemed a million miles away," I continued.

"Both figuratively and literally," Ian finished the thought. "We didn't give a shit," he mused. Back then our greatest fear was running afoul of the proctor and his dumbass rules."

"Times sure have changed," I said ruefully. "I'd give an arm and a leg… to have three feet on the floor be my biggest concern."

"We have a lot more important things to worry about," he nodded in agreement. And with that, not a single other word need be said as we sat there in silence for a few moments, both of us just looking down glumly.

It was painfully true: The War was inching closer and closer, practically at the campus doorstep. Uncle Sam had already claimed his first victims. Who was going to be next? We lived in dread.

Over the next few days, I found myself with much too much time to think. I couldn't get the war scenario out of my mind. I was obsessed with the "what if--" possibilities all the time. Whether I was lying in bed at night or driving across campus; daydreaming in a boring lecture class or sitting in the sauna, I kept asking myself, "What if--?" over and over again. I even recalled the "what if--?" syndrome which had preoccupied me with the freshman swim test. The consequences of this outcome were *slightly* more serious.

Concrete sequential that I am, I was constantly searching for escape routes *just in case* I suddenly found myself in jeopardy-- and then playing them and replaying them repeatedly. I couldn't share this burden with my parents; I knew they were worried sick over the possibility that their only son could be drafted. Nor did I want to let them know how terrified I was. I changed the subject every time they brought it up, even injecting forced humor into the conversation. By the end of that week, I had become even more preoccupied; occasional thoughts had morphed into ruminations.

I decided to round up Ian and Jordan. Maybe together we could sort things out for once and for all. I volunteered to take them to the place where we always did our best thinking: the diner. And mired in the same downer of a mood that I was in, they didn't need much convincing.

As soon as we were crammed into a small booth in the back, I placed our standing order: "Two eggs up, greasy home fries, and high test coffee-- times three. Hold the cow on two of 'em." No time or patience for small talk, we got right down to business. Ian was just as on edge as was I, and although he didn't show it as much, Jordan had become worried as well.

"I'm seriously thinking about ROT-C," Ian shared with us in a rare serious moment.

"What the hell is that?" Jordan asked quizzically.

"R.O.T.C. Reserve Officers Training, ROT-C as it's called," Ian patiently explained.

I didn't know all that much about it, but I did know that it was a hot topic of conversation on campus.

"It's the gentleman's way out, I hear," Ian said somewhat hesitatingly. "It lets you remain at college without having to board the Saigon Express."

I rolled my eyes at the words "gentleman's way out." There was nothing "gentlemanly" about what was going on. At that moment I recalled Norma's brother's telling us how ROT-C was his escape route. Although he hadn't put it in those exact terms. The waitress brought our orders at this point.

"OK. So what's the catch?" Jordan asked skeptically, diving into his potatoes. "There's gotta be one," I added, already chewing.

"It means some training on campus, meetings thereafter, and, ultimately, weekends on call after graduation," Ian detailed the deal step by step.

"Sounds like an insurance policy that would allow us to finish up at Cornell, no matter what," I ventured in.

"Yeah. But that's assuming we're not called up. And there's another down side," Ian went on.

"I knew it: no free lunch. There are strings attached. So what's the premium on this policy?" Jordan wanted to know.

"There'll be a huge time commitment to be made for years to come after college," Ian explained.

"That's assuming we get to *finish* college," I quickly pointed out.

"Trauma now, or trauma later," Jordan threw up his hands. "Choose your poison, fellas. It's one big crapshoot. Where should I place my marbles?"

Jordan was right. It could be a gamble; we'd have to play the odds. Furthermore, I still didn't see myself in uniform, as a gentleman, so to speak, or otherwise; nor was I all that enthused about the prospect of committing all that time. Still, ROT-C provided some protection against being drafted in the immediate future. It could buy some time, so I couldn't rule it out altogether. But what was a better bet? Ultimately I'd have to play the odds.

"Sounds to me like a stay of execution," I concluded, having bandied about that term before.

"I think that I'm going to declare myself a C.O.," Jordan blurted out.

"A *what?*" Ian asked.

Even I knew this one. "In essence, this declaration means that you are willing to go on record that the prospect of combat is against your principles."

"That shouldn't be too hard. Ian doesn't have any principles," Jordan interrupted. We all laughed, lightening the mood but for a moment. Then it was back to business.

"Sounds easy enough. But--" Ian interrupted me before I could finish the thought.

"There's no free ride. This option also has some strings attached, too. So what's the catch this time?"

I knew what they were. For one thing, I wasn't totally sure that I could pass the litmus test for being an objector.

"Uncle Sam isn't just rubber stamping "C.O.," I cautioned the others before there was a rush to euphoria. "Otherwise, everyone'd go that route. A thorough examination-- or should I say interrogation-- comes first."

"You mean to tell me that most of the guys on this campus aren't legitimately opposed to the War? What's the problem?" Ian appeared quizzical.

"This war or *any* war?" I challenged him. Ian didn't have an answer for that.

"Well, it still sounds good to me," Ian continued. "How the hell did we get knee-deep in Vietnam, anyway?"

I really didn't want to go there, but I felt compelled to answer him. As much as I was moving off the fence, I was not totally convinced that the United States didn't have at least some role in Southeast Asia.

"Aren't you a little suspicious of the motives of some of the protest groups?" I asked both of them.

"OK, OK," Jordan interjected with a sigh. "He's on the Commie kick again."

"Look," I answered back. Most of the groups are sincere; but we need to know who's behind some of the others."

"*You* need to know," Jordan corrected me.

"So because of those doubts," Ian responded with some exasperation in his voice, "you'll tank the whole anti-war movement."

"I *didn't* say that," I protested. "Just be a little bit cautious before you jump in whole hog."

"I think that there is a saying, 'Don't throw the baby into the bathroom,'" Jordan tried to feign being philosophical.

"I think you *mean*, "Don't throw the baby out with the bath water," Ian corrected him. And we all laughed again, which broke the tension for a moment this second time.

The consensus was that if push came to shove, we'd all consider this route. But personally, it was troubling to me.

"Well, there's a third possibility," I suggested, eager to get off the sore subject of C.O. status. "We can enter an 'essential profession.'"

"Like medicine," Jordan said.

"Well, that leaves you out, Shakespeare. Rocks for Jocks took care of that," Ian reminded me of my disastrous ride in the Science Department, and we all got yet another laugh. Anything even remotely connected to science was verboten for me. Let alone the sight of blood. I even winced at Jordan's dousing his potatoes with ketchup.

"Yeah, but teaching is something I've been considering all along," I said with a spark of enthusiasm. Although it had been on my short list of prospective careers even before the specter of Vietnam appeared, now I greatly resented the idea that the threat of being drafted would be the determining factor.

"You've been on the fence about the classroom all along. What would be so bad about going into teaching? Ian reminded me. "Look at the bright side. You haven't been able to decide-- so let the decision be made for you."

"But I don't want the decision 'made' for me! And I haven't completely ruled out journalism or maybe even something in television," I quickly added.

"Oh, those two are really *essential* professions that'll save your ass," quipped Ian.

"So, as I said, don't *you* make the decision-- the decision's made *for* you," suggested Jordan, always looking for any easy answer.

However, fear of the draft seemed to have had the opposite effect. I resented the idea that I had to make this choice under duress, making a decision that would affect a lifetime, not because I wanted to, but because I *had* to. I explained that I still needed more time to pick a career.

"You might not have that luxury of time, brother," Ian advised me, almost wistfully.

"Well," I announced to them, in a declarative tone, "I've temporarily shelved teaching as a career path."

Ian put his hand to his forehead, as if he were having a vision: "Ah," he said, "I see this as your brand of protest."

"And what about you?" I quickly asked, just to get the focus off me. A nerve had been struck and it turned out to be an extremely painful one.

"Oh, yeah," Ian said in a deep, theatrical voice. "Acting is another *essential* profession. It'll definitely save me from Nam. Maybe they'll send me to entertain the troops," he said sarcastically as he shook his head in disgust.

"Wouldn't you consider anything else?" I pursued it.

"I don't like *anything else*," he snapped back with a twinge of anger and resentment, though not aimed at me. "I know what I want to do. I'm not going to let this damn War change my life." Now he, too, was angry, in the precisely the same way I was. "I have no intention of spending my life doing something I really don't want to do just to get out of the draft."

"Yes," Jordan jumped in. "Just to avoid the draft. I'll do *whatever* it takes. I'm not ready to suit up in a body bag just yet." He struck the word "whatever" with a major underscore. Jordan had been a bystander during much of the dialogue, listening, not saying all that much. But these words were sobering. By far he was the most taciturn of the three of us. This time, though, he hit the nail on the head.

"Isn't it better to make some sacrifice than risk--" he didn't even want to say those awful words and didn't finish the sentence. Neither did we. The ending was perfectly clear to all of us.

"Well, we could all get married-- and have some kids," I tried to change the subject again.

"Now *that* is out of the question!" Ian exclaimed, slapping his hand on the table.

"I'd rather wade through the rice paddies," Jordan agreed, and again the three of us roared, which broke the tension for a second yet again.

"Well, I'm not even close, so there's nothing to talk about," I lamented. Once again, there wasn't anyone on the horizon, just the bevy of highly forgettable blind dates.

"Even if there is, I have absolutely no intention of getting hitched at 21, let alone having a kid. I'm *still* a kid!" Ian asserted and we hooted in agreement.

"Can you see me taking care of a baby?" Jordan mused.

"You can't even take care of yourself!" Ian added, producing yet another round of hilarity.

"I want to be a father someday," I went on. "But I'm just not ready for that role right now."

"Can you imagine someone call us 'Dad'?" Ian snickered. We barely manage to handle ourselves.

"After all these years, doing the laundry is still a major undertaking," I reminded them.

"But, I ask you--" interrupted Jordan, grounding the conversation again.

"Uh, oh. Another 'but.' What's it this time, Mr. Conscience?" Ian asked with a touch of sarcasm in his voice.

"Let's face it," Jordan explained. "There are some guys who are rushing to the altar and chasing parenthood."

"I'd rather be dead," Ian declared emphatically.

"Well, you very well could be if--" I jumped in without thinking, and let that half-finished statement fade to black.

"Having my career decided for me is one thing. But it stops there. I'm not getting hitched to just anyone. Why don't *they* just find a wife for me, too?" Ian said with great bitterness. We all knew who the "they" was.

"Still better than that body bag," Jordan lectured him, cocking his head and raising his pointer finger.

Jordan was being the most realistic. Getting married and getting "her" pregnant might become the only alternative if it came down to a life or death decision. What would become of us if there was no other way out? We all knew that was a distinct possibility.

"If push comes to shove... if we have no choice..." I summarized. We all felt as though we were being backed into a corner.

"No, this isn't what I want in the grand scheme of things," Ian lashed out. His anger had exploded and come to the forefront, and he could no longer hold back. "This is supposed to be the best time in my life. That's a laugh. From one day to the next I don't know whether I'm going to be studying for exams, planning my future-- or shooting up people on the other side of the world. The future belongs to me? This is unadulterated bullshit. I can't make any decisions, without having to worry about the War. It sucks."

Ian was trying his hardest to control his temper, but he was losing the fight. His face was turning red and I could see tears well up in his eyes. I could also see that our ire had attracted the attention of other customers in the diner, most of whom weren't students and not at all, shall I say-- sympathetic.

The three of us sat quietly for a few moments and let our feelings subside. Although I wasn't nearly as outwardly emotional as Ian who wore his heart on his sleeve, I nevertheless felt precisely the same way. And I'm sure so did Jordan, although he showed it less outwardly. He had the tendency to keep things in side, bottled up. We were of three very different temperaments. But one thing we shared in common: Our futures had been usurped from us.

I drifted back to my high school graduation. At the ceremony, the principal concluded his speech paraphrasing words from a John Denver song:

"Given the chance to dream… It can be done.

The promise of tomorrow is real.

The world belongs to you: Go conquer it!"

I don't think this turn of events is what he had in mind. It sounded great back then. It was an open road and we could set the course we would take to determine our destinies. Well, the world no longer *belonged to us*! Somehow, I don't think that what was happening was what our elders had predicted.

Misery loves company. At least none of the three of us was in the first priority group as far as the draft lottery was concerned, although Jordan was smack in the middle of the pack… not that far from that first third… in a precarious position… and in the on-deck circle. There was, so to speak, some delay of game before any of us had to make one of these life-altering decisions. None of us had to pack our bags-- just yet.

So we tried to place ourselves in the shoes of the others, those with low lottery numbers and in near certainty of being drafted. We tried to imagine how they felt. What alternative were they going to pick to avoid being drafted? Were any of these options truly the lesser of several evils? Or, was it better to just give in, get drafted, and take your chances? Yes, there were those who were awaiting for the call and said that if it came, they'd proudly serve. I shuddered to think what I would do if and when I was forced to make a decision like that. And it could still happen any day; that was by far the scariest part of our day-to-day existence back in 1968.

None of these escape routes seemed very appealing to us; there were strings attached to all of them. I decided then and there that I would just live one day at a time, at least for the time being-- praying that I could, in fact, go on-- living.

By 1:30 A.M., we were overtanked on coffee, out of home fries, and devoid of things to say. Without another word, we asked for the check, left a hefty tip for occupying that table so long, paid the bill, and headed back to the house. Little was said on the ride up to the hill. But group therapy coupled with some buddy bonding had, in fact, helped to put things in perspective.

The prospects were frightening and we all survived from day to day with the threat of the War, the draft, and dying-- all hanging over us. I had heard all the stories about the horrors and uncertainties of the Depression and then World War II. But I couldn't imagine anything being worse than what we were going through. I was convinced that Vietnam was altogether different. What other generation endured anything as threatening as this? For a war we didn't believe in, for a future over which we were given zero control. Who else had gone through the fear of that unwelcomed knock on the door or letter in the mail, almost on a daily basis? What a horrible way it was to set out on life's course in the late 1960's.

APRIL, 1968

#49 – Other Campus Tensions Rising

As if the growing tempest over the War was not enough, there was another major conflict brewing: race relations on campus.

African-American students at Cornell faced an identity crisis: separatism vs. assimilation. And I was becoming increasingly sympathetic to the decision they faced about whether to go mainstream of not. Through the years, a number of leaders of the black community spoke at Cornell: Malcolm X, Bobby Seale, Stokely Carmichael, and Dr. Martin Luther King, Jr.

There had been a number of campus skirmishes over the past three years. But the assassination of Dr. King was a turning point. Students took over WVBR, the radio station. Several fires were set in Collegetown. And a most damaging one at Anabel Taylor Hall, the interfaith religious building. Destroyed in the conflagration was the renowned triangular altar which could be rotated to accommodate services for the three major religions. To me, that chapel had always been an icon, a symbol of religious "oneness" and racial unity where students of all faiths could pray together.

There were two other conflicts brewing during the late 1960's. One was the call for the formation of an African-American Studies

Program. However, some students argued that this was not enough; rather, they sought a separate college to be created by Cornell run for and by black students. This issue led to several major campus demonstrations and disruptions. Ultimately a middle ground was reached with the addition of an "Afro-American Studies Center." However, it failed to snuff out the underlying racial tension on campus which was mounting.

The second source of conflict dealt with "divestiture," a new term for me. Simply put, there was a call for Cornell to cut its ties with companies doing business with South Africa. It culminated in an ugly incident in which President Perkins, who had always championed the causes of black students, was violently pulled off stage by two students while speaking. The AAS quickly responded by saying that this action was not sanctioned by them. When the next speaker came to the podium and declared that Perkins should have been allowed to finish, he received a standing ovation.

As I said, racial tensions were heating up-- and would boil over a year later.

MAY, 1968

#50 – Very Bad Choices

Jordan's favorite word was "just."

"Lemme sleep just five more minutes..."

"Just two more chapters..."

"C'mon, just one more drink."

And it's the word "just" that brought him down in the end-- even without the War.

Jordan Sheridan came from suburban northern New Jersey. He had been one of the two dozen freshmen who started out in my pledge class and was one of the 20 who stuck it out to make it to and through the initiation. Jordan was a typical CAT: an easy-going, fun-loving, cool guy, with no airs about him. Nothing ever seemed to ruffle him-- except, of course, the danger of being drafted. That nonchalance earned him the popularity of just about all the other pledges as well as the older brothers in the house.

He could easily have been elected an officer for the coming year, but had absolutely no interest in this kind of responsibility. As a matter of fact, Jordan had very little ambition altogether. He just rolled with the punches and liked to have a good time. Simply put, "worry" was not part of his vocabulary-- except, as I said, when it came to the war stuff. Actually, he was successful at shutting that out, too. I noticed that when the topic came up lately, Jordan just shut down.

He was oceans apart from a guy liked me who took everything to heart. Nevertheless, we became tight friends; I guess that opposites attract. Having been a wrestler in high school, he got a lot of mileage out of my inauspicious introduction to the sport during freshman gym rotation and never missed an opportunity to rib me about it, although all in good fun. He particularly relished the story about Ralph-the-Creep's utter humiliation in front of the class.

Jordan was about 5'10" with wavy, dirty blonde hair, usually hidden by his trademark, a baseball cap worn backwards. I'd say he was better-than-average looking and built rock solid; the girls called him "cute." His winning smile also made him a standout. Those good looks, coupled with that easy-going personality, made it easy for him to have any girl he wanted and usually resulted in his hooking an arm around a co-ed's waist.

As I mentioned, at the start of sophomore year, he and Ian room ended up rooming together by default, when Jordan's roommate didn't return to Cornell at the last minute (rather, wasn't "invited" to return) and Ian needed a place to stay after the Gamma Rho fiasco. The two of them hit it off and remained roomies in the house for junior year as well. As Jordan bonded with Ian, all three of us became attached at the hip. In short, he was, as they say, a regular kind of guy and we had become fast friends. The freshman year quintet had been supplanted by this newly-minted trio.

One other thing was clearly evident about Jordan: He was from a well-to-do family and lacked nothing. Although he never flaunted it, it was obvious by the clothes he wore and the car he drove that money was no object. On the other hand, our friendship with Jordan did have to compete with his testosterone levels; to put it bluntly, he was girl-crazy. We could be in the Ivy Room at the Straight and he would just forget that he was with us and disappear with some flirtatious female.

You'd think we'd get fed up with him after a while; but it was tough to get angry, or at least stay angry, with Jordan because we knew he couldn't help himself. He would just get led away by the nose (or some other body part, as Ian used to joke), and forget we were there. Simply put, Jordan didn't have a mean bone in his body. And you could always tell when he was between co-eds because he'd be in a down mood, at least "down" for him. Yeah, that was a noticeable fault: occasional bouts of brooding and moodiness.

The pursuit of the Cornell co-ed was only his *second* passion. Hard to believe, but there was something even more important to him: hockey. Jordan lived and breathed the game. Intercollegiate hockey has always been Cornell's signature sport and a campus favorite. The only problem is that the size of Lynah Rink did not match its astronomical popularity among faculty, staff, students, and townies. Like Fenway Park and Wrigley Field, respective home of the Red Sox and Cubs, nobody seemed to want to modernize, expand, or touch it in any way. Every game was a sell-out-- and purchasing season tickets meant pulling an all-nighter on a wannabe buyers' line outside while defying the elements. Rain or shine, snow, sleet, or hail, Jordan was always one of the first to queue up.

He was also a very sensitive guy, in close touch with his parents and two sisters, one of whom had just graduated from Syracuse University, and a second who was a junior there. Jordan was the "renegade" who opted for Cornell instead. He often talked with fondness about his aunts, uncles, and grandparents as well.

There were many similarities between Ian and him, but the family connection certainly was a striking difference. I remember when Jordan got word that his grandmother had died on the Thursday before the long-anticipated Spring Weekend, the third of the big three gala social weekends. She had been in her upper 80's and in failing health. Nevertheless, Jordan dropped everything, notified his date that the weekend was off, and headed back to New Jersey to be with his family. A week later, he was still visibly shaken up when he got back to campus.

Ian, on the other hand, just couldn't fathom how Jordan had given up the long-awaited weekend for his grandmother "who was going to die sooner or later anyway." I cut him some slack on this insensitivity, since he had never known from close family ties. Actually, I think Ian was angry with Jordan for putting a damper on the party plans that the three of us had painstakingly worked out in such utter detail. But, as I said, Ian had no frame of reference for such family loyalty. I, on the other hand, fully understood what Jordan needed to do-- and admired him for having done it.

Ian, Jordan, and I spent a great deal of time together. On weekends, we tripled dated, went to fraternity functions together, and-- just hung out. During the week, we worked out at the gym, (they pumped iron-- I swam), frequented the usual haunts such as the Commons and Big Red, and-- just hung out. From time to time, several of the other brothers joined us. It was a solid group, and it further convinced me how I had made the right choice as far as a fraternity was concerned. One of the best decisions I had made.

A big change occurred, however, shortly after Spring Weekend. At first we thought Jordan was still mourning the death of his grandmother, but he bounced back from that loss quite quickly. Then we attributed this mood swing to something else that might have happened over the three days he was gone, but it became evident that that was not the case. Both Ian and I detected a major shift in Jordan's behavior and his attitude. As I said, he was prone to occasional brooding and moodiness, but nothing ever before like this. We blamed the shift on everything from girl problems to troubles at home. Or maybe it was that ongoing fear of the War and being drafted, which heretofore he had managed to partially mask. But up to now, Jordan had always been a resilient kind of guy, so we just assumed that given a day or two, he would return to his old self as he had done in the past. This time, though, was markedly different.

For the first few days after the big weekend, Jordan announced that he wasn't going to the gym or library with us. Twice thereafter, he told us he would meet us there and then never showed up, without offering an explanation when we caught up with him back at the house. He also found excuses to avoid hanging out with us so much on the weekends. Obviously it was nothing either one of us had done or said, because Jordan was treating both of us equally shabbily. As a matter of fact, he had become suddenly flippant with a lot of the guys in the fraternity. The rest of them brushed it off; we knew him better. Something was definitely wrong; but we were mystified as to what it was.

"Maybe we need to say something?" I approached Ian, posed as a cross between a statement and a question.

"I don't know," he shook his head in frustration. Look, he knows we're there if he needs us. He seems to be shying away from us, from everyone. Maybe he just needs some time alone. Let's give it to him."

"But *why* is the question," I persisted. "If something is wrong, we need to be there for him."

"Quit playing Dear Abby. If something's wrong, then he'll tell us-- when he's good and ready," Ian snapped at me in an exasperated tone. After all, the two of them were roommates. Ian had been rebuffed enough by Jordan. Three strikes and you're out, at least as far as he was concerned. "See yah," was his attitude. He didn't want to pursue this conversation any further and cut me off. That was the difference between the two of us. I've always tended to take on everyone's problems. Ian wanted to back off and give the guy some space.

I decided to go it alone. The next time I would get the brushoff from Jordan, I was going to approach him. It didn't take very long for that very situation to arise.

The following Wednesday night, the three of us had planned to have dinner on campus, catch a guitar concert at the Commons, put in at least an hour or three of obligatory study time, and end up at the diner downtown. Typical weeknight regimen. Jordan seemed to have bounced back to his old self. As a matter of fact, he was in a particularly upbeat mood that evening, so we kind of assumed that whatever had been bothering him had been resolved without our intervention. The storm had passed.

Therefore, we were more than a bit surprised when he once again failed to show up for dinner. As a matter of fact, he was a.w.o.l. for the whole evening. Ian and I followed through on our plans, and after some quality libe time, capped off by some more home fries at the diner, we headed back to the house shortly before Midnight.

"Tonight's the night. This was the last straw. I'm going to find out what the hell is bugging him," I told Ian with determination, hoping he'd join me.

"You're in this one by your lonesome, brother," he bailed out. Besides, he was too ticked off at Jordan for standing us up yet another time. When we reached the house, Ian disappeared into the living room to watch the boob tube. I headed for my room, just down the hall from Jordan's room. He arrived a few minutes later, as if nothing had happened. As soon as I heard the door open, I bolted down the hall.

"Hey-- so where were you tonight? We missed you," I gingerly asked him in a very light mood.

"Since when are you my keeper?" he pounced on me. I had never seen Jordan act like this before. He seemed almost belligerent. I didn't know whether to retreat or go for broke.

"We were supposed to meet-- you, Ian and me, on campus," I reminded him, implying, "Where the hell were you?"

"So I broke the date. Big deal," he sneered while throwing his arms up. "You, of all people, should be used to getting stood up," he said in a mocking tone. That was a blow beneath the belt, but not a knockout punch, and I wasn't down and out just yet.

This was no longer the same person I was used to hanging out with. But, I was still his friend, his brother-- no matter what he had become. Something was very wrong here, and I was more determined than ever to find out what it was.

"Jordan, forget about tonight. It doesn't matter. Who gives a shit?" I tried, changing directions altogether. "But something's going on here. Something's different," I said, hoping he'd grab the lifeline I was throwing him. Instead, he tossed it back.

"Screw you. Suddenly you're my shrink," he snapped at me a second time. This was so out of character for him. However, I *still* wasn't ready to give up on him.

"I'm not your shrink. I thought I was your friend," trying a little old-fashioned guilt. But that didn't work, either. As a matter of fact, this time he rolled his eyes and just ignored me altogether. So I tried another tactic, and cut to the chase.

"Jordan, what's the story? Something's up. Would you please let me in on it?"

At that point he turned at me, gave me a look of disdain, and snarled, "Get off my back."

"Jordan, I--" I tried.

"Bug off," he ordered, raising his voice for the first time.

"I'm not 'bugging off,'" I responded.

"Screw you," Jordan shouted, left the room, and slammed the door hard enough to cause some of the brothers to come out into the hall to find out what the shouting was all about.

I didn't see Jordan the next morning. But I did run into him the next afternoon at the Teagle gym. I sat down at the machine next to his and went through the motions. Working out is a great equalizer among guys; it was almost as if nothing had happened the night before. As a matter of fact, he was in a particularly upbeat mood. Either he had forgotten what took place between us, didn't care, appreciated my concern, or was oblivious to it. I had absolutely no clue as to which of the above it was. But it really didn't matter; the "old" Jordan was back, in a manner of speaking. So I decided to follow his lead.

"Plans for tonight?" he asked me as we left the steam room.

"Nothing special. I was "between dates," as the euphemism went. Actually, I was in a big, bad hitter's slump; this had been the longest dry spell without a decent hook-up since I had been at Cornell.

"Big party tonight in Collegetown. Northeast corner of Dryden Road. You know the place. Be there!" was his friendly command, leaving me no choice but to accept.

Since I had nothing better scheduled than a date with the television, I decided to take him up on this invitation. I viewed it to be his way of extending an olive branch. And just maybe I'd meet someone there to my liking.

I usually didn't go out on weekday nights, but for this invitation I was going to make an exception. I had some good vibes: a détente with Jordan coupled with a chance to advance my only social situation put me in a pretty good mood. I left Teagle and made a beeline for the library, where I got in a couple of much-needed uninterrupted study hours. I even worked right through dinner. If I was going out later, I had to hit the books then-- or else pay the price the following day.

"Where are you going?" Ian stuck his head into my room and asked me curiously as I was getting dressed to go out.

"Jordan invited me to this party in Collegetown. Want to join us?"

"And party with that pothead? he answered with part surprise, part disdain, rolling his eyes. "You're going to a party with *him*?" he seemed amazed.

I ignored that question, but was taken aback by what he said.

"And besides, I've got a *real* date tonight," he followed, rubbing more salt into my raw wound. All of a sudden, I was getting it from both sides.

What else is new, I said to myself. I could never keep up with Ian's marathon dating, as much as I would have liked to. Besides, who was Ian to call Jordan a "pothead"? He had never brought that possibility up before. But Ian hadn't seen the episode the day before, either. I was trying to sort this all out. It just didn't add up. I thought accepting his invitation was a good first step.

By this time, marijuana and other drugs had begun to invade and penetrate the Cornell campus. Pot was only the beginning.

Dr. Timothy Leary was espousing the use of all sorts of hallucinogens and psychedelic drugs, and like the Pied Piper, he was leading many into the river. Drinking was still the number one fraternity vice at this point, and the bars were full not only on the weekends, but on weeknights as well. But drugs, though not that widespread at first, were beginning to catch up in acceptability and they were becoming more and more popular.

There were all sorts of experimentation going on. And while talk about the War was atop everyone's list, drug use was fast becoming a close second. Some did drugs for recreation; many gave in to peer pressure; others succumbed to ease the boredom; still others sought to break down social barriers; and then there were those who used drugs for "medicinal purposes"-- as painkillers or an escape mechanism from the threats hanging over us and the constant fear with which we lived. Quite a catalogue of reasons. Or, should I say-- excuses. At first, when someone got the label of pothead or druggie, he (or she) was almost a pariah. But that didn't last all that long. At the very least, he (or she) was a curiosity item—little more.

With nothing better to do than stare at the tube, and a mere modicum of curiosity about what Jordan was really up to-- but more importantly the chance to just maybe meet someone new-- I decided to take him up on his invitation. I rationalized that it was a good opportunity to patch up a friendship which had taken a hard hit in recent days.

It was easier to park at the CAT house, take the fifteen-minute walk through campus, and then cross the stone bridge into Collegetown. It sure beat driving there and then wasting time going around in circles, trying to land a parking spot. I arrived at the destination at about 10:00 P.M. The long walk on this cool, crisp night gave me the chance to have some second thoughts: I really had reservations about going to this party where I didn't know anyone except Jordan.

Furthermore, the address was all too familiar; it took me to Dryden Road, a stone's throw from where Aubrey had lived, and re-opened some old wounds that had never really healed. I was forced to pass by the rooming house where I had been stood up on that gut-wrenching night when she performed her disappearing act, giving me no closure.

For a few minutes I stood outside the old Victorian house set twenty feet back from the sidewalk. I looked down at the crumpled-up piece of paper on which I had written the address. This was the place? Although I could hear some muffled voices inside, it was actually relatively quiet given the fact that a party was going on inside. Maybe I had copied down the wrong building number. Nevertheless, I walked up the steps and entered through a big, old wooden and glass door with a huge brass knob that could have used a good polishing.

Once inside, though, I could hear loud music, talk, and laughter. I opened a second door, leading to what was probably once the living room. There must have been 20, maybe 30 people packed in the parlor, which would have been crowded with just 15. It was really dark, darker than it was outside, and I couldn't make much out. Once my eyes adjusted to the dim light, I looked around and realized I didn't know a soul here. This was really awkward. I kept moving.

Where was Jordan? I just walked around, hoping to find someone I knew, or at least someone to greet me. But everyone was otherwise engaged, too busy to notice me. Apparently Jordan wasn't there yet. I gave some thought to leaving, but decided to stick it out at least for a while. So for about ten minutes I just wandered from room to room. No one acknowledged me; I got an occasional glance as if to say, "Who the hell is this guy? What's he doing here?" Nothing more. People went back to what they were doing.

I was feeling increasingly uncomfortable, ready to bail out, when I heard my name called.

"Psst. In here." It was Jordan. He was sticking his head out of a doorway, probably from what was once a bedroom, judging by its smaller size. I didn't recognize him for a split second. Except when he was in the gym, he always kept that baseball cap on.

I followed his lead. He pulled back one of those old-fashioned sliding wooden doors and I entered this crowded room. It was smoke-filled and there was a stench. No mistaking it. This was marijuana, and my first introduction to it.

"C'mon in, pal, he greeted me in hyper-friendly fashion." No introductions were made. Six or seven others, guys and gals, were scattered around the room, three on the bed, and three on the floor. A joint was being passed from person to person. Jordan didn't bother to introduce me. Besides, this group was too out of it to realize that anyone else had joined them anyway. A bomb could have gone off and nobody would have even noticed.

My stomach was churning, first from the thick, disgusting smoke, second from the putrid stench, and third, with not a clue as to what to do in this situation.

"C'mon over, "Jordan motioned to a spot of bare floor near where he was holding court with the others. "Try this."

Without any introduction or warning, he stuck the joint in my hand.

Frozen, I just held it in my hand for a few seconds.

'What the f--, are you trying to do, burn your fingers?" he snickered with surprise at my awkwardness. "It's not going to kill you. Take a hit. It's just pot," he almost ordered.

I continued to stand there frozen, motionless, not knowing what to do next.

"Take a fucking puff," he practically commanded, showing increased irritation in his voice. The others in the room remained in their trance, almost oblivious to the exchange between the two of us. They were going, going, gone to know what was going on.

I had heard about the spread of drugs on campus. I had made a conscious decision up until this point not to get involved. I was certainly *no saint!* It's just that I was afraid. Afraid of what pot or any other drug could do to me, afraid of getting addicted, afraid of advancing to other drugs, afraid of losing control, afraid of getting caught. *Afraid.* I was consumed with fear on all levels.

"Take a drag; it's just pot!" Jordan demanded angrily, seeming to lose his patience, practically directing me by now. I was on the verge of giving in, figuring I was probably the only undergraduate on this campus who hadn't tried this stuff. But at that point I snapped out of what must have seemed like a stupor. I threw the joint down, tore out of the room, ran out of the house, and started to walk back to campus, first at a brisk pace and then at a gallop, almost until I was out of breath.

The cool, clean, clear air smelled so good. I just wanted to walk, empty my lungs, *and* empty my head. I didn't fit in. I just didn't belong. Frankly, at that moment I just wanted to cry. This experience had made me feel like a total misfit. I was about as low as a guy could go, on so many different levels.

I managed to avoid running into Jordan for two days, although it took some fancy footwork considering we roomed on the same corridor. I wasn't ready to face him. I thought of avoiding the gym for fear of running into him, but I needed the workout to relieve the tension. Besides, he wasn't there the next day or the day after that, so I had nothing to worry about. Unlike the last time, it wouldn't be business as usual when we ultimately met.

When I did bump into him on campus on the third day, I got a cool reception, practically avoidance. It was during a library study break. He was with his minions at a table in the Ivy Room cafeteria. Strange, I thought to myself; he rarely went there. Just my luck he was there now. I made a split second decision, a wise one, to sit somewhere else and not join them. I carried my tray past his table and found an open one a few rows down. As I pulled away, I felt all those eyes on my back and thought I heard him mutter to his friends, "jerk."

It was time for some good counsel from brother Ian.

"Of course I've smoked pot," Ian answered quizzically. "Hasn't everyone around here?" I didn't answer that question. There were no secrets between us. We knew everything about each other. Well, almost everything. It had evolved into that type of friendship. Strange, I should feel embarrassed to tell him that I hadn't.

"Are you still smoking?" I probed further, also trying to get the spotlight off me.

"No," he said convincingly. I quit. I didn't have to ask him why; he volunteered the information.

"I don't trust myself," he explained. "One thing leads to another. Next thing you'll know I'll be doing heroin with Ol' Dr. Leary. Besides, a six pack gives me a better buzz."

I didn't feel comfortable pursuing this conversation any further and cut Ian off before he had time to ask me any questions. I had two decisions pending, and one was made already. This drug stuff was not for me. I kept thinking back to the sights and sounds and smells of that Collegetown room. Just the thought of it made me sick to my stomach. But I still had some unfinished business with Jordan. It would have been very easy to cut my losses. After all, he had jettisoned me, twice. Still, we had become close buddies and he was such a likable guy. If he was going down the tubes, I wanted to take one more shot at trying to save him.

"You're not the savior of the world," moaned Ian, reminding me, almost in a condescending tone

"Remember 'Plastered' in the dorms when we were freshmen?" I countered. "You used to say --after it was too late-- that we should have done something to help the poor bastard. Well, it's too late to help him. But it's not too late to help Jordan. And besides, he's our fraternity brother."

Ian didn't have a comeback for that one. He knew that I was right. We all had regrets about what we had done –or failed to do-- for that drunk on our freshman floor. Now, here was a chance as things turned out to do the right thing for Jordan.

I had made up my mind of what I was going to do, although I'd have to go it alone. Unfortunately, though, the way things turned out-- it wouldn't matter anymore.

THE FOLLOWING WEEK

#51 - Too Little, Too Late

I walked back to the fraternity house from campus that early spring afternoon. It was a beautiful day, a warm and sunny one, with the first hopeful signs that winter was finally losing its tenacious grip on central New York. The bitter chill was out of the air. The trees were bursting, about ready to bud, and there were even a few flowers already in bloom. Call it spring fever: the much-awaited season was about to break out. I was in better spirits for more reasons than one. I knew what I had to do about Jordan; I was just waiting for the right occasion to arise to do it.

As I turned the corner coming off the small side street leading from the suspension bridge connecting main campus to fraternity row, I sensed trouble right away. Two official cars, large black sedans, were irregularly parked in the fraternity driveway. In addition, there were two marked Ithaca police cars parked on the street in front of the house. Their motors were turned off, their lights weren't flashing, and their sirens weren't blaring, so I didn't make all that much of it. Not an emergency, I concluded. Still, I couldn't imagine what had happened. My first thought was that there had been some kind of break-in.

My pace and heart rate quickened as I walked down the gentle slope to the house and walked inside. It was midday and the place was usually deserted, except for Otis, the cook-du-jour, and a few of the guys who had no classes or who had decided to cut theirs. However, four of the brothers, all seniors, were seated in the living room, obviously being interrogated by the cops along with some University suits. I paused in the doorway to the living room to eavesdrop and find out what was going on. All four seemed highly agitated by this inquisition.

"We have to determine what kind of accident this was," were the first words I picked up, spoken by one of the two cops.

"Or, was this a hazing incident?" charged the University guy in a highly accusatory tone.

I stepped into the conversation and couldn't refrain from asking:

"Excuse me," I inquired and introduced myself as another one of the brothers. "What are you talking about?"

However, everyone, including the seniors assembled, totally ignored me as if I weren't there. Obviously this was serious stuff and I had interrupted them at a bad moment.

"The time of death was 3:15 A.M.," indicated the other cop.

"Or, at least that's when the body was discovered," went the first.

What body? Whose death? I cringed, desperately needing to know whom they were talking about-- but didn't dare interrupt again.

"This has nothing to do with pledging or hazing!" shouted the house president, almost in tears. "Besides, Jordan isn't… Jordan *wasn't* even a pledge. He was a full-fledged brother."

I was putting two and two together, not wanting to come up with the obvious four. Something had happened to Jordan. "Time of death" and "the body." My worst fears were confirmed seconds later.

"Then how did one of your fraternity brothers die?" demanded the two cops, almost as if in unison at a heightened decibel level.

"I told you," pleaded the president, crying uncontrollably by now. "I don't know," he repeated again and again. I didn't know whether those tears were out of terror or out of grief.

"They said he was walking by the stone bridge over the gorge in Collegetown," one of the other brothers tried to explain.

"He climbed up on the stone railing," added the president, trying to regain his composure.

"We begged him… we *pleaded* with him to come down," continued one of the other seniors, underscoring the word *plead.* "But he didn't hear us. Or, he just wouldn't listen."

"He said that he was just walking across the bridge," exclaimed the pledge master.

"He didn't seem to realize he was walking on top," sighed the president in a barely audible tone, looking down now with his head buried in his hands. "We wanted to pull him down, but we were afraid he'd topple over. We were terrified."

"Then he lost his footing," exclaimed the steward nervously. "And fell to the bottom."

"It was all over, over before we could do anything about it," concluded the president, now sobbing uncontrollably.

Jordan was dead. He had died in the wee hours of the morning, crossing one of the beautiful bridges crisscrossing campus. That stone bridge I crossed a million times leading to Collegetown. All of a sudden that bridge didn't seem so beautiful to me. It had been an instrument of death. But the bridge wasn't to blame. Jordan had jumped up on top of the stone railing. He probably had been under the influence and wasn't in control of all his faculties. Tried as they did, the other guys with him couldn't talk him down. He was in his own world. The details really didn't matter. My buddy Jordan lay dead a hundred feet below at the bottom of the gorge.

The University ruled that Jordan's fall was an accident. The fraternity was absolved of taking part in a hazing incident. It was not held responsible. No disciplinary action was to be taken against the house nor charges filed against any individual members.

Not that it really mattered. The brotherhood was in shock, no one more so than I was. We had lost one of our own. And not by the hand of the War-- at least not directly. CAT was in a state of abject mourning. Ian kind of gulped, feeling the guiltiest of all about what happened to Jordan. But I had no intention of rubbing it in with "could'ves and should'ves and I-told-you-sos." I had said we should have done something to help him. Now it was too late. If only we could turn back the clock.

The Sheridans had fought having an autopsy performed; however, it was de jure in an accidental death case. The campus was abuzz with the news. Word leaked out that drugs were deemed to be a factor in this incident and the story took a life of its own. Suddenly we were an outcast of the system; this was some mark against us. Nobody wore his CAT hat or sweatshirt for days after. I resented this "holier-than-thou" attitude on the part of some of the biggest abusers. Having the press camped at our doorstep only made things worse.

The funeral for Jordan was held in his hometown in New Jersey. I was torn for a day or two as to whether or not to attend, looking for any excuse to avoid being there: too emotional, too tired, too much work, too many tests. In the end, I decided not to go. I rationalized that it was too far away; besides, I didn't want to invade his parents' private grief as they dealt with the death of their only son. In retrospect, I should have gone. The truth was, it was still too fresh, too painful for me and I couldn't handle the prospect of being at his funeral.

Jordan's final words to me, "It's just pot," kept echoing. "Just." That's what got him in the end. I still hadn't figured out exactly where this friendship had gone awry and what we should have done differently. I *had* tried-- I tried to convince myself. What else could we have done? Again and again, I mulled over why so many classmates were going this route. Now the only thing left to do was wonder whether they buried Jordan with his baseball cap on.

LATE MAY, 1968

#52 – Aesthetically Speaking

Jordan's death numbified me, to coin a word. I was overwhelmed with several emotions. For one thing, I had lost another very close friend; for another, I started to second-guess myself whether I, personally, could have done more to prevent his tragedy; for a third, this whole new drug scene was bewildering to me. In the late 1960's, it was the forbidden fruit. Temptation, experimentation, peer pressure. As if the War was not scary enough, this added another layer of fear. I felt lost between two worlds. I also wondered whether there was a connection between the two. That one line was stuck in my thoughts: "Jordan's death was not *directly* connected to the War." But *indirectly*?

Once again, I started to question things: Were students turning to drugs to dull the pain and ease the hurt? Sort of self-medication? Or, just a way of getting back at those in authority? All of these doubts were gnawing away at me. This period, the end of my junior year, the spring of 1968, proved to be my most troubling time at college. Sadly, it should have been one of the happiest and most care-free.

But if I was struggling with these issues during the late spring of 1968, Ian's pain and suffering were far, far worse. At least I had tried to derail Jordan's course to self-destruction; Ian, on the other hand, had told me to, in effect, mind my own business. Now he was having major league regrets about being a bystander to his demise. Usually he had such a smooth veneer, but under pressure, it cracked easily, as it did again in the days following Jordan's death. Good old guilt. He was edgy, withdrawn, and short-tempered. At least he had acknowledged that his poison was a six-pack; he was a drinker, not a druggie, almost proud to say it back then. And in the days that followed, he buried his troubles at the bar.

Although the University ruled the cause of Jordan's death to be accidental, the whole matter didn't exactly help the already tarnished image of the fraternities, and proved to be another nail in the coffin of the declining Greek system. A pall hung over the house, and just about everybody couldn't wait for the semester to be over, hoping that the summer break would give us some time to at least heal, put Jordan's death behind us, if not forget about it.

Finals were fast approaching, and once again I took my mind off my troubles by studying for those exams every waking moment. It was a good form of escapism-- and, it seemed to work. After all, this was my last chance to improve my three-year average that would be "locked" should I decide to make a possible run at graduate schools. As it turned out, I would manage to finish up the semester with a 3.3 grade point average, despite one highly deflating C-.

I was devastated, to say the least, when I received that final grade for my Survey of Modern Art course. As was the Cornell practice, I had left the professor with a self-addressed postcard for him to mail back to me. This was the standard operating procedure in those days for those who didn't want their grade to be posted (identified not by name, but by Cornell I.D. number) on the department bulletin board, or have to wait until yearly transcripts were mailed home at the end of the summer. The last such vigil outside the department office came after the Geology fiasco. I don't know whether I was impatient to get my grade sooner or paranoid that someone might actually figure out my identity and ascertain that grade.

On the flipside of the postcard I wrote in block letters: "FINAL GRADE: _____." Just two days later, I got the card back. The professor had wasted no time in scoring our papers and getting his grades submitted. He had filled that line in with a big, bold **C-** without adding any other comment or greeting as other instructors were known to do. There were no such pleasantries as "Good job!" or "Have a nice summer." Just that C-. I was no handwriting expert, but it seemed obvious to me that he took great pleasure in recording that grade, as evidenced by the flourish on the minus sign.

I was absolutely devastated. To begin with, except for the Geology debacle, I had never before received such a low final grade. That C- would stand out like a sore thumb on my academic transcript and be damaging if and when I applied to graduate schools. Maybe I wasn't an art connoisseur or a Picasso-in-training, but I truly believed that I had deserved better. I went into this course for all the right reasons, knowing little or nothing about the subject, and emerged with at least a modicum of understanding. The professor, though weird to the point of being bizarre, was entertaining, and the lecture class was never boring. Viewing myself as aesthetically challenged, I could barely draw the proverbial straight line. While I still couldn't produce anything noteworthy of my own, at least now I could critique and evaluate the work of others.

The final exam grade was subjective, based on interpretation and the professor's assessment of my analysis of several pieces placed before the class. Who was to say I was right or wrong? Unlike the dreaded Geology practicum, where the rock identifications of marble or quartz were either "correct" or "incorrect," who, besides the artist, really knew what he was thinking when he created each piece?

This might as well have been a multiple-choice test, with no single answer better than any other. Furthermore, I had learned, as an English major who had written my fair share of interpretative and evaluative critiques, that all I had to do was state my case convincingly. As long as I could justify and back up my answers with solid reasons, it was my analysis that counted. Not according to *this* professor, however. There was no place for personal input.

So, I decided to make an appointment with him to find out where I had gone wrong and to exercise my right to question the grade. Professor Gleason was a tall, erect man who always seemed to be looking up-- except when he was looking *down*-- at his students. He was known for his histrionics and being overly effusive, with the tendency towards exaggerated gestures. I viewed him as more of a cartoon character than professor. His class presentation was more of a club act than a scholarly lecture.

The Fine Arts Department was housed in one of those stately buildings on the Arts and Sciences quadrangle, directly across from Goldwin Smith, the main building, and ironically located right next to the dreaded science hall. The professor's office, in turn, was relegated to a stuffy, windowless room in the basement. I found this to be rather peculiar, given his obvious seniority in the department. Location, location: A professor's place in the pecking order is often measured by such mundane things as the placement and size of his (or her) office. Yes, size counts. Where did this guy stand in the pecking order? Apparently-- very low on the totem pole.

As soon as I arrived for my appointment and Professor Gleason discovered what I had come for, he appeared to be a bit put out that anyone would dare to question his judgment. Convincing him to change his mind wasn't going to be easy. But I was armed for bear, determined to try and assured that I had a good case. The professor seemed to wince in pain as I made my presentation.

When I was done, he let out a sigh, and without comment, swiveled around in his chair. After retrieving a milk crate buried in the back of that cramped and cluttered little hole in the wall, he began sifting through a pile of papers that it contained until he produced my graded exam. I hadn't seen the test paper until that moment. Finals were not returned to the students; all you got back was the grade.

He scanned it for a few seconds with a look of disdain on his face.

"Here it is," he said in a rather disgusted tone, begrudgingly handing it over to me. He gave me a few minutes to peruse the paper while he impatiently tapped his foot and stared up and away, evidently put out by this whole waste-of-his-precious-time exercise. It didn't take me long to realize that two of the questions had received no credit whatsoever, so I decided to focus on them. After all, there was no place to go but up; partial credit was certainly better than a zero.

"Look at this one," I pointed to the very first essay, trying to bring him back to earth. "This one-- it didn't get any points at all. I wrote a page and a half about that piece. I think I answered the question," I stated with authority.

Professor Gleason put on his spectacles and with a frown indicative of his obvious annoyance and scorn, reread the first page, starting to shake his head more and more vigorously as he got to the second.

"Oh, no," he chided me, "You missed the point altogether. That's clearly not what the artist had in mind," he pronounced with even more contempt.

Missed the point altogether? Who knew what the artist could possibly have had in mind? Who's to say what a collection of cardboard toilet paper rollers... glued together in a haphazard mound... then spray-painted green and purple... and topped off by three maraschino cherries-- purported to be? I had been led to believe-- by the professor himself-- that modern art was in the eye of the beholder. Ergo I could interpret this piece of "art" to be anything I deemed it to be.

"You obviously missed the point *altogether*," he reiterated, peering down at me over his glasses, which had slid farther down his chiseled nose. He loved to underscore certain words in the most dramatic fashion.

"And what *is* the point?" I questioned in an almost mocking tone, fearing nothing further to lose anymore. After all, how low could he go?

"*Can't you tell?*" he stared at me wide-eyed with his mouth gaping open, his head slowly shaking from side to side like a metronome. Evidently he was shocked that a person could be so art-illiterate as not to see a couple that had climbed the financial and sexual (or "sex-u-al", as he pronounced the word) mountain to find true fulfillment and happiness.

"The shape... the texture... the colors... the cherries? You missed them all," he said almost in shock as he turned my paper face down. Case closed. "Next?" he said, even more matter-of-factly, obviously looking to be rid of me as quickly as possible.

But I wasn't going to be disposed of all that easily. Since I felt this was also going to be an uphill battle with little chance of success, I decided to go for broke and argue even more vigorously about the second essay. After all, I again had nothing to lose, or so I thought.

This commentary was about a painting, and I use the term charitably, consisting of about 25 or 30 large polka dots in four colors randomly spread out on a piece of newsprint. That was it. Frankly, a second grader could have produced this piece-- and I said as much in my analysis, which needless to say, had irked him. Once again, he pulled the paper from my hands and reread my answer, gasping almost in horror.

"Obviously you had absolutely no clue whatsoever about this one, either," he sneered disparagingly. He then followed with a diatribe as to how these dots in four colors represented the four phases of the artist's life struggles. Each of the four colors represents a different battle, a different conflict, a different period in his life.

"*Don't you see?*" he put the paper face down and turned to me with his head shaking in disbelief that anyone could be so clueless.

"If that's what the artist was trying to communicate, why didn't he just say so?" I answered back. "Don't make me guess." All of this was too reminiscent of my playing guessing games in those required English courses in which I had similarly suffered. It was not like me to challenge a professor. But he had pushed all the wrong buttons, and I was not yet ready to give in.

The professor bristled at my response. I remained respectful, but I wasn't going to surrender so easily. Then he clinched the deal: "Consider your grade *charity*," he said in a condescending tone, implying that maybe it should have been even lower than it was.

I was up for a fight, ready to pursue this either with him or the head of the department, but it was clearly a no-win situation, so I tendered him an anemic thank you for his time and walked out with my tail between my legs.

That was my final foray into modern art. It was a world in which I clearly didn't belong. To this day, every time I enter an art museum, Professor Gleason comes to mind. My own home is furnished and decorated in the classic style, probably subconsciously due to this ill-fated dabbling into this period. My wife once thought about buying a contemporary-style coffee table made of cork, but I uncharacteristically put my foot down. And as you can guess, that C- still stands as a monument to my supposed ignorance of this subject as well as testimony to my failure to convince the professor otherwise.

Ironically, I fared far better in the Elementary Drawing and Painting elective I subsequently took to fill up my schedule, earning a B, even though that course was more of a challenge, albeit for different reasons. In the Modern Art class, all I had to do was passively interpret; in the drawing class I had to actively produce. Fortunately, though, the professor appropriately graded each student based on his or her individual progress. For someone like me, who could barely distinguish a line from a dot, there was no place to go but up.

Our first assignment was to draw a bowl of fruit. My still life drawing of a bunch of bananas actually resembled bananas, or at least I thought so. Ian scrutinized my masterpiece for several minutes before making a guess.

"Two canaries mating?"

I thought he was kidding, so I told him to try again.

"I don't know; to me, it looks like two birds screwing," he insisted.

For our second project, we were assigned to draw a self-portrait. I was satisfied that my finished product at least looked like a human being, although nobody I showed it to thought that it even remotely resembled me.

"Otis!" guessed Ian in earnest, scratching his head, trying his hardest to figure who was the subject of the picture.

"No," I shook my head, more than a little disappointed that it wasn't obvious to him that it was a painting of me.

"Wait a minute!" He shouted. "I've got it! It's a portrait of the new cook?" he said not very convincingly.

"The new cook is 70 years old," I corrected him, this time with my frustration showing through.

"Well, it beats me," he said, about to give up. "Hey, maybe it's a picture of that tree next to the dumpster?" he tried one more time. This time I didn't even answer him.

"It's a picture of-- me," I finally had to tell him, more than a little let down.

After a pause and some more head scratching, he asked: "Then what are those two little circles? I thought those were the knots on the tree."

"I was wearing my eyeglasses," I was forced to explain.

However, the third assignment proved to be the highlight of the course. Professor Cassidy announced that it would involve "life drawing."

"What's that?" I whispered to the guy sitting next to me.

"That's a polite way to say we're going to be sketching *nekked* people," he whispered back.

"At our next class, we will have a live nude model," routinely announced. "She will pose for two 45-minute sittings."

She. That's all we had to hear. It was anything but routine to a dozen love-starved college guys. We started banging on their desks like pubescent boys at their first peep show. The professor totally ignored this outburst, probably used to this juvenile response by now. The girls just shook their heads in disgust.

"I trust nobody is going to cut class next time," he added with feigned indignation.

That was a sure bet. This was Tuesday; on Thursday at this very time, she would be posing. The class, 26 in size, was about evenly split between guys and gals. My classmates, at least half of them, were psyched; and so was I. The speculation began as soon as we moved out of the classroom into the hall.

"Blonde, brunette, or redhead?" I wondered.

"Who the hell cares?" said another. "As long as she has her clothes off."

"I wonder if she's a student," I asked.

"Probably. I hear they pay $25 an hour for a model."

Those were really big bucks in those days."

"I'll pose for that," laughed this big fat fellow who could've used a cold shower about then.

"Nobody would pay a cent to look at you," piped in a third-- and everyone else roared with laughter.

Thursday rolled around. Nobody was absent, nobody was late. This time we made sure to be on time for class. It took place in a small studio with two dozen or so battered easels arranged in two concentric semi-circles on a paint-stained wooden floor facing a small stage raised a foot or two off the floor, just to offer a better view of the subject.

"Good afternoon ladies and gentlemen," Professor Cassidy cheerfully greeted us as if this were any other day. But it wasn't *any other day*. "I trust you know why we have gathered here," he said in his usual matter-of-fact manner.

My male classmates didn't have to be told, again responding by beating their desks like bongo drums. The professor just nodded with a sigh; once again the females in the class just shook their heads in utter revulsion.

"In a few moments I will be introducing Elizabeth. You will have 45 minutes to work on your sketch." By this point, the guys in the class were practically panting.

"I think they're in heat," I heard one of the gals sitting behind me mutter under her breath.

"This is the closest they can get to getting any," whispered another.

"Why don't you bring down your friend Ian to model for us?" coyly suggested a third.

"I've seen him naked plenty of times," I said matter-of-factly. "Nothing special to look at it," I countered, which evoked a muffled giggle from the three of them.

We heard all the belittling comments from the co-ed side, but couldn't care less. Sour grapes on their part.

"They're just jealous," remarked the fat fellow.

"Let me bring in our model now," Professor Cassidy continued. At this point, a little old woman opened a door and entered from stage left. She was wearing a heavy white terry cloth robe that was at least two sizes too big for her. There was no expression on her face. She was probably thinking to herself, "Let's get on with this so I can get my $25 and get the hell outta here." On cue from the professor, she untied the belt and dropped the robe to the floor.

"What is this?" the fat fellow elbowed me in the ribs.

"This, I think, is the model," I answered him back, just as surprised.

"This is a *model*?" he asked in disbelief. "A model is supposed to be-- young, supple, firm, perky, voluptuous..."

This old woman hardly fit that description. She was small, wrinkled, sagging, and with grey thinning hair resembling a steel wool pad. The teeth, of which she had only a few far and between, were very yellowed. She *was* the model.

"I think you'll find Elizabeth very, uh, interesting to draw," the professor snickered, anticipating our surprise. In the meantime, the girls in the class were trying to contain their laughter. They had gotten one over on us this time.

EARLY JUNE, 1968

#53 – On Deck

My junior year was almost over. About a year from now, I would be a college graduate. A very scary thought for me. One thing was for certain: I had no intention of wasting the summer of 1968. There would be no typing, filing, or running errands-- no matter how much those temporary agencies were willing to pay for my services. Even the enticement of a free lunch couldn't lure me. This was it, my last chance to test the waters before jumping into the job pool-- and my toes weren't even wet. In retrospect, I should have spent the past two summers as an apprentice or intern to help me decide what I wanted to do with the next 40 years of my life. I was stepping into the on-deck circle of the world of work, and I wasn't even holding a bat. It was a scary proposition.

I finally stopped kicking myself about the last two summers; they were past tense. Despite my parents' protestations, I had been too tempted by the prospect of pocketing extra spending money to see the bigger picture. But I sure as hell wasn't going to make the same mistake this summer. I would be graduating from Cornell with a degree in English, which was not one of the most practical majors, second only to Philosophy in its lack of utilitarianism. I continued to see the same three options open to me: journalism… teaching… television. But which one? I wasn't one iota closer to a decision.

My father underscored the importance of this choice:

"There are 24 hours in a day," he used to say. "You spent about eight of them sleeping. That leaves sixteen. Of those sixteen, at least eight are spent on the job. Not to mention coming and going, bringing work home, and socializing with your colleagues. More than half of your life revolves around your career. Make this decision *very* carefully," he cautioned me. This was advice I was going to heed. And then there was the old adage, "If you love your job, you'll never work a day in your life."

So where *did* my passion lie? I loved kids and I loved to write. Hey, maybe I could teach kids to write? But then what about television? Yeah, I loved to *watch* it. But television as a *career*?

WINTER, 1959

#54 – Crunch Time: Making That Decision

"Minnesota Mining and Manufacturing proudly presents - Tic Tac Dough! And now, here is the star of Tic Tac Dough--Jack Barry!"

That's how the staff announcer introduced my favorite television program at the top of the hour. A hardened game show addict even as a kid, I had seen the program on television dozens of times. We're talking about the mid to late 1950's well before VCRs and DVRs were ever heard of.

One of the fringe benefits of being sick and getting to stay home from school was remaining glued to the tube and watching daytime television from sun-up to sun-down, including a full slate of game shows during an era when that genre predominated. As soon as my parents were out the door and on their way to work, I made myself cozy and comfortable on the couch in the living room, propping myself up on two pillows with my quilt. Sore throat… fever… maybe even strep. I was deemed too sick to go to school, but certainly *never* too ill to watch television.

Let the games begin! I started at 9:00 A.M. and went through the whole day until late in the afternoon when Kate Smith came on and sang, breaking the string. *Tic Tac Dough, Treasure Hunt, The*

Price Is Right, To Tell the Truth, Truth or Consequences, Concentration, Name That Tune, Let's Make a Deal, Match Game, Play Your Hunch--even *Queen for a Day* was part of my repertoire.

I was hooked: game show addict, just eleven years old. I count identify every program, sponsor, emcee, announcer, and even the models. I constructed my own Game Show Network, decades before there was one on cable. I remember being at a loss from 1:30 to 3:00 P.M., experiencing strange withdrawal symptoms when there was nothing on except meaningless (to me, anyway) soap operas on the big three networks. For ninety minutes, I had to suffer through cartoon frolics on the local stations. But by 3:00 P.M., I was back in business. Some people are hooked on the soaps; my penchant was-- and still is-- the game show.

Many of these were broadcast on the NBC network and produced at the NBC studios at Rockefeller Center in New York City. I relentlessly badgered my parents to send away to NBC for tickets so that I could sit in the audience at one of these broadcasts. There was no such thing as videotaping then; everything was "live." But alas, I learned that I was not old enough to be admitted. However, as soon as I crossed over that age boundary (not a day later), I had them write away for tickets.

There was a long waiting list, I was told, so I would have to be patient. Every day as soon as I arrived home from school, I checked the mail. At last the day came; there was an envelope with the colorful NBC peacock logo in the return address corner. I ripped it open, practically destroying the contents in the process. Two tickets to *Tic Tac Dough*! I started to count the days. I still remember the subway ride from Brooklyn to Manhattan and the trip to Rockefeller Center from where NBC broadcasts.

Ticket holders queued up in the lobby more than an hour before show time. "Hurry up, hurry up," I pushed my father as we came out of the subway turnstile, up the steps, and onto street level, still a block or two away from our destination. Hurry up-- and wait. People had gotten there even earlier than we had. The line, which had already formed in the building's shiny and sparkling concourse, seemed endless, snaking around the entire ground level. After all this anticipation, was it possible that we were not going to get in? I hadn't been prepared for that possible huge disappointment. These weren't tickets for reserved seats at a Broadway show.

The first floor at Rockefeller Center was lined with elegant boutiques and fancy specialty shops, so there was plenty to look at while we waited. To kill time, I ogled every passerby, hoping to catch a glimpse of some celebrity, but no such luck. At last the NBC pages pulled back the ropes, counted us out like sheep, herded us into huge elevators, brought us upstairs, and escorted us down a few steps into the taping studio.

So this was it. I still remember my first impressions. To begin with, there was the relief that we had made it inside. Second, and to my surprise, was the realization that the set of the show was so small. TV exaggerates space. The stage looks so big at home; but how much room do a game board, emcee and two contestants actually take up? Third, from the steeply pitched audience section, I could see up and over the game board and set and was amazed at the frenzied activity going on behind the scenes. Lights were being adjusted, microphones were being hung, the game board was being put into place, props for the commercials were being set up on the side, the doors through which contestants entered were being opened and closed, and the contestants themselves were on the sidelines being touched-up by make-up artists.

All sorts of technical people, easily identifiable by the headsets they wore, were frantically racing around, obviously trying to make the deadline of air time. Again, this was "live" television; there was no videotape safety net to fall back on back then. At the top of the hour, the show was on the air, ready or not. That "live" element added even more excitement to the proceedings.

There looked to be a million lights hanging above us, a million cable wires below us. Actually, the view of the stage itself was eclipsed by several huge cameras in front of us. The studio audience could also watch the program on enormous monitors suspended from the ceiling, that were placed between large "Applause!" signs that lit up at the appropriate times. What you see in person at the television studio is very different from what you watch at home. It was then and there that I decided that this fast-paced world was for me; I wanted to get into some aspect of television production. I think my parents were hoping that the trip to NBC would get the TV bug out of my system for once and for all; instead, if anything, it made it far worse. From acute... to chronic!

No, going to see the show didn't cure my addiction. Ever since that day when I went to see *Tic Tac Dough* "live!" I thought I knew the career path I wanted to follow. I wasn't so interested in what went on-- *on* the set-- as I was intrigued with all the workings *behind* the scenes and the illusions that were created, culminating with what the viewer got to see on that tiny screen at home.

"Wanting" and actually "doing" are two different things. Throughout my Cornell college career I tried my hand at some freelance writing, submitting everything from news feature pieces to game show ideas. These submissions were soundly rejected, returned unopened with a terse statement that unsolicited material was not considered, or just discarded without a response altogether.

Although Cornell had its own radio station, I never got involved, which in retrospect was a huge mistake on my part. I did, however, "com-pet" (a Cornell term) for the *Cornell Daily Sun* and worked my way up to movie reviewer. It was a novelty at first, seeing my byline once a week and receiving feedback about my reviews from fellow students and even my professors; but scribbling notes in a murky, mildewed, pitch-black theatre and then having to race back to the *Sun* office to prepare a full review by the 1:00 A.M. deadline was far from glamorous and detracted from the fun of movie-going. But that was my dues-paying, so to speak, and I did it dutifully, aware that this lack of amenities came with the newspaper territory.

As I said, going to see *Tic Tac Dough* didn't cure my addiction to television and games shows, in particular. Ever since that day when we went to see the program broadcast *live* at the NBC studios, I knew what I wanted to do with my life. Or, so I thought.

LATE JUNE, 1968

#55 – At Last, a Break

So I persevered with my fledgling, albeit unsuccessful attempts at freelance writing, still wavering between teaching and television as possible career paths, with journalism now falling to a distant third. Other people collected coins or stamps; I collected rejection letters. And with graduation starting to come into sight, it was time to focus not only on freelancing, but also on a "real" job in television.

My objective, then, was to get a summer internship at one of the networks or local television stations with the hope of catapulting it into a full-time job after Cornell. Wishful thinking.

There were no word processors in those days; as a matter of fact, I was considered lucky to have an electric typewriter, given to me as a graduation gift after high school, something that was the envy of the majority of my classmates who still two-fingered it on the old, slow manual models. Methodically and mechanically, I pounded out letter after letter after letter of application to each of the three networks, all of their local affiliates in the greater metropolitan area, every one of the local independent stations serving New York City, as well as a number of large production companies that supplied programs to them. This was all before the proliferation of cable stations and the formation of the newer networks, so the number of employment possibilities was far more limited than it is today. I don't know how good a writer I was, but I was determined, and with all that practice, soon became one of the fastest student typists on campus.

There were two paths to follow if I was indeed serious about seeking a career in the television industry. The first was to try to get a job at any network or station in New York. Any job, performing any function, no matter how menial-- and then prove myself to be indispensable. Salary? Responsibilities? Inconsequential. "Just get your foot in the door," I told myself. Be low man on the totem pole and then work your way up. Prove that they "can't go on without you"; that would become my mantra. For example, NBC bragged how many of its big-name stars had gotten their start as pages or tour guides. Sounded good; if it worked for them, maybe it'd work for me.

The second method of entrée was to get out of the Big Apple and head for a local station in Anytown, USA. My sights were set on the proverbial Podunk. Learn the business, become a jack-of-all trades, rise quickly through the ranks, and then (hopefully) make a lateral move at a much higher level to New York or another big city. Write the news, type the news, report the news-- and then clean the control room and studio at the end of the day. After four years in upstate New York, itching to get back to the Big City, and smitten just a bit by the glamor bug, I opted to search for an internship via the first route.

Apparently, though, I wasn't the only one with such grandiose ideas; there were many others who were drawn to a career in television, or "communications," as it was starting to be called. Letter after letter was soon after followed with rejection after rejection. My collection was growing. A few were personalized; most were cold, dispassionate form letters. But they all delivered basically the same message: "Sorry-- nothing available. Not now, not in the foreseeable future. Good luck in your future endeavors." As if to say,

"What 'future endeavors'? Stop wasting your time." Either those companies did not offer summer internships to begin with, or those positions had long-since been filled.

The implication was that my "endeavors" were not going to be in the television industry. My plans for a summer internship were going bust; I was scoring goose eggs. I rationalized that I might have been more successful if I had started applying much earlier in the year. The typing pool was looking better and better; at least it was a sure thing-- and maybe I could still find a firm that offered that free lunch.

As the rejection letters continued to pile up, I became resigned to the fact that the prospects for a summer internship were dimming, and, worse, that it would be practically hopeless to break into television after graduation. In effect, the career decision had been made for me by default: I would go for the teaching. I had given TV the old college try. Not so terrible, I tried to convince myself, but I had to admit, I was extremely disappointed, at least at that moment.

It was time to dust off my resume for the temporary agencies and bone up on my typing. Nevertheless, each day I leafed through a stack of mostly junk mail, eyeing the return address in the upper-lefthand corner. But the string of rejection letters had just about petered out. As I said, some companies didn't even have the courtesy to respond.

"Call it quits, buddy," Ian advised me. If anyone knew, he did, with his dad in the business. For a while, I was hoping that just maybe *he* could open some doors for me. But Ian hardly spoke to him at all, and certainly was in no position to ask him to help me out. I know he would have if he could have.

"Jobs go to those on the inside, or those with connections," he explained. Well, I could play neither card and was ready to throw in my hand.

"So how does one break the cycle and get some experience... if you have no experience?" I pushed him further. He just shrugged his shoulders.

"Give up," continued to be his best advice, with a slap on my back as he walked away, seeming to lose patience with my tunnel vision. And that was precisely what I was about to do.

It was then that my big break came from one of the big networks during finals week and just before heading back home. The letter came in an envelope that looked no different from all the others that contained cold, dispassionate rejection slips. As a matter of fact, I didn't even bother to open it up right away. Bad news could wait, I figured. When I got up to my room, I casually opened the envelope, resigned to the seemingly inevitable.

But this letter was different. No internship offer, not yet, anyway:

> *"Kindly call the news director at the Broadcast Center at your earliest convenience."*

What was this all about? Suddenly there was a glimmer of hope; after all, I reasoned, why would they have me call to get the bad news. Still, having been repeatedly disappointed, I didn't want to jack up my hopes.

I nervously dialed that number in New York. A switchboard operator connected me to the extension I was told to call. The minute or so on hold seemed a lot, lot longer. Finally my contact got on the line. After very few pleasantries, he cut to the chase.

"The producers are piecing together a staff for a new series, a cross between a documentary and magazine show. No surprise: Most of the jobs are going to those who have already paid their dues in lower-level positions and are coming up the ranks at the network," he explained.

"OK, OK... get on with it," I said to myself. So why is he telling me all this? Where did I fit in? It was starting to sound like rejection-via-telephone rather than form letter. Get to the point already.

"Given all that is going on in the late 1960's, the producers don't want *everyone* from the inside. With all that was going on on the *outside*-- particularly the college campuses-- they are scouting for someone who had that perspective. That's where *you* fit in."

Bingo! Bullseye! For once, I was in the right place at the right time. I was offered a summer internship as a production assistant on the staff being assembled in preparation for a fall debut.

Euphoria! I didn't know exactly what I was going to be doing. Frankly, I really didn't care. I would have done almost anything for that first break. Now I was going to be working in network news. I would work my tail off, prove to the higher-ups that they couldn't function without me, and hopefully have a job waiting ten months later after graduation. Now, *finally*, I had my future all planned out.

Easy come, easy go. Unfortunately, things didn't work out the way I had planned. My elation was short-lived. During finals week, I was flying high; then, abruptly, I had my wings clipped and my bubble burst. With my bags figuratively packed and my sights set on New York and the network newsroom, I received a telephone message to call that news director guy again. I had that sixth sense that something was wrong-- and was I ever right. The bosses had decided to shelve the project for now, leaving me out in the cold. Hired and fired even before I started! I rationalized that it had all been too good to be true.

Ian tried to console me. "That's the nature of the TV business. Here today, gone tomorrow. Ride the wave while you're on one. You don't know how long it will last. Now just put yourself in the shoes of those people at the network who were counting on these jobs. Imagine how they must feel."

He meant well, but his "misery loves company" lecture just didn't do it for me. Yet again I dug through my dresser drawer to find the telephone numbers of those temporary employment agencies and started to dust off the keys on my typewriter. Well, at least one byproduct of the abortive internship search was that my typing speed was way up; that alone would earn me a few more cents per hour.

But then followed a second break. Although the network had absolutely no commitment to me since I hadn't clocked even a minute of work and could have cut me loose then and there, I was offered something else, as a sign of good faith and just to get my foot in the door.

Something else? In the same vein? Not exactly. I would be the cue card boy for *Piggily Wiggily*, one of the children's shows produced at the network's broadcast center. Appreciative as I was for not being axed altogether, nevertheless this was not exactly how I had envisioned putting my Ivy League education to good use, not to mention gaining a valuable summer experience. I had said that I would be willing to do almost anything to break into television. But this was pushing the envelope. *Almost* anything.

Ironically, I had been a huge fan of Piggily Wiggily himself (itself?) when I was a kid. But holding up cue cards for this man-child dressed in a porcine costume was more than I could stomach. Maybe typing, filing, making coffee, running errands, and doing other menial tasks weren't all that bad after all. Especially if there was that free lunch.

How did you spend your summer vacation? I could just imagine my buddies' exchanging war stories come next September.

"I was a volunteer at a local children's hospital."

"I interned in investment banking."

"I shadowed the assistant district attorney."

Uncomfortable pause.

"I held up cue cards for Piggily Wiggily."

"Uh, weren't you the guy I seemed to recall saying he would be willing to do almost *anything* to break into television?" Ian was quick to remind me.

"I know what I said," I answered him back. "*Almost* anything. But this--?" I sheepishly replied. Ian was right. How low was I willing to go? I snapped up the job.

I profusely thanked my contact guy, but I couldn't help but gingerly asking: Wasn't there something else I could do? *Anything* else? I kept reminding myself that I was willing to do anything to break into the industry. Well, this was the yeoman test. Not that I wanted to appear ungrateful or look a gift horse in the mouth, but--. To this day, I haven't forgotten that there was someone out there who was willing to stick his neck out and give a newcomer a chance.

"What does this guy owe me, anyway?" I asked Ian wondering, as if he knew anything more.

"Maybe he's hot for your bod," Ian laughed raucously.

"Shut up!" I joshed back.

"I told you to quit working out so much," he went on. "Look what you've become."

"Yeah. Still a tall, scrawny kid who can barely bench 50 pounds," I said.

All I could do was laugh at this point. But I *did* wonder why this guy was going the extra mile for me. Nevertheless, in the process of letting him know how appreciative I was, I slipped in the suggestion to keep me in mind "just in case" *anything else* opened up even remotely connected to the News Division. *Anything* else.

And something else did. To my amazement, Personnel, a.k.a. "Human Resources," came up with yet another alternative: desk assistant back in network news. This was an entry-level level position paying $80 per week (before taxes and various other deductions). But a paid internship: almost unheard of.

"I'll take it!" I declared, not missing a beat. I couldn't think of better way to spend the summer. After all, how many second chances would I get? Even a cat has only nine lives.

I subsequently found out why this guy was sticking out his neck for me. He had walked in my shoes some ten years earlier, following his passion. As a matter of fact, once upon a time he had been on the verge of throwing in the towel and ditching his dream. But one of the head honchos at the network had gone to bat for him. The rest was history. He vowed then and there to do the same thing for the next guy in line-- and the next guy just happened to me. (And, by the way, he, too, was a Cornellian.)

I vowed then and there that in the future, I would do the very same thing for some young kid waiting for a break. And I never did forget. It's been a guiding principle for me for my entire life.

SUMMER, 1968

#56 – The Pot Boils Over

As I started my summer internship in the news business, I was in the enviable position of observing much of what was happening on the outside-- from the inside. And it was a volatile two months.

The network studios, located in New York City's midtown, reminded me of the Emerald City in The Wizard of Oz. The building was like a fortress and security was as tight as a drum. But once I made my way inside that armory, I discovered an entire city, complete with a full commissary, a few stores, a post office, and even a barber shop. Sound stages to the left, smaller production studios to the right, offices and engineering facilities straight ahead.

Wherever I was taken on my orientation tour, I saw familiar faces from television. I must admit, I was a bit star struck at first and tried not to gape. But the glamor and glitz soon wore off as I discovered that they were people who put on their pants one leg at a time, just the way I did, and most (although not all) were down-to-earth regular-type guys (and gals) who related equally well to everyone, from their bosses on high to us lowly desk assistants at the bottom of the food chain.

The final stop on the circuit tour was my home base, the network newsroom, an expansive space bustling with activity. It was divided by an imaginary line between television and radio. At the long, rectangular desk sat two editors, one for radio and one for television, side by side. They were the big bosses-- and I reported to them.

My first shift was at the radio desk, serving as "slave" for whichever reporter or correspondent was on the air for his (in those days they were almost all male) tour of duty. My "professional" duties included picking up and rolling the wire copy (from the Associated Press, United Press International, and Reuters), running errands through the building, making appointments, answering all in-coming telephone calls to the news desk, and most important of all, doing seemingly endless coffee runs between the newsroom and the commissary. On occasion, I was even sent out of the building to pick up dry cleaning. In short, I was the "gopher" (*go* for this, *go* for that, etc.)

I was relieved that I had already compiled about 90 college credits for such demanding, intellectually challenging responsibilities. But if this was how I would earn my stripes and break into the business, so be it. And although the job itself was far from glamorous, it was in a glamorous setting, in a glamorous part of town. I was precisely where I wanted to be. This time, things had worked out the way I had hoped.

It was explained to me that I would work five days a week. But I was quickly alerted that those five days were not necessarily Monday through Friday. As a matter of fact, given my lowly status on the totem pole as an intern, they would be anything but. The broadcast news division is open for business 24/7 and I was the newest hire. I assumed this to mean that I would have to work weekends; I assumed correctly: Tuesdays and Wednesdays would be my days off. So much for spending time with my friends on Saturday nights. Furthermore, I was alerted to the fact that I could be assigned to any one of three shifts: 9:00 A.M. to 5:00 P.M., 5:00 P.M. to 1:00 A.M., or the dreaded (unless you're an owl) overnight, 1:00 A.M. to 9:00 A.M. I was forewarned of all of these ground rules. “Fine, fine,” I said to myself; I was precisely where I wanted to be. I’d tap dance on the editor’s desk if the big boss told me to do so.

The schedule for the desk assistants was posted two weeks in advance on a small bulletin board in the back of the newsroom. If I needed to change my schedule, I had to work out a trade with a fellow desk assistant. Otherwise, the schedule was in stone: “No exceptions,” I was told repeatedly and forcefully during my orientation. I was also advised that it was a cardinal sin to arrive even a minute late, since the “d.a.” going off duty couldn’t leave until his replacement had arrived-- which meant paying the dreaded overtime. But none of this stuff mattered one bit; I was *in*. Nor did the unorthodox scheduling bother me in the least. This was the television business and what I had been aspiring to. I had prepared myself for starting at the bottom, whatever it took. Of course, I couldn’t get much lower than this.

While I rarely got a day tour, I did manage to usually avoid the excruciatingly painful and dull overnight, except when I had to barter with another d.a. for a Saturday night off to attend a friend’s wedding. I usually pulled the evening shift (5:00 P.M. to 1:00 A.M); this turned out to be perfect for me, given the fact that this fast-paced time slot was where it was happening-- with all of the preparations for the nightly network news broadcast taking place on the TV side.

The overnight shift did, however, have some perks. My favorite task was compiling the “who’s where”-- listing all the network correspondents stationed all over the globe and then listing their contact information across six continents. In those days, the foreign bureaus were much larger and this was a yeoman task, which I actually enjoyed. London, Rome, Paris, Madrid, Berlin Warsaw, Calcutta, Cairo, Jerusalem, Istanbul, Saigon, Sydney-- vicariously I traveled around the world performing this job.

The overnight also afforded me an opportunity very few people have: to walk on the moon. Well, not exactly, but *sort of.* July, 1969 is also remembered for the moon landing and for its coverage. A replica of the moon had been built on the very top floor. Several reports were delivered from that spot. I couldn't resist! In the middle of the night, I slipped out of the newsroom and made my way up to the model used for animation. If only there were cell phone cameras in those days… I would have had some pictures to show my grandchildren in the future!

That summer would be one to remember for more reasons than those mentioned above. Not only did I get a front row seat to the news business, but I also made terrific contacts. But just as significant was the fact that it was a particularly newsworthy one, capped off by the highly volatile Democratic National Convention in Chicago. At the same time, the anti-war movement was moving full speed ahead and it found a ready stage at that convention. There was as much drama taking place on the streets outside as well as inside the convention hall itself. Demonstrations were breaking out all over the country and the national debate as to our involvement in Vietnam was coming to a boil. All this was happening while our involvement was becoming deeper and deeper, with more and more troops being sent in, more and more money being pumped in.

With a presidential election coming up in November, there were so many political developments that you needed a scorecard to keep track of the players, who were changing on a daily basis. Just maybe, reasoned the doves, with do-or-die Johnson out of the White House, some closure could be brought to the war. On the flipside were the hawks, who were as militant as ever about remaining in Vietnam, finishing what we had started, and adamant about America's not losing a war

With LBJ's surprise announcement "I shall not seek and will not accept a second term," it became a free-for-all; the field suddenly became wide open and there was some hope, particularly among the growing student resistance, that the end of the War just might be in sight. Draft card burnings were ritually performed on college campuses, accompanied with the chant, "Hell no, we won't go."

JFK's brother Robert, peace candidate Eugene McCarthy, and Hubert Humphrey were the leading contenders vying for the Democratic nod. What a horse race it was turning out to be. Without a doubt, the War was the number one campaign issue and polarizing the country more and more.

However, the presidential election was but one major story. The year 1968 was to see not one, but two assassinations. In a speech a day before he was gunned down, Dr. Martin Luther King, Junior proclaimed, "I see the Promised Land; I may not get there with you…" Sadly, he was prophetically right, another victim of violence, as I mentioned earlier.

And then on live television, hard to believe, a second Kennedy brother was gunned down, this time during the heated June primary elections. The reaction shots of young campaigners, hearing the news "Robert Kennedy has been shot" in both the Kennedy and McCarthy headquarters, told the grim story.

The pot boiled over at the Democratic Convention in Chicago. Inside, the party was bitterly divided, as Senator Hubert Humphrey emerged victorious; Edmund Muskie was chosen as his running mate. Outside the convention, thousands upon thousands of anti-protesters were assembled. However, the helmeted National Guard and Chicago police were ready for them. On cue, the riot began as all hell broke loose. The news footage of that moment in time-- a bitterly divided Democratic Party inside… and the protesters and police polarized outside-- preserved an ugly moment in our nation's history.

All of this happening at such a rapid pace-- coupled with having the opportunity to observe these events unfold from a seat inside the network newsroom-- I couldn't have possibly asked for more.

By the end of the summer of 1968, a severe case of senioritis was prematurely overtaking me. Although I loved Cornell and was eagerly anticipating my senior year, I viewed myself as a lame duck. What an experience this had been-- not only observing one event after another, but also seeing how they were reported to the American people.

Alas, by August it came to an end. Having to turn in my network identification card and resuming "civilian status" was a crushing experience. To this day, I remember the empty feeling I had leaving the building for the last time. That internship had exceeded my expectations and I longed to going back to the network full-time the minute I graduated. Instead of eliminating television as a career possibility, this experience had done precisely the opposite-- sharpened that interest and made the yearning even stronger.

Of course, I was *assuming* there would be a job-- and that was a rather huge assumption. But now there was a significant difference: At least I was working from *within*. The bosses had seemed very pleased with me; and why shouldn't they have been? I was always on time… I rolled the news copy tightly…. I answered the telephone with authority… and I delivered piping hot coffee. What keen professional skills I had acquired! Above all, I had observed newsmakers up-close and personal. What a way to have spent the summer. The big cheeses at the network told me to get back in touch with them in the early spring. There could be no guarantees, they cautioned me, but at least I had acquired what I had sought: my "in."

Now my sights were set much farther than Ithaca, NY. I began wishing away the year ahead so that I could come back to New York and begin my career in television. I had been given a break, and I was not going to screw things up. Little did I know that this whole process was going to be accelerated in a way that I would never have imagined.

PART IV

Senior Year

SEPTEMBER, 1968

#57 - Big Men On Campus

Seniors. Now the big men on campus, we made our plans for the year ahead, vowing not to let classes or course work get in our way *too* much. Of course, I needed a powerful antidote for that severe case of senioritis that was afflicting me. I had my work cut out for me with dual English and Education majors and student teaching on the horizon. Yes, I *still* wanted to keep Education open as an option; for some reason, I couldn't seem to let go of it. It was my safety net, even though I now had made some inroads, albeit baby steps, into the television industry. So this year was not going to be a breeze. Nevertheless, I had every intention of making it as memorable as possible. And, that it would certainly turn out to be, but in ways totally unexpected.

Still no contact with Kip; I had to assume the worse. Brant stayed in close touch; no progress, though, in his college pursuits. He always ended up back at square one. Dwayne? Sadly, for me, anyway, I had little or no contact with him. He was increasingly preoccupied with political action.

The issue of living arrangements had been of paramount importance and a subject for discussion right through the previous spring. One thing was certain, though. I wasn't spending a third year living at CAT. I still loved the fraternity, but residing there for two years was more than enough. I had enjoyed the rank and privileges that went with being an upperclassman dorming there. But by the end of the junior year, I had outgrown some of the shenanigans that were part 'n parcel of fraternity living. CAT had served me well, very well, but it was time to move on. After one year in Humboldt Hall and two at the house, I wanted to experience independent living off campus. Ian was of the same mind, and as the school year had winded down, he had recruited two other brothers to join us in an apartment search.

We had put the brakes on that hunt following the tragedy of Jordan's death. It would take some time to recover from that blow. Furthermore, I was mildly reluctant to room with Ian, after all this time *still* not 100% recovered from the Holly betrayal. Yeah, friends, but--? Maybe I still needed some distance. However, since *almost* all was forgiven by now, and since the other two guys he had rustled up to go in on the deal were so easy-going, I caved and agreed to join them.

Despite all our talk, we had waited much too long. The better apartments had long since been scooped up. Once again, as it had been the previous year, procrastination was our undoing. Apartment-hunting had taken place much earlier. Nevertheless our search was finally on; we had to come up with something.

I could tell that Ian and the other two were becoming increasingly exasperated with me. They did the groundwork; I just made excuses and found fault with everything they came up with, apprehensive about leaving the security of the fraternity house womb:

"It's too far from campus."

"There aren't enough bedroom."

"The bedrooms are too small."

"The bathrooms smell."

"The kitchen looks like early Flintstones."

"The toilet bowl is cracked."

"Ralph and Alice Kramden must have lived here."

"Will the bugs help pay the rent?"

"There's no parking."

"The place hasn't seen a mop and a broom since it's been built."

"The super is an s.o.b."

I think the three of them were weary of hearing my excuses and about to give up on me, ready to recruit a different fourth.

"Look, brother, you're not *buying* a place. It's just somewhere to hang your hat for ten months," quipped a highly exasperated Ian.

"No," I reassured him. "I want to move out of the house. I really do. I just haven't liked anything you've shown me."

Two days later, Ian returned with an ultimatum.

"We're going to show you one more place. If you don't like this one, then you're going to be stuck in CAT until you go on Social Security."

I hopped into his firetruck red Corvette, still skeptical that he had found anything markedly different. What was so special about this one, I wondered to myself, still looking for an escape route and any reason to back out.

"Where are you taking me?" I asked quizzically. I had expected yet another trip to Collegetown, the site of most of the student apartments. Instead, Ian turned left up fraternity row and then hung another left two blocks down.

"Why are we going to the Heights?" I questioned again, more than a little confused. We had turned into the Cayuga Heights section, the "Beverly Hills" of Ithaca, home to many of the professors.

Ian didn't answer, but instead motioned me with a signal of his right hand to be patient. He was driving a bit faster than he should have been on those winding roads; I could see he was eager to get to our destination. There was no further talk; I used the ten-minute drive to gaze at the beautiful colonial homes set back from the road on spacious and lushly landscaped grounds, many elevated enough to have a panoramic view of the lake and valley below. Where *was* he taking me?

At last we turned off North Triphammer Road, one of the main arteries that crisscrossed Cayuga Heights, and onto Colonial Oaks

Drive, and finally into one of the driveways on the gently sloping street. One home was more beautiful and elegantly manicured than the next.

"What are we doing here?" I asked him, even more surprised than before. "Are we were going to meet the real estate agent at his house?" I reasoned. He didn't answer me, just smiled, and motioned me to follow him, which I did.

"This, is Professor Ford's new home," he indicated with a sweep of his outstretched arm.

"So what the hell are we doing here?" I repeated my question, still perplexed as I kept in step, tailgating him up the gravel double driveway toward a house set way back from the road. There was no apartment here.

"Ford had the place built, planning to move in for the upcoming year. Then he decided to extend his leave of absence at the last minute. I think he's living in Italy, shacking up with some chick half his age. In the meantime, the real estate agent was told to sublet it for another ten months. Take a look for yourself."

This was the kind of place I'd aspire to-- someday in the distant future. Talk about turning the clock ahead. The four-bedroom colonial was brand-spanking new and had that new house smell of varnish. We could be residing in it before its rightful owner. There was a separate room for everything: laundry room, family room, library, even a home office. Now, strangely, I could be living in grand style, even before graduating. Quite a motivator to work hard and go for the gold after Cornell. Ian gave me the cook's tour, room by room.

"Man, if you find something wrong with this place, then you're doomed to live in the fraternity house for the rest of your existence."

He was right. I'd have the classiest digs of any student on campus. The rent was a bit steep, but not totally unreasonable, and certainly not a deal breaker.

"It's a go!" I nodded with a smile.

The only obstacle was the real estate agent; he was very reluctant to rent to four college guys.

"I don't know about this," he kept muttering over and over again, while shaking his head. It wasn't looking good.

But Ian, always the actor, knew this guy's Achilles heel and played him.

"It's kinda late to be renting, dontcha think? Most students have apartments by now," Ian prodded. "This place isn't exactly on a student's budget. You could end up getting stuck with its being empty for the whole year." Fat chance of that happening, I thought to myself.

Still, the agent kept stroking his chin deep in thought. It *still* didn't look very promising for us. But after mega assurances-- and mega bucks supplied by our parents put down as a security deposit-- the contract was signed.

With four bedrooms, each of us got our own space. We drew lots; I got the second smallest, but it was more than ample in size. Frankly, it could have been a closet. I didn't care because it was mine alone, reminiscent of how I felt at the beginning of sophomore year. The four of us got along great, not that it mattered one iota, given the fact that the four of us were rarely there at the same time. As a matter of fact, it was rare when more than two of us were in the house together. By senior year, with social commitments, classes, social commitments, lab and libe time, social commitments, campus activities, social commitments, part-time jobs, social commitments, etc. etc., we were going more than we were coming.

The house had a complete brick kitchen, but it might as well have been mothballed, with most of us taking our meals either on-campus, off-campus, or occasionally at the fraternity house. It was just too inconvenient to come all the way back to the Heights just to eat. That was the single drawback: It was a good fifteen-minute drive to campus. But it was well worth it; at least it was a fancy place to hang our hats and bring out dates.

September 1968: What an auspicious start to senior year. There was no place to go-- but down from here.

OCTOBER, 1968

#58 – Another Option

While I had taken a giant step forward toward a career in television thanks to my summer internship, I *still* hadn't ruled out teaching as a career. The classroom continued to be a draw. And I kept reminding myself that with a relatively "safe" draft lottery number, I had the luxury of deciding for myself what was really best for me. "Follow your passion," my parents kept advising me." But I had better decide soon: I was approaching the finish line. Graduation was now months away and I had to make a commitment one way or the other long before that.

Both my mother and father were high school teachers-- and the obvious question was whether I would follow in their footsteps. They were both career educators who put their heart and soul into the classroom. By the time they had retired, my father accrued almost 47 years of service, my mother almost 30. I observed first-hand that contrary to the public's perception --and misconception-- a teacher's workday did not end at 3:00 P.M. or on Friday afternoon. That's when they first started grading papers, planning for the next day's lessons, and doing a slew of clerical tasks. A comedian changes his act every few months; a teacher has to write a new "act" every day. And, usually there are several different "acts" to prepare.

But they always appeared to love what they were doing, probably because they felt that they were making a difference. They were truly consummate professionals and even as a little boy I could see how seriously they took their jobs.

So, education was in my DNA and the idea of entering teaching kept crossing my mind. I think that my father, who survived the Great Depression, would have been delighted to see me in a civil service job.

"The pay might not be great," he reasoned, "But at least there is some sense of security. And besides, it is very rewarding." My mother, also a committed professional, on the other hand, while not outwardly opposed to my teaching, was more of a dreamer; she encouraged me to follow my heart into journalism, communications, or some other writing career. This was one decision in which they did *not* stand united. I wish that they had; it would have made mine all the easier.

As I've noted, some of my Cornell classmates were considering teaching as a career, at least for the time being, but for less altruistic reasons. It could be a legal escape route from the draft. I can't say I blamed them-- and probably would have done precisely the same thing had I been in their position. Hence, as I mentioned earlier, a whole generation of young men who never would have thought of teaching as a livelihood, if had not been the fear of being drafted hanging over their heads, was suddenly lining up for Education courses as a means of avoiding Vietnam. Enrollment swelled in those classes.

Immediately following my television internship this past summer, I had come close to jettisoning Education as a minor. My mind was pretty well made up. But with no guarantee of a job and the clouds of war still hanging over us, I figured I had nothing to lose by going for it. In short, a safety net-- an insurance policy.

English majors at Cornell had a unique opportunity to pursue a dual concentration, with just enough Education credits to get their teaching certification. Thanks to some Advanced Placement credits from high school and getting my requirements out of the way, I would be entering my senior year with quite a few elective credits open to me. The obvious path, then, was to go for the teaching certificate, not because I *had* to, but because I *wanted* to and had the luxury of doing so, to keep that option open at least for a while longer. In short, *why not?* A good use of my elective credits, I reasoned.

The basic Education courses had been palatable; most of them were in psychology and measurement and I found them mildly interesting. Wisely I got most of them out of the way by the end of the junior year. I took the bare minimum to qualify for student teaching in my senior year.

In the fall, I was assigned to the English Department at Ithaca High School. The neatly laid out campus had a mini-quadrangle for each subject. English was the largest. A college town has to have a first-rate education system if it is going to attract and keep top professors-- especially true for a city like Ithaca, out in the boondocks. During orientation, I was introduced to the dozen or so members of the department. It was an interesting mix. Some were professors' wives who had lived in Ithaca for several years, but always faced the prospect of packing up and moving on if their husbands got promotions elsewhere, or worse, didn't get tenure. It appeared to be a nomadic existence. Others were wives of graduate students who were using their teaching credentials to pay the bills while their husbands were finishing up their doctorates before finding that first job and then relocating. And a few were career teachers who had grown up in town, come up through the system, and had returned to their home high school to teach. It was an eclectic mix.

Note the pronoun "she"; teaching was still a female-dominated profession during this period. There was just a handful of men. Also note that the turnover rate was fairly high for the aforementioned reasons. Except for the locals, those connected with the

University always faced the possibility of picking up stakes and moving on.

Mrs. Marguerite Osborne was the Coordinator of the English Department and served as liaison to Cornell, overseeing the student teachers at the junior and senior high school. She was in her upper fifties, maybe sixty, the widow of a Cornell engineering professor who had spent most of her professional life in the Ithaca area, rising through the ranks from teacher to chairperson to the current coordinator position. I soon learned that although she and Dr. Osborne never had children of their own, they viewed their students and the members of their respective departments as their "family" and treated them as such, especially at holiday time. In addition, Mrs. Osborne never, ever missed a birthday, usually with a homemade cake.

Originally there had been eleven student teachers in our platoon, nine females and two males. But my buddy dropped out over the summer leaving me the lone guy in the group. Each of us, we were told, would be assigned two six-week classroom experiences over the fall semester.

I was eager to find out what had been lined up for me.

"You're going to handle two ends of the spectrum," she explained. "You'll start out with a twelfth grade 'T' class."

"Seniors, not bad," I thought, pleasantly surprised at trying my hand with the older kids, right off the bat. "But a 'T' class. What's that?" I asked.

"Terminal," she blurted out with zero hesitation.

A class of *terminal* students. How depressing, I thought to myself. I was surprised there was such a thing in a public high school.

"I'd better explain that," Mrs. Osborne quickly jumped in with her cherubic smile. "In our school, 'T' *does* mean 'terminal'-- the students are going to *terminate* their education after high school. They are not planning to go on to college. We have six tracks: from High Honors, down to-- Terminal."

What a relief, I said to myself. Still, wasn't there a better way to label them? It was an awesome thought, having such a homogeneous group of youngsters placed all together. But this was 1968 and "tracking" was not a dirty word back then.

"What will I do for the second half of the semester?" I inquired, figuring there was no place to go but up. "You're going to jump to the other end of the spectrum. You'll take my sophomore class. It's the High Honors. The cream of the crop. Many of the professors' children are in there. Bet you'll recognize many of the names. It's like running a junior faculty meeting," she sort of giggled.

From worst to first, overnight, at least in terms of ability level. I certainly would have a wide range of experiences and was eager to begin. Not so fast!

Grant Kleiner would be my first cooperating teacher. He was a gentle, laid-back man with long, coarse grey hair combed back over his head and a neatly trimmed matching beard. A pair of frameless spectacles was perched on his nose. He usually wore plaid flannel shirts, buttoned to the top, with no tie. He often wore a cowboy vest and jeans. He always wore boots.

The game plan was for me to observe him teach for a week and then start to take over. I had expected to jump right in and was a bit disappointed about the seven-day delay, but quickly realized that I had a great deal to learn before taking over the controls.

There were 19 students in this class. It was a motley crew. Most were children of local farmers, University service employees, town folk, or assembly line workers from the gun factory. I wondered why they had no aspirations to go beyond high school. Had they tracked themselves -- or -- had they been sifted, sorted, and so-identified earlier on? Whatever the case, it was clear that this was the end of the educational line for them.

The seniors *adored* Mr. Kleiner. It wasn't so much that he was a great teacher-- which he was. But I could see right from the start that the students knew that he liked and respected them. That was the first lesson I learned: the rapport between teacher and students;

without it, there's nothing. All of the book knowledge in the world means diddlysquat. Students have a way of knowing if their teacher sincerely cares about them. He or she may get angry, lose patience, and even yell; and the students, in turn, may get their backs up. But none of that lasts very long. At the end of the day, literally, if they sense that their teacher is willing to jump through hoops out of caring, that's all that matters. It's a lot like parenting. When I think back to my own favorite teachers, the same criteria hold true.

It was then and there that I realized that this ingredient was first and foremost as a correlate of a teacher's success: nurturing. He shepherded then, he guided them, at times he chided them, but above all he cared for them. And they learned. His paternal style was something I wanted to emulate. But I also realized that I was a mere three, maybe four years older than they. A few of them looked even older than I! I took copious notes, not so much about what Mr. Kleiner (I never thought of calling him "Grant" and he never suggested that I did) taught (which was on a very fundamental level), but on how he approached each and every individual in the class. Yes, they learned from the textbook; but more important, he taught them lessons about life.

Mrs. Osborne asked me what I thought of Mr. Kleiner. I told her how impressed I was with the way he handled the students. I could see that she had paired me with him for a reason.

"He seems to know everything there is to know about the kids, almost as if they were his own," I said.

"But they *are* his own," she added with a twinkle in her eye. "I'm sure you will have a wonderful experience with Mr. Kleiner's students."

On the following Monday, I taught my first lesson. Mr. Kleiner sat in the back left corner of the classroom and observed every move that I made. I felt as though I was under a microscope, his eyes as well as the scrutiny of his students. It must have been a culture shock for these kids to see a young guy like me-- just a few years older than they-- in front of the room in jacket and tie. For one foolish moment, I had entertained the crazy idea of dressing like him. But just for a moment; that wasn't me and I think that these students were sophisticated enough to have seen through that veiled attempt at copying him.

If Grant Kleiner was country, then I was city; he was Burl Ives and I was Ryan O'Neal (back then, anyway!) I still remember what I wore that day: a burnt orange Shetland sweater over a white shirt and striped tie with brown corduroy pants and a tan camel-hair blazer. (I figured the tie would age me a bit, add on a few years, and draw a clear line of demarcation.) The kids looked me up and down. All I wanted at that moment was to win their confidence. But I could see it was going to take some time. "That's something a teacher has to *earn*," Mrs. Osborne had told me over and over again.

And that I did over the days which followed. I was given considerable latitude as to what I would do with them. These students didn't study the same structured curriculum followed by their classmates in the other tracks. There weren't any literary titles these students had to read or senior term papers they had to write. The "terminal" label still haunted me. Very shortly they would be entering the working world. So I decided to equip them with every skill possible to get an upper hand on the job market.

To set the tone for the unit to follow, I arranged field trips to two of the biggest employers in the county: the local gun factory and New York Telephone. The kids got to see firsthand what the world of work was really like. Most of them were gaping, having never seen mass production and an assembly line before. And watching rows of operators working under the watchful eye of the "chief" was also a rude awakening:

"You don't just get up out of your seat when you feel like it," something I pointed out and they observed for themselves. It was truly and eye-opener.

Painstakingly I introduced them to the want ads, deciphering all the short forms, explaining all the abbreviations. It was like teaching a foreign language. Then each student identified from the newspaper a dream job and wrote a business letter applying for it. That, in turn, led to a composing a resume, filling out an application, and requesting an interview.

All of the teaching materials were homemade and printed on an antediluvian rexograph machine whose purple ink reeked. Whenever I passed out a handout, the students sniffed it before they looked at it.

The preparation for these classes seemed endless. No sooner had I completed the next day's lesson when it was time to ready the following one. I couldn't seem to get ahead. So much for a teacher having banker's hours. It never ended; but those demands didn't bother me in the least. This was what teaching was all about-- and I was into it.

I kept glancing over to Mr. Kleiner for his blessing. He never smiled; it wasn't in his character. But he quietly nodded his approval each step of the way from that same seat in the back left corner of the room. I also sensed that Mrs. Osborne was getting good reports. I was flying sky high-- until we came to the interview lesson.

"What kinds of questions are they going to ask?"

"What happens if you don't know an answer?"

"What should you wear?"

"Can you ask how much money you're going to make?"

"What about a pension?"

"Whoah!" I couldn't resist, although I appreciated their enthusiasm. "You haven't worked a day and you're worried about a pension?" The rest of the class laughed with me. Our connection had begun to take hold.

The kids bombarded me with questions even before we began the process. They were certainly motivated. I tried to put the brakes on and back them up a bit.

"We'll get to all of that. But the best way to learn about an interview-- is to do one. Let's practice. Who would like to be the first brave volunteer?"

Gil Clarke's hand shot up. He was a cocky, confident kid, the son a local plumber who planned to follow in his father's footsteps.

His future was pre-determined. Gil looked a lot older than his 18 years. Given his size, unshaven face, unbuttoned shirt almost down to his navel, and grubby appearance, he looked to be considerably older than a high school senior. Frankly, he looked older than me! But he was still a boy, only in a man's body.

I quickly rearranged the furniture in the front of the room to create an interview setting. Gil was really into this; he went out into the hall.

"Knock, knock." He sashayed in and slumped into the seat. The kids laughed; so did I. Humor plays a big part in teaching-- something else you don't learn in the textbooks or Education courses.

"Gil, that's not going to get you the big bucks." That's all I had to say. Take two. He went out the door and into the hall again.

"Knock, knock." This time he went to the other extreme and played the sophisticate, with a grand entrance. Better this, I reasoned, so I joined in with his classmates' whistles and applause. He sat down and assumed the role of the interviewee very nicely. I asked him a series of pre-planned questions about himself, his knowledge of the hypothetical job, and his plans for the future. He fielded those quite well, although with short one- or two-word answers. I had to get him to talk and open up more. So I tried a different approach. Then came the zinger.

"I like to know a bit more about my employees," I went on, trying to get him to go beyond those staccato responses. "I want to know more about your interests, your background, your beliefs. You read the papers, Gil, and listen to the news. You know what's going on. So tell me: What do *you* think of our involvement in the War?"

Suddenly there came a stone-cold silence. The class literally froze-up. On cue, Gil locked up. Mr. Kleiner sunk into his chair; his steely grey eyes sunk back into his head, but not before they pierced right through me. What a difference a moment had made. *But what had I said?* I had obviously struck a raw nerve. After all, this was a question being discussed, something on everyone's mind. High schoolers, certainly seniors, could handle this, couldn't they? I was certain it had been discussed in Social Studies classes. Furthermore, a question like one this *could* come up on an interview. My sole purpose with that question was to pry him open, get him to talk. One-word answers at an interview could be a deal-breaker. I was desperately trying to convince myself that I had done nothing wrong.

Still, I got no response from him-- or from anyone else in the room, for that matter-- so I quickly changed the subject to something inane and far less controversial, like "Have you seen a good movie lately?" just to bring the class back down to earth and to get Gil to speak. But the damage had been done and the lesson lost. And it was beyond repair or recovery.

The remainder of the period dragged on interminably. The students had been transformed into mannequins. Usually I ran out of time; now I couldn't wait for the bell to ring. As soon as it did, they flew out the door, leaving me to reset the classroom furniture back to its original arrangement on my own. By the time I was finished, even Mr. Kleiner had slipped out of the room. Still unsure of what crime I had committed, I made a beeline to Mrs. Osborne's office, just around the corner. I was fearful that I would find that Mr. Kleiner had beaten me there, but fortunately that was not the case. He was not one to report everything to her.

I recounted precisely what had occurred, starving for her approval, or at the very least, an explanation. Had I committed some cardinal sin by asking that one question? Mrs. Osborne leaned over and took my two hands in both of hers. She looked me squarely in the eye.

"I understand what you were trying to do, to get Gil to open up. There probably was nothing wrong with that question," she calmed me down, both with her response and her beautiful smile. "Except in *that* classroom. The War… the War has already touched it. Mr. Kleiner's son is in Vietnam right now." Then she paused; what would follow was obviously harder to say. "Gil has already lost a brother there."

How tactless had I been? But how was I to know? I'm not sure whether I was more upset at my own insensitivity or about having instantaneously destroyed my relationship with the class. The closest I had come to losing someone in Vietnam was Kip. And I didn't know for sure whether he was dead or alive. Indirectly, Jordan, too. But now this...

I slept very little that night, dreading going back to school the next morning, even contemplating phoning in sick for the next two days and then allowing a weekend to pass before I returned to class. I reasoned that time heals all wounds. But time also wounds all heels. And I felt that I had been a heel. In the end I decided avoidance wouldn't work; I had to own up to my mistake, hope it wasn't a fatal flaw, and face the music as quickly as possible.

However, apparently Mrs. Osborne had worked her magic. Mr. Kleiner greeted me as if nothing had gone wrong the previous day. And even the class bounced back nicely. Still, I felt as though I was walking on eggshells with this group for the next few weeks. The following unit dealt with poetry-- and I scrupulously steered clear from anything that in any way smacked of being political or controversial. That's certainly not the way to teach. But I was understandably very gun shy for a while.

My last day with English 12T came. I was extremely sad to have to say goodbye to these kids; I had grown very attached to them. I hadn't expected to feel that way. So quickly, they had passed into and out of my life. The students threw me a surprise party and chipped in to buy me a tie tack with the letter S, a gift that I still cherish to this day.

ABOUT THE SAME TIME

#59 - Final Fall Weekend

As enmeshed as I was in student teaching, there was still plenty of time for diversions, especially of the female variety.

"So who's the lucky gal who gets to go with you on our final Fall Weekend fling?" I asked Ian a bit mischievously, knowing my customer, his wild libido, and strange dating habits all too well by now.

"Never mind *me*. Have I got someone for *you*!" he volunteered.

Immediately I was skeptical. If "she" was so wonderful, why wasn't Ian going out with her? As far as I knew, he was between girlfriends again. I had good reason to doubt his motives, given his track record. Besides, I didn't want his sloppy seconds.

"Trust me, bud, this is the girl for you," he said excitedly. "You'll meet my date; she's one of her sorority sisters. You have to trust me on this one."

Trust Ian: The two words didn't belong in the same sentence. Well, it sounded plausible. And I had stalled so long that I was coming up on the big weekend with the picks of the litter already scooped up. I could always ask a freshman, but I really didn't want to rob the cradle. I could also sit back in our house and watch television, but this was my final Fall Weekend. I had come a long way from Diana, Buzz, and three feet on the floor three years ago. Figuring I had nothing to lose, I nervously agreed to subscribe to Ian's attempt at matchmaking.

"Okay," I said somewhat cautiously and with more than a modicum of skepticism. The very next day, I saw what Ian was talking about: Liza was a knockout. She was a tall and slim brunette, with wavy dark shoulder-length hair and large brown eyes. Her skin was near-perfect; her figure, too. She was on the tall side. I'm about six feet and she was only a few inches shorter. My height must have clinched the deal. Never mind why she didn't have a date by now; I had discovered that some of the prettiest girls sometimes get passed over just because everyone *assumes* they are taken. Whatever the reason, she would be mine, at least for the weekend.

Apparently Ian had done his advance work building me up, and Liza seemed even more eager for this match than I. He also arranged to take care of all the party details and itinerary for the weekend, having become a cross between a matchmaker and event planner.

We were in the midst of an Indian summer. The fall foliage season was at its peak. But instead of the cool, crisp weather that was typical of this time of year, it was uncharacteristically warm. On Friday night, there was a cocktail party on the lawn back at the fraternity house, followed by a buffet dinner prepared inside by the cook-of-the-month, not even worth mentioning, because he (or she) would be gone before long. After supper, a hayride had been arranged out in the countryside, in some farmlands just south of Ithaca. The weather was ideal and Liza and I had a fantastic time together. I'd have to include that night on my "Top Ten List" of Cornell experiences.

On Saturday afternoon we went to the football game, me in shirtsleeves, and she in shorts. We were cheating the season. The game was followed by the annual Fall Tonic concert in Bailey Hall. Precisely the same event for one of my first dates with Diana. But that was ancient history. The only thing that remained the same were the terrific a cappella singing groups that performed everything from haunting Gregorian chants to football fighting songs, each followed by a resounding ovation from the pumped-up crowd.

Right after the concert, Liza and I quickly changed and parted company with the fraternity schedule. It was great to have wheels! We four senior roommate couples took our dates for dinner at one of the finest (and most expensive) restaurants in the downtown area. We got back to campus and Barton Hall just in time for the Janice Joplin concert, which, frankly, was the one thing I could have lived without. The crowd went wild. I'll admit it; to me, it sounded like a lot of shrieking. I couldn't understand the lyrics, even though we had half-way decent seats Ian had managed to wangle.

He kept telling me it was because me were so close to the deafening, humongous speakers, but I wasn't convinced that was the reason. How the music had changed, first from those mindless love songs of the early sixties... and then again from the protest songs of just two years ago... and now to this hard rock. I liked the strumming guitarists who at least had a perceptible message; I just wasn't into stuff. In short, I had been left back at the starting gate.

But I was a member of a very small minority; the sold-out armory went wild. Actually, I really didn't care who was performing. I was with Liza, courtesy of Ian. This was one more attempt by him at reconciliation, yet another peace offering. Maybe things do work out for the best in the end, I concluded.

Saturday night was the three-year anniversary of Buzz' comin' out party: how things had changed, how I had changed. So much had happened since the fall of 1965. For one thing, I didn't have to operate under the proctor's social scrutiny. We went back to my place and my own space at the house in the Heights. I couldn't help but telling Liza, with a straight face that we had to have three feet on the floor which startled her a bit-- but then quickly explained what I was talking about. Fortunately, that "rule" was no longer in force.

Fall Weekend culminated in a Sunday brunch back at the fraternity house. We seniors had really outgrown this stuff by now and stayed just the polite amount of time. Most of the upperclassmen parted company after an hour. The glorious weekend was coming to an end.

But not for Liza and me. We decided to prolong things and capitalized on the beautiful weather, which was even warmer on Sunday. I'm not usually spontaneous, but we got a crazy idea to go over to Flat Rock, a shallow waterfall under that one-lane bridge traversing a narrow gorge. We parked the car and walked down to the falls, which wasn't very far, stripped down to our bathing suits.

Flat Rock was so named because of the horizontal bed of rock in the stream which then turned straight down and formed a ledge against which you could lean and let the gushing water run over your back. In the summertime this was a very busy spot, but was virtually abandoned once the weather changed and the school year got under way. There was no one else there this day. The only sign of civilization was an occasional car passing over the bridge above. We had the falls all to ourselves, the only ones wise enough to defy the seasons.

Liza and I sat back against the rock, holding hands. We didn't have to say anything. The only sound was the rushing water.

"So what are you going to do after graduation?" she finally broke the silence.

"Still not sure." I explained how torn I still was, even at this late date with the finish line creeping closer and closer. "I have a double major right now. I really enjoy the teaching. But I think I'd like to do something in television, if I can make that happen."

"Me too," she said decidedly. "Oh, how I'd love to break in." I recalled that Ian had told me that she was tied into the theatre program. But I didn't know to what extent.

I told her about my internship last summer; she seemed very interested, herself looking for that first big break.

"I guess I'll have to do some commercials or some modeling and hope to get discovered," she sighed. I winced when she used the word "modeling," thinking of Aubrey; but with Liza, I just knew whatever she did would be classy and on the up and up.

I shared with her my game plan to return to New York, hoping that a real job would open up at the network where I interned.

"I thought you liked Ithaca so much," she said in a questioning tone.

"Oh, I do," I said. "But if I'm taking the TV route, then New York is the place." She seemed to get the picture.

"I'll go wherever the jobs are," Liza said resolutely. That answer pained me. Hey, we had just met and three days later I'm worried about where she's going to settle? I didn't even know where she had grown up. Talk about rushing things! But this relationship just might be going places. At that very point she wrapped her left ankle around mine, so now we were intertwined by hand and foot... and soul. It felt awfully good.

There was no more talk for a while. But I was suddenly serious, big time, about this girl and wanted to know more about her plans. So I went first, hoping that by revealing more about my hopes and dreams for the future, she'd do the same.

"I think I'll go back to New York, find that perfect job, get married, buy a huge colonial in the suburbs, and fill it with a bunch of kids. You know-- the American Dream," I mused tongue-in-cheek, although I really meant it. All that was missing from the picture was the picket fence. I was afraid she would brand me as kind of boring. In the end, I would have gladly settled for that reaction.

"I'm not going to have any children," she said matter-of-factly. That line hit me like a ton of bricks and my back shot up just a bit. Here we were drawing closer and closer and closer. All right, I tried to convince myself, this was only our first weekend together, but at least it had possibilities. If there was one thing I knew for sure, I wanted to have kids. After a beat, I gave her some room to back-off.

"Maybe not now, but someday you'll want to have children," I suggested.

"Not now, not *ever*," she sternly corrected me. "I know just where I'm going and there is just no room for kids to come along for the ride."

"Don't you want to have a baby of your own?" I asked with curiosity.

"Yeah, I love to hold babies. *Other people's* babies. But not mine. I just don't have that maternal instinct. There are other things I need to do," she said rather blithely and cut me off at that point, making it patently clear she didn't want to discuss this matter. I had been put on notice that it was to be strictly off limits.

I was only 21 years old-- and still unsure of where the future would take me. I still didn't know what I wanted to do with my life. I didn't have any notion where I was going to live or settle. I was even confused about what was going to happen after graduation. In this climate, I didn't even know what to expect the *very next day* with the specter of the draft hanging over all of us.

That's the way it was back then. True, there were very few things about which I was certain regarding the future. But this was, without any doubt, one of them: Someday I wanted to be father. Not today, not necessarily tomorrow, maybe not in the foreseeable future. Eventually. I wanted to perpetuate the breed and replicate the childhood I had had.

I am a pretty easy-going guy, always the compromiser. That is one of my strong suits, so I have been told. This, however, was a point that was non-negotiable in a marriage. Yes, I kept saying to myself as I processed this pronouncement, this was only our first weekend together. Who knew if there would even be another date? Maybe I was going too far and too fast. Why was I preoccupied with marriage-- let alone having children-- with someone I had just met? Just have a good time, no strings attached, Ian was constantly coaching me. Besides, having kids isn't for everyone. Many women were passing on motherhood; it was just another option and a good one for many. If Liza belonged to that group, so be it. But she was different from all the others I had dated; from the beginning, I had fallen for her and felt this relationship had strong possibilities.

So I quickly changed the subject to something more neutral. But Liza's obstinacy stuck in my craw. Yeah, first date. Suppose this grew into something more lasting. We had hit it off, big time. I think she felt the same way. The chemistry was instant and we had so much else in common. Then why get started with something that was going nowhere-- and then get hurt one more time? I had been bruised enough. So, I deemed, it was fair game to pursue the subject.

I tried a compromise approach.

"There are a lot of things I want to do before I settle down. Get my head on straight, for one. Decide what I'm going to do with my life when I finally grow up," I tried humor to lighten things up. There was no response.

"Travel," I continued. "Go to graduate school, maybe. I want kids, but not right now." Maybe the time variable would bridge the gap, I hoped.

"I don't want kids-- *ever*," Liza made it abundantly clear. And that was her absolute right. There was no room for discussion.

The rest of the afternoon dragged on. Was this a lame duck relationship doomed from square one?

THE NEXT DAY

#60 - Life Coach

"For heaven's sake, you're not marrying the girl!" Ian said half-laughingly, although he was more than a bit exasperated with me. "You just met her. Marriage? Forget about everything else. For once, don't screw this up! When will you ever learn? Just have a good time! Man, you deserve it. You've paid your dues several times over."

That was the big difference between Ian and me: He lived for the moment; I lived for the future.

"But suppose this develops into something more," I said in a questioning tone.

"You'll worry then. How many times have I told you? Worry is a wasted emotion. You seem to like her-- she certainly likes you." Ian had done his research; Liza felt the same way about me. Maybe he was right. I half-heartedly nodded as he spoke.

"Enjoy yourself. Get in on the action. Don't use it, you're gonna lose it. You don't want it to atrophy!" he kidded me.

Well, he was right about that. Still, it was easy for him to say. I hadn't been getting much action. Frankly, I hadn't been getting any at all. Yet I couldn't invest, emotionally, in a relationship that could be dead end. I was willing to compromise about almost anything else, but not this: where to work, where to live. But having a family, or rather *not* having one-- was just not on the table, and not up for discussion. And I already had endured enough blows and disappointments over the past three years. Was I setting myself up for yet another one? I was understandably gun-shy.

"Look," he tried again. "Put it out of your mind. Go out on a few more dates. Who knows? Maybe it'll end on its own. Let the relationship run its course."

"And maybe it won't," I persisted. "Then what happens?"

"Then you'll have plenty of time to make a decision as to whether or not you should bail out. You're not booking the honeymoon just yet. Don't worry-- I'm not calling the caterer."

Easier said than done. I waited a day or two to call Liza. Then a day or two more. A week passed. A second week. I never called her again.

No, I never called Liza, but I thought about her a great deal. I kept asking myself what might have been. Just maybe... Should I cave on this point? But there was absolutely no room for compromise. I fully respected her wishes; yet I wanted to have children *someday*. That was just something I had always taken for granted. Why get started in a relationship in which we both could get hurt? Why look for trouble?

I was getting in, deeper and deeper. I recalled how badly I had gotten burned by Norma. I had no business even getting started with a girl from that background. That should have taught me something: Tread more cautiously. Hadn't I learned my lesson? As I said, I was different from some guys; I couldn't live just in the present. It was my nature to worry about what would come next.

Ian simply couldn't fathom why I was so unbending. Then again he didn't come from the wonderful home life I had and I don't think that this would have been as big an issue with him as it was for me. He seemed both angry and fed up with me at the same time. He was forever trying to make-up for the Holly debacle of two summers ago.

I think he viewed this Liza-fix-up as clearing his "debt" and at long last getting it stamped "fully paid" for once and for all.

Fortunately, student teaching was all-consuming and provided a diverting distraction. I dreaded running into Liza again. On this big campus, it was distinctly possible that I might never see her. That, however, wasn't the case. I didn't have long to wait for that first encounter. The following week, I saw her at the Straight-- with another guy. Apparently it hadn't taken her long to get over me. She greeted me warmly, but like an old friend, not a boyfriend. She even introduced me to her next-in-line.

Sound familiar? I had experienced this very same scenario before. Easy come, easy go. So, we had managed to get this first meeting over with relatively easily after the break. It didn't seem to faze her in the least. There had been this coolness, aloofness, detachedness about her. Too fast, too soon. I concluded that I was just another in the long string of guys she had dated. I wondered whether she even remembered my name. This was my final foray into the Cornell dating pool. To my amazement, this time I ended up feet on the floor-- all three of them. Really, I was OK.

THROUGHOUT THE FALL, 1968

#61 - Student Teaching—Act II

My fellow student teachers made up a diverse bunch. They had gone into Education for a variety of reasons; they really ran the gamut. Some were in it out of idealism; others because of the draft; still others by default, because it was the line of least resistance, with not the slightest clue as to what they wanted to do. Those were, by far, the weakest links. You need *passion* to make it as a teacher.

Our platoon, a motley crew, met once a week for "seminar" to share our classroom experiences. Privately, we referred to it as "group therapy." Sitting on the other side of the teacher's desk for the first time, we hadn't expected the classroom to be so demanding-- or so draining.

This seminar was certainly unorthodox. Instead of meeting on campus in a standard classroom, we met at the home of Agnes J. Abbott, the Director of Student Teaching. She lived alone in a quaint, rustic, warmly furnished cottage right on the lake, just off campus. It had stone walls with an English garden in front-- very British.

This wasn't a house-- it was a museum. And it was so orderly, with a place for everything and everything in a place. Just like my bedroom. The most striking piece was her antique wooden desk in the old secretary style, with pigeonhole cubbies for everything. Her parlor, as she called it, was in the rear of the house, with a huge picture window that faced a small yard, which in turn extended up to the bank of the stream and offered an unobstructed view of the waterfalls. Just a stone's throw from Flat Rock and the site of my afternoon tryst with Liza.

Seminar met every Thursday afternoon from 2:00 to 3:30 P.M., time to exchange war stories. Weather permitting, we sat around a picnic table in Miss Abbott's yard. And during the first weeks of October, the view had been nothing short of spectacular. This was the peak of the foliage season, and the surroundings contributed greatly to the enjoyment of this class.

As I said, teaching was far more challenging than any of us had expected it to be. We all looked forward to this time for "commiseration," as we came to call it. Coffee, tea, punch, and cookies were always served, which added to the informality. Little wonder this became my favorite class.

I was intrigued by Miss Abbott's lifestyle. It was so orderly, so regimented. It was so antithetically different from anything most people ever experience. She and Mrs. Osbourne were cut out of the same mold, actually the same one in which I had grown up in the 1950's, but had long since been discarded by the rest of the world.

A different activity was scheduled for every day of the week, with no deviation from the routine. That's how Agnes Abbott lived her life. Church bingo on Monday night, quilting on Tuesday night, University lecture series on Wednesday night, folk dancing on Thursday night, and so forth. Sunday morning was reserved for church, followed by a big lunch at a local restaurant with her sister who lived in Slaterville Springs, some 20 minutes back east in the farmlands. Dinner was followed by a quiet evening at home, maybe some television viewing, and then finally time to get ready for the week ahead.

And so Monday morning would roll around and that precise same routine would start all over again. Life had a rhythm. The regimen never, ever changed, it never deviated a bit. Everything was so measured out. Day after day, week after week, year after year. The cycle of the four seasons flowed much the same way. She seemed to relish them all, extracting the most joy out of each.

Back then it all seemed so dull to me. Although we were all fond of Miss Abbott, we privately poked fun at her lifestyle. Now, in retrospect and as I myself get older, her way of life doesn't seem all that bad and I think her routine is something our frazzled, frenzied, stressed-out modern society in perpetual motion with so many moving parts could learn from: those simple, less complicated ways. Routine... regimen.

At each of these sessions, we were encouraged to share our successes and failures, or, as Miss Abbott called them, our victories and our defeats. She said very little; she smiled a lot and nodded her head. I'm sure that she had heard many of these same stories year in, year out. The plot remained the same, only the cast of characters changed. But if they were familiar to her, she never let on, never yawned, and never looked bored. Confession is good for the soul. For example, I bared my soul and shared my interview-lesson debacle. I'll bet that story was a first, even for her.

This group became quite cohesive, predictable given these weekly bonding sessions, and soon developed a mission all its own. We were trying to save Penny, our weak sister, who was simply terrified of getting up in front of her class. By the middle of the month, she *still* hadn't taught her first lesson and both Mrs. Osborne and Miss Abbott were more than a bit concerned. Our classmate Melody, a very confident and self-assured young woman who had jumped right in and made a big splash, suggested that Penny should start more slowly.

"Just give a spelling test. All you have to do is dictate the ten words-- and then sit down. On the next day, you'll try to do a little bit more." We all agreed that Melody was on to something, and that this was a good idea. Break the ice... put your toe in the pool-- we encouraged her. Penny gave a hesitant nod of assent.

The next day, Miss Abbott relayed this game plan to Mrs. Osborne who concurred that it was a good idea-- frankly, the *only* idea left. She, in turn, passed the word on to Penny's cooperating teacher, who was also at wit's end.

Time came for the spelling test. Penny was nowhere to be found. She had frozen-- and bolted. Teaching is definitely not for everyone; it was definitely not for her. That left just ten of us still sitting in Miss Abbott's parlor.

LATE NOVEMBER

#62 - The Other End of the Spectrum

There was no break from the time I finished with Mr. Kleiner's 12Ts until I started with Mrs. Osborne's high honors sophomores the very next Monday. There could be no time off if I was to complete the required student teaching hours before the winter break. I could have extended them into January, but this was my senior year and I was contracting an ever-worsening bout of senioritis.

Yes, I did recognize the names of many of my new students. They were the offspring of some of Cornell's most acclaimed professors-- microversions of the very same. And were they bright! I had to stay one step ahead of them. Nor did I have to make any decisions about what topics were off limits to them. They asked me anything and everything that was on their minds with zero inhibitions.

"What do you think of the War and would you go if they drafted you and where would you run if you had to run away and would you shoot a gun if they told you to and did you ever smoke pot or anything else and what about sex in high school and and and…." They really pushed the envelope: no holds barred-- everything except the Bill Clinton boxers or briefs question, and I'll bet they would have asked me that one, too, if it were today. (I would have sidestepped the question by telling them that I wear underoos.)

I guess it was a novelty for them to have a teacher, young and male, and from that bastion high atop the hill, Cornell. They wanted to know my views about every subject imaginable. This was the end of 1968-- and there was plenty to talk about. I sensed that their political comments reflected what they heard around the dinner table at home. Mrs. Osborne cautioned me that with a high-achieving group such as this one, it was a yeoman challenge to keep them on task. They would go every which way but straight. But somehow I managed.

The objective, not of my choosing, was to cover a three-week unit on Shakespeare's play *The Tempest,* not one of his most noted works. I jazzed it all up, with everything from a model of the Globe Theatre to rented Elizabethan costumes. The preparation was endless; I spent hours planning each lesson. I don't know who learned more about Shakespeare and his plays-- the students or their teacher.

The last day with this class also ended with a party, albeit on a grander scale than the one with the 12Ts. The kids organized a breakfast, brought in music, and presented me with cards and gifts. That was nice, but it was secondary. Obviously I had made some impression on them. And *that* is what I had discovered teaching is all about. Just when I was beginning to lean and lock in towards something in television… student teaching far exceeded my expectations. This extremely positive classroom experience only made my career decision, coming ever closer, all the more difficult.

EARLY DECEMBER, 1968

#63 – Off the Fence

By the fall of 1968, the mood of the country had reached a feverish pitch. Almost everyone had taken sides regarding the War by then, with fewer and fewer still sitting on the fence. It seemed that the louder the protests, the more adamantly Washington turned a deaf ear. A new president, Nixon, was taking office. But nothing really changed. Tension was everywhere; there was a single topic of conversation, from the coffee shop to the barber shop, from the classrooms to the gyms. Even fraternity row was no longer immune. Suddenly there was a subject more important than rushing or hazing. Everyone had a stake in the outcome; everyone had an opinion and was not hesitant to share it.

The country appeared to be at the breaking point. I am ashamed to admit now that I was one of those still not wholeheartedly committed to the anti-war effort. "How come?" My children and grandchildren might ask me someday and I would have to explain that the right answer was not all that clear-cut, not to me, anyway.

But it was becoming increasingly evident that this was an evil war. However, *not* so transparent were the anti-American forces who were egging the protesters on. While most of the anti-war sentiment was engendered from idealism, particularly on the college campuses, there was this other piece that deeply troubled me. To be blunt, I distrusted the motives of some of the dissenters whom I deemed to be enemies of America. Separating the two became my issue and a tremendous source of internal conflict.

"Let's go to Washington," Ian declared, thrusting a flyer in my face detailing a huge peace demonstration that had been scheduled for the days ahead. It was promoted to be the largest demonstration to date. Up until this point, I continued to be one of those people in the middle, not quite ready to take sides. While it was evident that I would continue to remain relatively safe thanks to the good graces of the lottery, the ugly statistics were getting to me-- and so was my conscience.

The number of casualties was continuing to mount, and just as distressing, there appeared to be no end in sight as our government constantly pumped more money and military into what seemed to be a losing cause. So, whether it was wanting to be part of history, making a statement myself, or simply satisfying my curiosity, I decided to jump on board and join those heading for D.C.

And while it had taken me some time, maybe too much time, to stand up and be counted, I would now become one of the protesters. Actually, Ian and I made the trip in two legs. Rather than taking one of the charter buses leaving from Cornell, we elected to drive south to my home in Brooklyn the night before, and then catch one of the buses leaving from New York City the next day. Smart move on our part; I am very glad that we did it that way. The contingent leaving from campus was homogeneous, more of the same, made up almost entirely of students.

It was whole different world on the buses leaving from the Port Authority in Manhattan. No snake charmer this time! It was a veritable snapshot of the protest movement. Yes, there were still plenty of professors, teachers, and students of all ages. But there were also doctors, nurses, lawyers, engineers, architects, car dealers, appliance repairmen, secretaries, and even a magician. There were mothers of college-age children, there were mothers rolling baby strollers, there were single women with no children. There were people from all walks of life representing every race, religion, and creed. It was a true slice of the American pie. The group couldn't have been more diverse; yet there was a single thread, one common denominator that drew them all together. They wanted the War to end and they wanted it to end then and there.

Every single seat on our coach, just one of the many chartered for the trip, was filled with this diverse crowd. The driver was the last to board. He didn't look too pleased to be there, to put it mildly. I don't know whether it was the fact that he was pressed into service on his day off to handle the overload, or his utter disdain for the cause. Whatever the reason, he could barely mask his annoyance. He was 50-ish, solidly built, with little or no neck. His square head rested on his broad shoulders. He wore a neatly pressed grey uniform with an American flag pin on the left lapel-- in sharp contrast to the anti-war signs and symbols the rest of us were sporting. His one distinguishing feature was a pencil-thin salt 'n pepper mustache on his upper lip. He sized up the crowd, all the while munching on a toothpick, just the way Buzz used to do. Then he made his standard speech to the riders, without even a word of introduction or greeting.

"Let's make it perfectly clear. You're riding on *my* bus. There ain't gonna be any smokin', cussin, drinkin' or druggin'. Do I make myself understood? If you can't abide by my rules, you might as well git offfa this bus here 'n now." This edict was strangely reminiscent of the assistant proctor's proclamation to the incoming freshman some three years ago. But how times had changed! We were no longer passive sheep and we didn't have to swallow this diatribe, only tolerate it. My fellow passengers just sat there staring at him, either out of curiosity or in disgust. There was nothing to say. Not seeing any response, he nodded, and took his seat behind the wheel. The engines were revved up and we were out of there and heading south.

The bus ride to the outskirts of the Capital took slightly under five hours. Each person or group did its own thing. Some read, knit, played cards, listened to music, or just slept. One guy in the back of the bus strummed some protest songs on his guitar and a few of the riders sang along. The driver appeared to wince in pain, but didn't do anything to stop it. Bags of pretzels and chips and baskets of fruit and nuts were passed up and down the aisle. There was muted conversation and considerable joking, although it was far from a party atmosphere. I would best describe the mood as intense. The people were pumped up; they just wanted to get to Washington, do what needed to be done, and then get home.

I was one of those who slept most of the trip. Ian, with his long legs, claimed the aisle seat to stretch out more; even on this raw day he wore shorts and a hooded sweatshirt. I guess Floridians have a different body temperature, because I was already chilled and we were still inside. My mother had told me I wasn't dressed warmly enough; as usual, I didn't listen to her-- and as usual she turned out to be right. I used the cold window as a head rest and dozed off, but it was an interrupted sleep. Between the noise on the bus and the contorted position, I kept waking up.

From time to time I scrutinized the driver. I tried to read his mind, having the distinct feeling that he was absolutely contemptuous of this outing, probably one of those "hawks" who was staunchly behind the war effort, right or wrong. Once or twice when the decibel level got a bit high, he roared back to the riders, "Will yah tone it down a notch back there!" A sympathizer, he wasn't.

Traffic slowed to barely a crawl on approach to D.C., given the fact that so many people were converging from all directions. It was a chilly, raw, overcast morning when we arrived, unusually cold for Washington at that time of the year. It felt like snow, but there was none in the forecast. It was just a miserable day, weather-wise, anyway.

Obviously there had been considerable planning by the authorities for this event; the charter buses, pulling in from all over the country, were lined up in an orderly manner not far from the White House, where they were permitted to discharge their passengers. As I got off the bus, I could barely move. There seemed to be wall-to-wall people. The passengers from our bus immediately scattered; there was no attempt to stick together. It was as though each was on his or her own mission. The news reports later said that there was as many as a half a million people assembled, but as I looked around at the massive crowds and tried to keep pace with Ian's long strides, it felt like even more.

The demonstrators came from all parts of the United States, and had arrived via every mode of transportation imaginable: plane, train, car, bus, motorcycle. It looked like a convention. Many brought placards or wore apparel (hats, T-shirts) announcing their affiliation and where they came from; others had banners or flags; and still others (like us) brought only themselves. Judging by the number of sweatshirts, I would say the majority were college students-- as well it should have been, given the fact that they had the greatest stake in the outcome. Veritably, this was a life and death matter for us.

The two-finger peace sign was ubiquitous, as were black arm bands. There were those who wore vests literally covered with buttons of all types, protesting anything and everything, from the War to environmental concerns. Civil rights was also being protested, although there was absolutely no question that it was the anti-war sentiment that was Topic A today. A few people had donned the American flag as a scarf or shawl, but definitely not as a sign of patriotism or respect. It certainly was a diverse group in every way imaginable. But they were united in one purpose: for the United States to get out of Vietnam-- *immediately.*

This was supposed to be one of the biggest peace demonstrations ever held in the United States. And although it was meant to be peaceful, given the tension in the air and the high stakes involved, the government was prepared just in case things got out of hand. The presence of the military was evident, with helmeted troops and armed National Guardsmen stationed everywhere, standing by.

As the morning wore on, protestors continued to stream in. The throngs of people very slowly inched along towards their final destination, the grassy hill at the base of the Washington Monument. Ian and I, together with the rest of the protesters, were herded along like cattle.

By early afternoon, everyone had settled in. The speeches began. There were politicians, show business personalities, peace activists, clergymen, and civil rights leaders. The crowd was receptive to all the speakers, but tended its loudest ovation to Senator Eugene McCarthy, the unsuccessful presidential candidate who wanted an immediate end to America's involvement in the War. Other politicians and show business personalities showed up as well and were warmly received. Between the speeches, the crowd was entertained by a never-ending parade of lesser-known folk singers, rock bands, and other performers. And yes, there was that magician. There was little, if any, down time.

It was wall-to-wall people, standing shoulder to shoulder, touching both physically and spiritually. They came from all walks of life, so different in appearance and yet all with the same purpose in mind. Ian and I found a patch of grass and grabbed it before it got gobbled up. Most of the throng watched the podium. But there were "side shows" going on among the crowd which were just as interesting. A few protesters sat in circles and lit candles, seemingly oblivious to everything else going on; a handful had their eyes closed, held hands, and seemed to be deep in prayer, also blocking everything else out. And there were those who burned their draft cards and even the American flag amid muted chants of "Hell no, I won't go."

But perhaps the most commanding image, at least for me, was a petite, African-American woman who sat on the ground all by herself sobbing uncontrollably. She must have been 45 or 50 years old, but appeared considerably older than that, with curly white hair and glasses hanging on her chest from a string around her neck.

Also dangling from her neck, on a string, was a worn photograph of a smiling young man. At first glance, I thought it was one of those ID badges some people wear for work, but quickly realized it was something else. She was modestly dressed, in a limp print dress which draped her slight frame; she also had severely worn slipper-like shoes and frayed stockings rolled up at the knees. I looked at Ian, he looked at me, and without a word between us, we both bolted up, risking our piece of turf, to see what was wrong.

"I lost my son," she said softly amid those sobs. She knew we had come over to comfort her, but she just continued to stare straight ahead. We didn't need any acknowledgment. "It's too late for my boy, but the killing has to stop, it has to stop, before anyone else dies!" She momentarily raised her voice and then resumed her muffled sobs. At this point she clutched the tattered photo of her son that hung on the chain on her chest. I had the sense that she had very little else in her life except for him. We both put a hand on one of her shoulders, a silent show of sympathy, support, and recognition, and then, after a few heart-wrenching seconds, walked away.

That was the defining moment, the turning point for me in this whole, long divisive process. First Kip, now this poor woman-- whom I had just met and whose son I didn't even know. The tragedy of the War had once again been personalized; it had another new face.

It certainly was a strange mix of sights, and sounds, and smells. From time to time, usually between speakers or acts, chanting began somewhere in the crowd and spread quickly.

The print and broadcast media captured many of the images: There were more "Hell, no, I won't go!" slogans or "What do we want? Peace! When do we want it? NOW!" Homemade placards were also bobbing up and down. For example, "Save face-- or-- save lives?" Or, "Will Vietnam be enough? What's next?" And, "War is not healthy for children and other living things."

In the meantime, the guitars were strumming the melodies of the anti-war songs that had become mainstream music during this era. Instead of warming up as the day wore on, it seemed to get colder; small bonfires were lit to keep us comfortable on this raw fall day that befit the mood. All of this was going on simultaneously in an almost carnival-like atmosphere with a cacophony of sounds.

However, this protest was not one-sided. Just as fervent were those who supported the War and came out to make themselves heard. This demonstration was not going to go unchallenged. Counter demonstrators, albeit far fewer in number, were on the periphery of the crowd, and charges of "traitors" and "Communists" could be seen on their placards and shouted from time to time at those assembled. Once again, the media recorded such signs as:

> "Support the Pentagon!"
> "Communism = Enemy of Freedom!"
> "America is Worth Saving!"
> "Put Victory Back in our Vocabulary!"
> "Heroism, not Hanoism!"

Pictures of McCarthy and other political doves appeared on their signs, but with the words "Traitor!" or "Wanted for treason!" superimposed over them or red lines drawn diagonally across their faces. Many of the counter-protesters were from the VFW, American Legionnaires, or veterans of World War II and the Korean War.

Here is where I stood apart from the crowd: I was at least sympathetic and understanding --if not in agreement-- with the viewpoint of the counter-protestors; I could understand how they felt, having fought for America. They were sincere in their support of the President. But, I reasoned, this War was far, far different from Korea or WWII. That's where we parted company. Why couldn't they comprehend that? Their sole focus was the American flags they waved or sported as lapel pins. America-- right or wrong. No, America was very *wrong* when it came to this war, was the conclusion I was finally reaching.

Tensions continued to mount with verbal sparring between the two groups increasing. I kept thinking back to the Democratic Convention in Chicago in August, a confrontation that turned into a riot. I was fearful that any spark could ignite the heated and fueled emotions here. The cops and guardsmen continued to be on stand-by, serving as a buffer between the two groups just in case tempers flared. All in all, though, this was a peaceful demonstration which seemed to gel the anti-war sentiments.

From time to time, angry exchanges erupted on a small scale. One guy, held up by the traffic and obviously quite exasperated jumped out of his car shouting, "I wish I could step on my gas pedal and run all of youse down." The media caught it all. I didn't know whether he was angrier about the massive traffic delays or the protest itself. Ian vainly attempted to address a middle-aged well-dressed woman who was with the counter-protesters, handing out leaflets to anyone who would take one. He walked over her and tried to engage her in a conversation.

"Excuse me," he interrupted her, "Do you understand why we are here today?" he politely attempted to reason with her.

"I know and I don't care," she snapped at him, barely making eye contact, continuing to leaflet.

"Well, all these people obviously feel very strongly to have made the trip today," he refused to give up.

"Look," she brushed him off, "I can't stand them. I can't stand the way they dress, I can't stand the way they speak, I can't stand the way they smell, I can't stand the way they cuss, and I *certainly* can't stand the way they think. I just can't stand them." And she just turned away from Ian, who shrugged at me with a hopeless "what-else-can-I-say" expression.

More pro-war leaflets were passed out, but most people either tore them up or threw them to the ground.

Several college students next to us started dispensing small American flags affixed to a soda straw to anyone in the crowd who would take one. Puzzled at first why they would be displaying any symbol of patriotism on this side of the rally, I quickly found out what they were up to. Each person took one-- and then used a match or cigarette lighter to set the small flags on fire. In the eyes of the counter-protesters, this was a gross act of disrespect that just crossed the line and was more than they could tolerate.

"Traitors-- you're a disgrace to our country," they shouted at them with ire.

"You're desecrating our flag," screamed another, nearly hysterical.

"Better than a body bag," a bearded protester yelled back, raising a clenched fist.

That exchange was a signal for the parade marshals to lock arms and form a human barrier between the two sides. Once again, tensions were high; any spark could ignite them. I expected a nasty explosion to follow. Fortunately, both sides retreated. But the taunts continued.

"After Vietnam? Thailand? Cambodia," from one side.

"Get out of America! Go join the Commies," from the other.

Ian had taken his turn in arguing with one of the counter-protesters, but that attempt had been futile. I wasn't so brave. Still, when an older man, a grandfatherly type approached me with a pro-America flyer, I decided to give it a shot. I would have expected him by his appearance to be one of us, but he was one of *them.* Timid as I was, I felt I could take him on.

"Look," I tried to get his attention for a moment. "The President keeps promising to end our participation and turn the War over to the Vietnamese. How many more lives are going to be lost before that happens? There's no end in sight."

"We shouldn't have been there in the first place," he actually agreed with me, to my initial surprise; that's where the meeting of the minds ended. "But if we walk out now, all that money and all those lives will have been lost in vain. America will leave in disgrace. We can't let that happen," he pronounced with fierce determination.

So that's what it was all about: Let's get out now --vs.-- just a little more, and a little more, and we'll complete the job. But how much is a "little bit more"? How many more lives lost? How much money wasted? We were sinking into this abyss, with no lifeline to pull us out. At this point, other protesters and counter-protesters entered the fray.

"Listen," one middle-aged man, matter-of-factly instructed the crowd, "Only those people with draft-age sons have the right to make the decision whether we should be over there in Vietnam in the first place."

"You're only protesting because you're afraid your son might die!" a member of the opposition tried to shout him down.

"Damn right!" he yelled back proudly. "I'm a father, first." Once again the parade marshals stepped in, just in case. But again, everyone backed down and tensions abated, at least for the moment.

By 8:00 P.M., just about every one of the protesters on both sides was back on the planes, trains, buses, cars, and motorcycles taking them home. The exodus from Washington, D.C. had begun. With a few minor exceptions, the day had been a peaceful one. The ride back to New York was far more tranquil than the trip down. The driver turned down the lights on the bus, probably hoping that we were all worn out and would go right to sleep. He was right about this. Both physically and mentally exhausted from the day's activities, most just wanted to doze off. I eyed the driver and imagined him muttering to himself about these spoiled college kids and their fellow anti-war, anti-American protesters.

Frankly, I didn't give a shit what he thought. If I hadn't come, I still would have remained a member of the silent majority. I was there-- and my presence made my statement. No longer could I be called one of those "muddled in the middle." Those who hadn't made themselves known, who hadn't spoken up-- actually gave support to the President with their tacit approval. And in my mind, that is where I had stood, at least until that defining moment.

Yes, I *still* doubted the true motives of some of those who protested. But I couldn't let those doubts outweigh the real issues and stop me from taking a stand. Finally, I jumped off the fence. That image of the poor little black woman sobbing for her dead son became my personal peace symbol and enabled me to join the protest. My inner conflict was finally over; I felt a degree of satisfaction, and, finally, a sense of peace.

But I was just one person. The Administration certainly wasn't swayed by the protestors. The White House claimed that it had received thousands of calls, letters, and telegrams, *supporting* its Vietnam policy. There were even those who later accused the protestors of treason, claiming that this public display of discord was a morale-booster for the enemy and thereby served to prolong the War.

When I got back to campus, I relived the demonstration again and again by watching and listening to the reports on television and radio as well as reading about it in newspapers and magazines. The coverage combined to create indelible images that have remained with me and aided me in reporting what happened and recording this account.

In the days that followed, the Veterans of Foreign Wars, American Legion, and other groups decried the demonstration and called for counter-protests in support of the President. Opinion polls taken in the days after revealed a nation becoming even more and more deeply divided.

JANUARY, 1969

#64 - Flying Solo

I thought that my last day at Ithaca High School would come in mid-December. Wrong again. I had been more than a little disappointed that Mrs. Osborne had missed the party her class had thrown for me because she had a wicked case of the flu. It was extremely rare for her to be absent, so she must have been pretty sick. Lucille Gherkin, the ace reliever in the substitute bullpen, babysat me and the class even thought there was absolutely nothing for her to do but join in on the fun.

Over the weekend, the principal called me. Mrs. Osborne was a lot sicker than first thought. Her flu had morphed into pneumonia and she would be out of school much longer than expected. They thought it was foolish to bring in a substitute for this class, since I had been with the students all this time. So he arranged for me to receive emergency certification now that my student teaching was behind me. I would cover her two classes until the December break-- as a substitute teacher and at substitute pay, pro rata for two classes (about $18 a day). Who cared about the money? I was flattered to receive such an unusual opportunity and thrilled to be going back to I.H.S. as a "real" teacher.

My sleep was a restless one on that Sunday night. Though I had been in charge of these same students-- I had been the student teacher with an experienced pilot flying next to me in the cockpit. For the next two weeks, I'd be going solo. After Friday's farewell, the class was more than a little surprised to see me back on Monday morning.

Of course, teaching at the high school in the morning meant missing a "few" classes. Fortunately, though, I had not used many cuts this semester. So after completing this second stint, I said goodbye to the students for a second time. With that first paycheck in hand, I was finally finished, or so I thought.

But now a fast-approaching career decision was going to be even tougher to make. I felt as though I was being pulled in two different directions. I also felt somewhat guilty, knowing that others, directionless at this point, would have given almost anything to be in my shoes and the "tough" position I was in. The conflict was about to become even more complicated.

A few days later, I received a call from Mrs. Osborne.

"I'm feeling much better, though not 100%." Nice, but why did she have to call to tell me this?

"I'm going to be adding your name to the list of substitutes for the English Department," she continued.

Now *that* was a surprise.

"But I'm not... certified," I hesitated to remind her.

"You certainly are!" she reminded me. "That emergency certification doesn't suddenly disappear just because I'm back."

There was, however, one *minor* detail: What about my spring classes? If possible, I would work out my schedule so that I would be available at least two days per week or perhaps just the afternoons for half-day work. I thanked her, got off the phone as fast as I could, grabbed the course catalogue and spring semester class roster, and came up with several different scenarios which would free me up enough to substitute at the high school. *When* the classes met was now more important than *what* they were given the circumstances.

There was no such thing as a teacher shortage back then, especially in a college town such as Ithaca with professor and grad student wives starving for work. The mad rush to enter the teaching ranks from those looking to avoid the draft further crowded the field. How different things are today! Substitute service was in great demand back then, so being placed third on the priority list was an "honor," if you'd call it that.

As I said, Lucille Gherkin, the wife of a used car salesman, was the first call out the bullpen; she was warm and nurturing and everyone liked her, so much so, that the students felt guilty giving her a hard time. She was followed by Binney Finch, the wife of one of the botany professors, who was called second. She was a little biddy with a short-cut pixie hairdo in silver. The kids called her "Sergeant Finch." Little wonder; she barked orders and maintained complete control, which made her in demand, too-- although she was the antithesis of the motherly Mrs. Gherkin.

It was, you might say, a precipitous fall after that. Then came "Mrs. Ditz," who was known to have her shoes stolen and hidden on the window ledge outside the classroom on more than one occasion. I was inserted before her in the lineup, bumping several others down a notch in the pecking order-- to their dismay. It was very cut-and-dried back then.

Mrs. Tuttle was the district clerk. Her husband called the hog prices on the local radio station at 6:00 in the morning and she called the substitutes at about the same time, so they certainly shared a "common calling." Substitute teachers don't rise to the sound of the alarm clock; they get used to the telephone ringing at an ungodly hour. I eagerly awaited that first call. But I was going to have to be very patient. Teachers were rarely absent in those days. Besides, I was limited in terms of my availability.

MID-JANUARY, 1969

#65 - Combat Pay

The first call came during final exams week at Cornell. Fortunately, most of my courses culminated in term papers rather than tests, so I was free to work. The ringing of the phone jarred me at first. My housemates were just "thrilled" with that early wake-up call. Well, I was on my way.

That was just the beginning. I had successfully arranged my spring schedule-- four classes and a tutorial-- so that I would be available on Tuesdays and Thursdays-- selecting my classes by day and time rather than by professor and content. (More about that coming up.) I judiciously stockpiled all my cuts so that I could take two-or-more-day assignments that extended beyond Tuesdays and Thursdays. And it's fortuitous that I did. February opened the door and *in flew enza*, a potent strain similar to the one I had suffered through during my freshman year after the wrestling fiasco. A fierce outbreak hit the high school, zapping both students and teachers, and I was getting called almost every day, frequently booked in advance.

I knew all of the dozen or so English teachers by now and enjoyed the variety of a different program each day. In turn, the students knew me and it was still a novelty for them to have a young male substitute. On the other hand, teachers in the other departments in this large school *didn't* know me-- and on more than one occasion I was stopped for a hall pass. Once, there was even an attempt to evict me from the men's room while I was "conducting business." I don't know who was more embarrassed, my befuddled colleague or I. Little did I know then how flattered I should have been. How I'd welcome a mistake like that now.

Only once during the semester did I get called for a subject other than English: Typing. That's what they still called it in those days; it soon after became "Keyboarding"; then "Computer Applications"; now it's mutated into "Digital Input Technology." I wondered what some big shot in the State Ed Department got paid to come up with that new course title.

I guess they didn't have any "typing" substitutes. Miss Elfrieda Feeney, the head of the Business Education Department, was a large angular woman whom I had seen looming around the building, a rather scary creature, and had never said two words to, not even "hello." You know the type; she telegraphed the message that she didn't like men-- and she definitely didn't like me.

She met me in the Main Office at check-in. Although I was facing away, I couldn't help but notice that she practically scowled at Mrs. Tuttle, giving her a disapproving glance, for assigning me to her department. Mrs. Tuttle returned with a shrug of the shoulders, as if to say that I was the best thing she could come up with. I think that they were both more than a little apprehensive about having a male in this all-female department. I felt about as welcome as the fox in the hen house; she made me feel as though I was invading the girls locker room, off limits to guys.

Although I scrupulously followed the lesson plans that had been left on the most sanitary looking desk I had ever seen, I felt Miss Feeney's eyes on me all day. All I had to do was administer typing drills to the five classes, walk around the room, and make sure the students were doing what they were supposed to be doing: "a-s-d-f, a-s-d-f, a-s-d-f." This was tough stuff. If only my own junior high school typing teacher could see me now! I recalled my own less-than-successful experience in her classroom. How ironic that she had thrown up her hands in frustration when it came to getting me to improve my form. Would she ever have been proud…

For the entire day I caught glimpses of Miss Feeney lurking outside, peering through the window of the classroom door, spying on me from the hallway, all the time with that sour puss seemingly stuck on her face. Once or twice I nodded in acknowledgment, even giving her a wave with my pointer finger, just to unnerve her; but then I decided the best thing to do was ignore these espionage tactics. She obviously was trying to catch me doing something wrong, coming close when she bolted into the room and told me not to sit on the teacher's desk.

"It is an ungentlemanly thing for a man to sit that way in front of all those girls," she chastised me in a threatening tone. No surprise; try hard as I did, I knew I wouldn't get through the day without incurring her wrath.

After the last period, I made a beeline for the main office where I politely told Mrs. Tuttle that I really preferred to stick to the English Department from that point on. Knowing her customers, particularly Miss Feeney, she understood precisely what I was talking about.

Mrs. Tuttle respected my wishes-- except for one desperate call on a Monday night and a fervent plea to a take an assignment at the junior high school in the downtown area on the following day. Actually, the district clerk who calls the substitutes has a lot of "power" in the pointer finger and had been dialing me more often than not out of turn, so I didn't want to turn her down and appear ungrateful. How I wish I had.

I arrived at the junior high school (middle schools hadn't been invented back then) at the usual starting time-- not realizing that this building began its day 45 minutes later than the high school to permit the same buses to do a second run. Nobody greeted me, welcomed me, or as much as offered me a cup of coffee, for which I had a dire need. I patiently waited in the main office until one of the assistant principals, a harried chap, handed me a substitute manual and handwritten schedule for "Mrs. Rich-- Eighth Grade Social Studies." I would be "teaching" (and I use the term liberally) periods 1, 3, 6, 7, 8. In teacher parlance, this is what is known as a "bottom heavy schedule," with most of the teaching periods after lunch. Worse, I would be doing, or at least attempting to do, the exact same lesson five different times.

Mrs. Rich had dutifully left for me a twenty-minute filmstrip (that's the precursor to a DVD) about the explorer Magellan, which was to be shown to each of the five classes, and then followed with a worksheet containing ten questions for the children to complete. Seemed simple enough. The opening bell rang, the halls swelled with kids, and her first-period class of 13-year-olds exploded into the room. They stopped short at the door; they could smell blood.

"A sub!" That is a familiar battle cry among junior high school students-- and a call to draw arms.

"Ooh, they sent a young one," sized up another, licking his chops. I was fresh meat. I attempted to gain control of the class and introduced myself as the substitute for Mrs. Rich. For a few seconds there was a delayed reaction, a pause-- and then all hell broke loose.

"She's not Mrs. Rich, she's Mrs. Bitch," corrected the first student.

"Do we have to work today?" inquired the next.

"Are you married?" asked a third.

"Can I go to the bathroom?" cried out a chorus of kids.

"Why do we have to do work today?" shouted several others.

"Hey, do you know your fly is open?" one pointed unabashedly.

Foolishly I took the bait and looked down at my zipper, which led to more raucous laughter and applause.

Hard to believe, but it was downhill from there. I quickly turned out the lights to show the filmstrip hoping that it would focus attention. It had the opposite effect. When the lights came back up, most of the students were on the floor, wiggling and squiggling under their desks. Heaven knows how many children were conceived in that class on that day.

The same scene was re-enacted four more times. Things got no better; actually, they got worse, if that was possible. The three classes in the row at the end of the day were totally off the wall. At least I had had an intermission in the morning. Furthermore, by 6th period, word had spread that "Mrs. Bitch" was absent so the students had time to "prepare" for me. They came armed *and* sugared-up after lunch. At the end of the day I left Mrs. Bitch's planbook and keys on the counter and walked out, vowing never to darken the doorstep of a junior high school again.

I didn't have to. Word of my less-than-successful junior high school debut filtered back to the high school. Mrs. Tuttle was informed that I had "control" problems. What was I, incontinent? I was furious. Where was that elusive elementary school "self-control button" when I really needed it?

"Never mind," she comforted me. I was doing just fine with the high school students. "That's where you belong, and that's where you will stay."

FEBRUARY, 1969

#66 - The Last Lap

I worked an average of two days a week through the early spring. I could have worked even more, but I didn't want to miss *too many* of my Cornell classes. It wasn't the money, still a mere pittance; nor was it the experience. I was asking myself a question: Was this what I wanted to be doing for the rest of my life? I used this quandary as an excuse to accept the calls. And the answer kept changing from day to day.

In early April, Mrs. Osborne sent me a note to stop by her office. Now what had I done? I had become a bit paranoid after the disastrous interview lesson in Mr. Kleiner's class, then the debacle trying to teach typing to all those girls under the thumb of Miss Feeney, and followed by the nightmarish experience at the junior high school. But this time, very good news awaited me.

"Mrs. Whitaker's husband has taken a position as chair of his department at the University of Arizona in Tucson. She's putting her house up for sale, leaving Ithaca, and giving up her teaching job in the department." Then she paused for a beat: "It's yours for the asking."

I was dumbstruck. Anyone else would have killed for that position, particularly in those crazy days and at that wonderful school. However, this was a double whammy. Not only wasn't I certain whether I definitely, absolutely, positively wanted to go into teaching-- but

I had never before entertained the idea of settling in Ithaca. The thought had never even crossed my mind. Yes, I *loved* it-- as an occasional tourist, summer visitor, and four-year student. But to *live* there? Was this boy from Brooklyn ready to give up city life and move, for the foreseeable future, to the country? I still had that "in" in television, and was not prepared to give that up. All of a sudden, not one, but two life decisions were hanging over me. How I wished I hadn't gotten that offer! Too much, too soon; I was on overload.

My mind worked overtime from that moment on. The reality of graduation set in. After all, the school year was entering the homestretch. Up to that point, I had been stalling on that life decision; I could do that no longer. In short, I was a mess.

A teaching career was the line of least resistance. I had originally taken the Education courses because the dual major worked so well into my schedule. Way back, a teaching license seemed to be a good thing to hold in my pocket, given the uncertain times and protection it afforded against the draft. But having been a "winner" in the lottery, that didn't have to be the deciding factor. I thoroughly enjoyed my internship at the network; but the teaching experience had proved to be just as rewarding, although in an altogether different way. And, yes, just maybe I could see myself settling in Ithaca. The days seemed to pass faster and faster and I was running out of time. My head was spinning:

Should I go right to work and cash in my chips at the network, hoping they still remembered me? "Out of sight, out of mind," I reasoned. Strike while the iron is hot.

Should I remain in Ithaca and take this tempting offer to be a full-time teacher at a top notch college town high school? It was an opportunity which most people in my shoes would have killed for.

Or, should I go to graduate school full-time and get my master's out of the way? That route would buy me some time with a stay of execution about an ultimate career choice.

But in what field? English? Education? Journalism? Drama? Communications? These were the leaders of the pack among a crowded field of options.

And where? New York? Ithaca? Someplace else? I had half-heartedly submitted several applications for master's programs, just to keep that option open.

On the other hand, should I go for a teaching job in New York City while going to grad school part-time?

Or, should I look for some other kind of job --any job-- back in the City, while I got my act together and head on straight?

Or, just maybe take a year off-- what is now come to be called a "gap year"-- to sort things out?

Or, perhaps chuck it all and sell hot dogs at Yankee Stadium?

Or--, or--, or... Should I? Should I? Should I? My head was spinning, swimming with ideas. There seemed to be an overwhelming sea of possibilities and combinations. My parents told me to do what I wanted to do; they would support me in any decision. "Follow your dreams," is all that they said. That was nice, but only made things tougher. Privately I knew what my father and my mother independently wanted me to do. However, this was a decision I had to make for myself. For once, I wished they had been more insistent. I almost wanted someone to make my mind up for me: "This is the right thing to do." But was there a "right"? In the end, where did my passion lie?

I didn't dare discuss this dilemma with classmates or friends; as we entered the home stretch of our Cornell existence, many of them had *no* offers to speak of, or were still in jeopardy of being drafted. In their eyes, I had nothing to complain about; they would have traded places with me in a nanosecond. I had to keep my mouth shut. Frankly, I could have used some guidance. These were life-altering decisions with far-reaching implications.

I continued to stall right through late winter and early spring. However, things would happen in the next few weeks which would result in all those decisions being made *for* me.

SPRING SEMESTER, 1969

#67 – Saving the Best for Last

Besides student teaching and the other obligatory Education courses, I had saved the best for last. I thought back to freshman year and all that advice that the upperclassmen had passed along about picking courses and professors. As a freshman and sophomore, I had dutifully fulfilled my distribution requirements, part 'n parcel of a liberal arts education: English writing seminar, social science, natural science, cultural arts, foreign language, yada, yada, yada. All of this to supposedly make me a well-rounded person-- if not an employable one. And I still bore the battle scars from Geology 101 to prove it.

Then, by the end of my sophomore year, I had made sure to complete all the prerequisites to qualify as an English major. I suffered through those abstruse lectures in which a professor could dwell on the meaning of a single poetic image for fifty minutes. But I dutifully did that, too.

Slightly obsessive compulsive and definitely anal retentive, I had made checklist after checklist, and met with my academic advisor on several occasions to make sure that I was following all of the complicated regulations. I got the sense he was sick of seeing me stop by so often. Finally, I had checked and rechecked all the requirements

for that combined English/Education major, just to mak
sure that I wouldn't come up to the finish line a credit or two short, a horror story I had been forewarned had happened to others. So with everything seemingly in place (and, I must admit, a pretty solid education under my belt), at long last, it was my turn to finally take a course that *I wanted* to take. And the icing on the cake was that it fit into my "compact" schedule.

The Education side of my double major called for some sociology/psychology elective. "Abnormal Psychology," or "Nuts 'n Sluts," as it was more aptly dubbed, it was going to be. I had heard upperclassmen talk about it for years; it was one of those legendary courses that you "have" to take, not mandated by Cornell, but rather according to generations of students who had passed through before me. This course would have been fertile breeding ground for some of those wild and wacky reality shows of today. There wasn't a single area of deviance that we didn't touch, at the rate of one per session.

The popular professor, who enjoyed a huge following, was certainly entertaining; this was one class nobody wanted to cut. His course outline resembled the TV listings for some of those talk shows on now; the lecture hall looked more like the studio audience for Jerry Springer than a college classroom; and the assemblage of students made for a ripe audience. On some days, I felt as though I needed a shower after class. It proved to be "engaging," for want of a better word and, as things turned out, extremely embarrassing.

In addition to a take-home final, our course grade would be based on a group project on an assigned area of social deviance. Even the method of topic selection was unorthodox. The students were randomly assigned to groups. Then, one member of each group was called to the lecture hall stage to pick an envelope out of a box. That student opened the envelope and announced (usually with some fanfare by the audience) the assigned topic to rousing applause, as well occasional whistles and catcalls, by his or her classmates

I was "blessed" to be hooked up with a group assigned to "bestiality"; blessed, because several of my classmates drew even kinkier subjects, if that was possible. Unfortunately, what was normally a private matter "among consenting adults," i.e., my group of four, became a very public one.

The ditzy grad student who had been assigned to assist the professor published the list of topics-- with the names of the students assigned to each topic-- along with their telephone numbers. Normally, this is a common "sharing" practice at college to facilitate communication among classmates, but definitely *not* in a course like this one, for obvious reasons.

This list was first posted throughout the Sociology building, soon after multicopied and appeared all over campus, then spread like wildfire throughout Collegetown, and ultimately circulated across fraternity/sorority row. Just imagine what would have happened if the Internet of Facebook existed back then. The list proffered such services as "incest," "cross dressing," "ménage a trois," and a variety of other non-conformist acts-- all complete with student names and telephone numbers. You can imagine some of the phone calls that we received, mostly from pranksters, and, worse, others who were serious about procuring our advertised services. On the list, for example, was my name... telephone number... and "bestiality."

"Hey," Ian called to me more than a bit puzzled. "There's some jerk on the phone who wants to know whether you'd rather do it with a cow or a sheep. Whaddya want me to tell him?"

ABOUT THE SAME TIME

#68 – "You Can Take the Boy Out of Brooklyn..."

Also at the start of the spring semester, Ian was badgering me to take a two-credit theatre course with him, one that he needed to complete his major requirements in the Drama Department.

"C'mon," I bet it'll be a gut for you he egged me on. "No papers, no heavy reading. An easy A." He made it sound really attractive, especially to a second-term senior.

I didn't need the course, but coincidentally it, too, fit in perfectly with my plan to keep my class schedule limited to just two days so that I would be available for substitute teaching. What the hell, I said to myself, and gave in to him.

"Stage Dialects" was a performing course in which we had to learn to abandon our way of speaking and adapt a foreign accent for acting purposes. Professor Chatsworth, who herself spoke a veritable Katherine Hepburn English, explained the premise.

"All languages can be reduced to about 40 sounds. This is the phonetic alphabet. Once you learn the phonetics, you can translate any script into that dialect. That's all there is to it." Her own speech was so perfect; she enunciated each and every word so beautifully. Cornell legend had it, though, that Olivia Chatsworth, hailing from

Westport, Connecticut-- was *really* Libby Lazarus, transplanted from the Bronx, New York.

It sounded simple enough to me. In the first few sessions, we were drilled on the 40 phonetic sounds-- and then one by one, started to apply them to Italian, German, British, and even Cockney accents. This class was certainly unconventional. After a while, we were taught to do the same for Japanese, Chinese, Russian, and several other exotic tongues. We didn't have a clue as to what we were saying. But supposedly we were pronouncing the words correctly via the international phonetic language. For all we knew, we were reciting curse words. This, she told us, is how actors prepare for a part requiring a foreign language or dialect.

For the final exam, we were given an appointment time and told to report to the little theatre in Goldwin Smith Hall. Our assignment had been to prepare the same 100-word speech, of our own choosing, in any five dialects. At the given time, we went onto the stage, stood at the podium, and delivered the five soliloquies.

Professor Chatsworth sat in the back of the empty theatre with her clipboard. When my turn came, I strode up to the stage, stood erect at the podium, cleared my throat, and delivered what I had rehearsed: the opening of the Gettysburg Address in the five dialects I had chosen-- German, Italian, Irish, U.S. southern, and Cockney.

In between dialects, I quickly looked up at the professor. She was frozen, expressionless, almost with a pained look on her face. When I was done delivering the Cockney version, the fifth and final dialect, she had her glasses off. After a few moments, obviously trying to figure out what to say to me, she offered a brief critique. Tightly clutching her glasses against her chest, pale almost to the point of being white, she delivered her assessment short and to the point:

"Thank you, young man, for trying. But no matter *what* dialect you speak, it still comes out sounding like Brooklynese."

So much for listening to Ian.

MARCH, 1969

#69 – Culture Shock

We would be entering the last lap. It was in the early spring of our senior year when Ian introduced me to the next in line of his long parade of girlfriends. His pattern was always the same; he would start off head over heels about one, get hot and heavy for a few weeks, stick with her for several months, and then for whatever reason, lose interest, dump her, and move on to the next.

Ian was the type of guy who always had to have a girl at his side--but then would find some excuse to cut himself loose. I sensed that even he didn't know exactly what it was that he was looking for in making the relationship more lasting. I was beginning to think he was afraid of the "C" word: commitment.

The latest in the string, however, was different from the others on two counts. First, Ian had been secretly dating her for nearly almost four months, a new record for him. As a matter of fact, this romance even survived the winter break; when spring semester rolled around, they returned to campus after being apart for more than a month and picked up where they had left off in the fall. He had never brought her to the apartment or the house, but I didn't give it much thought until I met her for the first time.

Second, Chanice was an African-American, born in Nigeria, currently living in Atlanta. Again, this was 1969, and crossing the race barrier was not all that common. But it seemed not to concern Ian in the least. Unfortunately, as we were to learn, the rest of the world, back then, was not quite as accepting.

Chanice was short, petite, and had a tight "afro" hairstyle as it was called in those days. She had sparkling eyes and a cute smile. I could see why Ian was so drawn to her. To boot, she was very bright and fun to be with. Star quality, they certainly drew attention when they crossed campus interlocked arm in arm.

Ian had this habit of seeking my approval. Sometimes he made me feel like his father. I know that he had met considerable resistance from both of his parents insofar as Chanice was concerned. Why he even informed them was beyond me.

"For once they agree on something," he lamented in disgust. "Don't get me wrong," he would imitate his mother lecturing him. "She may be a lovely girl. I'm sure she is. But I'm concerned about the problems you'll face in the future." His father was no better: "Marriage has enough problems; just look at your mother and me. You don't have to begin with the deck stacked against you." Try as they did, they couldn't get him to break up with Chanice.

My first thought was that his attraction to Chanice stemmed from his open defiance of his parents, a sign of rebellion, almost a way of getting back at them just because they disapproved. If, on the other hand, they had given Chanice their blessing, he would have responded by dumping her. But I was lousy at playing amateur psych; Ian was sincere-- and I could see why. I saw that he was truly in love with her. None of his other relationships had lasted this long. He dug his feet in, determined to make this one work.

When he brought Chanice to the fraternity house for the first time, he got a mixed bag of reactions. Remember, this was 1969. A few of the brothers were totally accepting as brothers should be, even going out of their way to make Chanice feel welcome; one or two were outright rude; and the majority eyed the pair with distant curiosity. Sound familiar? This was precisely the reception Aubrey had received when I brought her to CAT.

Role reversal; just the way Ian had greased the way for us, now I had to do likewise for the two of them. But Ian just ignored them all and overcompensated in trying to make Chanice feel welcome, fawning all over her. If she was uncomfortable, she certainly didn't show it, and seemed to appreciate the overtures made to her, ignoring the one or two knuckleheads who couldn't mask their disapproval. Simply put, she was resilient.

The couple met hostility from some unexpected places. Some of our classmates expressed annoyance that Ian had "crossed the line." There were also some pretty catty remarks from the sister sororities who couldn't fathom a hot property like Ian forsaking one of "them" for "her." Personally, that behavior outraged --disgusted-- me the most.

Ian tried not to show it, but sensitive as he was, he was hurt by the slings and arrows and lack of acceptance from so many different corners. I was amazed at the callousness that surfaced from all quarters. We had several heart-to-heart talks late into the night as I tried to prop him up. Supposedly, a college campus is an enlightened place. It was a rude awakening. But, I repeat: This was 1969. We've come a long way since then.

In the end, Ian just didn't care. He was in love with Chanice, she was in love with him, and that's all that mattered. Screw the rest of the world. Together they could make this work. And somehow this challenge to be accepted only drew them closer and made them even more determined to fight the world and be committed to each other.

Even though officially I was Ian's big brother in the fraternity, as I've noted, there was a strange kind of role reversal: It was Ian who usually doled out the advice to me, most about dating and relationships. However, one Sunday night following a big party weekend, he sought me out to play his father and I could tell right away that the weight of the world was on his shoulders.

Ian pulled up a chair and sat on it backwards, his feet straddling each side, his chin resting on the back. When he assumed this position, I immediately knew something was up, big time. Whenever we got into a heavy discussion, that's how he would sit. So I was prepared for something coming-- but not for what he was about to spring on me.

There was silence for a few minutes. I was going to let him speak first, when he was good and ready. I sensed that something else had happened between Chanice and him. Maybe they had another ugly encounter over the weekend. Perhaps racism had reared its ugly head. Or, maybe they broke up. I knew *something big* was up. But I wasn't at all expecting what he would unload.

"She's pregnant," he blurted out. "She's pregnant," he repeated, this time louder and angrier. As if he had nothing to do with it. It was almost as if to say, she did this to herself. But I wasn't going there. I didn't know how he expected me to respond. Was he looking for approval? Advice? Solace? I took it for granted that the baby was his; that didn't seem to be the issue, so I didn't dare question that. That few seconds of silence while I tried to come up with the right thing to say were deafening. Obviously he was waiting for me to say something. Acknowledgment? Acceptance? Approval? Surprise? *What did Ian want from me?*

"Are you absolutely sure?" I spoke in a low tone, thinking that was a benign enough question.

"Yes, I'm sure, he snapped back angrily. "I'm the only one. She's going into her third month." By now I knew him well enough not to take this outburst of temper personally. Ian was hurting. He was scared. Worse, he was panicking.

"Maybe she's just late," I tried.

"We'd know that by now," he muttered, looking down. "She waited until after the weekend to tell me. Anyway, she's not showing yet so she didn't want to ruin things. You know how she is. Chanice went for the test at the clinic last week. There's no doubt about it."

"Didn't you guys use-- protection?" I sheepishly asked.

"Of course I bagged it," he snapped at me. "But you know there's no guarantee. Just my lousy luck to be in that 1%."

This certainly was not the time to give him a lecture about birth control.

"Then what are you going to do?" I continued.

"What am *I* going to do about it?" he replied. Suddenly it wasn't his problem.

"I meant the both of you," I clarified.

Ian didn't answer. Instead, his eyes welled up with tears. There was no easy answer.

I waited a few seconds and then deliberately changed the subject. "Do you love Chanice?"

"You know that I love her," he answered in a disapproving tone almost implying that it was a stupid question.

"Enough to marry her?" I probed further.

That question, he didn't answer. Again, he looked down, and I could see a tear slide down his cheek. This was so out-of-character for his macho image. In three years I had rarely seen this sensitive, more serious side of Ian. After his initiation trauma, following the draft lottery, and again when Jordan died in that accident. Then, after a few seconds of thought, he looked up and at me, squarely, straight in the eyes.

"I don't know," he said suddenly so softly. "I just don't know." We both sat in silence for a few more moments just to reflect. Ian looked cornered; he looked trapped.

"Are you ready to spend the rest of your life with her?" I broke the silence.

Ian didn't answer that question; he had drifted off into deep thought.

"And there's a third person to consider," I had to remind him.

"That's if we decided to keep the baby," he quickly added.

"What is that supposed to mean?" I asked.

"It's 1969; let me remind you-- abortion is legal in some places," he said, almost annoyed that I hadn't raised this option.

"You would consider that?" I asked, with a bit of surprise in my voice. Of course I had heard of girls who had gone this route. But having to consider such a decision had never hit so close to home before. I was feeling his pain.

"But I'm not ready to get married," he suddenly declared rather assertively. "And I'm certainly not ready to be a father," he rationalized.

"There's a new life at stake here," I reminded him.

"Oh cut the moral bullshit," he took a swipe at me.

"Ian, you're going to make a great father someday, but--"

"Don't patronize me, either," he shouted me down, at the midpoint between anger and fear. It was clear he didn't want to get into a discussion of the abortion issue. I didn't take his ire personally. He was caught between the proverbial rock and hard place, with no safe place to go.

"It's hard enough bringing up any baby. But an interracial baby could have even a tougher time in this world," I added. At least back then.

"You sound like my mother," he snapped back. I could see what was coming; Ian was obviously trying to convince himself --and me-- that an abortion was the best way to go. Erase the mess... call a do-over.

But I recanted: "The world is becoming much more accepting these days," I advised him. "Maybe eliminate the race factor from the equation." However, he didn't respond to that observation.

I wasn't going to go there, so I went in a different direction. "Might I ask you...?" I said, almost in a playful way. "Have you and Chanice talked about this? She does have a *small* say in the decision."

Ian took a gulp; he turned his head away from me. It was obvious that he didn't want to deal with this now. There was enough on his plate already. But I wouldn't let him off the hook.

"Ian, what does *Chanice* want to do?" I repeated the question, this time more forcefully. He had come to me for advice and counsel; I was going to give it to him whether he liked it or not.

"She wants to keep the baby," he said slowly and deliberately after a long pause.

"Does she want to get married?" I continued my examination of the witness.

He didn't answer, so I repeated the question.

"Does she want to get married?" I demanded to know a second time.

There was a short pause, a moment for reflection.

"She's not sure," he finally fired back, almost with disgust.

"Well, it sounds to me that neither of you is ready for the "M" word. So maybe you need to take that choice off the table."

Ian lifted his chin from the chair for the first time and looked at me squarely in the eyes.

"You really think so?" he asked pointedly.

Suddenly I felt like Dear Abby giving life-altering advice. But I felt confident in what I was saying.

"Well, neither of you seems ready to get hitched," I concluded. "At least if one of you was sure that you could make this thing work..." I was trying to be rational.

"Hey, wait a minute. You didn't ask for this-- but it could solve your draft woes for once and for all. Remember--"

Ian cut me off: "Take that out of the mix. I don't want the War to be the deciding factor." History repeating itself: That's exactly how I had felt about whether or not to pursue teaching as a career. He felt precisely the same way.

How fate works in strange ways. A pregnancy would have made this predicament a great deal easier to solve if Ian had ended up with a low lottery number. Then there might not have been anything to decide. But, how ironic: He hadn't.

So the subject shifted yet again: "Then what about the baby?" he asked plaintively.

For the first time, he was talking about "the baby."

"Well, *what* about the baby? Is it fair to bring him or her into that kind of relationship? And is it fair to the two of you?"

"So then abortion *is* the only route to go," he concluded.

"No! That's not what I said." He had taken my reasoning and twisted it.

"Look, buddy," I quickly jumped in. "There are other options. You could put the baby up for adoption." Adoption: yet another possibility.

Marriage? Adoption? Abortion? His future... Chanice's future... the baby's future. All this was more than Ian could handle; he was on overload and just didn't want to talk about this anymore. Without even as much as a goodbye, he bolted out the door.

Ian was wrestling with these life-altering decisions. What about the other half of the equation? There were *three* lives at stake here. I sensed what Ian wanted; but what about Chanice? Rather than push him any further, I decided to find out for myself and invited her to meet me at the Commons, which had previously been the backdrop for so many personal dramas. Chanice knew how close Ian and I were; she readily agreed to meet me there.

I made a point of being on time, not the norm for me. But Chanice had arrived even earlier. I observed her for a few seconds from the top of the steps. She was mindlessly stirring a cup of hot chocolate, looking very pensive. I slid into the seat across from her.

We exchanged a couple of minutes of small talk. The two of us had become close as well, often a threesome, occasionally double dating. There was a brother-sister relationship between us. But today I was playing the role of negotiator. Or, more precisely, mediator.

"I think I know what Ian wants," jumping right in

But Chanice didn't even respond to that statement as I might have expected she would have. She seemed to know what he wanted. Had he consulted her?

"Did he tell you what *I* want?" she turned and looked me right in the eyes.

I could see why Ian had fallen for her hook, line, and sinker. She was beautiful both on the outside and on the inside. And what you saw is what you got. There were no pretenses about her. This was one straight-shooter.

"I'm not absolutely sure," I confided, although I did have more than an inkling.

"Well abortion is *not* an option," she said, setting up one of the ground rules from square one. And this time there was a fire in her eyes with the word "not." Rarely had I seen her anger surface and temper flare.

"Ian doesn't know if he, or you, for that matter-- are ready for marriage," I tried. "And he's certainly not ready to be a father."

"Either we get married. Or I put this baby up for adoption," she blurted out. Chanice was very straightforward. She made no bones about it: There were just two possibilities. Take it or leave it. She had made up her mind.

But what a turn of events! After all the earlier gut-wrenching stress in search of an escape route, the draft lottery was not a determining factor as well it could have been. Ian had one of the higher numbers and seemed relatively safe from a call-up. As I said, if he had been at immediate risk, this decision to quickly get hitched and have a kid might have been considerably easier.

When all was said and done, for Ian, marriage, at least at this moment in time, was anathema and definitely off the table. He had made up his mind; he wanted her to turn the clock back and get an abortion. For Chanice, that was *not* an option; it was simply out of the question. She was willing to get married-- something Ian was definitely not prepared to do. They were poles apart, at loggerheads. With a baby at stake, not to mention a friendship and relationship as well, I felt as though I was caught in the middle. Time was also of the essence. They were at an impasse with nobody budging.

THAT NIGHT

#70 - Irreconcilable Differences

I reported back to Ian as soon as I returned from my meeting with Chanice at the Commons. This was a complicated matter, literally a life and death one. Actually three lives were at stake. His head was spinning. While I certainly couldn't make a decision for him, I could help him sort things out.

"Forget about abortion," I advised him.

"What do you mean *forget* about it?" he shouted angrily, as if that were my decision to make. I was only the go-between. But I knew how upset he was and let him use me to let off steam.

"It's either the two of you get married, or, she's putting the baby up for adoption. Those are your only choices."

"Oh, that simple," he said in a mocking tone. "You make it sound so easy. And besides, is that Chanice's decision to make?" he raised his voice a decibel higher. Suddenly he was taking some ownership of the problem.

"Ian, in the end, it *is* her decision to make, if you guys don't get married." It did, in fact, sound so simple. I think that Ian was somewhat relieved that the options had been reduced to two. They were two helluva choices-- but at least they were down to just two. He wasn't going to be able to play the abortion card anymore. Chanice had put her foot down. But Ian had a big foot, too. And while he couldn't get her to change her mind, he wasn't ready for marriage. Or, for being a father. He was saving both of those events for later in life. It had nothing to do with Chanice, how much he loved her, or the fact that she was black. He just wasn't ready to settle down, get married, support a family, or be a father. This wasn't the time. It pained him greatly that this baby, his baby, would be born, and he wouldn't be part of its life.

"You'll be a father later on when the time *is* right," I tried to console him.

"Don't shovel that crap at me!" he lashed out. But again, I knew I was just his convenient punching bag and dutifully took the blows.

Chanice took a leave of absence for the remainder of the school year. She ultimately decided not to return to Cornell. Her family, though surprised at this turn of events, was supportive in the end. As a matter of fact, her parents offered to take and raise the baby, but she was dead set against that as well. Chanice was a very proper and responsible young woman. She had created this problem and took ownership; it was her duty to solve it.

Now was the time to find a suitable couple to raise this baby. She found a reputable agency that gave the birth mother a role in selecting the adoptive parents, and took it upon herself to interview prospective mothers and fathers, asking very tough questions. Sadly there was considerably less demand for an interracial baby, at least back then, but there was a fair number of applicants, if that's the proper word. I learned all this from Ian, who periodically received updates from Chanice, albeit in a business-like and matter-of-fact way. She felt that she owed him at least that.

Chanice had made her choice of parents. She was convinced that she had found the perfect couple to raise her... *their*... child. That baby boy was born on schedule. Once again, she dutifully informed Ian of his arrival and placement. She also told him that she wasn't coming back to Cornell, but would complete her on in Atlanta come the fall. That was the very last r Ian or I ever heard of or from Chanice-- and their

SPRING, 1969

#71 – Growing Malaise on Campus

Up to this point, I've talked about the growing divide over the War in Vietnam. But there was another pot simmering and it was about to boil over: race relations on campus. Earlier in the year, the spark had been the disciplining of several black students who had been charged with disorderly conduct and destruction during disruptions in December.

Tensions continued to mount during the spring. Ultimately, reprimands had been given to three students while acquitting others. There was a rash of false alarms across campus. But the low point-- and a most horrendous one-- came at Wari, the black women's co-op, which had opened in 1968. A six-foot high cross, wrapped in cloth, was left burning on the porch of the building. A horrific image that would trigger an equally horrific response. The camel's back was about to be broken.

FRIDAY, APRIL 18TH, 1969

#72 - Parents Weekend

April 19th: quite a day in United States history. The siege in which 76 died at the Branch Davidian Cult Compound outside Waco, Texas…. the truck bombing at the Federal Building in Oklahoma City, which killed 118… the eve of the Columbine massacre… Charles Manson's sentencing for the murder of Sharon Tate… and, the television premiere of the Simpsons. There are other notable events-- but all of this together is more than enough. However, something else would now be added to this hall of shame.

Yes, something *else* happened on that date-- April 19th in the year 1969. It was something which not only profoundly changed Cornell University, but redefined the college protest movement as well. It certainly had a life-changing impact on me.

The story begins the day before, on the 18th. It was the third weekend in April, Parents Weekend, my fourth and final one, and my father was coming to visit. By senior year, most students simply skip this event; it is really targeted for the underclassmen: been there, done that. However, my parents were glad for any excuse to make a visit to campus, and I actually looked forward to it. Since my maternal grandfather was ill, my mother had decided at the last minute to remain back in Brooklyn with him, so my father made the trip up alone.

Procrastinator that I am, by the time I had gotten around to trying to make a motel reservation for him in the area, everything was booked solid. There wasn't a hole in the wall to be had. Ithaca had much to offer, but it wasn't New York or Boston, or some other large city with pages and pages of listings in the hotel guide; the sleepover pickings were slim to none in those days.

"Listen carefully as our menu options have recently changed." I had to endure that lecture over and over again as I dialed the reservations number for each chain in the Finger Lakes region and impatiently responded to each of the prompts. When I finally did get to speak to a "live" operator, the answer was the same each time: "I'm sorry that everything is booked at that location, but I can get you the nearest property in our chain-- 30 miles away."

With a chipper voice, the representative informed me of my only choice, practically panting to book the reservation. Well, the best she could come up with was a room in Cortland to the north or in Elmira to the south. If I took one of those two places, we'd spend more time in the car than on campus, shuttling back and forth, so I politely declined. I was on the verge of telling my father not to come. Then, thanks to a tip from one of my fraternity brothers, at the eleventh hour I was able to reserve one of the few guest rooms on the top floor of Willard Straight Hall, the student union building.

This was a pleasant surprise: After all these years, I never knew that the student union building housed such guest quarters. Spartan as it was, the place did offer proximity to campus. As a matter of fact, you couldn't get much closer to the action: It was in the very heart of it. That was the good news I told my father, as I sheepishly escorted him to his accommodations for the weekend.

"Well, you're not going to be spending much time in here, anyway," I said with a sigh and quite apologetically as I showed him the bed, dresser, lamp, and sink that made my freshman dorm room look palatial by comparison. But he never complained about these things:

"It's clean, it's a place to stay, it's close to campus, it's good enough," he said with a smile as he saw my revulsion. "After all, I'm not moving in; it's just for two days," he tried to derail my guilt trip. But fate works in very strange ways; little did I know that this turn of events would give my father and me a front row seat not only to Cornell history, but to American history as well.

The Straight housed just about every student service imaginable, including a cafeteria, browsing library, bank, barber shop, post office, music room, game room, meeting rooms, art gallery, information booth, student desk, ticket office, observatory deck, ride board --and the list goes on-- which made it the number one student hangout. It was at the center of the large and sprawling campus. Every Cornell student probably passes through or passes by at least once a day.

Geography is important to this story. North, South, East, West-- the Straight is at the crossroads. It is located on a small street, Central Avenue. A stone's throw north are the two main libraries (graduate and undergraduate), the College of Arts and Sciences quadrangle, and the bell tower which stands at attention and can be seen from just about every campus location. It appears in many of those picture perfect postcards of Cornell, the symbol of the University. (It appears on the cover of this book, too.)

The front of the building faces east towards the chapel, bookstore, and quadrangles of several of Cornell's other separate colleges. Collegetown is about a block or two away to the south, leading out of Ithaca, and to Route 79, the road to civilization, that two-lane highway through the farmlands, heading southeast to Binghamton and the Interstate to New York. The rear of the Straight points west to the Lake Cayuga, crowning Libe Slope, looking down at the West Campus "boys" dorms (as they were called in those days) and facing the other side of the lake and town.

Dad's arrival date, Friday, April 18th, was uneventful. We had dinner together at one of the local Italian restaurants in town. Hard as he tried, he couldn't stop yawning and I could tell that he was having trouble staying up, exhausted from the seven-hour marathon trip I had suffered through so many times. This is the price you pay for going to college in the wilderness.

"The bus stopped in every town in eastern Pennsylvania and then some," he complained. "Every time I managed to doze off, we seemed to make another stop."

"But remember when I was a freshman, how you and Mom begged me to take that bus instead of driving with a stranger," I gently chided him. Yes, he recalled those battles that had taken place almost four years ago. Now he knew firsthand what I had tried to avoid like the plague. But I have to admit, looking back to freshman year and recalling that nightmarish ride with "Leon-the-Mercenary," it was safe, reliable transportation.

So we called it an early evening; I settled Dad in at his room in the Straight and then headed back to my place to get some studying done. The game plan called for him to go right to bed, get a good night's sleep after the exhausting trip, and then we would meet for a big breakfast in the morning downstairs in the Ivy Room. It was a good thing he was so tired; there wasn't even a TV in the room, which would have been a serious deprivation for me. Well, I tried to convince myself, maybe he would browse through that huge stack of newspapers and magazines I had put into a care package for him to ease my guilt. The best laid plans for this weekend... such was not destined to happen.

With the other guys in our Cayuga Heights "mansion" already out for the night with their parents, or more likely, their dates, I decided to capitalize on the quiet time and get some much-needed reading done. This, was a first! During my four years at Cornell, I rarely, if ever, studied anywhere but the library; the bed, the television, and the refrigerator were all temptations-- far too powerful distractions for me to resist. It was avoidance at its worst. I'd find any excuse not to hit the books.

The second semester --my final semester-- was coming to a close and I was still battling that severe bout of senioritis, with one lengthy research paper and one comprehensive final looming on the horizon. I just wanted to get them over with. The textbook I was studying wasn't exactly light reading, although I did manage to knock off almost 100 pages before I started to doze off. I don't know whether it was the fact that the content was as dull as dishwater, I was extremely tired, or a combination of the two.

The next thing I knew, it was past 1:00 A.M. I had pissed the rest of the evening away. Creature of habit that I was, I set my alarm clock radio to get me up at precisely 8:00 A.M. each day for the network news. Unless I got a call to substitute at the high school, that was my daily routine. By the time the headlines were read at the top of the hour, I was ready to climb out from under the covers and face the world. But I was not going to make it to 8:00 A.M. on this particular day, the morning of April 19th.

SATURDAY, APRIL 19TH, 1969

#73 –Day #1: The Takeover

The shrill ring of the telephone jolted me out of a deep sleep. The clock radio flashed 5:45 A.M. For that split second, I didn't know where I was. No one likes to have sleep interrupted or the silence of the night shattered by the loud ringing of a telephone-- especially me. It's frightening: Nobody is calling to chitchat or report good news at that hour of the morning. Even as a substitute teacher, I had never gotten accustomed to being awakened with the roosters. Besides, this was Saturday morning. I wasn't being called to work. What was this, a wrong number? A prank? Who could possibly be dialing me at this ungodly hour?

The telephone was on the floor, buried under a pile of underwear, the logical place for a slob like me to keep it. I nearly tripped on the cord as I stumbled out of bed and tried to find it in the dark. I caught it on the fourth ring. It was Dad on the other end. His message was quick and to the point.

"I'm downstairs at Willard Straight Hall," he stated matter-of-factly. Then, after a long pause: "I think I'm being held hostage. Don't worry, though." Another pause. "Everything will be OK." And then I heard a click, followed by a dial tone. He had hung up. Or, was *ordered* to hang up.

"Everything will be OK." Those were the only words that registered. I had become a deep, sound sleeper. To make matters worse, I was still zoned out after the previous night's hitting the books. Dad said he was "OK." OK-- so I went back to bed. That's about all that I could process at that early hour.

Like clockwork, literally, the radio alarm went off at 8:00 A.M. and jarred me from that deep sleep a second time. Station identification….musical jingle…. "This is the World News Roundup from New York. Dateline: Ithaca, NY. A group of students has taken over Willard Straight Hall, the student union building at the heart of the Ithaca campus. First reports are that parents and employees are being held hostage…"

That's all I had to hear. Now-- I was wide awake! In a matter of seconds, I put two and two together to form a frightening four and flew out of bed. First that call from my father-- now this headline. *He was one of the parents being held hostage at the Straight.*

Given its strategic location and prominence, it was no surprise that the student union building would be the target of a takeover. In a state of panic and dread, I threw on some clothes, any clothes that were lying around, and raced toward my car, still zipping up my pants, buckling my belt, and squeezing into my sneakers all at the same time as I fumbled for the keys and tried to open the door.

I couldn't get to campus fast enough, breaking every traffic rule in the book along the way as I sped through Cayuga Heights, barely negotiating some wide curves, and made the trip in about half the time it usually took on a normal day. This, was *not* normal. So what if a cop stopped me? I wished one would. This was my father; maybe a policeman could get me to the Straight sooner.

Wild thoughts overcame me now that I had a few minutes to think and process everything: Who was holding him? Why were they holding him? Was he safe? How was I going to get him released? In what condition would I find him? Had he been hurt? How badly? Or, even--? All these questions raced through my mind as I raced across campus. I had lots of questions, but no answers, and I was becoming increasingly alarmed as I imagined the worst possible case scenario.

I was coming closer, crossing the bridge that led to campus. The light was red. But it was still early on a Saturday morning and there wasn't another car in sight, so I looked both ways and ran it. The campus was eerily quiet. The rest of the world didn't yet know what I knew. That would change very dramatically very shortly.

I charged across East Avenue, hung a right at Campus Road, barreled down the hill, and pulled into the lower parking lot of Willard Straight Hall. The sun was officially up, but it was a cold, grey, raw Ithaca morning when I got there. Daybreak was fighting a thick and dark cloud cover with some light precipitation, in good keeping with the events that were about to unfold. It was "Ithacating," as I described that weather condition before.

I pulled up at breakneck speed, stopping short, just in time, or my car would have landed in the downstairs lobby. The sound of those screeching brakes cracked the stillness of the morning.

The lower parking lot was still deserted. Didn't Dad also say he was being held "downstairs"? The Straight was a big building. At first I was moving around aimlessly. Where was I to look? Whom was I to ask? The doors to the lower level seemed to be bolted shut. Strange, I thought. They were never locked before. So I decided to run around to the front of the building. As I turned the corner, there was my father standing alone on the south side, calmly and patiently, although shivering slightly in his tweed coat and familiar blue beret. What a relief; I had found him. After a tight hug, my questioning began:

"Are you OK? Did they hurt you?" I fired at him, not yet knowing who the "they" was.

"I'm fine," he reassured me. "Just a little cold."

"What happened?" I asked, still in disbelief. Didn't you say--?"

"Can I get a cup of coffee?" he practically begged.

But perhaps selfishly, I ignored his request. I just needed to know what had happened to him first.

"When you called me, you said--"

He finished the sentence: "After a few minutes, the parents were led out of the building."

I could see he was also a little shaken up. Who wouldn't be? Dad was a strong man from hearty Russian stock and he had survived his share of travails in his 60 or so years, but this was out of the ordinary, certainly not the norm.

"Where's the rest of your stuff?" I asked.

"I don't know. All I want is a cup of coffee. Can we get one now? Let's go into the cafeteria." This would be easier said than done. Little did we know that the building had been locked on all sides; nobody was coming or going then and there.

Now that I had ascertained that Dad was all right, the next step was to figure out what was happening. It didn't take long to discover; a group of 50-100 black students from the AAS, African-American Society, had entered Willard Straight Hall through an unlocked door, chained and wired the others doors shut, and barricaded themselves inside. Dwayne Jennings, my freshman dorm-mate, was one of them; hours later I was to learn that he was in the vanguard. The building employees and the parents occupying the guest rooms upstairs had been evicted from the building. My father was one of those parents.

Rumor had it that some students were carrying weapons, although I didn't know that for sure. Shortly after 6:00 A.M., they were in complete control of Willard Straight Hall. We weren't entering the building, for that cup of coffee, or for anything else.

For what purpose they had taken over the building, we still did not know. Up to this point, campus disturbances had been breaking out all across the country, from Berkeley to Columbia, with protests increasing in number and intensity. Sit-ins, rallies, riots, teach-ins, takeovers, traffic blockades, demonstrations, draft-card burnings: all part of the sixties protest movement and modus operandi. With students feeling that their necks were on the chopping block, they were also feeling their oats-- becoming increasingly frustrated with

Washington and also increasingly militant. Those in power didn't seem to get it: *This well-educated generation wasn't going to passively accept this loss of control sitting down.* They were going to attempt to seize it back.

Many college-age men of that era felt their very own survival was in jeopardy and would stop at nothing to make their point. The *armed* take-over of Willard Straight Hall amped things up to a new and dangerous level. The stakes were suddenly higher. Why not-- there was, after all, little to lose. Or, was there?

All along, the protests had been simmering; now it was about to come to a boil-- and it would happen right before me, on the Cornell campus. Furthermore, with my father held as one of the hostages, this had become up-close and personal. Although the anti-war movement had been gaining momentum across the country, our campus had been spared, immune, at least up until now. Perhaps its out-of-the-way rural location, often the beaten track, had given it an extra layer of insulation which the big cities didn't have.

But what happened in the early morning hours of April 19th was a first. Heretofore, the demonstrations, though massive, had been relatively peaceful. For the first time in American history, we would find out that the students were armed. Secondly, we were to learn that this action was not *directly* connected to the War, not at all. But the students were feeling empowered; no longer would they be passive against what they deemed were *any* injustices. Suddenly, we were in uncharted waters. This was not the civil disobedience that had characterized other campus disturbances. As we were about to find out, now there was the threat of violence.

As the sun continued to fight its way up in the eastern skies, word spread like wildfire about the Straight takeover. This was no longer a Cornell story, an Ithaca story, or even just a national story. It was unprecedented-- and all the world's attention would become focused on our campus and the drama that was unfolding there. The quietude of that early Saturday morning had been destroyed;

the peace and tranquility of the Cornell campus had been shattered. The plaza in front of the Straight started to swell with people, streaming in from all over. I shouldn't have been surprised at this turn of events; deep down, I felt that this had been long in coming. With no safety valve to let off steam, the pressure cooker was about to explode.

In addition to the obvious student interest, there was considerable press attention as well. Correspondents from print and broadcast media were dispatched to Cornell and camped out within hours. The big cities hadn't been immune to demonstrations: New York City had its Greenwich Village... San Francisco had its Haight Ashbury… But Ithaca? This remote and rural location in a sleepy upstate town seemed to be such an unlikely place for the most volatile protest to date now in the making.

By 7:00 AM, a number of students from the SDS, Students for a Democratic Society, the group which had spearheaded the anti-war protests up until now, arrived at the Straight and started picketing in front of the building in support of the black students inside. As the hours passed, the number of SDS pickets increased. How ironic that the large red and white "Welcome Parents" banner still hung over the entrance *outside* and served as a backdrop to the far from welcoming drama that was unfolding *inside.*

Word spread that James Perkins, Cornell's president, had called an emergency meeting of the members of his administrative team as to how to handle the sudden crisis. In the meantime, about two dozen members from the Delta Upsilon fraternity headed for Willard Straight Hall in an apparent attempt to retake the building. They found a broken window on the south side, coincidentally near where I had found my father standing, and made their entry through it. Scuffles broke out inside and it was later reported that makeshift weapons (such as billiard cues) were used in the fisticuffs, with injuries sustained among both the black students and fraternity members. The white students were ultimately driven out of the building and forced to retreat. This violent confrontation and unsuccessful attempt to liberate the Straight only heightened the tension as the situation continued to deteriorate hour by hour.

According to one account, a leader of the takeover shouted to the crowd in front of the building: "If any more whites come in… you're gonna die here… with a reign of terror like you've never seen." The University's administration demanded an immediate end to the building occupation. No such luck; that wasn't happening.

By midday, there were more questions than answers. Up until this point I hadn't known the specific reason for the revolt. We knew the underlying causes for other protests; but what had been the immediate cause of *this* particular takeover? We soon found out. As I explained before, in the early morning hours of Thursday, April 18th, three black students had been reprimanded by the University for misconduct during a demonstration demanding an autonomous black college at Cornell. This had been followed by that cross burning at Wari House, the black women's cooperative. According to the *Cornell Sun*, the protest stemmed from having black people judged without a jury of their peers and without any legitimate judicial body to make the ultimate determination. The subsequent threat on the lives of the black women had further enraged the students.

A formal list of demands was forthcoming. The three most significant were the nullification of disciplinary action taken against those three black students… an investigation of the cross burning at Wari House… and re-opening discussions about housing the poor in Ithaca, (a demand eventually withdrawn). But an additional demand was tacked on shortly thereafter: An investigation of the attack by the Delta Upsilon students who had invaded the Straight to reclaim it, was subsequently added to the list and obviously added fuel to the fire already blazing.

On the University's side, the administration was facing *two* issues: first, responding to the black students' demands to liberate the Straight; second, subsequently dealing with the students involved in the takeover

Since my fraternity brothers had made the sleeping arrangements for my father, they all knew that he was staying at the Straight; they became increasingly concerned when they heard the report of the takeover, which now had a life of its own. They also put two and two together, this time to get five. Worried about what had happened, Ian, as well as the other guys from the house, made a beeline for campus to track us down. They were relieved to see that my father had not been harmed and that we had been reunited.

It was still all too fresh for us to know what to make of the situation. The demand for an investigation of the cross burning certainly seemed legitimate, we concluded. But a take-over of a building to protest the reprimands? Some people were having a tougher time justifying that. I fully understood the ire of the black students. At the same time, I also related to the University's stance about gross violations of the rules. Talk about a "lose-lose" situation-- being between a rock and a hard place…

All this time, the rumor mill was working overtime ramped up by reports of retaliation against the blacks to reclaim the building. Still barricaded inside, the students received ominous reports of what was happening on the *outside.* In addition, the aborted attempt by Delta Upsilon and other fraternity men to retake the building generated further fear, spiking the tension even higher. As a result, feeling threatened, those inside decided to arm themselves. By nightfall, students in Willard Straight Hall were observed unloading rifles and shotguns with telescopic sights, gun cases, and hatchets through the back door of the building. *The college protest movement in America had entered a new era.*

It would be the *Cornell Sun* as well as *The New York Times* which would keep us well informed, both during and after the takeover: "This is a brand new ball game with the introduction of guns and other weapons," one of the administrators nervously announced to the throng of onlookers, faculty, students, and the press, camped outside the Straight.

That evening, leaders of the SDS and IFC (Interfraternity Council) sponsored a teach-in. The actions of the AAS were justified on the grounds that the students had been "victims of a breakdown in the University's judicial system." Rumors continued to spread, now about bombs, false alarms, and even worse, a sniper (which, thankfully, turned out to be untrue).

Although my father's captivity was brief and left him relatively unscathed (except for that errant cup of coffee), he was still a bit shaken at being awakened, taken from his room, and then forcibly evicted from the building, so I decided to drive him to New York rather than relegating him to another seven-hour marathon bus ride back to Brooklyn.

Needless to say, I really would have preferred to have remained on campus given all that was going on minute by minute, but my good-old guilt kicked in about sticking him on that bus. I distinctly recall traveling east on Route 79, pulling away from Ithaca, and seeing a caravan of police and sheriff's deputies traveling in the opposite direction-- so incongruous on this normally tranquil stretch of country road. Reportedly, they were carrying rifles, riot sticks, and tear gas. It gave me a frightening premonition of the potential confrontation that was brewing.

Never before had I made the trip in four hours, but I did this time. As soon as my father was settled back home in my mother's charge, I turned right around to get back to the action at Cornell, despite my parents' protestations to spend the night and return refreshed in the morning.

"How can you drive through the night after driving all day?" they plaintively begged me to stay over and get some sleep. This time, however, those arguments fell on deaf ears. They didn't stand a chance; I didn't feel even a twinge of guilt about ignoring their exhortations. I knew they meant well, but--. I had dutifully brought

Dad back home; now I wanted to get back as quickly as possible and watch firsthand the drama that was unfolding, history in the making. It was very strange being in the eye of a hurricane, the center of a storm that the whole country was watching.

SUNDAY, APRIL 20TH, 1969

#74 – Day #2: Taking Sides

The campus was starting to become increasingly polarized-- not only in responding to the demands of the protesters, but also dealing with their major breach of discipline. President Perkins and his crisis team were determined to negotiate a settlement to end the takeover. The phone lines were burning up as conversations took place among the members of the administration in Ithaca, Faculty Council, and Board of Trustees, scattered all over.

On the one side, there were those who felt the University should use whatever force was necessary to "recapture the building and regain control from these gun-toting hooligans." They wanted the authorities to move in immediately, demanding that the local police (on standby in a parking lot in downtown Ithaca), State Troopers, or National Guard do whatever was required to liberate the Straight, restore the administration to power, capture the hostage-takers, and punish them to the fullest extent possible. This, was a categorical imperative: there were to be no ifs, ands, or buts.

At the other extreme were those who said that never before had weapons been introduced in a campus demonstration; the sight of those guns pointed out the windows was awesome, and they pleaded with Cornell's president to do anything in his power to accede to the protesters' demands and secure the release of those in jeopardy, thereby assuring the safety of all. "Losing face" should not be a concern when the "loss of life" is at stake. The gist of their argument was that this could very quickly turn into a bloodbath. Although they certainly didn't condone the students' actions, they could understand their frustration and furor.

The Cornell community-- faculty, staff, and students-- was deeply divided, in a state of siege, and to a degree, a civil war of its own. The chasm was widening; everyone seemed to have an opinion as to what must be done *immediately*.

That additional demand issued by the hostage-takers that the white fraternity brothers from Delta Upsilon be punished for trying to retake the Straight exacerbated the already volatile situation: Why should *they* be the ones who are punished? This new condition added fuel to the fire.

The SDS students remained on guard through the night. The rumor mill continued to crank overtime. By this point, the campus was on high alert. Just the thought of that bastion of student activity, Willard Straight Hall, being occupied by a group of armed students was a terrifying one.

Word spread that the Dean of the Faculty, Robert Miller, had come up with a compromise to end the armed standoff. He proposed convening the full faculty the next day, Monday, to nullify the judicial penalties against the three black students *if* the AAS leadership would agree to end the occupation of Willard Straight Hall. He said that he himself would resign from his position if he couldn't get the faculty to go along with this agreement. It appeared that the stalemate had been broken. But easier said than done; that was not going to happen.

By Noon, the following agreement had been proposed, based on the demands I cited above: First, the reprimands against the three black students would be nullified; second, the AAS would participate in the formation of a new judicial system; third, students would not be prosecuted for the Straight takeover; fourth, the University, however, would not interfere with any civil prosecution that could arise.

According to press reports and those who chronicled the events, several additional points were added: (1)the University would incur the costs of repairing the damages to the Straight as a result of the takeover; (2)the Wari House would be provided with 24/7 protection; (3)Two investigations would follow-- one of the cross-burning, and the other of Delta Upsilon's attempt to liberate the Straight; (4) Effort would be made provide legal aid for any students who faced civil action because of the takeover.

I had been on the inside, so to speak, since my father was one of the parents held originally. Now, for a second time I had some insights. I knew Dwayne Jennings; at least I thought I did. I tried to get inside his head and second-guess what he and his fellow leaders of the AAS would do next.

By early afternoon on Sunday, the black leaders agreed to the deal and said that they would leave the Straight. However, they would *not* agree to the request to go without their weapons, arguing that they needed them for protection. It was about 4:00 P.M. when approximately 100 students, walking six or seven abreast, emerged from the front of the building. I will *never, ever* forget that sight. The students marched out in military formation, silently, carrying rifles and bearing other weapons such as clubs and spears. They exited stone-faced, with little emotion, no visible signs of defiance, certainly not with any jubilation. After all, the deal had not yet been sealed. This was the picture that appeared in newspapers, magazines, and on newscasts throughout the country-- and is an image that is etched in the memory of every Cornellian of that era.

They turned left (north), marching between the two libraries, across the Arts Quadrangle, across the Triphammer Bridge leading off campus and to the women's dorms, and finally to their destination, the African-American Students headquarters. It was there that the agreement was signed between the Dean of the Faculty and the AAS leaders to end the occupation-- with a line of armed AAS students nearby.

The key point in the agreement was the nullification of the penalties against those students. In addition, the promise was made to hold the AAS leadership harmless for the occupation just ended. As with most negotiations, there were no "winners" per se. At least the confrontation was over. Or so I thought. Wishful thinking; sadly, I was wrong.

Dwayne had gotten what he wanted, or so it was agreed. I was glad that he had been a deal-maker in defusing this highly volatile situation. Hard to believe, but I actually felt a tinge of pride that my former friend was instrumental in defusing this powder keg. Also hard to believe, I still felt some bonding with one of my first friends at Cornell. Relieved, the Cornell community breathed a collective sigh of relief, believing that the crisis was over.

Far from it. The faculty still had to vote on the agreement. That, was the sticking point. It was hoped that the imminent threat to life, both of blacks and whites, would get the faculty to go along with it. In short, there was fear of bloodshed.

But Cornell was becoming an increasingly divided campus-- not only between, but within groups. Support for the agreement was far from unanimous. The Faculty Council, Faculty Committee on Student Affairs, and many prominent professors voiced fierce opposition to Cornell's capitulating. In essence, it had come down to this: guaranteeing the safety of the student body vs. negotiating with armed militants. The administration had been left with a no-win situation. On the one hand, there was the desire to end the standoff; on the other, the administration didn't want to be seen as weak or appear to having been brought to its knees.

In the interim, President Perkins issued a "law and order" edict banning firearms and building occupations. But it was too little too late. The proverbial horse was out of the barn by then. By this point, there didn't appear to be a graceful or face-saving way out.

MONDAY, APRIL 21ST, 1969

#75 – Day #3: The Deal Falls Apart

President Perkins invited the Cornell community to attend a convocation that afternoon in Barton Hall, the armory, prior to the faculty meeting when the vote would take place. The only other times I had been back in here were for Freshman Convocation in 1965 and then a few big weekend concerts.

At the appointed time, we streamed into the cavernous building. It was an SRO crowd with reportedly twelve thousand students, faculty, staff, and locals waiting to see what would happen next. There wasn't an inch of space to be had. Nobody wanted to miss this. However, President Perkins' message was *not* what the crowd expected-- leaving many shocked. Instead, he delivered a spirited speech about the "challenges Cornell faced"-- never referring specifically to the events of the past three days.

The air was thick with tension; nobody knew what to expect next. I had seen news footage of the protests on other campuses, with a speaker addressing throngs of students on college quadrangles at sit-ins, protests, rallies, and demonstrations, holding those audiences spellbound in the palm of his hand. Those were voluntary assemblages; here the stakes were quite a bit higher. This was altogether different because of that added variable: weapons. They had upped the ante. As the demands of the officers of the AAS were read, the vast majority of students voted "yes" with clenched fists. It was an awesome sight. One meeting down, one to go.

A few hours later, the faculty convened down the street in Bailey Hall, that stately building with white pillars around the curved front. I attended several concerts, such as Fall Tonic, there as well; in addition, a number of the very large lecture classes I had taken had been scheduled for its huge, high capacity auditorium. This faculty meeting was going to turn out to be the largest in the history of the University, with over 1,000 members present.

There was no meeting of the minds; it was a bitterly divided group, with hardliners emerging from both sides. It all boiled down to this: While sympathy was expressed for the plight of the black students and this incident in particular, the consensus was that it was impossible to dismiss the penalties, given the use of arms, threat of force, and the seizure of a campus building. To now repeal the reprimands of the three students *under the gun, literally*, would endanger the University.

A substitute motion was proposed condemning the building seizure and the appearance of weapons on campus-- as well as the cross-burning incident at the Wari Co-op. The plan was for reps from the AAS to meet with those from the Faculty Council under "non-pressurized circumstances" to revisit the demands. The vote came. This *counter* motion passed-- overwhelmingly. As threatened, unable to deliver a signed agreement, Dean Miller resigned.

No, the Dean of the Faculty was *not* able to deliver on the promise he had made to the AAS leaders to end the takeover. Now, they felt that they had been "taken," betrayed-- just to get them to vacate the building. The lines were being drawn even more markedly than before and a showdown was brewing. As the faculty moved *out* of Bailey Hall, several thousand students moved *in* at a meeting called by the SDS condemning the faculty vote and in support of the AAS and its takeover. A veritable impasse: *nobody was blinking.*

Tensions reached a new nadir that night when one of the black leaders was interviewed on radio and said that the faculty had better reconsider its position or the University had one hour to live: “We’re going to demonstrate that we will die in the process, but by G-d, we will not die alone.”

From this point on, reports started to differ. To this day, there are various accounts of what actually occurred. Perhaps that can be attributed to the fact that no two people saw things precisely the same way. Perception is reality.

As I best recall, students started to file back into Barton that evening. For all intents and purposes, they had taken over this building. The AAS leaders came to the podium and repeated similar sentiments to those expressed on the radio interview: “Black people have done all the dying; now it has come time that the pigs are going to die, too.”

Dwayne strode to the podium. There was fire in his eyes. The more militant students, feeling that they had been “duped” to end their occupation, were enraged by the faculty’s reneging on what they though was a sealed deal and demanded “Action now!” One of the more moderate SDS leaders urged calm until the faculty had time to meet a second time. “Give them a chance,” was the message being conveyed. However, he appeared to be in the minority. The campus was in a stage of siege. I wondered how the University was going to hold up under this pressure.

TUESDAY, APRIL 22ND, 1969

#76 – Day #4: A Second Vote

The lines were drawn. The AAS refused to meet with the Faculty Council. Classes were canceled; "discussion groups" took their place. The various faculty departments met separately during the day. There was little consensus. Many departments accepted the nullification, while the Government and History Departments dissented, saying they'd refuse to teach if the faculty voted to nullify the reprimands. There was no room for compromise.

Later in the day, more gasoline was thrown on the fire when an AAS spokesperson was interviewed on Cornell's radio station, WHCU. Both the President and the University were accused of "suppressive tactics," tantamount to martial law. Several key officials and professors were branded as racists: "And as racists, they will be dealt with." Finally: "Before this is over, [they] are going to die in the gutter like dogs."

According to reports, the faculty was "ordered" to meet that night and reverse Monday's vote: "After nine o'clock, it's going to be too late… Cornell has three hours to live." At 7:30 P.M., to break the stalemate, the Faculty Council voted to call a meeting for the next day.

Word circulated of threats to other professors who were not supporting the nullification of the penalties. On the other hand, several faculty members, furious that the University had "abdicated academic freedom" and had failed to respond to these threats, indicated their intention to resign from Cornell.

The rest of the day on Tuesday was used to politic and change minds. But if anything, the faculty became even more split, more deeply divided, and more polarized during the next 24 hours. Views became even more hardened. How to handle the situation-- responding to the demands coupled with the takeover and the threat of violence-- was debated from one end of the campus to the other. The two issues were intertwined. The students intended to use those guns if those demands were not met. It boiled down to this:

Do you give in to guarantee the safety of so many?

On the other hand, how do you negotiate with those who threaten violence?

That issue of academic freedom was introduced into the mix. Debates sprung up all over campus. Perhaps my most vivid memory was a heated exchange between two professors with diametrically opposing views who happened to cross paths on the Arts Quadrangle in front of Goldwin Smith Hall. The tone of their voices was angry, the decibel level high. They immediately drew a crowd around them. It was just one of many fierce and impassioned discussions just like it. The press captured many of these verbal fisticuffs:

"You don't negotiate with terrorists under the threat of violence!"

"The lives of our students are at stake. We must do whatever it takes to guarantee their safety."

"The reversal of the nullification vote is tantamount to appeasement."

"Negotiate now, get even later!"

"How can you possibly reward those who have violated the law?"

"Is it worth the risk to public safety to uphold the rules at a time like this?"

"This so-called settlement is being violently wrenched from the University."

"Academic freedom is non-negotiable."

"The principles of academic freedom are secondary to safety."

"The risk of students dying and the use of guns is enough to call for compromise."

"Condemn the administration for capitulating!"

"For the sake of reason, don't jeopardize our students on principle!"

"We can't stand on principles with guns pointed at our heads."

"The one thing the University cannot survive is the death of principle."

These were just a few examples of the impassioned sentiments voiced by the faculty that were expressed that day and reported by the print media. Once again, to this day, I acknowledge the *Sun* and *Times,* as well as the Altschuler/Kramnick chronology (referenced earlier) for their factual, accurate, objective reporting of these flare-ups.

The SDS called for another meeting Tuesday night at Goldwin Smith Hall… which had to be moved to Bailey Hall… and ultimately to the huge armory, Barton Hall to accommodate the thousands of students who showed up. At Midnight, there was a collective sigh as the AAS announced that it would hold off on its threatened actions until after the faculty meeting the next day. There were a number of passionate speeches, most notably from professors in support of the students. They also threatened to go on strike-- but if the nullification *didn't* take place-- unlike their colleagues who would said they would strike and/or resign if it *did.*

This Barton Hall convocation lasted through most of the night. However, there were two sides to the story, with counter-protests and demonstrations demanding punishment for those responsible for the Straight seizure. Teach-ins took place over. It was a campus divided.

President Perkins appealed to the faculty to "clear the slate and create a new judicial system by which we can all abide…Join me in the effort to move this University from the edge of disaster towards a new and harmonious community." He received a standing ovation.

In the debate which followed, some professors announced their decision to change their votes to "for nullification"-- although some did so out of fear. The black students had guns... reportedly some fraternity members had guns... and armed police were on standby to move in on a given signal. The campus was a powder keg. The fear was, that if a match was struck, it could easily blow up.

WEDNESDAY, APRIL 23RD, 1969

#77 – Day #5: The Tide Starts to Turn

The tide was starting to turn. More and more professors were siding with the majority of students, either out of fear of violence or convinced by their students that in the end, it was the right thing to do. The Committee of Concerned Faculty was formed to urge nullification of the penalties, tantamount to complete amnesty.

But there were still hardline dissenters: "If they are going to destroy this University, I say let them try. President Perkins has promised to preserve order and he no doubt has the means available to do it if there is a will to do it." Still others expressed shock and dismay at Cornell's "surrender at gunpoint to terrorist tactics" and denounced the University for its failure to defend academic freedom.

The vote was taken. The nullification motion passed by a large majority, a voice vote reported to be about two-to-one.

The crowd in Barton Hall continued to grow. When word arrived at approximately 2:00 P.M. that the faculty had reversed its decision, the crowd roared its approval. When President Perkins arrived, he sat on the floor patiently waiting his turn to speak. "After all, we're now *all* equals," I heard someone comment defiantly. When

Perkins did get to address the assemblage, his tone was celebratory, expressing hope that this painful chapter in the University's history could now be put in the past. Perkins, along with AAS and SDS reps, all embraced.

Dean Miller rescinded his resignation; however, several top Government professors tendered theirs. Small groups continued to meet to talk about what had happened. There needed to be time to decompress. Among the topics discussed were "transforming the University… ending racism… and giving students a greater role in governance." These teach-ins continued for quite some time.

THURSDAY, APRIL 24TH, 1969

#78 - Day #6: The Deed is Done

The nullification went into effect. Evidently the consensus was it was more important to protect lives than preserve the rules. How would that good old proctor have reacted to this severe breach of conduct? Even those professors who voted for the amnesty agreed that the price had been high-- but it was not greater than the price of human life. In the end, the threat of violence had been just too great not to nullify. After five days of turmoil, tension started to subside. But campus life was not about to return to normal. There was a teach-in on racism at Barton, attended by several thousand students, at which "injustices of racial life at Cornell" was the subject.

FRIDAY, APRIL 25TH, 1969

#79 – Day #7: Picking Up the Pieces

About one week later after the Straight takeover, calm was being gradually restored. Tragedy had been averted, but at a huge price; the resolution had taken its toll. For one thing, a few high-profile professors had followed through on their threats to resign; as I said, the Government Department took the hardest hit. For another, many professors, still embittered by the outcome, said that they would cease normal instruction until they could teach without feeling threatened or restrained by the presence of weapons on campus. The faculty was given the option to continue instruction on a voluntary basis, albeit with no tests, papers, or grades. The restructuring of Cornell was about to begin.

Another teach-in was held, this one sponsored by the History and Government Departments. Much of the discussion focused on *why* the nullification vote had succeeded in the end: "Behind men armed with guns... was the sordid spectacle of [President Perkins] physically bullied from the platform because he expressed views which some of his listeners didn't happen to like."

Some members of the Class of 1969 immediately departed campus-- never, ever to return. Echoing the sentiments of the professors who had abruptly resigned their posts, they were not going to forgive the administration for its "weak-willed" stance against a bunch of "crazy terrorists." Their decisions were based on either getting a head start on their post-college plans, or simply their utter disgust with the handling of the situation and the desire to get as far away from Cornell as possible. Many of the more politically conservative members of our class proclaimed that were finished with the University-- forever. Just imagine how the brothers of Delta Upsilon must have felt.

For all intents and purposes, classes were done for the semester. Those that weren't canceled altogether continued on a pass-fail basis. Since this was my senior year, classes at Cornell were over for me-- period. What an abrupt, anti-climactic end to my college career, as far as academics was concerned, anyway. Since the professors had that option to continue instruction on a voluntary basis, with students given the chance to get pass-fail grades, there were no tests or papers in most classes.

But I decided to stick around campus. What was the rush to leave? For one thing, I was just not yet psyched to cut my ties with Cornell. I just wasn't ready to go home. This was *not* how I had envisioned my senior year winding down: It was just too much of a letdown. Although I was excited about the future, there was still some ambivalence and I was also saddened at the thought of leaving Cornell and Ithaca, even in June. Second, I was coming up to the finish line with "the" decision to make about that future. Up to this moment, I thought I had a little more time. All of a sudden, I was put on the spot. Third, I was just plain curious as to what would happen next in the daily drama for which I had been given this orchestra seat.

I opted for continuing my favorite English course-- without having to be concerned about papers, finals, or grades hanging over my head. It was a very odd feeling, something that I had never experienced throughout my 17 years of schooling, during which I had become conditioned to grub for grades and worry about attendance, lateness, cuts, tests, quizzes, and papers. Education with no ulterior motive: a novel idea.

I went to that Modern Poetry class and this time hung on every word the gifted lecturer spoke without having to take a single note. It was a liberating feeling, one to which I certainly was unaccustomed. I had originally shunned this course, after my foray into the world of modern art and the disastrous grade it produced. Now, there was nothing to lose, nothing to worry about. Mercenary that I was, I told the registry in the Ithaca School District that I was available for additional days of substitute teaching. All in all, it was a very strange way to close the book on the Cornell chapter of my life.

Actually, this period turned out to be one of relative calm after the stormy protests. A degree of normalcy had been restored, with a weekend concert going on as scheduled. Things remained peaceful for the next few weeks. Preliminary plans took shape for some of the proposals agreed to after the Straight takeover. One would be the formation of a University "senate." However, many of those deliberations took place behind closed doors. Furthermore, what was enacted out in public had a small audience: The campus had already begun emptying out. My education at Cornell was coming to a close, albeit in a very unexpected and unorthodox way. How anticlimactic.

President Perkins had weighed the emotional arguments of both sides, sided with the faculty vote, and subsequently given in to all of the demands. Shortly thereafter he was relieved of his command as President, a nice way to put it, by the Board of Trustees of Cornell. He was attacked by some members of the Board, professors, and conservative students. His so-called celebratory "victory" was called a "surrender."

Even some government officials and politicians tossed in their two cents, with Perkins attacked from all corners. President Nixon condemned the occupation, calling on college administrators to stand up to this kind of situation. Attorney General Mitchell reportedly went so far as recommending that college violence be made a federal crime. New York State Governor Rockefeller signed legislation banning guns from college campuses. The press was no more supportive, terming to what took place as "Cornell's capitulation" and "anarchy at Cornell."

I don't know how many of those "big shots" were on campus observing the takeover firsthand or merely getting their information from incident reports issued by the administration or secondary press accounts. Yes, the handling of the situation was widely debated. It must have been very easy to criticize Perkins from a distance for "caving in" to the student protesters and not standing up to them. One had to be there to comprehend the situation: the eerie sight of those guns pointed out the windows-- accompanied by the threats to use them. It was an awesome, no-win decision. If I had been in President Perkins' place or in the shoes of the faculty, I doubt that I would have done anything differently. He was forced into a corner, a lose-lose proposition. But to this day, I believe the health and safety of those for whom he was responsible-- became priority one. As one commentator so aptly put it, "The decision was made to protect human life above the reputation of the University."

Willard Straight Hall is on Central Avenue, between West Avenue, where the old west campus freshman dorms are located, and East Avenue, the main drag that cuts through campus. After the takeover, Central Avenue was closed and became a pedestrian mall, much the way Pennsylvania Avenue near the White House has been cut off to traffic-- and it's my guess-- for much the same reasons.

END-OF-THE-SCHOOL-YEAR, 1969

#80 - Graduation

Graduation went off as scheduled, although quite a few members of the Class of 1969 were not present for the commencement ceremony. Either they had begun their post-graduate activities ahead of schedule, returned home early with no more required classes, or were just too disgusted with the University's capitulation weeks earlier to stick around. Then there were those others, like Brant, who hadn't made it to the finish line because of academics. And then there were those who were missing because they had been drafted as the long arm of Uncle Sam reached onto campus and plucked them off. Some, like Kip, had left the University never to return.

So, for one reason or another, there were plenty of empty seats, literally and spiritually, at graduation. If attendance had been taken, there would have been a very different and diminished roll call from the three thousand freshmen who stood end-to-end on the football field in the fall of 1965. I couldn't help to think back to the fearsome fivesome and how we had been inseparable almost four years earlier. Look to your right, look to your left; who would have expected the line-up to look like this as our college careers came to a close?

No surprise: Ian's parents couldn't make it up for the big day, so he joined my parents and me the night before for the ceremonial last supper. He still acted as though nothing had happened between us. Much had been forgiven after the Holly horror show, but the friendship, though steadily on the mend, had taken its hits, been irreparably damaged, and could never quite be precisely the same, even though over the past two years he had done cartwheels to make it up to me.

I felt sorry for Ian, but the absence of his mother and father, even at a milestone occasion like this one, didn't seem to bother him in the least. Either that, or he was just used to it. Instead he just tagged along with me and my parents. In any event, we met the next morning for the usual picture-taking rituals before hiking over to the line-up on the Arts Quadrangle in preparation for the processional.

Rain was coming down in buckets at sunrise-- ironically, just the way it had on move-in day some four years ago. I thought that we were going to be cheated out of the traditional outdoor commencement ceremony, relegated to --of all places-- Barton Hall, the site of so much drama over the past four years. That would have added insult to injury, further dampening our spirits. But the way it had happened so many times before, the rains abruptly stopped, blue skies sailed down from the North, and it turned into a picture perfect day, at least for the start of the ceremony.

The Cornell graduation is a lot like the Olympics in that the pomp and circumstance of the opening ceremony is just as important, if not more so, as the event itself. Weather permitting, the commencement takes place in the football stadium. Given the number of graduates on the field and their family and friends in the stands there to watch, no other venue could hold such a crowd.

The choreography is incredible. About an hour before the actual ceremony starts, the processionals get underway; each college lines its students up at a different part of campus and then the march to the football field begins. Another great aerial shot! It looks like a parade, with parents waving and taking pictures from the sidelines. As soon as their sons and daughters pass by, they scurry to find seats, or at least standing room, in the football stadium.

The chimes at McGraw Tower can be heard everywhere on campus playing fast and furiously: a mix of Cornell favorites alternating with sounds of the sixties. Simultaneously, several of Cornell's bands are heard playing on the quadrangles of the various colleges. Quite a cacophony-- yet a stirring one, heightening the electricity already in the air.

Once they've reached the stadium, the students from each college are introduced, led in, and circle the track before taking their seats on the field facing west. As each school enters, a booming baritone, in the most mellifluous tones, can be head over the public address system.

"Now entering the arena are the candidates for graduation of the College of Engineering…." A few minutes later, "Now entering the arena are the candidates for graduation of the College of Arts and Sciences…." And then, "Now entering the arena are the candidates for graduation of the School of Nursing." It really does look like the opening ceremony at the Olympics.

The process is repeated until all of the separate colleges of the University, undergraduate and graduate, make their grand entrance circling the track under their respective banners and flags. Quite a colorful spectacle, all set against that familiar backdrop of the lake, valley, and west hill. It's nothing short of breathtaking. Pomp and circumstance at its best!

The actual ceremony itself is relatively brief. Following a "State of Cornell" speech by the President, as well as several student presenters, the members of each college stand and are declared "graduates of Cornell" by their respective dean.

Don't like Ithaca weather? As I've mentioned several times, just wait a few minutes and it's bound to change. What had evolved into a sunny day quickly turned the other way yet again, deteriorating into a heavy overcast with storm clouds gathering and rolling south over the lake. How ironic-- much like the storm clouds of Vietnam had gathered and loomed over us.

Nature has always been a major player with a big role in Cornell's extravaganza; so why not today? A steady drizzle started to rain on us midway through the proceedings. The ceremony is terminated only in the case of thunder and lightning and since such was not the case, we had to endure the downpour. There was a stirring rendition of the alma mater, "Far above Cayuga's waters...." which did then, and always has, given me goosebumps. Caps were tossed, graduates let out a wild, resounding shout of glee-- and, *it was all over.*

My parents and I exited the Stadium and miraculously found each other in a matter of minutes at an agreed-upon location that we had the common sense to designate the night before. Good idea, given the thousands of students and their family members milling about, hugging, kissing, crying, and taking pictures, with many friends saying goodbye to one other for one last time.

But I had done all of that already. Now after four years, it was finally time to say goodbye to the University as well as farewell to Ian-- as both this rite of passage and our Cornell being and existence had come to a close and we would go our separate ways.

I noticed that as hard as he tried to hide them, tears welled up in his eyes. I had seen that display of emotion from Mr. Macho only several times before. Was he sad, or sorry? Honestly, I just didn't feel quite as bad, but went through the motions just the same. For one thing, as much as I loved Cornell, as well as the past four years, I was ready to move on and start the next chapter in my life.

Nor was this the time or place to tell Ian how I truly felt about what I deemed a betrayal; that time had long since passed. Even though that fury had been festering all these months, if I hadn't had the nerve to speak up before, now certainly wasn't the moment to lay it all out. As I keep saying, much had been forgiven if not forgotten; but the bonding just would never or could never be as tight between us, at least as far as I was concerned.

I looked around at all that hugging and kissing going on. Frankly, I felt a twinge of envy and emptiness; there really weren't too many people left for me to say goodbye to. I had said farewell to my housemates the evening before; I had said goodbye to my fraternity brothers at a big blowout two nights ago. But some of my closest friendships and personal relationships had run aground. Looking for an excuse to escape that momentary feeling which unnerved and upset me, I had the perfect excuse in what was now a heavy, steady drenching.

"Let's get on the road," I signaled to my parents, while not rushing me at this emotional moment, were all too glad to get out of the pouring rain. We made a hasty exit, headed for the two cars that were already packed up, and prepared to depart from Ithaca for one last time. My college education was now officially over and my Cornell career was in the record books.

SEPTEMBER, 1999

#81 - Back to the Present

President Rhodes was finished speaking and the tumultuous ovation he received startled me and brought me back to the present tense. The audience was wildly applauding not just for this speech, which had been a knockout punch, but also for all his years of service to our beloved Cornell, which was about to come to an end.

I thought back to my own Freshman Convocation. So much had happened to me and Cornell during the intervening years. It was a lifetime. Now, I turned to the left and looked at my son. What would he face during his four years on the Hill? I looked beyond him at my wife; although she hadn't been part of the Cornell experience, she had been the cornerstone of everything I had built thereafter. She had helped make many of my life's dreams come true. And then I turned to the right and looked at that former classmate I bumped into just before the President had started to speak. *Who was that, anyway?*

It was Brant. *Brant?* Of all people, what in the world was *he* doing back at Cornell? Few of his dreams had become reality. He never came close to graduating. But now he was getting a second chance through one of his children. Brant, one of the fearsome fivesome, who was now starting all over again with me all these years later as both of our kids would be classmates. *How ironic!* Of t four, who would have guessed that it would have been *he* who had returned. How coincidental-- that not only had our paths crossed this way again, but also that we had found each other this way, to boot. Life, at least the Cornell part of it, had come full circle.

But Cornell had become a very different institution since we had started out as freshmen. I had been given the chance to observe first-hand its evolution. To its *revolution.* I had come on the scene at a time when nobody questioned anything. You did precisely what you were told to do. The boys were in the boys dorms and the girls were in the girls dorms. Rarely did the twain meet. That infamous Cornell couple, Brunhilda and the proctor, took great pains to make sure of that! Skirting the three-feet-on-the-floor rule on Fall and Spring Weekends was about the biggest challenge we faced in 1965. Except for prelims, dateless Saturday nights, the freshman swim test, and fraternity rush-- we had few worries in the world. Back then, everything else was right with the world.

All of that was about to suddenly change-- and I had gotten to see it all up close and very personal during my tumultuous stay on the Hill. Four years later, we questioned everything; students accepted nothing at face value. Men and women not only lived in the same dorms, but on the same floors. *Who cares?* The administration had absolutely no interest or influence as to their comings and goings. From 1965 to 1969, I had been an eyewitness to all these drastic changes and 180-degree turn. In April 1969, I was afforded a front row seat. I was "privileged," for want of a better word, to observe an evolution firsthand.

What was the single greatest impetus for this transformation? The War in Vietnam? Civil Rights movement? Women's lib? Probably all three of them. The conditions were ripe for revolution and the American university was the perfect setting for it to happen, Cornell in particular. College campuses overnight had become pressure cookers for change and the pot exploded on the Hill. Honestly, I don't know if it all was for the good. But it doesn't matter; besides, nobody is asking me. Cornell will never go back to the way it was. Why should it? The only question is: Where will it go in the future?

The year was 1969: America was not the same… Cornell was not the same…and I certainly was not the same.

TODAY

#82 – A Lifetime Later

How quickly the years have passed by. As a recent graduate, a brazen 21-year-old, in 1969 I felt that I had all the time in the world. By 23, I had found my life's companion and soulmate. During my four years at college, I had searched in vain, turning up every stone, looking for that person. My romantic exploits, or lack thereof, would make great material for a *Lifetime* movie.

However, when I got back to Brooklyn, I found that she had been right under my nose all this time. Turns out that we had gone to high school together, but given the graduating class of almost 1,100, we didn't know each other. Two years later, we were married. Compulsive planner that I was, we agreed to travel for three summers before starting a family. Spontaneity was never my strong suit. I was always accused of being so rigid; yet another example.

Together we saw the world. And back then we *did* have all the time in the world. It seemed limitless, never-ending. One summer we covered the Mediterranean: Israel, the Greek Isles, and then on to Italy, and Switzerland. The next summer we covered the British Isles and Scandinavia. And for the third, we traveled up and down the Pacific Coast, from British Columbia to San Diego. They were all whirlwind tours. But we did get to see it all, traveling on our own, living from day to day, and operating on a shoestring budget. *And, we had a ball!* I distinctly remember leaving Florence, Italy and mentioning what places we would revisit when we came back and were not in such a rush. Dream on…

But little did I understand back then that we wouldn't be returning so fast. As our three sons came along, we had to put long-distance traveling on hold. Not that I am complaining, though. Far, far from it! Without the slightest doubt, those middle years have been the most wonderful, fulfilling, and meaningful years-- the anchor of my life. I would have given up *anything* else to be a husband and father.

Still, to put things in perspective, with the boys grown, daughters-in-law and granddaughters in the family portrait, we're coming out of the tunnel on the other end, and are planning trips anew (although now it's not on $5 a day!) and we're letting the travel agents arrange them for us. No more baggage handling for me.

Ah, middle age! But time seems such much more precious. After passing 40… 50… and now 60… I've started to hear some footsteps; there is a sense of mortality we didn't feel in 1969 with all the time in the world, and with that world waiting to be conquered. Very little, or so we thought, was standing in our way back then.

By the way, I was offered and ended up taking the job at Network News. But I didn't stay very long. Not because I didn't love the job and my colleagues. On the contrary; I wanted to get a master's degree in broadcasting. My boss tried to talk me out of it; he told me that I'd learn more in one day in the newsroom than I would in two years in the classroom. He may have been right, but I wanted to earn that sheepskin.

I left, went to grad school at night, and taught English by day. I never stopped. I've spent more than 35 years in Education. No regrets; it was a most rewarding career. But I must admit that I have often thought back to the fork in the road and wondered what would have happened if I had stayed with radio and television. Well, now that I am retired-- I am going to try to find out.

EPILOGUE

What ever happened to the Class of 1969? With the best of intentions, I had set out to go to each of my five-year college reunions. But something always seems to pop up that prevented me from attending. An obligation at work… a graduation… a close friend's wedding-- whatever. There always seemed to be a conflict. I just never got there for the fifth, tenth, fifteenth, or twentieth, promising myself each time, "Wait 'til the next" five years later, and then another five years later, and so forth. They seemed to roll around more quickly each time.

And so the years...the decades... flew by. A lifetime had passed; by hook or crook I was determined to make it to my 25th alumni reunion and find out how life had turned out for everyone else. Yes, we did manage to make it back this time.

Buzz? I don't know and I couldn't care less. His name came up on several occasions during the weekend. After all, he had been a legend in his time, and as his roommate, I earned a degree of notoriety as well. I heard some wild and crazy tales about how what had happened to him, but just assumed it was all speculation. The stories that were concocted were all too wild and crazy, even for Buzz. I was just lucky to have been rid of him as quickly as I was in the fall of 1965. Never heard from him or of him again.

Diana? I learned a great deal more about her. I see her name in the 1969 class column in the *Cornell Alumni News* magazine from time to time. Both she and her husband are lawyers, deeply committed to environmental concerns. There is no mention of children; just not on their agenda. I don't think that she was at the Reunion. Reunions were just not her "thing." Just the way fraternities weren't. Frankly, I didn't look for her, not even out of the corner of my eye.

And Norma? "We" were just not meant to be. She had left my life just as quickly as she had entered it. I did run into her at the Reunion and the meeting was cordial enough. After all, there had been no hard feelings between us. No surprise: She was back in Tennessee with her husband Ken and a household full of children. Ken, yet another clone of her two brothers, had gone into the family business, also a foregone conclusion. I didn't even ask about her parents, although she volunteered that "Daddy" was gone now and Ken had taken over the business. I chuckled to myself: Imagine me running a munitions plant. Norma had taught briefly. But with money no object, she was now a full-time mom and grand dame of Memphis society. She was a nice girl, but we were from two such different worlds. I was happy for her that she had found what she was looking for.

Dwayne was at the Reunion. He was there in jacket and tie, now wearing glasses, sporting a crew cut, and a bit more filled out, to put it euphemistically, than the lanky guy I recalled from dorm days. He had gone Establishment after all these years, now working for corporate America. In the end, he had become one of "us."

We were at the Saturday afternoon barbecue at the Cornell plantations with several hundred other sixty-niners and their spouses or significant others. Dwayne was in a conversation about twenty feet away; he spotted me immediately, excused himself, and approached with a warm greeting, instantly wiping away the years of contempt, rudeness, and bare tolerance he had directed at me. It was the "old" Dwayne from freshman dorm days.

I can't say that I returned this sudden display of warmth in kind, although I wish I could have. I don't forget so easily. I have been told that among my flaws, holding grudges is one of them; to which, I plead guilty. I don't have the power which some people do to wipe away bad memories. They stay with me. Forgive? Forget? Just a little? No, neither.

Although I had learned to be understanding and sympathetic to Dwayne and what he had been going through, most notably the University's failure to provide support for the first wave of African-American students to arrive on campus, I had taken the brunt of his transformation and was left with quite a bruising. But I have to say that deep down he was a *really* good guy, and I was truly sorry that our friendship had imploded.

Maybe Dwayne thought my chilly reception was due to the role he had played at Cornell on Parents Weekend in April 1969. But if so, he was wrong; on the contrary-- what he did during the uprising was his business, and if anything, I respected the fact that he had tried to play the role of peacemaker. I had finally come to understand the frustration he was experiencing during those years. I certainly wasn't innocent in the breakup of our short-lived "bromance" and perhaps that's why he had come down so hard on me. I bore a sense of guilt, too, as to why our friendship had gone south. And, I regretted it.

My feelings for Dwayne were purely personal. I had great memories of how we had started out together as incoming freshmen and the good friend he was to me. But I hadn't forgotten the way he treated me after he left the dorms or when we were in that Government class together. I couldn't just pick up where we had once left off as corridor mates and eradicate all the other stuff in between. I very coolly returned his greeting, didn't even introduce him to my wife, who was standing at my side, and then abruptly excused myself to get on the buffet line under the tent, with fried filet of sole far more appealing to me at the moment than being with him. Still, it stung-- for which I partly blame myself to this day.

"What was *that* all about?" she asked inquisitively.

"Nobody." I replied, a bit sorrowfully. "Nobody important." Dwayne and I haven't seen each other since. Frankly, I don't expect to ever see him again. I am sad about that. I just wish that our friendship had had a longer shelf life. Perhaps you can sense my ambivalence and misgivings that I hadn't met him more than half way.

Brant is another story altogether. Of course, he wasn't at the Reunion; he didn't belong there. But he worked hard at staying in touch with me. He married soon after my (not his) graduation. Brant never did finish college. He became a father six months after the wedding-- doing the responsible thing in those days. That was Brant, never catching a break, always trying to go by the book. That marriage didn't last long; neither did the next. But he was the marrying kind and tried it again until he got it right. He and his wife now live in Pikesville, Maryland, the parents of three girls (as well as the son from his first marriage). He is also the youthful grandfather of a baby boy.

Brant looks barely a day older than when we first met in 1965. And he is still trying to find himself. He has worked at various sales jobs, moving from one company to the next, always starting over. As a matter of pride, he refused to take over his folks' business, even though it was offered to him on a silver platter and would have put him on Easy Street. He's practically back to where he started after busting out of Cornell some 30 years ago. Big dreams-- with little or nothing to show for them after a lifetime of false starts. He has his regrets that in some ways, life just passed him by. Whenever he begins his "what might have been" speech, I cut him off, pointing to his personal successes. At least he has derived tremendous satisfaction from his present wife, children, and grandson, and to a degree has had his aspirations fulfilled through them. And, now our kids turned out to be Cornell classmates, so we have that permanent bond and connection.

Kip? I only wish I knew. As I said earlier, I never heard from him again and always found an excuse to avoid contacting his parents to ask how things turned out. At times, I've been tempted to contact the Alumni House to find out, but have restrained myself for fear of discovering the truth. Ironically, he was the one who had everything going for him to make it *really* big. After his departure to Vietnam and all those unanswered letters, I just assumed the worst. The fact that he never returned to Cornell leads me to believe that his story does not have a happy ending. Still, I'll keep a glimmer of hope alive.

I make a feeble attempt at keeping up with Ian. To be honest, he tries harder than I do. But it's been getting more and more difficult as of late. He settled in California, in the Santa Barbara area, not far from where his mother lives. But he rarely sees her, so he says. It's my theory that he ran away from the stormy domestic situation with his parents. In any event, he has rarely returned to the East.

Despite a string of romances (about which he shared with me far more many details than I cared to know-- much too much information), he never settled down and is single to this day. Ian would come right up to the finish line, but never crossed it. He kept telling me I would be his best man at his wedding; I never bothered getting my tux pressed. I have often wondered what made him so afraid of commitment. He went west for an acting career, but it never amounted to anything. That's a forgotten dream by now. Financially, however, he has made it big --very big-- managing a large real estate conglomerate in the San Joachim Valley.

It's commonplace to say, "We kept in touch despite the miles." Easily said, hard to do. You have to work at that type of friendship. And it takes a dual commitment. There's just so much a relationship can withstand the test of time and distance. Yes, you call, you exchange birthday and holiday cards. But you're not there for the important stuff, the personal stuff, and the benchmark life cycle stuff that getting older is all about. At first I invited him to all my family functions, but he always found an excuse for not coming, so I gave up asking. Frankly, I think that he was relieved that I stopped inviting him. And so as the months and years have pedaled by faster and faster, we maintain a telephone friendship, barely.

I saw Ian at the Reunion. He still had his boyish good looks, charismatic grin, and was maybe a pound heavier, although not even. There was but an occasional grey strand in that full head of sandy brown hair. But there was one noticeable different now: I detected an ever-so-slight sadness to him. Though professing how much he relished his carefree independence, me fears he dost protest too much. Somehow, somewhere I think he would have liked to have settled down.

The class president called for our attention: "Will everyone please gather outside the party tent. It's time to take the Class of 1969's Reunion picture." As I slowly worked my way outside amid the crowd, I reminisced about what was-- and what might have been-- for the five of us starting out together as freshmen on the majestic Cornell campus, as the storm clouds of war gathered in the fall of 1965.

ABOUT THE AUTHOR

Steven S. Kussin was a high school principal for 21 years. Currently he is the education reporter for WCBS Newsradio 880 in New York, an adjunct professor at Hofstra University, a weekly columnist for the Herald chain of community newspapers, and an educational consultant for many school systems. This book is his second; his first was a manual for school administrators: How To Build the Master Schedule in Ten Easy Steps. He looks forward to turning this novel into a screenplay-- and then beginning work on a second one.

Steve received a Ph.D. from New York University, an M.S. from Brooklyn College, and a B.A. from Cornell University. He and his wife Sharyn live on Long Island. They are the proud parents of three sons (Todd, Eric, and Lonnie)-- all of whom graduated from Cornell as well... two daughters-in-law (Alyssa and Laura)... as well as the grandparents of two granddaughters (Rebecca and Kaylee).

41118542R00257

Made in the USA
Middletown, DE
04 March 2017